Studies in the History of Medieval Religion
VOLUME LIV

WOMEN AND MONASTIC REFORM IN THE MEDIEVAL WEST, c. 1000–1500

Studies in the History of Medieval Religion

ISSN 0955-2480

Founding Editor
Christopher Harper-Bill

Series Editor
Frances Andrews

Previously published titles in the series are listed at the back of this volume

WOMEN AND MONASTIC REFORM IN THE MEDIEVAL WEST,

c. 1000–1500

DEBATING IDENTITIES,
CREATING COMMUNITIES

EDITED BY
JULIE HOTCHIN AND JIRKI THIBAUT

THE BOYDELL PRESS

© Contributors 2023

All Rights Reserved. Except as permitted under current legislation
no part of this work may be photocopied, stored in a retrieval system,
published, performed in public, adapted, broadcast,
transmitted, recorded or reproduced in any form or by any means,
without the prior permission of the copyright owner

First published 2023
The Boydell Press, Woodbridge
Paperback edition 2025

ISBN 978-1-83765-049-1 hardback
ISBN 978-1-83765-284-6 paperback

The Boydell Press is an imprint of Boydell & Brewer Ltd
PO Box 9, Woodbridge, Suffolk IP12 3DF, UK
and of Boydell & Brewer Inc.
668 Mt Hope Avenue, Rochester, NY 14620–2731, USA
website: www.boydellandbrewer.com

Our Authorised Representative for product safety in the EU is Easy Access System Europe –
Mustamäe tee 50, 10621 Tallinn, Estonia, gpsr.requests@easproject.com

A CIP catalogue record for this book is available
from the British Library

The publisher has no responsibility for the continued existence or accuracy of URLs for external or third-party internet websites referred to in this book, and does not guarantee that any content on such websites is, or will remain, accurate or appropriate

In memory of Nicky Ramsay (1953–2022),
for whom a garden was always a delight.

Contents

List of Illustrations ... ix
List of Contributors ... xii
Acknowledgements ... xv
List of Abbreviations ... xvii

1 Debating Identities: Women and Monastic Reform in the Medieval West, *c.* 1000–1500 ... 1
    Julie Hotchin and Jirki Thibaut

2 Liturgy and Female Monastic Hagiography around the Year 1000: A *lecture croisée* of the *Life* of Liutrud, the *Second Life* of Glodesind of Metz and the So-called *Pontificale Romano-Germanicum* ... 24
    Gordon Blennemann

3 Remakers of Reform: The Women Religious of Leominster and their Prayerbook ... 57
    Katie Anne-Marie Bugyis

4 The Materiality of Female Religious Reform in Twelfth-Century Ireland: The Case of Co-located Religious Houses ... 81
    Tracy Collins

5 Women as Witnesses: Picturing Gender and Spiritual Identity in a Twelfth-Century Embroidered Fragment from Northern Germany ... 98
    Julie Hotchin and Vera Henkelmann

6 *Mulieres Religiose* and Cistercian Nuns in Northern Italy in the Thirteenth Century: A Choice of 'Order' ... 132
    Elena Vanelli

7   Circulation of Books and Reform Ideas between Female Monasteries in
    Medieval Castile: From Twelfth-Century Cistercians to the Observant
    Reform   154
    Mercedes Pérez Vidal

8   Women, Men and Local Monasticism in Late Medieval Bologna   180
    Sherri Franks Johnson

9   Building Community: Material Concerns in the Fifteenth-Century
    Monastic Reform   202
    Jennifer Edwards

10 Who Made Reform Visible? Male and Female Agency in Changing
    Visual Culture   227
    Katharina Ulrike Mersch

11 Nuns, Cistercian Chant and Observant Reform in the Southern Low
    Countries   249
    John Glasenapp OSB

Index   271

Illustrations

Tracy Collins, 'The Materiality of Female Religious Reform in Twelfth-Century Ireland. The Case of Co-located Religious Houses'

Map 4.1 Locations of co-located religious houses in Ireland established by c. 1144 (by author). 90

Table 4.1 List of co-located religious houses in 12th-century Ireland, established by c. 1144. 91

Fig. 4.1 View of the upstanding remains of the nunnery at Ardcarn, Co. Roscommon, noting extensive low earthworks in the background. Photo: author. 94

Fig. 4.2 View of the Nuns' Church, Clonmacnois, Co. Offaly. Photo: author. 95

Julie Hotchin and Vera Henkelmann, 'Women as Witnesses: Picturing Gender and Spiritual Identity in a Twelfth-Century Embroidered Fragment from Northern Germany'

Fig. 5.1 Embroidered fragment with 'Scenes of the Life of Christ'. Berlin, Kunstgewerbemuseum, Inv. No. 1888,470. © Kunstgewerbemuseum, Staatliche Museen zu Berlin. Photo: Stephan Klonk. 102

Fig. 5.2 Fragment of embroidered border with *praepositus*. Formerly Berlin, Schlossmuseum (without Inv. No.; lost in 1945); image now Berlin, Kunstgewerbemuseum. © Kunstgewerbemuseum, Staatliche Museen zu Berlin. Photo: Archiv Kunstgewerbemuseum. 107

Fig. 5.3 *Pater Heinricus*. Detail from Berlin, Kunstgewerbemuseum, Inv. No. 1888,470. © Kunstgewerbemuseum, Staatliche Museen zu Berlin. Photo: Stephan Klonk. 112

Fig. 5.4 Samson and St Severus. Detail from Berlin, Kunstgewerbemuseum, Inv. No. 1888,470. © Kunstgewerbemuseum, Staatliche Museen zu Berlin. Photo: Stephan Klonk. 112

x   ILLUSTRATIONS

Fig. 5.5   Martyrdom of St Andrew with *praepositus* Gerhard and nuns of Lamspringe. Wolfenbüttel, Herzog August Bibliothek, Cod. Guelf. 475 Helmst., fol. 148v, last quarter of the 12th century.   117

Fig. 5.6   Scenes of the Resurrection with figures of nuns. Detail from Berlin, Kunstgewerbemuseum, Inv. No. 1888,470. © Kunstgewerbemuseum, Staatliche Museen zu Berlin. Photo: Stephan Klonk.   121

Mercedes Pérez Vidal, 'Circulation of Books and Reform Ideas Between Female Monasteries in Medieval Castile. From Twelfth-Century Cistercians to the Observant Reform'

Fig. 7.1   The Lorvão Beatus. São Mamede de Lorvão, codex 44, PT/TT/MSML/B/44, f. 17r. 'Quando este apocalypse entra as matinas a se de começar aqui no Refeitorio'. © Arquivo Nacional da Torre do Tombo, Lisboa.   164

Fig. 7.2   Beatus, Saint, Presbyter of Liebana, Commentary on the Apocalyse. Spain, probably Toledo, *c.* 1220; Las Huelgas. The Morgan Library & Museum. MS M.429. Purchased by J. Pierpont Morgan (1837–1913) in 1910, f. 142r. Photo: The Morgan Library & Museum, New York.   166

Fig. 7.3   Sancti Spiritus de Toro. Beatriz de Portugal's tomb, first quarter of the 15th century, detail of Saint Catherine of Siena. Alabaster (155 x 229 x 71cm). Photo: courtesy of Diana Lucía Gómez-Chacón.   172

Fig. 7.4   Miscellaneous volume, Guillaume Perrault, *Libro del criamjento e enseñamiento de los religiosos*, translated by Pablo de Santa María in 1421, and dedicated to 'soror doña Leonor priora del mosterio [sic] de santosprtos [sic] de toro'. Biblioteca Nacional de España, Madrid, MSS/21626, fol. 100v. © Biblioteca Nacional de España, Madrid.   173

Fig. 7.5   Ground plan of Santo Domingo el Real de Madrid, hypothetical reconstruction of the state of the monastery in the mid-16th century with lodgings of Constanza de Castilla. Source: Author's reconstruction based on the ground plan of 1869. Ayuntamiento de Madrid, Museo de Historia de Madrid, Inv. No. 2695.   177

Sherri Franks Johnson, 'Women, Men and Local Monasticism in Late Medieval Bologna'

Table 8.1 Monasteries in Bologna in 1400.   189

Jennifer Edwards, 'Building Community: Material Concerns in the Fifteenth-Century Monastic Reform'

Table 9.1 Abbesses of Fontevraud and Sainte-Croix. 212

Katharina Ulrike Mersch, 'Who Made Reform Visible? Male and Female Agency in Changing Visual Culture'

Fig. 10.1 Heiningen, Embroidery with Philosophy and the Seven Liberal Arts, 1516, London, Victoria and Albert Museum, Inv. No. 289-1876. © Victoria and Albert Museum, London. 230

Fig. 10.2 Lüne, Embroidery with the Resurrection of Christ, 1504–7. © Museum für Kunst und Gewerbe, Hamburg. 234

Fig. 10.3 Lüne, detail of the bench cover with the legend of St Bartholomew (LUEKO Ha 001), 1493. © Kloster Lüne. 242

Fig. 10.4 Wienhausen, woven wall hanging depicting the hunt of the unicorn and the *hortus conclusus* (WIEN Ha 14), c. 1500. © Kloster Wienhausen. 247

John Glasenapp OSB, 'Nuns, Cistercian Chant and Observant Reform in the Southern Low Countries'

Map 11.1 Reformed Benedictine and Cistercian monasteries of central Belgium. Courtesy of Hans Blomme. 255

Table 11.1 Transmission of reform, from Marche-les-Dames to Forest Abbey. 256

Fig. 11.1 Beaupré Antiphoner, initial 'B' with St John the Baptist for the non-standard first Vespers responsory 'Baptista Christi et praecursor', W. 760, fol. 122v. © The Walters Art Museum, Baltimore. 260

Fig. 11.2 Excised leaf from the Beaupré Antiphoner for the feast of St Catherine. © Ashmolean Museum, University of Oxford. 261

The editors, contributors and publisher are grateful to all the institutions and individuals for permission to reproduce the materials in which they hold copyright. Every effort has been made to trace the copyright holders; apologies are offered for any omission, and the publisher will be pleased to add any necessary acknowledgement in subsequent editions.

Contributors

Gordon Blennemann is Associate Professor in Medieval History at the University of Montreal. His research and publications focus on the social implications of hagiography and liturgy and the history of religious women throughout the Middle Ages. More recently he has been interested in festive culture in early medieval Europe.

Ann-Marie Bugyis is an Assistant Professor in the Program of Liberal Studies at the University of Notre Dame. She is a historian of Christian theology, liturgical practice and material culture, who is particularly interested in reconstructing the lived experiences of religious women in the Middle Ages through their documents of practice and other material remains. She is the author of *The Care of Nuns: Benedictine Women's Ministries in England during the Central Middle Ages* (Oxford, 2019), and a co-editor of *Women Intellectuals and Leaders in the Middle Ages* (Woodbridge, 2020) and *Medieval Cantors and Their Craft: Music, Liturgy, and the Shaping of History* (York, 2017).

Tracy Collins is currently a state archaeologist with The National Monuments Service, Ireland. She was previously a co-director of Aegis Archaeology, an archaeological services company, and a full-time temporary lecturer at the Department of Archaeology, University College Cork. She has a special research interest in church archaeology and medieval female monasticism, which is reflected in her monograph, *Female Monasticism in Medieval Ireland: An Archaeology* (Cork, 2021).

Jennifer C. Edwards is Professor and Chair of History at Manhattan College in Riverdale, NY, where she teaches medieval and ancient history. Her research examines medieval European women and gender, power and authority, religion and health. She is the author of *Superior Women: Medieval Female Authority in Poitiers' Abbey of Sainte-Croix* (Oxford, 2019), a runner-up for the Society for Medieval Feminist Scholarship 2020 book prize. Her 2014 article 'My Sister for Abbess: Fifteenth-Century Power Disputes over the Abbey of Sainte-Croix,

Poitiers' in the *Journal of Medieval History* won the Society for French Historical Studies William Koren, Jr. Prize. She is currently working on a book project, 'Holy Healing: Saints and Leprosy in the Middle Ages', and a Reacting to the Past game on Christine de Pisan, the *Querelle des Femmes*, and the Hundred Years War. She earned her PhD and MA from the University of Illinois at Urbana-Champaign and her BA from the University of Massachusetts at Amherst. She is an associate editor for the *Medieval Feminist Forum* and serves on the Advisory Board of the Society for Medieval Feminist Scholarship.

Br. John Glasenapp OSB is a monk of Saint Meinrad Archabbey and Director of the Institute for Sacred Music at the Saint Meinrad Seminary and School of Theology. He earned his PhD in Historical Musicology from Columbia University with support from the Alliance-Council for European Studies and the U.S. Fulbright Commission to Belgium. His research focuses on Cistercian chant, musical authority and reform, the later histories of manuscripts and exchanges across religious groups and institutional boundaries.

Vera Henkelmann is an Associate Postdoc Fellow at the Max Weber Centre for Advanced Cultural and Social Sciences at the University of Erfurt. She studied art history, medieval and early modern history as well as prehistory at the University of Bonn. She holds a PhD in art history from the University of Dortmund and was awarded the dissertation prize of the University of Dortmund for her thesis *Spätgotische Marienleuchter: Formen, Funktionen, Bedeutungen* (Regensburg, 2014). Her special field of interest is medieval sacred art, including textiles and jewellery, as well as lighting devices in the context of liturgy, piety and spirituality.

Julie Hotchin is an Honorary Lecturer in the School of History at the Australian National University. Her research examines medieval religious women, manuscript culture, and women's intellectual and devotional practices. She is a co-editor of *Partners in Spirit: Women, Men and Religious Life in Germany, 1100–1500* (Turnhout, 2014), *Women and Work in Premodern Europe: Experiences, Relationships and Cultural Representations* (New York, 2018) and a special issue of the *Journal of Religious History* on 'Religous Devotion, Gender and the Body in Europe, 1100–1800' (2020).

Sherri Franks Johnson is Assistant Professor in the Department of Religious Studies at the University of California, Riverside. Her research interests include the history of women's monasticism in the late Middle Ages and the veneration of Marian images in early modern Italy.

Katharina Ulrike Mersch is senior lecturer for the history of the Middle Ages at the Ruhr-University in Bochum. She was previously substitute professor at the universities in Frankfurt am Main and Göttingen. She studies the history of women's convents in a cultural perspective, which informed her book about visual communication, *Soziale Dimensionen visueller Kommunikation – Stifte, Chorfrauenstifte und Klöster im Vergleich* (Göttingen, 2012). Her research also focuses on medieval conceptions of crowds and religious exclusion within the broader frame of social history: *Missachtung, Anerkennung und Kreativität. Exkommunizierte Laien im 13. Jahrhundert* (Ostfildern, 2020).

Mercedes Pérez Vidal received her PhD in Art History in 2013 from the University of Oviedo, with a dissertation on the Dominican female monasteries of medieval Castile. Her research focuses on the cultural history and art history of female monasteries, specifically the relation of art and architecture to liturgy, nuns' libraries and manuscript production, and the networks of cultural transfer between the Iberian Peninsula and other territories. She has been a postdoctoral fellow at the National Autonomous University of Mexico (2014–15) and the Heinrich Heine Universität in Düsseldorf (2017–2019), and a Marie Skłodowska Curie Actions fellow at the University of Padua (2015–17). She is currently Ramón y Cajal Senior research fellow and lecturer at the Autonomous University of Madrid. She is the author of *Arte y liturgia en los monasterios de Dominicas en Castilla Desde los orígenes hasta la reforma observante (1218–1506)* (Gijón, 2021), and the editor of *Women Religious Crossing between Cloister and the World. Nunneries in Europe and the Americas, ca. 1200–1700* (Leeds, 2022)

Jirki Thibaut is interested in female religious life in the Early and High Middle Ages. She received her PhD in History in 2020 from Ghent University (joint PhD with the University of Leuven). Her dissertation focused on how women religious negotiated their institutional identity in ninth–eleventh-century Saxony.

Elena Vanelli recently completed a PhD in Medieval History on Cistercian nuns in Northern Italy at the University of Hamburg. She is now Lecturer of Ancient and Medieval History at the University of Kassel and is working on a digital edition of the 'Decretum Burchardi' in a Project of the Akademie der Wissenschaften und Literatur Mainz.

Acknowledgements

A COLLABORATIVE project of this nature incurs many debts of gratitude. This volume is the result of a broad international collaboration, and its realisation is due to the generous support of many people and institutions. Earlier versions of several chapters in this collection were presented at a series of sessions entitled 'Debating Identities, Creating Communities: Materialities of Female Monastic Reform in the Medieval West' at the *International Medieval Congress* at Leeds in 2019. We would like to thank the speakers and audience for the lively and fruitful discussions that teased out and sharpened the connections between the papers and that, in turn, strengthened the themes of this volume. Further thanks go to the Australian National University, the University of Ghent, and the University of Leuven for enabling us to pursue this project. This volume emerged out of the project 'Re-evaluating Female Monasticism's 'Ambiguous Identities' in the Ninth-to-Eleventh-Century West', funded by the FWO (Research Foundation Flanders), which was led by Steven Vanderputten. We are also grateful to the many libraries and archival institutions that facilitated the research published here.

We consider ourselves fortunate to have been able to discuss this project with many colleagues and friends, whose constructive remarks, frank and sometimes challenging questions, and endless support were crucial to realise this publication. Our special thanks go to Steven Vanderputten, whose input and insight were invaluable in the early stages of this project, and to Claire Renkin, whose perceptive comments and encouragement nurtured this project at critical junctures. Further, we warmly thank the editorial team of Boydell & Brewer, and especially Elizabeth McDonald and Caroline Palmer, for their patience and thoughtful guidance through the editorial process, and Frances Andrews as series editor for Studies in the History of Medieval Religion. We are also grateful to the anonymous peer reviewer for their constructive remarks that focused our thinking in the project's final stage.

Further, we want to thank our contributors. They conducted most of the research for this volume during the Covid-19 pandemic. This international crisis posed considerable challenges for every researcher, and we want to thank our authors for their persistence, resilience, patience and commitment to the aims and ideas explored in this volume.

We'd also like to acknowledge the support of our partners. They, too, have lived with this project for longer than they may have anticipated and their ongoing encouragement has been integral to bringing it to fruition.

Abbreviations

ADV	*Archives Départementales de la Vienne*
AS	*Acta Sanctorum ordinis sancti Benedicti in saeculorum classes distribute*, ed. Jean Mabillon (9 vols, Paris, 1668–1701)
ASMi	*Archivio di Stato di Milano*
BHL	*Bibliotheca Hagiographica Latina Antiquae et Mediae Aetatis* (2 vols, Brussels, 1898–1901)
BnF	*Bibliothèque Nationale de France*
CHMM	Alison Beach and Isabelle Cochelin (eds), *The Cambridge History of Medieval Monasticism in the Latin West* (2 vols, Cambridge, 2020)
HAB	*Wolfenbüttel, Herzog August Bibliothek*
KBR	*Brussels, Koninklijke Bibliotheek/Bibliothèque Royale*
MGH	*Monumenta Germaniae Historica*
PL	*Patrologiae Cursus Completus: Series Latina*, ed. Jacques-Paul Migne (22 vols, Paris, 1844–88)
PRG	*Pontificale Romano-Germanicum*
UB	*Urkundenbuch*

CHAPTER 1

Debating Identities: Women and Monastic Reform in the Medieval West, c. 1000–1500

JULIE HOTCHIN AND JIRKI THIBAUT

AROUND the turn of the tenth century, a sister from Hohenbourg in Alsace composed a *Life* of the community's holy founder, St Odile (died c. 720).¹ Odile is depicted as a charismatic leader with persuasive speech. One scene recounts how, when the newly formed community gathered to determine the manner of religious observance to guide their lives, Odile asked the sisters 'whether they wished to live the canonical or regular life'. Although this choice did not exist at the time of the events described, the *Life* nevertheless records that the women unanimously opted for the regular life as an expression of their piety. St Odile is said to have cautioned her sisters against adopting the constraints this would entail. Acknowledging their desire to 'bear every difficulty and harshness for the name of Christ', she warned them against this course as 'our successors would curse us' because their location, at the top of the Hohenbourg, made it difficult to obtain water 'without great effort'. Persuaded by her practical argument, the sisters yielded and elected to retain the 'canonical dress'.²

Odile's dialogue with the sisters at Hohenbourg offers a tantalizing glimpse

---

¹ Wilhelm Levison (ed.), 'Vita Odiliae Abbatissae Hohenburgensis', *MGH. Scriptores rerum Merovingicarum: Passiones vitaeque sanctorum aevi Merovingici*, vol. 6 (Hannover, 1913), pp. 24–50. Sabine Klapp comments on the contested dating and unknown authorship of the *Vita* in Sabine Klapp, *Das Äbtissinnenamt in den Unterelsässischen Frauenstiften vom 14. bis zum 16. Jahrhundert. Umkämpft, verhandelt, normiert* (Berlin, 2012), p. 51, n. 14; Rosamond McKitterick, on the other hand, argues in favour of a female author in Rosamond McKitterick, *Books, Scribes and Learning in the Frankish Kingdoms, 6th–9th centuries* (Aldershot, 1994), p. 28.

² 'Vita Odiliae', c. 16, pp. 45–6. Translation is our own.

into community dynamics and wider social and religious expectations about the role and function of female religious institutions. In representing women debating what form of religious observance the nascent community would adopt, the *Life* is representative of a wider culture of debate about the institutional and spiritual identity of monastic women. In presenting the adoption of the canonical life as a pragmatic decision influenced by the logistics of the location, the author of the *Life* may have intended to justify the canonical life to counter efforts to introduce the Benedictine Rule to the community at Hohenbourg.[3] If so, this anecdote shows how contemporary pressures facing the author shaped the narrative of St Odile and the community's origins, lending authority to the present community who drew on their founder's legacy to legitimise their way of life. But the sisters' decision in favour of a particular observance also needs to be seen as an expression of political agency. Odile's argument to maintain autonomy, expressed through the rationale of being able to freely obtain water outside the cloister, projected the practical realities of the contemporary community upon its first members. Odile's argument hence created an authoritative tradition upon which they could draw to legitimise their own practice in contemporary debates.[4]

The negotiated reality in this exemplar from the *Life* of St Odile is not unique. Scholars have drawn attention to the ways in which women religious participated in and steered the debates about their institutional and spiritual narratives of the self. The extent of women's ability to determine their forms of communal religious life is crystallized in transformative processes often referred to as reform. As this example shows, women asserted their voice in debates about the ideas and

---

[3] The circumstances in which the *Vita Odilia* was written are unknown. Fiona Griffiths posits that the work may have been written as an attempt to 'resist or forestall' the introduction of the Benedictine Rule: Fiona J. Griffiths, *The Garden of Delights. Reform and Renaissance for Women in the Twelfth Century* (Philadelphia, 2007), p. 31. For the context of debates about the canonical and regular life for women religious in the tenth century, see Steven Vanderputten, *Dark Age Nunneries. The Ambiguous Identity of Female Monasticism, 800–1050* (Ithaca, N.Y., 2018), pp. 4–10, 65–134.

[4] The canonesses of the *Stift* of St Stephan in Strasbourg similarly drew on the legend of St Odile as a model to legitimise their way of life in the context of internal debates about reform and disputes with the bishop of Strasbourg in the mid-fifteenth century. A tapestry depicting the *Life* of St Odile was commissioned, perhaps by the abbess Agnes von Rathsamhausen (r. 1462–5), as a collective self-assertion of the community's identity and privileges. See Martina Backes and Barbara Fleith, 'Zur Funktion von Heiligenviten in Text und Bild in Elsässischen und Südwestdeutschen Frauenklöstern des Mittelalters am Beispiel des Odiliakultes', in Jeffrey F. Hamburger, Carola Jäggi, Susan Marti and Hedwig Röckelein (eds), *Frauen - Kloster - Kunst. Neue Forschungen zur Kulturgeschichte des Mittelalters* (Turnhout, 2007), pp. 165–75. For the internal disruption generated by debates about reform at St Stephan, see Klapp, *Äbtissinnenamt*, pp. 92–5, 171–5.

structures that shaped their religious lives, as they embraced, rejected or adapted to calls for 'reform' contingent on their circumstances.[5] Nevertheless, studies of women's engagement in monastic reform, while focusing on different periods, regions and monastic observance, have rarely intersected, and fundamental questions regarding women's roles and exercise of power within the contingencies of religious reform are ripe for further examination. This volume aims to examine the diverse attitudes and responses of women religious to spiritual and institutional change over time and from a comparative perspective.

The central aim of *Women and Monastic Reform* is to re-evaluate and enlarge our knowledge of women's involvement in spiritual and institutional change in monastic communities over the period *c.* 1000–*c.* 1500. Contributors draw on a range of visual, material and textual sources to reappraise critically how female monastic communities reflected, individually and collectively, on their spiritual ideals and institutional forms across this timespan. In doing so, authors address two key questions animating current research into women and monastic reform: the reconceptualisation of reform as a contingent and negotiated process determined by local circumstances; and interpretations of women religious as active participants in reform processes, who responded to expectations from their local social, economic and political contexts to remain socially relevant. Collectively, *Women and Monastic Reform* contributes to current strands of scholarship that model a more inclusive way of acknowledging and valuing the capacities of historical women in processes of transformation.

Reform as a Negotiated Reality

Earlier traditions of the historiography of monastic reform tended to interpret medieval monasticism as a progressive succession of reform movements.[6] This concept can be summarised briefly. Classic overviews of monastic reform history usually take as their starting point the Carolingian clerical and ecclesiastical elite who sought to homogenise monastic life, only then to jump to the new monastic movements such as Cluny in the long tenth century, which were held to embody the ideals of homogeneity. The impulse for monastic reform, according to this narrative, reached its culmination in the age of monastic orders in the twelfth and

---

[5] See literature cited below in footnotes 26–30.
[6] See the critical historiographical discussions in Emilia Jamroziak, 'The Historiography of Medieval Monasticism: Perspectives from Northern Europe', *Religions*, 12:7 (2021), 1–13; Felice Lifshitz, 'The Historiography of Central Medieval Western Monasticism', in CHMM, pp. 365–81; Steven Vanderputten, *Monastic Reform as Process. Realities and Representations in Medieval Flanders 900–1100* (Ithaca, N.Y., 2013), pp. 1–13; Id., 'Monastic Reform from the Tenth to the Early Twelfth Century', in CHMM, pp. 599–617.

thirteenth centuries, which consequently manifested in new (semi-) monastic experiments in the thirteenth to the fourteenth centuries, and finally led to the Observant reform in the fifteenth century.[7] This view of monastic history as a cyclical narrative was profoundly influenced by the accounts of contemporary reformers, many of whom were members of religious orders and whose outlook deeply influenced later versions of events. Although the proponents of reform of religious life varied widely, they shared a commitment to renewed adherence of the rule or customs of regular religious life. These urgings for reform were often expressed in the rhetoric of 'returning' monastic communities to an order's origins; existing practices and moral behaviours were criticised as failing to reflect apostolic models of collective religious life, while monastic lifestyles were considered to be insufficiently ascetic and humble.[8]

Critical approaches to the concept of reform have questioned its utility as a descriptor of historical change. First, reappraisals of monastic reform have drawn attention to the fact that calls for reform were often a rhetorical construction. The idea that the lifestyle of a specific community had strayed from an ascetic ideal and was therefore in need of spiritual renewal could serve as a justification for reformer activists, whether ecclesiastical or secular, to intervene in a community in order to serve their own individual political and/or socio-economic agenda – regardless of whether or not their lifestyle was seen as problematic by contemporaries.[9] For this reason, Felice Lifshitz has characterised reform 'as a

---

[7] This characterisation of the cyclical nature of monastic reform is drawn from Ortwin Huysmans, 'Tutor ac Nutritor. Episcopal Agency, Lordship and the Administration of Religious Communities. Ecclesiastical Province of Rheims c. 888–1073' (unpublished Ph.D. dissertation, University of Louvain, 2016), p. 5. This concept of monastic reform as a cyclic phenomenon has been influential; see Clifford Hugh Lawrence, *Medieval Monasticism: Forms of Religious Life in Western Europe in the Middle Ages*, 3rd edition (Harlow, 2001 [1984]). For a critical historiographical discussion of the history of monasticism, see Steven Vanderputten, *Medieval Monasticisms: Forms and Experiences of the Monastic Life in the Latin West* (München, 2020); and the studies cited in the footnote above.

[8] See also the classic essay by Kaspar Elm, 'Verfall und Erneuerung des Ordenswesens im Spätmittelalter', in J. Fleckenstein (ed.), *Untersuchungen zu Kloster und Stift* (Göttingen, 1980), pp. 188–238, translated by James D. Mixson as 'Decline and Renewal of the Religious Orders in the Late Middle Ages: Current Research and Research Agendas', in Kaspar Elm and James D. Mixson (eds), *Religious Life between Jerusalem, the Desert, and the World: Selected Essays by Kaspar Elm* (Boston, 2016), pp. 138–88; and Beach and Cochelin, 'General Introduction', pp. 1–15; Vanderputten, 'Monastic Reform', pp. 599–617; Lifshitz, 'The Historiography', pp. 365–81; Huysmans, 'Tutor ac Nutritor', pp. 7–8.

[9] Vanderputten, 'Monastic Reform', p. 599; Ulrich Andermann, 'Die unsittlichen und disziplinlosen Kanonissen. Ein Topos und seine Hintergründe, aufgezeigt an Beispielen

self-interested discursive strategy periodically utilised by activists to legitimise their own political and spiritual agendas'.[10]

Further, the legacy of a linear model of monastic history that presents a succession of ever more developed forms of regular life (and their decline) is now being fundamentally revised by interpretations that argue for a radically diverse picture of reform based upon regional and local studies. Turning to studies of change in organisations informed by social and anthropological approaches, Steven Vanderputten and Michael Vargas have argued that approaches to monastic reform need to examine an organisation's informal dynamics and how it was situated within local contexts to fully understand how any attempt at institutional change unfolded.[11] For example, in his ground-breaking work *Reform as Process*, Vanderputten argued that a reform was not a 'flashpoint event'[12] that was hierarchically imposed. Rather, he argues, institutional change of the kind historians identify as reform was a gradual and cumulative process that was embedded in localised and contingent circumstances. There was no reform system or standardised reformist template; reform was a messy and indeed fractured reality that evolved differently across period and region, and even community.[13] This approach is reshaping our conceptualisation of the field, as scholars increasingly shift attention from univocal or agonistic narratives of reform to 'wrestle with the ambiguous and contradictory spaces in the middle'.[14] Hendrik Dey encapsulates this profound historiographical shift as '"bringing chaos out of order" to reveal

---

sächsischer Frauenstifte (11.-13. Jahrhundert)', *Westfälische Zeitschrift*, 146 (1996), 39-63. Julia Barrow also problematises and discusses the semantic meanings of the term reform and its evolution over time. See Julia Barrow, 'Ideas and Applications of Reform', in Thomas Noble and Julia Smith (eds), *The Cambridge History of Christianity. 3: Early Medieval Christianity, ca. 600-1100* (Cambridge, 2008), pp. 345-62; Ead., 'The Ideology of the Tenth-Century English Benedictine "Reform"', in Patricia Skinner (ed.), *Challenging the Boundaries of Medieval History. The Legacy of Timothy Reuter* (Turnhout, 2009), pp. 141-54.

[10] Lifshitz, 'The Historiography', p. 373.

[11] Vanderputten, *Reform as Process*; Michael A. Vargas, *Taming a Brood of Vipers: Conflict and Change in Fourteenth-Century Dominican Convents* (Leiden, 2011), pp. 22-7, especially p. 23.

[12] Vanderputten, *Reform as Process*, p. 9.

[13] Ibid., pp. 1-13; Id., 'Monastic Reform', pp. 599-617; See also Jamroziak, 'Historiography'; and Martha Newman, 'Reformed Monasticism and the Narrative of Cistercian Beginnings', *Church History*, 90 (2021), 537-56.

[14] Christopher M. Bellito and David Zachariah Flanagin, 'Introduction', in *Reassessing Reform: A Historical Investigation in Church Renewal*, ed. by id. (Washington, 2012), pp. 1-13, at p. 11.

the "remarkable range of experiences and practices" that characterised medieval Western monasticism'.[15]

In line with the shift in research from studies of reform as top-down and unified processes into more sophisticated, complex and dynamic interpretations that allow for the play of interactions at a local level, scholars also highlight the importance of historical contingency and how it informs a negotiated reality of reform.[16] Although much of contemporary reformist literature represented events as unfolding towards an inevitable conclusion, in reality institutional and spiritual change unfolded through multiple dialogues, options and decisions. Historians have pointed to the rich culture of debate in monastic communities, in which monastics discussed, adapted and negotiated reform precepts. Our source record does not always grant us insight into the interpersonal dynamics behind these processes; nevertheless, there is a growing awareness that sources can implicitly hint at and, in some cases, even explicitly document the culture of negotiation and debate that was inherent to reformist interventions.[17] While women's role in these processes of change was often eclipsed in earlier scholarship, scholars are now foregrounding their involvement; the following section directs attention to how scholarship is redefining our understanding of women's involvement in reform.

---

[15] Hendrik Dey, 'Bringing Chaos out of Order: New Approaches to the Study of Early Western Monasticism', in Hendrik Dey and Elizabeth Fentress (eds), *Western Monasticism ante litteram: The Space of Monastic Observance in Late Antiquity and the Early Middle Ages* (Turnhout, 2011), pp. 19–40, at p. 20, cited in Lifshitz, 'The Historiography', p. 368.

[16] This approach has been developed most fully in recent scholarship by Steven Vanderputten; see, for example, *Id.*, *Reform as Process*; and *Medieval Monasticisms*, pp. 166–7.

[17] Katrinette Bodarwé, 'Immer Ärger mit den Stiftsdamen: Reform in Regensburg', in Eva Schlotheuber, Helmut Flachenecker and Ingrid Gardill (eds) *Nonnen, Kanonissen und Mystikerinnen. Religiöse Frauengemeinschaften in Süddeutschland. Beiträge zur interdisziplinären Tagung vom 21. bis 23. September 2005 in Frauenchiemsee* (Göttingen, 2008), pp. 79–102; *Ead.*, 'Eine Männerregel für Frauen. Die Adaption der Benediktsregel im 9. und 10. Jahrhundert', in Gert Melville and Anne Müller (eds), *Female Vita Religiosa between late Antiquity and the High Middle Ages. Structures, Developments and Spatial Contexts* (Münster, 2011), pp. 235–74; Elizabeth A. Lehfeldt, *Religious Women in Golden Age Spain: The Permeable Cloister* (Aldershot, 2005); Claudia Märtl, '"pos verstockt weyber"? Der Streit um die Lebensform der Regensburger Damenstifte im ausgehenden 15. Jahrhundert', in Lothar Kolmer and Kurt Reindel (eds), *Regensburg, Bayern und Europa: Festschrift für Kurt Reindel zum 70. Geburtstag* (Regensburg, 1995), pp. 365–406; Vanderputten, *Dark Age Nunneries*; *Id.*, 'Debating Reform in Tenth- and Early Eleventh-Century Female Monasticism', *Zeitschrift für Kirchengeschichte*, 125:3 (2015), 289–306; and Anne Winston-Allen, *Convent Chronicles: Women Writing about Women and Reform in the Late Middle Ages* (University Park, 2004). Winston-Allen provides a useful detailed bibliography that lists editions of sources published in regional journals.

Women and Monastic Reform: New Approaches

In discussing reformist interventions into or within monastic communities, earlier generations of scholars paid less attention to how women religious navigated the tensions of institutional change. Female religious institutions were – much in line with the 'limited visibility' women had in monastic studies in general – often ignored in early studies on monastic reform.[18] When women religious were incorporated into the main narrative of reform, historians tended to appraise them, as Fiona Griffiths puts it, as 'objects of reform rather than as potential supporters or even initiators of it'.[19] Women were thus defined at best as passive bystanders of the changes affecting their lives or, in some cases, even as being mired in a state of spiritual decline and hence in need of reform.[20]

In the latter decades of the twentieth century, scholarship on women and monastic reform was influenced by the concerns of women's history and shifting interpretations of 'reform'.[21] Women's history offered new methodological approaches and asked different questions of the sources so as to place women back into the historical record. Studies of convents that drew upon their rich archives, libraries and material remains were well suited to these investigations.[22] Motivated by the desire to identify the experiences of women religious, historians also addressed questions of female agency in relation to reform. Historians such

---

[18] See the historiographical discussion in Fiona Griffiths, 'Women and Reform in the Central Middle Ages', in Judith M. Bennett and Ruth M. Karras (eds), *The Oxford Handbook of Women and Gender in Medieval Europe* (Oxford, 2013), pp. 447–73, and especially pp. 449–51 on the traditional historiographies on women and monastic reform; and Lifshitz, 'The Historiography', pp. 374–5, citation at p. 374.

[19] Griffiths, 'Women and Reform', p. 449.

[20] An example of a study that proceeds from the premise that the state of women's religious life warranted an intervention or reform is Gudrun Gleba, *Reformpraxis und materielle Kultur: Westfälische Frauenklöster im späten Mittelalter* (Husum, 2000). Gleba's study is rich with detail about women's pragmatic literacy and how reform processes unfolded.

[21] Griffiths, 'Women and Reform', p. 449. On the influence of women's history and scholarship on the history of religious women, see Elizabeth A. Lehfeldt, 'Why Nuns aren't Funny', *Sixteenth Century Journal*, L/1 (2019), 69–75.

[22] The literature on women's monastic material and written remains has burgeoned since the 1990s; representative studies include Alison I. Beach, *Women as Scribes: Book Production and Monastic Reform in Twelfth-Century Bavaria* (Cambridge, 2009); Katrinette Bodarwé, *Sanctimoniales litteratae: Schriftlichkeit und Bildung in den ottonischen Frauenkommunitäten Gandersheim, Essen und Quedlinburg* (Münster 2004); Roberta Gilchrist, *Gender and Material Culture: The Archaeology of Religious Women* (London, 1994); and Wybren Scheepsma, *Medieval Religious Women in the Low Countries. The Modern Devotion, the Canonesses of Windesheim, and their Writings* (Woodbridge, 2004), and the literature cited in the notes below.

as Suzanne Wemple and Jane Tibbets Schulenburg, amongst others, identified the causes of a putative decline for women religious with the misogynistic structures of medieval society, and of the church in particular. In this narrative, the interventions of reformist ecclesiastics were held to have restricted religious women's economic autonomy and spiritual expression.[23] Research in this vein reflected broader concerns in women's history to investigate how women countered efforts to curtail and limit their autonomy, resulting in an important strand of research that focused on women's resistance to efforts to impose reform, and in particular enclosure, upon their communities.[24] The continuing appeal of the transgressive nature of these narratives is evident, as Elizabeth Lehfeldt observes, in the view that 'misbehaving nuns were nuns with agency and a story'.[25]

Over the last two decades, scholars have successfully challenged the view that reform was irrelevant or even hostile towards women religious. Earlier views that assumed that male ecclesiastical elites and traditional orders increasingly aimed to restrict the presence of women in the church out of concerns about sexual purity have given way to more nuanced interpretations of gendered participation in different liturgical forms.[26] Moreover, women's attraction to new forms

---

[23] Suzanne Wemple, *Women in Frankish Society. Marriage and the Cloister, 500-900* (Philadelphia, 1981), pp. 127-48, 165-75, 189-97; Jane T. Schulenburg, 'Strict Active Enclosure and Its Effects on the Female Monastic Experience, *ca.* 500-1100', in John A. Nichols and Lillian T. Shank (eds), *Medieval Religious Women. Bd. 1: Distant Echoes* (Kalamazoo, 1984), pp. 51-86; Jo Ann McNamara, *Sisters in Arms: Catholic Nuns through Two Millennia* (Cambridge, 1996). See also the discussion in Griffiths, 'Women and Reform', pp. 450-1. On the other hand, research in the tradition of local history in Germany, for example, has integrated research into women's religious institutions into wider social, economic and political narratives of change. For an overview of regional historiographical approaches in *Landesgeschichte*, see the discussion in Sigrid Hirbodian and Alison Beach, 'Research on Monasticism in the German Tradition', in CHMM, pp. 1140-53.

[24] The practice of enclosure varied widely by time and place. For orientation see Erin L. Jordan, 'Roving Nuns and Cistercian Realities: The Cloistering of Religious Women in the Thirteenth Century', *Journal of Medieval and Early Modern Studies*, 42:3 (2012), 597-614; Julie Ann Smith, 'Clausura Districta: Conceiving Space and Community for Dominican Nuns in the Thirteenth Century', *Parergon*, 27:2 (2010), 13-36; Heike Uffmann, 'Inside and Outside the Convent Walls: The Norm and Practice of Enclosure in the Reformed Nunneries of Late Medieval Germany', *The Medieval History Journal*, 4:1 (2001) 83-108; and Edmund Wareham, 'The Openness of the Enclosed Convent: Evidence from the Lüne Letter collection', in Manuele Gragnolati and Almut Suerbaum (eds), *Openness in Medieval Europe* (Berlin, 2022), pp. 271-88.

[25] Lehfeldt, 'Why Nuns aren't Funny', citation at p. 71.

[26] See the historiographical discussions in Griffiths, 'Women and Reform', pp. 449-56; Gisela Muschiol, 'Gender and Monastic Liturgy in the Latin West (High and Late Middle Ages)', in CHMM, pp. 803-15; and the further literature in notes 43 and 45.

of religious life that emerged from impulses for spiritual renewal has been well documented, including female involvement in monastic and mendicant orders,[27] in semi-religious movements, such as the beguines or recluses,[28] or as patrons and benefactors of reform for monastic communities of both sexes.[29] This has led to increased attention into how women's responses to reform not only bring their

---

[27] As Beach and Cochelin have also noted: 'The tendency to see women as marginal to – or even problematic for – the work of orders is popular in contemporary histories and encourages the continued relegation of religious women to their own, separate chapters in monastic surveys'; as a consequence of which female monasticism is too often seen as a 'side-growth' of the monastic 'family tree'; in 'General Introduction', pp. 5–7, citation, pp. 6–7. Representative studies of women and their interactions with new religious orders include Maiju Lehmijoki-Gardner, 'Writing Religious Rules as an Interactive Process: Dominican Penitent Women and the Making of their Regula', *Speculum*, 79 (2004), 660–87; Anne E. Lester, *Creating Cistercian Nuns: The Women's Religious Movement and its Reform in Thirteenth Century Champagne* (Ithaca, N.Y., 2011); Catherine M. Mooney, *Clare of Assisi and the Thirteenth-Century Church: Religious Women, Rules, and Resistance* (Philadelphia, 2016); and Bert Roest, *Order and Disorder: The Poor Clares between Foundation and Reform* (Leiden, 2013).

[28] The arguments of Herbert Grundmann, *Religious Movements in the Middle Ages: The Historical Links between Heresy, the Mendicant Orders, and the Women's Religious Movement in the Twelfth and Thirteenth Century with the Historical Foundations of German Mysticism,* trans. Steven Rowan (Notre Dame, 1995), have been revised and extended. For example, see Letha Böhringer, Jennifer Kolpacoff Deane and Hildo van Engen (eds), *Labels and Libels: Naming Beguines in Northern Medieval* Europe (Turnhout, 2014); Tanya Stabler Miller, *The Beguines of Medieval Paris: Gender, Patronage, and Spiritual Authority* (Philadelphia, 2014); Alison More, *Fictive Orders and Feminine Religious Identities, 1200–1600* (Oxford, 2017); and Walter Simons, *Cities of Ladies: Beguine Communities in the Medieval Low Countries, 1200–1565* (Philadelphia, 2001). For research into recluses see Anneke B. Mulder-Bakker, *Lives of the Anchoresses: The Rise of the Urban Recluse in Medieval Europe,* trans. Myra Heerspink Scholz (Philadelphia, 2005); and Frances Andrews and Eleonora Rava, 'Introduction: Approaches to Voluntary Reclusion in Medieval Europe (13th–16th Centuries)', in *Quaderni di storia religiosa medievale,* 24:1 (2021), 7–30, and articles in this special issue.

[29] For an overview see Hedwig Röckelein, 'Founders, Donors, and Saints: Patrons of Nuns' Convent', in Jeffrey F. Hamburger and Susan Marti (eds), *Crown and Veil: Female Monasticism from the Fifth to the Fifteenth Centuries,* trans. Dietlinde Hamburger (New York, 2008), pp. 207–24; Erin L. Jordan, *Women, Power, and Religious Patronage in The Middle Ages* (New York, 2006); Jonathan R. Lyon, 'Nobility and Monastic Patronage: The View from Outside the Monastery', in CHMM, pp. 848–64; and Karen Stöber, 'Female Patrons of Late Medieval English Monasteries', *Medieval Prosopography,* 31 (2016), 115–36. For a case study that examines a founder's influence on normative models see Christina Andenna, 'Sancia, Queen of Naples and *Soror Clara*: A Life Lived Between Secular Responsibilities and Religious Desire', in Lezlie Knox and David B. Couturier (eds), *Franciscan Women: Female Identities and Religious Culture, Medieval and Modern* (New York, 2020), pp. 115–32.

roles in power relations into sharper focus,[30] but also contribute to new questions that seek to understand varied models of male clerical engagement in nurturing, directing or restraining religious women's lives.[31] These strands of research have played an important role in restoring our historical understanding of women as individual people and examining their options within specific contexts.

One risk in approaching women's involvement in monastic reform is that the narratives are reduced to binaries, whether of women as proponents or as opponents of the changes affecting their lives. That women found themselves regularly in situations of oppression, subject to forced and unwanted change which diminished their autonomy, is unquestioned. But this was not the only experience; it is necessary also to examine why some women saw benefits and others constraints arising from interventions into their institutions, and what individual women stood to gain as well as lose.[32] Examining how nuns negotiated the tensions between autonomy and repression is central to understanding the varied

---

[30] Studies that examine aspects of women's power in various contexts of reform include: Jane Carroll, 'Subversive Obedience: Images of Spiritual Reform by and for Fifteenth-Century Nuns', in Therese Martin (ed.), *Reassessing the Roles of Women as 'Makers' of Medieval Art and Architecture* (Leiden, 2012), pp. 705–37; Jennifer C. Edwards, *Superior Women: Medieval Female Authority in Poitiers' Abbey of Sainte-Croix* (Oxford, 2019); Sigrid Hirbodian, 'Reformschwestern und Reformverliererinnen. Strategien und Handlungs-möglichkeiten geistlicher Frauen in den Reformen des 15. Jahrhunderts', in Andreas Bihrer and Dietmar Schiersner (eds), *Reformverlierer 1000–1800: Zum Umgang mit Niederlagen in der europäischen Vormoderne* (Berlin, 2016), pp. 449–73; Mooney, *Clare of Assisi*; Lehfeldt, *Women in Golden Age Spain*; Vanderputten, *Dark Age Nunneries*; and Winston-Allen, *Convent Chronicles*.

[31] See, amongst others: Fiona Griffiths, 'Men's Duty to Provide for Women's Needs: Abelard, Heloise, and their Negotiation of the Cura Monialium', *Journal of Medieval History*, 30 (2004), 1–24; Ead. and Julie Hotchin, *Partners in Spirit: Women, Men and Religious Life in Germany, 1100–1500* (Turnhout, 2014); Fiona Griffiths, *Nuns' Priests' Tales: Men and Salvation in Medieval Women's Monastic Life* (Philadelphia, 2018); Meri Heinonen, 'Between Friars and Nuns: The Relationships of Religious Men and Women in Johannes Meyer's *Buch der Reformatio Predigerorderns*', *Oxford German Studies*, 42:3 (2013), 237–58; and ead., 'Men in the Communities of Dominican Nuns – Sister-Books Discussing Priests and Friars', *Journal of Religious History*, 40:4 (2016), 589–609. On the repressive implications of reform for some women, see Tamar Herzig, 'Female Mysticism, Heterodoxy, and Reform', in James Mixson and Bert Roest (eds), *A Companion to Observant Reform in the Late Middle Ages and Beyond* (Leiden, 2015), pp. 255–82, and Rabia Gregory, 'Thinking of Their Sisters: Authority and Authorship in Late Medieval Women's Religious Communities', *Journal of Medieval Religious Cultures*, 40:1 (2014), 75–100.

[32] For a synthesis of critical approaches to research into women and power over the last two decades see Marie A. Kelleher, 'What Do We Mean by "Women and Power"?', *Medieval Feminist Forum*, 51:2 (2015), 104–15.

experiences of women and monastic reform.[33] The outcome of these questions is not always as clear or straightforward as we would expect or might have hoped for. Indeed, historians have increasingly pointed towards the fluid, even ambiguous monastic identities of women religious – which, as Alison Beach and Isabelle Cochelin have observed, makes them 'hard to place within a single order or to characterise with a single term'.[34] Recent studies increasingly employ this concept of fluid identity as a vector to study how women navigated tensions of historical change, placing them at the forefront in recent histories of monastic and religious renewal.[35] As a result, we see how spiritual credibility and socio-political viability could be more important factors shaping women's choices (to the extent that they exercised choice) than any strict adherence to a specific rule, or even order, congregation or tradition. As Bert Roest noted on the Observant reform in the fifteenth century, 'it was more important that monastic communities were able to sell their spiritual, socio-political, and economic relevance to their surroundings', and indeed some communities, such as noble foundations of canonesses, were equally able to do so without aligning with a reformist movement.[36]

In focusing on monastic reform as a negotiated reality, *Women and Monastic Reform* enriches the current vein of research that challenges earlier assumptions of reform as negative or irrelevant for women, directing attention instead to women as active participants responding to wider processes of religious, economic and social change. While recognising the limited use of 'reform' as a broad

[33] On this point see Kathryne Beebe, 'Observant Reform in the Late Middle Ages', in Bernice M. Kaczynski (ed), *The Oxford Handbook of Christian Monasticism* (Oxford, 2020), pp. 300–13; see also Vanderputten, *Dark Age Nunneries*, p. 7.

[34] Beach and Cochelin, 'General Introduction', p. 8.

[35] See, for example, Vanderputten, *Dark Age Nunneries*; Jirki Thibaut, 'Rectamque Regulam Servare. De ambigue observantie en heterogene identiteit van vrouwengemeenschappen in Saksen, ca. 800–1050' (unpublished Ph.D. dissertation, Ghent University, University of Leuven, 2020); More, *Fictive Orders*; Sherri Franks Johnson, 'Negotiated Unions and Hostile Takeovers: Studying Religious Women's Choices in Late Medieval Italy', *Viator*, 44:2 (2013), 267–82. See further also: Katherine Gill, 'Scandala: Controversies Concerning Clausura and Women's Religious Communities in Late Medieval Italy', in Scott L. Waugh and Peter D. Diehl, *Christendom and its Discontents. Exclusion, Persecution, and Rebellion, 1000–1500* (Cambridge, 1996), pp. 177–203.

[36] Bert Roest, 'A Crisis of Late Medieval Monasticism?', in CHMM, p. 1186. On canonesses see Andermann, 'Die unsittlichen und disziplinlosen Kanonissen'; Sigrid Hirbodian, 'Religious Women: Secular Canonesses and Beguines', in Kaczynski (ed), *Handbook of Christian Monasticism*, pp. 285–99; Klapp, *Äbtissinnenamt*; and Gabriela Signori, 'Leere Seiten: Zur Memorialkultur eines nicht regulierten Augustiner-Chorfrauenstifts im ausgehenden 15. Jahrhundert', in Gabriela Signori (ed), *Lesen, Schrieben, Sticken und Erinnen. Beiträge zur Kultur- und Sozialgeschichte mittelalterlicher Frauenklöster* (Bielefeld, 2000), pp. 149–84.

label to refer to historical change, we nevertheless consider that it remains useful to refer to a close study of specific circumstances. Contributors interpret 'reform', therefore, as a negotiated reality occurring within the societal context of each individual community and its historical traditions and identity. Authors examine how female communities debated reform precepts concerning their manner of living, in the process creating models of community with spiritual resonance and relevance to them. Although these processes of transformation could at times result in considerable restriction, even violence, for some individuals, female institutions could and did remain viable and socially relevant. The range of adaptive strategies women adopted invites us to explore the spaces for negotiation and how individual women, with or against male associates, navigated the pressures of religious change. Collectively, the volume provides new insights into how female responses to reformist interventions into the internal discipline and organisational structures of their religious communities were conditioned by local, social, political and religious circumstances. In doing so, this volume enlarges our understanding of women as active agents in the debates affecting their lives, highlighting how the ways in which women religious dealt with reform were more ambiguous and inconsistent than previously has been assumed.

Chronological and Geographical Scope

This volume offers a broad chronological and geographical approach. It includes 'snapshots' of reform from western Europe, reaching from Ireland to Spain, and spans the period from *c.* 1000 to *c.* 1500. Across this span, it is crucial to note that the experiences and strategies of negotiating reform were not the same for every period, region or even community. Hence, *Women and Monastic Reform* does not claim to be comprehensive in its coverage of the topic across this period; the diversity of experiences and the circumstances of monastic reform are simply too great to address in a single volume. Contributors present case-studies that offer new insights into how reform in female monastic contexts is understood in order to further stimulate research into how women participated in debates affecting their manner of religious life and the institutional forms in which they sought to practice it.

In adopting a wide-angle lens to look comparatively across time and space, this volume aims to identify continuities and parallels as well as differences in the experiences of monastic women and how they crafted religious and social identities that gave expression to their narratives of self. In focusing on local variability, the case-studies comprising this volume advance our understanding of what women envisioned and accomplished as they negotiated shifting social and spiritual landscapes.

Sources

Our understanding of women's (and men's) experiences of monastic reform is necessarily determined by the sources that survive. Contributors to this volume employ a rich and wide-ranging body of evidence. Sources analysed include liturgical and devotional manuscripts, economic and legal records in archival collections, built remains, textiles, art historical evidence, hagiography and historical narratives. The nature, extent and variety of sources differ markedly across the chronological breadth of this volume, from the more limited material in the early period to the richer availability of evidence, textual and material, produced by and for women in later centuries. The introduction of new liturgical forms and disciplinary observance frequently generated an increase in nuns' literate activity, as education in literacy (Latin or vernacular) and theological knowledge was necessary to prepare nuns to fulfil their liturgical duties.[37] Research in the last two decades has demonstrated amply the breadth of material produced by and for women, especially sources written or produced by women that render their activities visible or that shed light on their attitudes and engagement.[38] This diversity of sources also produces innovative methodological approaches in response to questions such as how do we uncover a female voice or female agency in a collaborative production? How do we address the silence or rhetoric of female

---

[37] The scholarship on nuns' literacy, writing and education is vast. For orientation and individual case studies see the three volumes arising from the 'Nuns' Literacies' project: Virginia Blanton, Veronica O'Mara and Patricia Stoop (eds), *Nuns' Literacies in Medieval Europe: The Hull Dialogue* (Turnhout, 2013); *Nuns' Literacies in Medieval Europe: The Kansas City Dialogue* (Turnhout, 2015); and *Nuns' Literacies in Medieval Europe: The Antwerp Dialogue* (Turnhout, 2018).

[38] Representative examples of research into textual sources that are reshaping our understanding of nuns' cultural and intellectual participation in reform include: Eva Schlotheuber, *Klostereintritt und Bildung: die Lebenswelt der Nonnen im späten Mittelalter; mit einer Edition des "Konventstagebuchs" einer Zisterzienserin von Heilig-Kreuz bei Braunschweig; (1484–1507)* (Tübingen, 2004); and the project 'The Nuns' Networks: Editing and Producing an In-Depth Catalogue of the Letters from Lüne Abbey (c.1460–1555)', led by Henrike Lähnemann and Eva Schlotheuber. This digital edition will edit and catalogue the correspondence of the Benedictine nuns of Lüne to make this extraordinary collection of letters accessible to scholars (http://diglib.hab.de/edoc/ed000248/start.htm [accessed 27 December 2022]). For reform and nuns' textile production see Tanja Kohwagner-Nikolai, *'Per manus sororum'…: Niedersächsische Bildstickereien im Klosterstich (1300–1583)* (Munich, 2006), and for the material culture of devotion see June L. Mecham, *Sacred Communities, Shared Devotions: Gender, Material Culture, and Monasticism in Late Medieval Germany* (Turnhout, 2014). An important recent approach to the archaeology of medieval women's monastic life is Tracy Collins, *Female Monasticism in Medieval Ireland: An Archaeology* (Cork, 2021). See also the literature cited in the footnotes below.

voices in primary evidence? How can the analysis of material evidence add to our understanding of women's experiences in addition to the study of the textual? New questions are asked regarding familiar material too, as liturgical sources are used to untangle how women religious created an institutional narrative of the self, or how renewed scholarly attention to nuns' textile production demonstrates how female communities exploited the potential of this medium to negotiate identities. The following discussion addresses three groups of sources which have each been the subject of critical reappraisal in recent years and which form the basis of several studies in this volume: archival documents, liturgical sources, and material and visual culture.

ARCHIVAL DOCUMENTS

Investigating how historical subjects meshed reformist decrees and precepts with existing practices and local traditions requires a shift of focus from reliance upon centralised records such as those from orders and General Chapters, to sources that enable us to hear the 'voices' (however mediated) of people from 'below'.[39] This direction has been particularly important for uncovering histories of religious women, and for re-writing histories that locate women and other groups at the forefront of events. Charters and archival records provide a clarifying point of entry into this research.[40] As Scott Bruce notes, charters 'are expressive of a host of historical information that rarely surfaces in religious texts'.[41] Archival records, such as grants, charters and cartularies, enable us to plot the economic resources of communities, the ties a community maintained with lay and ecclesiastical stakeholders and other communities, and also how these evolved, became

---

[39] This methodological shift is one aspect of a wider 'turn' in the study of religious history, discussed by Christine Caldwell Ames, 'Medieval Religious, Religions, Religion', *History Compass*, 10:4 (2012), 334–52; and Giles Constable, 'From Church History to Religious Cultures: The Study of Medieval Religious Life and Spirituality', in Miri Rubin (ed.), *European Religious Cultures: Essays Offered to Christopher Brooke on the Occasion of his Eightieth Birthday* (London, 2008), pp. 3–16. Other examples, though not exhaustive, are Berman, *The White Nuns*; Lezlie Knox, *Creating Clare of Assisi: Female Franciscan Identities in Later Medieval Italy* (Leiden, 2008); Johnson, *Monastic Women*; Lester, *Creating Cistercian Nuns*.

[40] For a more general discussion on the preservation of archival records of female communities, see Katrinette Bodarwé, 'Gender and the Archive: The Preservation of Charters in Early Medieval Women's Communities', in Mathilde Van Dijk and René Nip (eds), *Saints, Scholars, and Politicians. Gender as a Tool in Medieval Studies. Festschrift in Honour of Anneke Mulder-Bakker on the Occasion of her Sixty-Fifth Birthday* (Turnhout, 2005), pp. 111–32.

[41] Scott Bruce, 'Sources for the History of Monasticism in the Central Middle Ages (c. 800–1100)', in CHMM, pp. 382–98, citation at p. 383.

stronger or loosened in a changing social, economic and political context.[42] Contributors to this volume also show how such archival records and documents of practice can be used to investigate different dimensions of institutional change, and how women religious negotiated the complex relationships and expectations of kin, patrons and external authorities in the process of adopting new rules to structure their lives. Sherri Franks Johnson's and Elena Vanelli's chapters draw upon charters to investigate the scope of women's agency in institutionalisation processes. They piece together evidence from local contexts to reveal insights into women's (and men's) spiritual aspirations, their scope for action within local lay and ecclesiastical networks, and the choices and accommodations they faced as their communities were confronted with structural changes for consolidation, regularisation or dispersal.

LITURGICAL SOURCES

The analysis of liturgical books and their exchange provides an important vantage point to investigate how women religious integrated new musical forms and spiritual ideas into existing liturgical practices.[43] Close examination of the material evidence of surviving manuscripts reveals glimpses into how women negotiated the devotional and liturgical changes affecting their communities.[44] The studies by Gordon Blennemann, Mercedes Pérez Vidal, Katie Bugyis and John Glasenapp in this volume employ codicological, paleographical and contextual analysis to shed light onto the selection, emendation and circulation of texts and books within and between female communities, showing us how individuals reflected upon reform ideas and whether to integrate them into their manner of living. These authors advance our understanding of women as liturgical actors, revealing how the form

---

[42] *Ibid.*, pp. 383–6; Lauren Mancia, 'Sources for Monasticism in the Long Twelfth Century', in Alison Beach and Isabelle Cochelin (eds), CHMM, pp. 668–70.
[43] Alison Noel Altstatt, 'The Music and Liturgy of Kloster Preetz: Anna von Buchwald's Buch im Chor in its Fifteenth-Century Context' (unpublished Ph.D. thesis, University of Northern Iowa, 2011); Jeffrey Hamburger, Eva Schlotheuber, Susan Marti and Margot Fassler, *Liturgical Life and Latin Learning at Paradies bei Soest, 1300–1425. Inscription and Illumination in the Choir Books of a North German Dominican Convent* (2 vols, Münster, 2017); and Ulrike Hascher-Burger and Henrike Lähnemann, *Liturgie und Reform im Kloster Medingen. Edition und Untersuchung des Propst-Handbuchs Oxford, Bodleian Library, MS. Lat. liturg. e. 18* (Tübingen, 2013).
[44] Beach, *Women as Scribes*; Henrike Lähnemann, 'The Materiality of Medieval Manuscripts', in *Oxford German Studies* 45:2 (2016), 121–41; June Mecham, 'Reading between the Lines: Compilation, Variation and the Recovery of an Authentic Female Voice in the *Dornenkron* Prayer Books from Wienhausen', *Journal of Medieval History*, 29 (2003), 102–28; Vanderputten, 'Debating Reform', 289–305.

and content of the liturgy that stood at the heart of communal practice and identity could become a prism for reform processes within female monasteries.[45]

MATERIAL AND VISUAL CULTURE

Contributors also draw upon material and visual sources, furthering our understanding of the lived experience of women religious. Analysis of the material evidence of monastic life helps us to discern women's attitudes, spirituality and self-image in the context of reform, and to consider how material things structured and informed a nun's sense of self.[46] A greater focus on a convent's material culture directs our attention to how nuns employed architecture, visuality and objects in their strategies to shape the spaces of their cloister and demonstrate their presence and power.[47] To this end, chapters by Tracy Collins and Jennifer Edwards analyse the organisation of and contests about monastic space to reveal how the arrangement and reconfiguration of space produced hierarchies of gender and power. These studies also show how different possibilities for women's monastic life were realised spatially, from the experimental forms of co-located

---

[45] For more on the liturgical and pastoral roles exercised by women, see amongst others Katie Ann-Marie Bugyis, *The Care of Nuns: The Ministries of Benedictine Women in England during the Central Middle Ages* (New York, 2019); Ead., 'The Practice of Penance in Communities of Benedictine Women Religious in Central Medieval England', *Speculum*, 92:1 (2017), 36–84; Jeffrey F. Hamburger and Eva Schlotheuber (eds), *The Liber ordinarius of Nivelles. Liturgy as Interdisciplinary Intersection* (Tübingen, 2020); Claire Taylor Jones, *Ruling the Spirit: Women, Liturgy, and Dominican Reform in Late Medieval Germany* (Philadelphia, 2018); Suzan Boynton, 'Monastic Liturgy, 1100–1500: Continuity and Performance', in CHMM, pp. 958–74; Gisela Muschiol and Alison Beach, 'Gender and Monastic Liturgy in the Latin West (High and Late Middle Ages)', in CHMM, pp. 803–15.

[46] Studies in the anthropology of religion argue that the material world is integral to belief; see, for example, David Morgan (ed.), *Religion and Material Culture: The Matter of Belief* (London, 2010). See also Mecham, *Sacred Communities*; Caroline Walker Bynum, *Christian Materiality: An Essay on Religion in late Medieval Europe* (New York, 2011); and Ead. 'Crowned with Many Crowns': Nuns and Their Statues in Late-Medieval Wienhausen', *The Catholic Historical Review*, 101:1 (2015), 18–40.

[47] In addition to Mecham, *Sacred Communities*, other representative studies include Kathleen Giles Arthur, *Women, Art and Observant Franciscan Piety: Caterina Vigri and the Poor Clares in Early Modern Ferrara* (Amsterdam, 2018); Corine Schleif and Volker Schier, *Katerina's Windows: Donation and Devotion, Art and Music, as Heard and Seen in the Writings of a Birgittine Nun* (Philadelphia, 2009); Stefanie Seeberg, *Textile Bildwerke im Kirchenraum: Leinenstickereien im Kontext mittelalterlicher Raumausstattungen aus dem Prämonstratenserinnenkloster Altenberg/Lahn* (Petersberg, 2014); and Olaf Siart, *Kreuzgänge Mittelalterlicher Frauenklöster: Bildprogramme und Funktionen* (Petersberg, 2008).

communities on the one hand to producing normative models of communal life on the other.

One form of material culture closely associated with female religious practice, especially in the context of reform, is textile production. Embroidered hangings performed key functions at times of crisis when a community's autonomy, customs or traditions were challenged and its members sought to legitimise their identity and privileges.[48] The importance of textiles as a vehicle for collective representation in female monastic culture is examined in chapters by Julie Hotchin and Vera Henkelmann, and Katharina Mersch. Their analyses of visual programmes and the contexts in which they were produced reveals how women employed this medium to express claims to female spiritual privilege, authority and piety.[49] These embroidered visualisations of female self-image and gender dynamics demonstrate how women's involvement in the production of liturgical textiles could give them 'a voice through a visible language'.[50]

Debating Identities, Creating Communities

The studies in this volume add texture to the emerging picture of how women religious responded to calls for spiritual and institutional renewal as political actors fully involved in their local social contexts. In bringing together authors from varying career stages we aim to show how the latest research is reframing the field. The approaches and conclusions presented here do not constitute a new narrative of women and reform. However much a synthesis of reform processes and responses from the standpoint of women religious and their supporters might be desired, it is, as said before, well beyond the scope of this volume. Authors do, however, document multiple shifts in emphasis and offer reappraisals that contribute to a more layered and nuanced understanding of women's endeavours to realise their desired forms of religious life. They bring a variety of critical

---

[48] Tanja Kohwagner-Nikolai, 'Patrons, Saints and Benefactresses: The Use of Tapestries to Create Corporate Identity in Late Medieval Nunneries', in Evelin Wetter (ed.), *Iconography of Liturgical Textiles in the Middle Ages* (Riggisberg, 2010), pp. 141–52.

[49] Jane L. Carroll, 'Woven Devotions: Reform and Piety in the Tapestries Done by Dominican Nuns,' in Jane L. Carroll and Alison Stewart (eds), *Saints, Sinners and Sisters. Gender and Northern Art in Medieval and Early Modern Europe* (Aldershot, 2003), pp. 182–201; Kohwagner-Nikolai, *'Per manus sororum'*; and Ane Preisler Skovgaard, 'The Fabric of Devotion: A New Approach to Studying Textiles from Late Medieval Nunneries', *Konsthistorik Tidskrift/Journal of Art History*, 90:1 (2021), 44–64.

[50] Stefanie Seeberg, 'Women as Makers of Church Decoration: Illustrated textiles at the Monasteries of Altenberg/Lahn, Rupertsberg, and Heiningen (13th–14th c.)', in Martin (ed.), *Reassessing the Roles*, pp. 355–91, citation at p. 391.

perspectives and share a commitment to analysing women's actions as political, strategic and adept at responding to their circumstances. Nevertheless, some common threads about female responses and debates about religious identity emerge, namely: female institutional identities, and male–female relations and gendered religious identities.

FEMALE COLLECTIVE IDENTITIES AND INSTITUTIONAL AFFILIATION

A primary theme addressed in this volume is how communities engaged with normative models of female religious life. Female institutional identities waxed and waned contingent upon local contexts and the perceived spiritual and political advantages of one or other models of religious life. Women made strategic and pragmatic choices in determining whether to adopt, reject or accommodate aspects of particular religious identities.[51] Authors stress the messiness of the processes through which communities sought to craft local identities and traditions in the context of wider changes, and the tenacity with which women and their male supporters influenced outcomes within the limits of their circumstances.

As several contributors show, liturgical texts prove to be an important prism through which to explore the dynamics of how a community engaged with normative models of female religious life. Blennemann's analysis of the reception of the image of the virgin martyr Agnes in the *Lives* of saints Glodesind and Liutrud from tenth-century Lotharingia, for example, reveals traces of wider debates about the legitimate scope of female spiritual activity such as teaching and instruction. Further insights into how women religious engaged with pressures to adopt models of female holiness at odds with how a community understood their role and spiritual action are presented by Bugyis in her analysis of a tenth-century devotional compilation attributed to Leominster. Her perceptive contextual reading of the compilation reveals it to be an unique expression of

---

[51] Examples of this research vein are Lucy C. Barnhouse, 'Disordered Women? The Hospital Sisters of Mainz and Their Late Medieval Identities', *Medieval Feminist Forum: A Journal of Gender and Sexuality*, 55:2 (2019), 60–97; Elizabeth Freeman, "Houses of a Peculiar Order': Cistercian Nunneries in Medieval England, with Special Attention to the Fifteenth and Sixteenth Centuries', *Cîteaux* 55 (2004), 245–87; Johnson, *Monastic Women*; More, *Fictive Orders*; Christopher M. Kurpiewski, 'Power in the Pursuit of Religion: The Penitent Sisters of Speyer and their Choice of Affiliation', in Heather J. Tanner, Laura L. Gathagan and Lois Lynn Huneycutt (eds), *Medieval Elite Women and the Exercise of Power, 1100–1400. Moving Beyond the Exceptionalist Debate* (Cham, 2019), pp. 199–223; Linda Rasmussen, 'Order! Order! Determining Order in Medieval English Nunneries', in Linda Rasmussen, Valerie Spear and Dianne Tillotson (eds), *Our Medieval Heritage: Essays in Honour of John Tillotson for his 60th Birthday* (Cardiff, 2002), pp. 30–49; and Vanderputten, *Dark Age Nunneries*.

collective identity in which a (likely) female scribe blends normative directives from the *Regularis Concordia* with local practices such that the women 'remade reform after their own likeness'.[52]

Contributors also trace how the circulation of liturgical manuscripts offers evidence of women's participation in wider institutional connections and debates. As Glasenapp and Pérez Vidal show, the exchange of liturgical books and transmission of texts could convey ideas and practices expressive of particular religious identities and generate solidarities between monastic houses. Books were important vectors to introduce and promote new liturgical practices or methods of spiritual formation, and close attention to their context and circumstances reveals a high degree of variability in the extent to which efforts to unify liturgical ideas were adopted in these communities. The chapters by these authors reveal how textual exchange between communities crossed boundaries of order and gender, demonstrating that common spiritual aims could be more important than order identities.[53]

Reformist debates about institutional forms of women's religious life are crystallized clearly in the questions about the relation between women religious and male orders. Women's implicit or explicit adoption of a specific order identity was, especially in traditional research, attributed to the imposition of a particular observance or to the resistance of male orders to accommodate women's requests to affiliate with them. Little attention was given to identifying the motivations that influenced women to opt for a particular affiliation – or not.[54] In the last two decades, studies on women's relations with religious orders stress the contingent processes through which communities were affiliated with or adopted institutional identities aligned with male orders.[55] Authors in this volume take up calls to

[52] See Bugyis's chapter, pp. 57–80, citation at p. 80.

[53] Anna Dlabačová. 'Transcending the Order: The Pursuit of Observance and Religious Identity Formation in the Low Countries, *c*. 1450–1500', in Bert Roest and Johanneke Uphoff (eds), *Religious Orders and Religious Identity Formation, ca. 1420–1620. Discourses and Strategies of Observance and Pastoral Engagement* (Leiden, 2016), pp. 86–109; and Julie Hotchin, '*Reformatrices* and their Books: Religious Women and Reading Networks in fifteenth-century Germany', in John N. Crossley and Constant J. Mews (eds), *Communities of Learning: Networks and the Shaping of Intellectual Identity in Europe, 1100–1500* (Turnhout, 2011), pp. 251–91.

[54] For a discussion of this, see the chapters of Vanelli and Johnson in this volume. Beach and Cochelin observe that 'much of the scholarship on *feminae religiosae* has focused on their inclusion – or exclusion from – various orders'; 'General Introduction', p. 5.

[55] See amongst others the literature cited in notes 27 and 35, and Barnhouse, 'Disordered Women?'; Elizabeth Freeman, 'The Fourth Lateran Council of 1215, the Prohibition against New Religious Orders, and Religious Women', *The Journal of Medieval Religious Cultures*, 44:1 (2018), 1–23; Johnson, *Monastic Women*; More, *Fictive Orders*; Knox, *Creating Clare of Assisi*; Hedwig Röckelein, 'Frauen im Umkreis der benediktinischen

examine how processes of institutional formation involved women and others in a series of intricate trade-offs as they weighed the perceived benefits of economic stability, privileges or legitimisation against the potential costs of autonomy, such as financial insecurity or the threat of accusations of heterodoxy. Women religious are shown to be pragmatic in how they advanced their interests and secured a place for their communities. Vanelli's study of the gradual transformation of lay religious communities into monastic houses that adopted a Cistercian identity situates women's choices against the backdrop of wider civic tensions and conflicts. By investigating how women navigated local ecclesiastical and civic politics in making choices about institutional forms, she argues that women's decisions to adopt a Cistercian identity need to be seen within the wider economic and political environment of Lombard towns. Debates about religious identities could also bring internal communal divisions into sharp relief. Pressures to adopt different religious observances, whether imposed externally or initiated from within, went to the heart of personal narratives of self and collective rituals through which corporate identity was formed. This is brought in sharp focus by Edwards. Her analysis of the debates generated within the convent of St Croix when pressures to adopt a new observance required the reorganisation of monastic space underlines how monastic identities were bound with familial, social and political ties.

By teasing out the multiple, overlapping identities of women's institutions within fluid religious landscapes, authors in this volume respond to Katherine Gill's call to contribute to 'more inclusive and varied histories' of women's religious institutions.[56] In response to this line of thought, Collins and Johnson demonstrate how close attention to patterns of institutional development contributes to a rewriting of earlier narratives. Collins counters traditional narratives of church reform in twelfth-century Ireland that attributed reform initiatives to clerical agents, influenced by continental models. Rather, her analysis presents a nuanced and complex picture of co-located monastic settlements in Ireland that evolved out of a variety of pre-existing or new arrangements. Johnson's chapter, on the other hand, adopts a broader angle to survey local episcopal efforts to organise religious communities at a local level. She adduces evidence to demonstrate that some male as well as female monasteries subject to episcopal authority fluctuated in their observance and institutional status over time, thereby countering

---

Reformen des 10. bis 12. Jahrhunderts. Gorze, Cluny, Hirsau, St. Blasien und Siegburg', in Gert Melville and Anne Müller (eds), *Female 'vita religiosa' between Late Antiquity and the High Middle Ages* (Vienna, 2011), pp. 275–328.

[56] Gill, 'Scandala', p. 201.

standard narratives that only female monasteries were marginalised or existed beyond the governance structures of male orders.

MALE–FEMALE RELATIONS

This volume also contributes to new histories that explore the interdependence between men and women in monastic life.[57] Female religious institutions were dual-sex to some extent because a clerical presence was required to provide sacramental services and to manage or assist with legal and business affairs. While ordained men serving in female monasteries could be a source of tension or anxiety, these men could also express respect and esteem for women's religiosity and the traditions of the female institutions with which their own identities and interests were bound.[58] Authors in this volume offer fresh insights into how reform could engender reciprocity between religious women and the men responsible for their spiritual oversight, such as how men enabled female spiritual leadership or collaborated with women on a shared spiritual mission. The contributions of Edwards, Johnson and Glasenapp, for example, illustrate how nuns championed reform initiatives, with ecclesiastical support, often assuming extensive spiritual and organisational authority as they extended their observance into other communities. Despite pressures to adopt recognised models of monastic life, female monastic leaders could also craft and gain approval for modified customs that reflected their practical concerns and devotional interests. These studies illustrate how a nun's social rank and the convergence of local reformist politics could enable some women to (re)fashion the rhythms of a community's practice and identity in their own image.

Ordained priests and monks were also drawn to women religious as an attribute of their spirituality, understanding their ministry to nuns as Christ's brides as a path to their own salvation.[59] From the twelfth century, monks and priests who lived alongside women in dual-sex monastic communities or ministered to women religious justified their arrangements in the face of criticism with references to recreating communities of women and men in the model of the early church.[60] Collins examines the material traces of this phenomenon in what she

---

[57] In addition to the works cited in note 31, see also Stephanie Monika Neidhardt, 'Die Beziehungen zwischen dem männlichen und weiblichen Zweig des Dominikanerorderns', in Eva Schlotheuber and Sigrid Schmitt (eds), *Zwischen Klauser und Welt: Autonomie und Interaktion spätmittelalterlicher geistlicher Frauengemeinschaften* (Ostfildern, 2022), pp. 95–113.

[58] The implications of this structural arrangement, which took many forms, are discussed in Griffiths and Hotchin (eds), *Partners in Spirit*.

[59] Griffiths, *Nuns' Priests Tales*, pp. 39–76.

[60] In addition to the work cited in note 59, see also Alison I. Beach, 'Women Among the

identifies as an experimental model of co-located male and female communities associated with the Augustinian order of Arrouaise in Ireland. Despite the lack of evidence about how these co-located communities emerged and functioned within their societies, they nevertheless present suggestive evidence of canons' willingness and commitment to minister to women religious. Collins's analysis raises numerous questions about how such communities may have interpreted and expressed their collective identities, how they may have interacted, and about female agency in the organisation and leadership of these communities. Hotchin and Henkelmann examine similar questions about gendered spiritual identities in their investigation of the iconography and context of a twelfth-century textile fragment from a (likely) female Benedictine community in northern Germany. The striking imagery of nuns and biblical women accompanied by clerics and holy figures associated with a ministry to women and evangelisation promotes reciprocity between women and men in a shared spiritual mission. The textile's visual programme expresses a sophisticated message about how the interdependence of gendered spiritual roles was imagined within a monastic community animated by religious renewal.

A central methodological question driving research into the production of material culture and devotional objects in the contexts of reform asks who had power to determine what identities were expressed, and through which media.[61] Mersch takes up this question through her investigation into the respective roles of women and men in producing objects that represent corporate religious identity. Seeking to identify 'who made reform visible', she explores the scope of female agency in producing artworks for female use. Her conclusions challenge notions that nuns were prevented by enclosure from participating in and acquiring the

---

Apostles? The Complexities of the Double Monastery', in *ead.*, *The Trauma of Monastic Reform: Community and Conflict in Twelfth-century Germany* (Cambridge, 2017), pp. 73–90, and Julie Hotchin, 'Female Religious Life and the Cura Monialium in Hirsau Monasticism, 1080 to 1150', in Constant J. Mews (ed.), *Listen, Daughter: The Speculum Virginum and the Formation of Religious Women in the Middle Ages* (New York, 2001), pp. 59–83.

[61] The essays gathered in Martin (ed.), *Reassessing the Roles of Women*, examine the issues involved in identifying the 'maker' of material objects. Jeffrey Hamburger explores the particular challenges of identifying women's agency in obtaining, choosing and selecting imagery for devotional purposes in the context of the *cura monialium* in 'Art, Enclosure and the Cura Monialium: Prolegomena in the Guise of a Postscript', in *Gesta*, 31 (1992), 108–34; and Anne Winston-Allen examines women's role in the exchange of images and developing shared visual cultures in the context of Observant reform in 'Networking in Medieval Strasbourg: Cross-Order Collaborations in Book Illustration among Women's Reformed Convents', in Stephen Mossman, Nigel F. Palmer and Felix Heinzer (eds), *Schreiben und Lesen in der Stadt. Literaturbetrieb im spätmittelalterchen Straßburg* (Berlin, 2012), pp. 197–212.

intellectual, design and artisanal skills to produce works that visualised collective spiritual identities. Hotchin and Henkelmann also take up this question, gesturing towards a possible collaboration between men and women in the conception, design and production of a luxury embroidered silk fragment. They, too, contest assumptions that nuns lacked theological training or design skills to picture their place in salvation history alongside men in visual media.[62] The material evidence of built remains, manuscripts and textiles, together with textual sources, contributes to a richer picture of how women and men understood themselves as working together to further spiritual renewal of the Christian church.

Conclusion

The essays gathered here revise traditional narratives of reform in which women religious were overlooked or dismissed as passive; in contrast, our authors foreground women at the centre of debates about what constituted viable models of collective religious life. The case studies in this volume upend notions of women's monastic life as in 'decline', bringing to the fore evidence of the myriad ways in which female religious institutions were esteemed for their intercessory, social and caritative roles within local societies. Far from being marginal, contests about the forms that women's religious life could take demonstrate how nuns were integral to local communities. Focusing on women's intentions and aspirations, this volume presents a vibrant picture of female political agility, uncovering how women – individually and collectively – responded to calls for spiritual renewal and negotiated their religious identities. Seeking to identify the voices of women in a variety of sources, the authors eschew a one-size fits all approach through detailed analyses in which evidence of female perspectives, aspirations and ideas add texture and nuance to our understanding of the history of women's monastic institutions. Finally, *Women and Monastic Reform* contributes to new narratives about how monastic women sought to realise their aims for collective religious life and demonstrates their continued significance for the medieval Church and society.

---

[62] Tanja Kohwagner-Nikolai also advances this argument in her consideration of gender and textile production: 'Per manus sororum? Überlegungen zur Genderfrage bei der Herstellung von Paramenten', in Ursula Röper and Hans Jürgen Scheuer (eds), *Paramente in Bewegung: Bildwelten liturgischer Textilien (12. bis 21. Jahrhundert)* (Regensburg, 2019), pp. 139–50.

CHAPTER 2

Liturgy and Female Monastic Hagiography Around the Year 1000: A *lecture croisée* of the *Life* of Liutrud, the *Second Life* of Glodesind of Metz and the So-called *Pontificale Romano-Germanicum*

GORDON BLENNEMANN

IN a fundamental essay published in 1991 on the significance of religious women's communities in early and high medieval Saxony, the late Michel Parisse called for a comparative perspective on the political, social and religious conditions of the conspicuous density of women's communities in Saxony.[1] In doing so, he referred to his home region of Lorraine, for which he – amongst others – used the term Lotharingia to describe its early medieval reality.[2] In terms of sheer numbers, Lotharingia is indeed closest to the Saxon situation, but chronologically its

---

[1] Michel Parisse, 'Frauenstifte und Frauenklöster in Sachsen vom 10. bis zur Mitte des 12. Jahrhunderts', in Odilo Engels, Franz-Josef Heyen, Franz Staab and Stefan Weinfurter (eds), *Die Salier und das Reich* (3 vols, Sigmaringen, 1991), vol. 2, pp. 465–502, in particular p. 465.

[2] Of interest here is the standard article on the connection between aristocracy and monastic reform: Michel Parisse, 'Noblesse et monastères en Lotharingie du IXe au XIe siècle', in Raymund Kottje and Helmut Maurer (eds), *Monastische Reformen im 9. und 10. Jahrhundert* (Sigmaringen, 1989), pp. 167–96. See also the following more recent publications on Lotharingia: Michel Margue and Hérold Pettiau (eds), *La Lotharingie en question. Identités, oppositions, intégration / Lotharingische Identitäten im Spannungsfeld zwischen integrativen und partikularen Kräften. Actes des 14es Journées Lotharingiennes, 10–13 octobre 2006* (Luxembourg, 2018); Tristan Martine and Jesska Nowak (eds), *D'un regnum à l'autre. La Lotharingie, un espace de l'entre-deux? Vom Regnum zum Imperium. Lotharingien als Zwischenreich?* (Nancy, 2021); Jens Schneider, *Auf der Suche nach dem verlorenen Reich: Lotharingien im 9. und 10. Jahrhundert* (Cologne, 2010); and

monasteries also refer back to earlier times. Examples of this are the Merovingian foundations of Remiremont in the Vosges and Sainte-Glossinde and Saint-Pierre-aux-Nonnains in the Carolingian *lieu de mémoire* Metz.[3] Women's monasteries like these combined stabilising power in the Carolingian core lands with supra-regional influence within the framework of the Frankish *regnum* and *imperium*. For areas such as Saxony, which were integrated comparatively late into the Frankish sphere of influence, the politico-religious structures of the ancient parts of the Frankish realm provided a framework of tradition and reference far into the post-Carolingian period.[4]

In this contribution – not least as an expression of gratitude to one of my academic teachers – I would like to take up Parisse's observations. I do not aim at a similarly broad investigation, especially since a comparative approach in a broad thematic perspective would go beyond the scope of the contribution as well as of this volume, even though recent studies on women's religious communities in Saxony and Lorraine invite us to do so.[5] The focus is rather on a partial aspect: the textual and ideological relations between liturgy and hagiography in the tenth and early eleventh centuries. Such an approach is complementary to studies in which the importance of relics and hagiographical texts as vectors of communication, the transfer of ideas and the spatial integration of new secular and ecclesiastical structures of power were elaborated – again primarily for the Carolingian period.[6] Following on from these studies, the observations in this article concentrate on

---

Thomas Bauer, *Lotharingien als historischer Raum. Raumbildung und Raumbewusstsein im Mittelalter* (Cologne, 1997).

[3] See on Remiremont Michèle Gaillard, *D'une réforme à l'autre (816–934): les communautés religieuses en Lorraine à l'époque carolingienne* (Paris, 2006), in particular pp. 265–304, and on Saint-Pierre-aux-Nonnains et Sainte-Glossinde Gordon Blennemann, *Die Metzer Benediktinerinnen im Mittelalter: Studien zu den Handlungsspielräumen geistlicher Frauen* (Husum, 2011), pp. 68–93.

[4] Caspar Ehlers, *Die Integration Sachsens in das fränkische Reich: 751–1024* (Göttingen, 2007).

[5] For Saxony namely: Jirki Thibaut, '*Rectamque Regulam Servare*. De ambigue observantie en heterogene identiteit van vrouwengemeenschappen in Saksen, ca. 800–1050' (unpublished Ph.D. dissertation, Ghent University, University of Leuven, 2020); and Ingrid Rembold, *Conquest and Christianization: Saxony and the Carolingian World, 772–888* (Cambridge, 2018). For Lotharingia see Steven Vanderputten, *Dark Age Nunneries: The Ambiguous Identity of Female Monasticism, 800–1050* (Ithaca, N.Y., 2018).

[6] For example, the two following monographs: Hedwig Röckelein, *Reliquientranslationen nach Sachsen im 9. Jahrhundert: über Kommunikation, Mobilität und Öffentlichkeit im Frühmittelalter* (Stuttgart, 2002); and Maximilian Diesenberger, *Predigt und Politik im frühmittelalterlichen Bayern: Arn von Salzburg, Karl der Große und die Salzburger Sermones-Sammlung* (Berlin, 2015).

religious and monastic aspects of these genres and raise questions about the shared significance of liturgy and hagiography for the definition and mediation of traditional as well as new ascetic and monastic models of life in the tenth century.

The debates which shaped these models are part of monastic and broader religious transformations traditionally labelled as the reform of the tenth and early eleventh century.[7] Concerning the impact of these transformations on the identity of religious women, more recent studies underline the (above all, episcopal) urge to reduce the variety of individual and institutional life forms and to restrict female agency in the debates about these transformations in order to confine their voices to the inner monastic sphere.[8] These developments obviously built on Carolingian precedents, but the socio-political reality of the post-Carolingian world changed the interplay between local contexts and overarching discussions. It is against this background that I would like to explore how old and venerable models of sanctity – namely the model of the late antique virgin-martyr – were used as argumentative tools in hagiography and liturgy, either as a means of ecclesiastical control of religious women or as a reference of authority by the women themselves. In this sense I adopt an approach that examines how people engage with texts and ideas, rather than imposing concepts such as reform as given facts at the outset of this investigation.

The focus is on a limited number of sample texts, some of which are well known. On the one hand, the article looks at the *ordines* concerning women in the so-called *Pontificale Romano-Germanicum* (henceforth PRG).[9] This has recently been reconsidered by Henry Parkes on the basis of a broad examination of the manuscript tradition, in critical discussion with the monumental edition of the PRG by Cyrille Vogel and Reinhard Elze, which in turn was based on the preliminary work of Michel Andrieu.[10] Amongst other things, Parkes has challenged the standard view that the PRG was produced in the Mainz monastery of St Alban's in the 960s, even as he emphasises the importance of Mainz as a place of

---

[7] See with a discussion of the historiography Steven Vanderputten, 'Monastic Reform from the Tenth to the Early Twelfth Century', in CHMM, pp. 599–617.

[8] See on this Vanderputten, *Dark Age Nunneries*, pp. 88–110; and Blennemann, *Die Metzer Benediktinerinnen*, pp. 75–93.

[9] Cyrille Vogel and Reinhard Elze (eds), *Le Pontifical romano-germanique du 10ᵉ siècle [Pontificale Romano-Germanicum saeculi decimi]* (Vols 1–3) (3 vols, Città del Vaticano, 1963–72) (henceforth: *Le Pontifical*).

[10] See Henry Parkes, *The Making of Liturgy in the Ottonian Church: Books, Music and Ritual in Mainz, 950–1050* (Cambridge, 2015), and the critical approach to the edition by Vogel and Elze: Henry Parkes, 'Questioning the Authority of Vogel and Elze's Pontifical romano-germanique', in Helen Gittos and Sarah M. Hamilton (eds), *Understanding Medieval Liturgy: Essays in Interpretation* (Farnham, 2016), pp. 75–101, which also offers a survey of the historiography.

liturgical reflection and manuscript production. Parkes generally underlines the great variety of text versions and contexts of use of the manuscripts, which rather speak to an interplay of different scriptoria and contexts of origin. Most recently, however, he has suggested Emperor Henry II and his political environment as initiators of the liturgical tradition of the PRG in the years between 1002 and 1009. The PRG might have been compiled for the first time for the newly founded bishopric of Bamberg as a gift for the cathedral there.[11]

In relation to the hagiography, the focus is on two *Vitae* of the second half of the tenth century, which describe the lives of religious women of the fifth and sixth centuries: Glodesind, founder and abbess of a nunnery in Metz, and Liutrud, a *Deo sacrata* and hermit in the Perthois (Champagne). As we shall see, there is evidence of cult traditions for both saints around the year 1000, both in Lotharingia and in Saxony.

The *Vita* of St Glodesind (BHL 3563)[12] was probably written by John of Saint-Arnoul, to whom the *Vita* of John of Gorze is also attributed, on the basis of an anonymous model written around 900 (BHL 3562)[13] at the request of the nuns of the monastery of Sainte-Glossinde in Metz.[14] The dossier also includes translation and miracle reports (BHL 3564), which, however, will not be analysed in our context. The *Vita* was written between 960 and 984. John's version of the dossier is found, amongst others, in the only known manuscript of the *Vita* of John of Gorze, which was copied around the year 1000.[15]

The hagiographical dossier of St Glodesind indicates that the nuns of Sainte-Glossinde resisted against the relics of their founding abbess being too widely

---

[11] Henry Parkes, 'Henry II, Liturgical Patronage and the Birth of the "Romano-German Pontifical"', in *Early Medieval Europe*, 28 (2020), 104–41.

[12] John of Saint-Arnoul, 'Vita sanctae Glodesindis secunda', ed. *AS, Iulii*, vol. VI (Antwerp, 1729), col. 210–12 (henceforth 'Vita Glodesindis secunda'), see on the text Monique Goullet, 'Glodesindis', in Monique Goullet and Martin Heinzelmann (eds), *Miracles, vies et réécritures dans l'Occident médiéval: Actes de l'Atelier "La réécriture des Miracles" (IHAP, juin 2004) et SHG X-XII : dossiers des saints de Metz et Laon et de saint Saturnin de Toulose* (Ostfildern, 2006), pp. 288–95. On John of Saint-Arnoul: Peter Christian Jacobsen (ed.), *Die Geschichte vom Leben des Johannes, Abt des Klosters Gorze*, MGH, Script. rer. Germ. in usum schol. sep. ed., vol. LXXXI (Wiesbaden, 2016), pp. 81–6.

[13] 'Vita sanctae Glodesindis prima', ed. *AS, Iulii*, vol. VI (Antwerp, 1729), col. 203–5 (henceforth: 'Vita Glodesindis prima'), see on the text: Goullet, 'Glodesindis', pp. 283–7.

[14] Despite the use of hagiographical topoi, this is obvious right from the beginning of the prologue: 'Multa iam diu prece sanctitatis vestrae, sorores in Christo carissimae, paulo immoderatius me perurgente, ne quid vestro denegarem amori, id demum effecit; quia quod petebatis non modo honestum, verum omnino constabat religiosum.': 'Vita Glodesindis secunda', col. 210.

[15] Paris, BnF, lat. 13766, fol. 1v–47 (dossier of St Glodesind) and fol. 49v–96v (*Life* of John of Gorze), see *Die Geschichte vom Leben des Johannes*, ed. Jacobsen, pp. 105–15.

distributed. Accordingly, only a few traces of her relics are found outside the monastery. In addition, however, we encounter indications of the significance of Glodesind as a historical and exemplary model in Lotharingia and beyond.[16] In our context, the interest of Bishop Hildeward of Halberstadt (968–96), who was educated in Metz, is particularly noteworthy: after the Slavic invasions of his diocese in 983, he wrote to Bishop Adalbero II of Metz asking him to send him relics of St Stephen and St Glodesind. The reason he gave was the protection these relics had given the city of Metz during the Norman raids in the ninth century. Both versions of the hagiographical dossier of Glodesind underline this episode and the visible work of Glodesind as patroness of the city of Metz.[17] Even though there is a lack of evidence to support this, it seems quite possible that Glodesind was known and venerated in Saxony through the mediation of individuals such as Hildeward.

While the story of Glodesind leads directly to the heart of Lotharingia, in the case of the versified *Vita* (618 decapentasyllabic verses) of St Liutrud, there are connections to Lotharingia via the author Dietrich of Trier.[18] Dietrich first lived in Mainz, founded the monastery of St Gangolf there in 960 and was provost of the cathedral by 961 at the latest. In Trier he is mentioned as a deacon or archdeacon before he was elevated to the metropolitan see in 965 with the assistance of Archbishop Willigis of Mainz.[19]

Liutrud belongs to a group of seven sisters named in the *Vita*, all of whom were consecrated virgins and for most of whom there is evidence of a cult of saints.[20] Besides Liutrud, St Pusinna stands out in this group. As early as 1958, Baudouin de Gaiffier pointed out the close textual connections between Liutrud's *Vita* and a previously unknown prose version of the *Vita Pusinnae*, which was probably written in the tenth century at the latest.[21] While de Gaiffier assumed that this

---

[16] Blennemann, *Die Metzer Benediktinerinnen*, pp. 57–8; and Bauer, *Lotharingien als historischer Raum*, pp. 570–5, with map at p. 36.

[17] With source references: Blennemann, *Die Metzer Benediktinerinnen*, p. 58.

[18] Dietrich of Trier, 'Vita sanctae Liutrudis', ed. Karl Stecker, in *MGH, Poetae latini medii aevi*, vol. V/1 (Hannover, 1937), pp. 155–73 (henceforth: 'Vita sanctae Liutrudis'). See on the text in general with a survey of the historiography: Wolfgang Kirsch, *Laudes sanctorum. Geschichte der hagiographischen Versepik vom IV. bis X. Jahrhundert* (2 vols, Stuttgart, 2004–11), vol. II/1, pp. 589–600.

[19] On Dietrich: Egon Boshof, *Das Erzstift Trier und seine Stellung zu Königtum und Papsttum im ausgehenden 10. Jahrhundert. Der Pontifikat des Theoderich* (Cologne, 1972).

[20] 'Vita sanctae Liutrudis', p. 157. On the different cult traditions see Kirsch, *Laudes sanctorum*, vol. II/1, p. 592.

[21] Baudouin de Gaiffier, 'La plus ancienne vie de sainte Pusinne de Binson, honorée en Westphalie', *Analecta Bollandiana*, 76 (1958), 188–224.

prose *Vita* was inspired by Dietrich's verse version of the *Vita Liutrudis*, Helmut Beumann has been able to show that both texts rather go back to a lost prose version of the *Vita Liutrudis*.[22] The *Vita* (BHL 310) of the Bishop of Châlons-sur-Marne Alpinus (died c. 510) could also have served as a model.[23]

The remains of Pusinna were transferred to the female community of Herford in 860, while those of Liutrud were transferred to the canons of St Paul's near Corvey in 864.[24] The relic translations formed the starting point for a rich cult tradition in Saxony to which, again, Hildeward of Halberstadt contributed amongst others.[25]

The question arises for which context and public the *Vita Liutrudis* was written. Beumann has emphasised the special closeness of Dietrich of Trier to the Ottonians.[26] Dietrich places his protagonist in close relation to St Maurice, who was of particular importance to the Ottonian dynasty.[27] Liutrud received relics of St Maurice in Agaune during her return journey from a pilgrimage in Rome, for which she built a basilica next to her hermitage on the *Mons Sigmari*, which she had received as an inheritance from her father Sigmar.[28] Beumann has therefore assumed that Dietrich recommended Liutrud to the Ottonians as an exemplary devotee of Maurice.

Against this idea of a primary function of the text as cult propaganda, Wolfgang Kirsch has rightly put forward formal arguments to propose an alternative.[29] The *Mons Sigmari* is not described in the *Vita* as a special place of veneration or pilgrimage, nor are there any references to the cult traditions of Pusinna in Herford or Liutrud in Corvey. Kirsch argues that Dietrich rather develops a hagiographical *exemplum* of *virginitas*, which was probably primarily addressed to a convent of women. We know that Dietrich was particularly committed to the women's

---

[22] Helmut Beumann, 'Pusinna, Liutrud und Mauritius. Quellenkritisches zur Geschichte ihrer hagiographischen Beziehungen', in Heinz Stoob (ed.), *Ostwestfälisch-weserländische Forschungen zur Geschichte und Landeskunde* (Münster, 1970), pp. 17–29; and reacting to Beumann: Baudouin de Gaiffier, 'À propos des vies des saintes Pusinne et Liutrude', *Analecta Bollandiana*, 89 (1971), 311–18.

[23] Röckelein, *Reliquientranslationen nach Sachsen*, p. 116.

[24] On the two *translationes* and the cult traditions in Saxony *ibid.*, pp. 190–224.

[25] *Ibid.*, p. 223.

[26] Beumann, 'Pusinna, Liutrud und Mauritius', p. 127.

[27] On the development of the cult of Saint Maurice and the Theban Legion under the Ottonians see Anne Wagner, 'Le culte des martyrs de la Légion thébaine dans l'Empire ottonien', in Nicole Brocard, Françoise Vannotti and Anne Wagner (eds), *Autour de Saint Maurice. Actes du colloque 'Politique, société et construction identitaire: Autour de Saint Maurice', 29 septembre–2 octobre 2009, Besançon (France), Saint-Maurice (Suisse)* (Saint-Maurice, 2012), pp. 405–17.

[28] 'Vita sanctae Liutrudis', p. 160.

[29] On the following, see Kirsch, *Laudes sanctorum*, vol. II/2, pp. 595–8.

monastery of Oeren in Trier, for which, however, no special cult tradition of Liutrud has been handed down. On the other hand, a cult of Liutrud does appear in the *liturgica* of the convent of Essen, which also hold relics of the saint and which was particularly close to the Ottonians.[30] Nevertheless, it is striking that the reference to St Maurice in the *Vita* emphasises above all the ideal connection between ascetic virginity and martyrdom.

In view of these far-reaching textual and cult-historical references, the question of the audience of the *Vita Liutrudis* should not be too narrowly defined. Whether in Essen or in Trier, such references point to the ability of hagiographical texts to present a view from regional and local contexts into a universal political-social frame of reference and thus to their integrative power.

The *lecture croisée* of the PRG and the two *Vitae* presented here takes up these observations and focuses on the question of the contribution of liturgical and hagiographical texts to the normative discussion on the female *vita religiosa* in the tenth century. Hagiography and liturgy are understood as complementary but sometimes also competing media in these debates. The texts' statements on the model of the consecrated virgin as well as on the liturgical forms of her consecration serve as an exemplary field of investigation. This is not primarily a contribution to the liturgical history of the consecration of the virgin in the narrower sense.[31] Rather, the aim is to relate hagiography and its function as narrated

[30] On this, see Katrinette Bodarwé, *Sanctimonales litteratae. Schriftlichkeit und Bildung in den ottonischen Frauenkommunitäten Gandersheim, Essen und Quedlinburg* (Münster, 2004), p. 203.

[31] On the *Consecratio virginum* see the still important monograph by René Metz, *La consécration des vierges dans l'église romaine: étude d'histoire de la liturgie* (Paris, 1954), in particular pp. 163-222 on the consecration of virgins in the PRG. See on this also: Nikolaus Gussone, 'Die Jungfrauenweihe in ottonischer Zeit nach dem Ritus im "Pontificale Romano-Germanicum"', in Jeffrey F. Hamburger and Carola Jäggi (eds), *Frauen – Kloster – Kunst: neue Forschungen zur Kulturgeschichte des Mittelalters; Beiträge zum Internationalen Kolloquium vom 13. bis 16. Mai 2005 anlässlich der Ausstellung "Krone und Schleier"* (Turnhout, 2007), pp. 25-42. On the *Consecratio virginum* in general see also: Philipp Oppenheim, *Die Consecratio virginum als geistesgeschichtliches Problem: eine Studie zu ihrem Aufbau, ihrem Wert und ihrer Geschichte* (Rome, 1943); Ludwig Münster, *Hochzeit des Lammes. Die Christusmystik der Jungfrauenweihe* (Düsseldorf, 1955); Adrien Nocent, 'Die Jungfrauenweihe', in Aimé Georges Martimort (ed.), *Handbuch der Liturgiewissenschaft, Bd. II: Die übrigen Sakramente und Sakramentalien. Die Heiligung der Zeit* (Freiburg, 1965), pp. 146-54; J. E. Enout, 'De virginum Consecratione quaestiones selectae', *Ephemerides liturgicae*, 76 (1962), 3-38; Ignazio M. Calabuig and Rosella Barbieri, 'Struttura e fonti dell' ordo consecrationis virginum', *Ephemerides liturgicae*, 96 (1982), 102-53; A. M. Triacca, 'Martirio: il significato salvifico-sacramentario della sua DYNAMIΣ-VIRTUS', *Salesianum*, 35:2 (1973), 247-300; Matias Augé, 'I commenti all' 'Ordo consecrationis

norm to the normativity of liturgical texts.[32] To this end, I follow fundamental recent work on textual and ritual relationships between hagiography and liturgy, as outlined by Gerard Rouwhorst[33] and Els Rose.[34] With regard to the example of the PRG, this approach also responds to Parkes's observation that a considerable proportion of the manuscripts of the liturgical tradition of the PRG probably never served liturgical practice, but were rather read as theoretical manuals.[35] Hagiography and liturgy thus intersected in two ways: as a practical manner but also as an ideal norm.

Female Ordines in the PRG

While this article concentrates on the consecration of virgins, the *ordo* of the *Consecratio virginum* in the PRG will first be considered with respect to the other *ordines* concerning women in the PRG. In the manuscripts there are a total of seven liturgical *ordines* that focus directly on religious women. In order, these are an *ordo* for the consecration of virgins,[36] an *ordo* for the mass for the consecration of virgins,[37] an *ordo* for the consecration of an abbess,[38] an *ordo* for the consecra-

---

virginum': nota bibliografica', *Ephemerides liturgicae*, 96:2 (1982), 184–7; Gabriele Kontzny, 'Die Jungfrauenweihe', in Teresa Berger and Albert Gerhards (eds), *Liturgie und Frauenfrage. Ein Beitrag zur Frauenforschung aus liturgiewissenschaflicher Sicht* (St. Ottilien, 1990), pp. 475–92; Gabriel Ramis Miquel, *Consagración de la mujer en las liturgias occidentales* (Rome, 1990); and despite the focus on the later Middle Ages: Eva Schlotheuber, *Klostereintritt und Bildung: die Lebenswelt der Nonnen im späten Mittelalter; mit einer Edition des 'Konventstagebuchs' einer Zisterzienserin von Heilig-Kreuz bei Braunschweig; (1484–1507)* (Tübingen, 2004). Publications on early medieval aspects on this matter are quoted later on in this chapter.

[32] On hagiography as narrated norm see Gordon Blennemann, 'Hagiographie: une norme narrée. Regards sur les Vitae de Jutta de Sponheim et d'Hildegarde de Bingen et le Liber visionum d'Élisabeth de Schönau', in Falk Bretscheider, Julie Claustre, Isabelle Heullant-Donat and Élisabeth Lusset (eds), *Enfermements. II, Règles et dérèglements en milieu clos (IVe–XIXe siècle)* (Paris, 2015), pp. 115–27.

[33] Gerard A. M. Rouwhorst, 'Hymns and Prayers in the Apocryphal Acts of Thomas', in Clemens Leonhard and Hermut Löhr (eds), *Literature or Liturgy? Early Christian Hymns and Prayers in their Literary and Liturgical Context in Antiquity* (Tübingen, 2014), pp. 195–212.

[34] See primarily her observations on the relationship between liturgical commemoration of the saints and hagiography in the introductory part of her edition of the *Missale Gothicum*: Els Rose (ed.), *Missale gothicum: e codice Vaticano Reginensi latino 317 editum*, Corpus Christianorum. Series Latina, 159 (Turnhout, 2005), pp. 189–328.

[35] See for instance Parkes, *The Making of Liturgy*, pp. 89–132.

[36] *Le Pontifical*, vol. I, pp. 38–46, cap. XX: *Consecratio sacrae virginis quae in epiphania vel in alvis paschalibus aut in apostolorum nataliciis celebratur.*

[37] Ibid., pp. 47–8, cap. XXI: *Item missa in natali virginum.*

[38] Ibid., pp. 48–51, cap. XXII: *Ordinatio abbatissae canonicam regulam profitentis.*

tion of virgins who remain in a domestic context[39] (whereby the first two *ordines e silentio* refer to virgins living in community), an *ordo* for the consecration of a deaconess[40] and finally an *ordo* for the consecration of a widow who has taken a vow of chastity.[41] After a series of *ordines* concerning abbots and monks,[42] the PRG offers another *ordo* for the ordination of an abbess.[43]

Not least due to the fact that a large part of the manuscripts is not available in digital form, it is not possible in our context to give a complete picture of the transmission of these seven *ordines*. Nevertheless, based on the critical apparatus of the edition by Vogel and Elze as well as the concordance tables prepared by Henry Parkes,[44] some general, albeit preliminary, statements can be made.

In his concordance tables, Parkes has placed twenty-three additional textual witnesses alongside the ten manuscripts that have been completely collated and the two that have been partially collated by Vogel and Elze. Besides the second *ordo* for the consecration of an abbess (which I don't consider in my account), the majority of these manuscripts transmit the first six liturgical forms of interest here *en bloc*, although almost never in the order given in Vogel's and Elze's edition. Moreover, only eleven manuscripts actually offer all six *ordines*. If one adds the textual witnesses that transmit four or five of them, the number increases, however, by a further eleven manuscripts to twenty-two. In these eleven textual witnesses, the *ordo* for the ordination of a deaconess and/or the *ordo missae* for the ordination of a virgin living in community are mostly missing, as this was possibly perceived as an unnecessary duplication. It is striking that only one of the twenty-two manuscripts mentioned omits the *ordo* for the consecration of a virgin living individually in a domestic context. Among the thirty-three manuscripts collated by Parkes, this *ordo* is missing in only nine textual witnesses.

All in all, it can be seen that the *ordines* concerning women were intended as a serial unit and that the various institutions and scriptoria that produced these manuscripts were interested in depicting the entire range of religious women's lifestyles beyond the monastic framework in the narrow sense.

---

[39] Ibid., pp. 51-4, cap. XXIII: *Consecratio virginum quae a seculo conversae in domibus suis susceptum castitatis habitum privatim observare voluerint.*
[40] Ibid., pp. 54-9, cap. XXIV: *Ad diaconam faciendam.*
[41] Ibid., pp. 59-62, cap. XXV: *Consecratio viduae que fuerit castitatem professa.*
[42] Ibid., pp. 62-76, cap. XXVI-XXXI.
[43] Ibid., pp. 76-82, cap. XXXII: *Ordinatio abbatisse monasticam regulam profitentis.*
[44] Henry Parkes, 'PRG Database: Concordance Tables for the *Romano-German Pontifical*' (https://henrybradshawsociety.org/prg-database/) [accessed 18 July 2021]. In the following I consistently refer to these concordance tables which offer the shelf marks of the different manuscripts.

Although the majority of the manuscripts presuppose, at least formally, the need to frame liturgically this diversity of religious women's ways of life, the devil is in the detail when it comes to the representation, classification and hierarchisation of these ways of life. The comparison of the various versions of the text (subject to more detailed studies of the manuscripts) reveals striking differences and shifts in meaning in this respect.

One of these shifts, which at the same time underlines the serial logic of the six *ordines* of interest here, deserves particular attention in our context: textual witnesses B[45] and G[46] of the PRG edition open the series of *ordines* relating to women – following the *titulus* of the *ordo* for the consecration of virgins – with a kind of preamble:

> All those, who have to be promoted to the holy orders, have to be consecrated by the bishop before the proclamation of the Gospel, because through them the preaching of the Holy Gospel has to be spread throughout the entire world. Virgins, however, and widows have to be veiled after the reading of the Gospel, because it is fitting to preach to them by means of the Gospel.[47]

To this general explanation and justification that virgins and widows, because of their position in relation to the Gospel and its proclamation, are to be consecrated after the Gospel reading, or more precisely that their *velatio* is to be celebrated after the Gospel reading, there is a complementary explanation at the beginning of the consecration of widows:

> Widows have to be veiled after the reading of the Gospel, because it is fitting to preach to them by means of the Gospel.[48]

Among the textual witnesses of the edition of the PRG, only the already mentioned manuscripts B and G offer both preambles. The explanation of the *velatio* of widows is found in all textual witnesses of the edition with the exception of

---

[45] Bamberg, Staatsbibliothek, cod. lit. 53.
[46] Eichstätt, Diözesanarchiv, cod. B 4.
[47] 'Omnes qui ad sacros ordines debent promoveri ante pronuntiationem evangelii ab episcopo debent consecrari, quia ab eis praedicatio sancti evangelii debet per totum mundum diffundi. Virgines autem et viduae post lectum evangelium debent velari, quia decet eas et per evangelium praedicari.': *Le Pontifical*, vol. I, pp. 38–9 (the translations of the PRG are mine).
[48] 'Viduae, post lectum evangelium debent velari, quia decet eas per evangelium predicare' (or *predicari* in the reading of manuscripts B, G and V [Vendôme, Bibiliothèque municipale, cod. 14]): *Ibid.*, p. 59.

manuscript T.[49] B and G are therefore in the minority with their statement that the *velatio* of virgins as well as widows is to be performed after the Gospel reading, for all other manuscripts make this restriction only for widows or completely exclude these general considerations.

René Metz has already pointed out this fundamental difference in the course of the liturgy of consecration between the various versions of the PRG, without, however, going into the underlying differences in interpretation.[50] Their significance goes far beyond the mere history of the text, as they seem to reveal a fundamental disagreement with regard to the position of consecrated virgins as readers and teachers of the Bible, or rather of the Gospel text as the essence of divine wisdom. If we understand the preamble, which only survives in B and G, as a contribution to a broader normative discussion on the question of the teaching authority of consecrated virgins *vis-à-vis* the Gospel and the biblical text in general, the other manuscripts reflect a contrary attitude: in contrast to widows, consecrated virgins very much belonged to the *sacri ordines* and were to take part in the proclamation and mediation or, in the narrower sense of the word *praedicare*, the preaching of the Gospel text *per totum mundum*. This choice of words refers quite clearly to Christ's Great Commission to the Apostles (Mt 28:16–20). This strand of the PRG's manuscripts thus took up a tradition going back to late Antiquity, which attributed to consecrated virgins a special ability to know and understand God and his wisdom.[51]

These elements of a discussion of ideas and norms in a liturgical context underline Henry Parkes's observation that a considerable part of the manuscripts of the PRG displays theoretical reflections rather than liturgical practice. This brings me back to the question posed at the outset, namely the relationship of this liturgical discussion of ideas and norms to other contemporary contributions to the normative framing of the female *vita religiosa*. My focus, as already announced, is on the

---

[49] Vienna, Nationalbibliothek, cod. lat. 701.
[50] Metz, *La consécration des vierges*, pp. 185–7.
[51] See on late antique concepts of *virginitas* the general remarks with the essential bibliography by Anne-Marie Helvétius, 'Le monachisme féminin en Occident de l'Antiquité tardive au haut Moyen Âge', in: *Monachesimi d'oriente e d'occidente nell'alto medioevo: Spoleto, 31 marzo–6 aprile 2016* (2 vols, Spoleto, 2017), vol. 1, pp. 199–201; Francisco de Borja Vizmanos, *Las vírgenes cristianas de la Iglesia primitiva: Estudio histórico y antología patrística* (Madrid, 2009); Susanna Elm, *Virgins of God. The Making of Asceticism in Late Antiquity* (Oxford, 1994); Cordula Nolte, *Conversio und Christianitas. Frauen in der Christianisierung vom 5. bis 8. Jahrhundert* (Stuttgart, 1995); Peter Robert Lamont Brown, *The Body and Society: Men, Women and Sexual Renunciation in Early Christianity* (New York, 1988); Kate Mason Cooper, *The Virgin and the Bride. Idealized Womanhood in Late Antiquity* (Cambridge, 1996).

versified *Vita* of St Liutrud by Dietrich of Trier and the *réécriture* of the *Vita* of St Glodesind of Metz by John of Saint-Arnoul.

Before doing so, however, it is necessary to recall some fundamental connections of the PRG to hagiographical traditions, which determined the form and content of the *ordo* for the consecration of virgins. They also serve as a starting point for my observations on possible intellectual and textual connections between the manuscript tradition of the PRG and the selected *Lives*.

Hagiographical Connections of the PRG

The hagiographical inspirations in the *Consecratio virginum* of the PRG have been known since René Metz's investigations on the consecration of virgins, but they have not aroused any further research interest.[52] On the one hand, Metz highlights quotations from the Latin *Passio* of the Roman martyr Agnes (BHL 156), probably written around 506-14.[53] These adoptions are found in four antiphons that were intoned by the virgins to be consecrated and/or the virgins participating in the liturgy, who already belonged to the community. Another hagiographical quotation comes from the Latin *Passio* of the Apostle Matthew (BHL 5690), which probably originated around the middle of the sixth century and is of Gallo-Frankish origin.[54] The quotation bears the title *Benedictio Matthei apostoli* in the

---

[52] Metz, *La consécration des vierges*, pp. 189-90, 203-6 and 211-12; Gussone, 'Die Jungfrauenweihe in ottonischer Zeit', pp. 31, 34-5, does not go beyond Metz's observations on this point.

[53] The text is to be found as appendix to the edition of the works of Ambrose of Milan in the PL (after the edition of the works by the Maurists): 'Passio sanctae Agnetis', Jacques-Paul Migne (ed.), PL vol. 17 (Paris, 1879), cols 735-42. A working edition can be found in Christine Phillipps, 'Materials for the Study of the Cult of Saint Agnes of Rome in Anglo-Saxon England: Texts and Interpretations' (unpublished Ph.D. dissertation, York University, 2008), pp. 205-63. On the text and its dating, see Cécile Lanéry, 'La légende de sainte Agnès: quelques réflexions sur la genèse d'un dossier hagiographique (IVᵉ-VIᵉ s.)' in *Mélanges de l'Ecole française de Rome. Moyen Âge*, 126:1 (2014), 17-25, at pp. 21-4; and ead., 'Les passions latines composées en Italie', in Guy Philippart (ed.), *Hagiographies. Histoire internationale de la littérature hagiographique latine et vernaculaire en Occident des origines à 1550*, Corpus Christianorum. Hagiographies (7 vols, Turnhout, 1994-2017), vol. 5, pp. 15-369, here at pp. 192-203 as well as, in more detail, ead., *Ambroise de Milan hagiographe* (Paris, 2008), pp. 347-83.

[54] Johann Albert Fabricius (ed.), *Codex apocryphus Novi Testamenti* (2 vols, Hamburg, 1743), vol. I, pp. 636-68. On the text see Dominique Alibert e.a. (trans.), 'Passion de Matthieu', in Pierre Geoltrain and Jean-Daniel Kaestli (eds), *Écrits apocryphes chrétiens, tome II* (Paris, 2005), pp. 808-35, here at pp. 811-14, and Els Rose, *Ritual Memory: The Apocryphal Acts and Liturgical Commemoration in the Early Medieval West (c. 500-1215)* (Leiden, 2009), pp. 170-4. The text is part of the so-called Collection of Pseudo-Abdias considered to be of Gaulish origin and dating from the end of the sixth century, see on

ordo. It refers to the words of blessing with which the Apostle Matthew consecrates the virginity of the Ethiopian princess Iphigenia and her companions in the narrative of the *Passio*. They are read out by the bishop in the *ordo* of the PRG.[55]

The *Passio Agnetis* is first encountered at the moment when the virgin to be consecrated is handed over to the bishop by her parents or relatives [*parentes*]. The virgin sings the antiphon 'Ipsi sum desponsata, cui angeli serviunt, cuius pulchritudinem sol et luna mirantur' ['I am betrothed to Him whom the angels serve, whose beauty the sun and the moon admire'], the second part of which ['cuius […] mirantur'] quotes directly from the *Passio Agnetis*.[56] The remaining hagiographical quotations accompany the *velatio*, the handing over of the *annulum* as a sign of the virgin's marriage to Christ, and finally the coronation. After the blessing and taking of the veil, the Virgin sings the antiphon 'Induit me dominus ciclade auro texto, et immensis monilibus ornavit me' ['The Lord vests me in robes woven of gold, and adorns me with boundless necklaces']. In the case of a group of candidates, each should intone the antiphon individually.[57] The entire text of the antiphon comes from the *Passio Agnetis*.[58] However, it is possibly inspired by Is 61:10: 'Et indumento iustitiae circumdedit me, quasi sponsum decoratum corona, et quasi sponsam monilibus suis' ['He … arrayed me in a robe of his righteousness, as a bridegroom adorns himself with a crown, and as a bride adorns herself with her jewels'].[59] The *Oratio post assumptum velum* is again followed by the antiphon 'Ipsi sum desponsata'.[60] Following a supplication, the third antiphon, 'Posuit signum in faciem meam, ut nullum praeter eum amatorem admittam' ['He has placed his seal upon my face so that I may receive no other lover save him'], is sung, the text of which is again taken entirely from the *Passio Agnetis*.[61] It is followed by the *Benedictio Matthei apostoli*.[62] After the taking of

---

this Dominique Alibert e.a. (trans), 'Actes latins des apôtres', in *Écrits apocryphes chrétiens*, Pierre Geoltrain and Jean-Daniel Kaestli (eds), *Écrits apocryphes chrétiens, tome II* (Paris, 2005), pp. 735–864, here at pp. 737–46, and Els Rose, 'Abdias scriptor vitarum sanctorum apostolorum? The Collection of Pseudo-Abdias Reconsidered', *Revue d'histoire des textes*, 8 (2013), 227–68.

[55] 'Et dicit episcopus benedictionem Matthei apostoli super eam [i.e. virginem]': *Le Pontifical*, vol. I, p. 45.
[56] Ibid., p. 39, cap. XX, n. 1. See on this also Metz, *La consécration des vierges*, pp. 189–90.
[57] 'Et si plures fuerint velatae, per singulas incipiatur eadem antiphona ut supra': *Le Pontifical*, vol. I, p. 44, cap. XX, n. 17
[58] Metz, *La consécration des vierges*, pp. 203–4.
[59] Ibid., p. 203, n. 143.
[60] *Le Pontifical*, vol. I, p. 44, cap. XX, n. 19.
[61] Ibid., p. 44, cap. XX, n. 21. See also on this Metz, *La consécration des vierges*, p. 205.
[62] *Le Pontifical*, vol. I, p. 45, cap. XX, n. 22. See on this Metz, *La consécration des vierges*, pp. 205–6.

the ring and the crowning with the *torques*, the fourth antiphon, 'Annulo suo subarravit me Dominus meus Ihesus Christus, et tanquam sponsam decoravit me corona' ['With his ring my Lord, Jesus Christ, has betrothed me, and like a spouse he adorned me with a crown'], inspired by the *Passio Agnetis*, is finally sung.[63] It combines a shortened quotation from the *Passio Agnetis* – there it says 'annulo fidei suae subarravit me' – with a slightly modified excerpt either from the already mentioned passage in Is 61:10 or from Ez 16:12: 'Et dedi inaurem super os tuum, et circulos auribus tuis, et coronam decoris in capite tuo' ['And I put a ring on your nose, earrings on your ears and a beautiful crown on your head'].[64]

The question of whether these hagiographical quotations are taken from older liturgical traditions or are original creations cannot always be answered unequivocally. There is much to suggest that the adoption of the Apostle Matthew's Blessing of the Virgins from his *Passio* took place in the context of the development of the PRG, for no evidence has yet been found to support its use in the liturgy of the Blessing of the Virgins prior to its use in the PRG.[65]

Metz assumed that the quotations of the four antiphons were also taken 'directly or mediated' ['directement ou par intermédiaire'] from the *Passio Agnetis*.[66] A series of antiphonaries of the ninth and tenth centuries, however, transmits an *Officium* for the feast day of the saint (21 January), in which all four chants appear, in part, even several times.[67] The oldest known, albeit fragmentary, manuscript tradition of the *Officium Agnetis* is found in the so-called Graduale-Antiphonary of Albi, which belonged to the cathedral Sainte-Cécile of Albi and was written around 890.[68] This rules out a direct adoption from the *Passio* and thus an editing of the antiphons especially for the PRG. On the basis of the comparison with the Graduale-Antiphonary of Albi, however, we can – with Metz – exclude the *Officium commune unius virginis* – probably dating back to the time of Gregory the Great – as the source of inspiration for the PRG, especially since only two of the four antiphons of the *Consecratio virginum* are found there.[69] This leaves the fact that the recourse to

---

[63] *Le Pontifical*, vol. I, p. 46, cap. XX, n. 25.

[64] Metz, *La consécration des vierges*, pp. 211–12.

[65] Ibid., p. 206.

[66] Ibid., p. 189, n. 89.

[67] For a detailed repertoire of the manuscript tradition of the *Officium sanctae Agnetis* (21 January) see 'Cantus: A Database for Latin Ecclesiastical Chant' https://cantus.uwaterloo.ca/ [accessed 18 July 2021].

[68] Albi, Bibliothèque municipale Rochegude, Ms. 44, fol. 73–73v, and the edition of John A. Emerson (ed.), *Albi, Bibliothèque Municipale Rochegude, Manuscript 44: A Complete Ninth-Century Gradual and Antiphoner from Southern France* (Ottawa, 2002), pp. 179–81; on the manuscript and its origins see *ibid.*, pp. xiii–lxvi.

[69] Metz, *La consécration des vierges*, pp. 203–4.

the hagio-liturgical tradition on Agnes as the basis for the design of the *Consecratio virginum* took place in the milieu which produced the PRG.

The references to the *Passio Agnetis* and the *Passio Matthei* are important innovations in form and content of the liturgy of the consecration of virgins. Metz has shown through his analysis of the content of the quotations from both *Passiones* that, in the context of the development of the PRG, the function of both texts as hagiographical *exempla* of the idea of the consecrated virgin's mystical bridehood with Christ was of a primary interest.[70] Indeed, both narratives present their protagonists Agnes and Iphigenia as exemplary brides of Christ who defend their fidelity to the heavenly Bridegroom against the lust of earthly suitors.

The quotations thus built on the stylisation of the consecrated virgin as the *sponsa Christi*, who, in eschatological expectation of her union with Christ, shapes her life as a virtuous battle to protect her soul against the sins and temptations of the devil. Its connection to earlier liturgical traditions is complicated given the immense diversity of the sources and the representations they convey.[71] And one has to keep in mind that martyrdom and the definition of the profession as second baptism were important complementary references to understand the symbolic nature of the consecration of virgins.[72] The PRG seems to synthesise somewhat older strands which, on the basis of the concept of the *sponsa Christi*, shaped the *Consecratio virginum* on the ritual and legal traditions of betrothal and marriage. The handing over of the *sponsa* by the parents to the bridegroom corresponds

---

[70] *Ibid.*, p. 190.
[71] For the Gaulish context the evidence has been synthesised by Gisela Muschiol, *Famula Dei. Zur Liturgie in merowingischen Frauenklöstern* (Münster, 1994), pp. 276–95; see also René Metz's articles on the early medieval context: René Metz, 'La consécration des vierges dans l'église franque du VIe au IXe siècle', *Revue des sciences religieuses*, 31 (1957), 105–21; *id.*, 'La consécration des vierges en Gaule des origins à l'apparition des livres liturgiques', *Revue de droit canonique*, 6 (1956), 321–39; and *id.*, 'La consécration des vierges dans l'église franque d'après la plus ancienne vie de sainte Pusinne (VIIIe–IXe siècle)', *Revue des sciences religieuses*, 35 (1961), 32–48. On the earlier times see O. G. Harrison, 'The formulas "ad Virgines sacras", a Study of the Sources', *Ephemerides Liturgicae*, 66 (1952), 252–73 and 352–66; Donald Dee Hochstetler, *A Conflict of Traditions: Women in Religion in the Early Middle Ages 500–840* (Lanham, 1992); Gabriel Ramis Miquel, 'La bendición de las vírgines y de las viudas en la liturgia céltica', *Ephemerides liturgicae*, 101 (1987), 145–9; *id.*, 'La consagración de las virigines y viudas en los Pontificales romanos', *Ephemerides Liturgicae*, 10 (1996), 97–140, and *id.*, 'La consagración de las virigines en la liturgica galicana y ambrosiana', *Ephemerides liturgicae*, 105 (1992), 59–76.
[72] Muschiol, *Famula Dei*, pp. 294–5, as well as Ramis Miquel, 'La consagración de las virigines'. On the definition of the *professio monachorum* as second baptism see Hubertus Lutterbach, *Monachus factus est. Die Mönchwerdung im frühen Mittelalter. Zugleich ein Beitrag zur Frömmigkeits- und Liturgiegeschichte* (Münster, 1995).

to the handing over of the virgin to the bishop, whereby the latter symbolically stands for the heavenly bridegroom Christ. The veil, ring and crown are also found as central symbolic objects in rituals of betrothal and marriage.[73]

The stylisation of the virgin as *sponsa Christi* and exemplary fighter of virtues against sins was developed by the apologists and patristics.[74] Ambrose of Milan and Prudentius' *Peristephanon* are two milestones in this development. In both, recourse to hagiographical *exempla* plays a decisive role. Among them we also find the Roman virgin martyr Agnes.[75] The Latin *Passio Agnetis* presents itself not least for this reason as a pseudo-Ambrosian letter to consecrated virgins on the saint's feast day.[76]

What is the nature of the relationship between the quotations in the PRG and the overall narratives of the two *Passiones*? The *Passio Agnetis* presents its protagonist as a twelve-year-old girl who has chosen Christ as her heavenly groom and therefore steadfastly resists the marriage proposals of the son of the prefect of Rome, who is not identified by name. The quotations from the four antiphons are integrated into the narrative. They are taken from the monologue of the saint with which she rejects the amorous advances of, and valuables offered by, the prefect's son, and styles herself as *sponsa Christi*:

> Depart from me, since I have already been taken by another lover, who has presented me with considerably better ornaments than you, *and betrothed me with the ring of his faith*: a man by far more noble than you in birth and honour. He has adorned my right hand with an inestimable bracelet, and

---

[73] Metz, *La consécration des vierges*, pp. 117-24, as well as Robert Schilling, 'Le voile de consécration dans l'ancien rit romain', in *Mélanges en l'honneur de Monseigneu Michel Andrieu* (Strasbourg, 1956), pp. 403-14; Johannes Petrus de Jong, 'Brautsegen und Jungfrauenweihe: Eine Rekonstruktion des altrömischen Trauungsritus als Basis für theologische Besinnung', *Zeitschrift für katholische Theologie*, 84:3 (1962), 300-22; and Adrien Nocent, 'Il mistero di Cristo nella Velatio sponsae e nella Velatio virginum', *Rivista Liturgica*, 55 (1968), 368-77.

[74] On the concept of the *sponsa Christi* see Metz, *La consécration des vierges*, pp. 117-24; Vizmanos, *Las vírgenes cristianas*, pp. 151-75; John Bugge, *Virginitas: An Essay in the History of a Medieval Ideal* (The Hague, 1975); Dyan H. Elliott, 'Tertullian, the Angelic Life, and the Bride of Christ', in Lisa Bitel and Felice Lifshitz (eds), *Gender and Christianity in Medieval Europe: New Perspectives* (Philadelphia, 2008), pp. 15-33; and Susanna Elm and Barbara Vinken (eds), *Braut Christi: Familienformen in Europa im Spiegel der sponsa* (Paderborn, 2016).

[75] See on Ambrose of Milan: Lanéry, *Ambroise de Milan hagiographe*, pp. 80-7, and on Prudentius see Cécile Lanéry, 'La légende de sainte Agnès: quelques réflexions sur la genèse d'un dossier hagiographique (IVe-VIe s.)', in *Mélanges de l'Ecole française de Rome. Moyen Âge*, 126: 1 (2014), 17-25, at p. 20.

[76] *Ibid.*, p. 21.

> encircled my neck with precious jewels; he has delivered priceless pearls for my ears, and surrounded me with spring flowers and glittering gems. *He has placed his seal upon my face so that I may receive no other lover save him. He has clothed me with a robe woven from gold, and adorned me with innumerable necklaces.* [...] *The angels serve him, the sun and moon wonder at his beauty.* The dead are restored to life by his odour, the infirm are strengthened by his touch: he whose power never fails, and whose wealth never decreases. I preserve my faith for him alone, I commit myself to him with total devotion: whom when I have loved him I am pure, when I have touched him I am clean, when I have received him I am a virgin.[77]

The excerpt from the monologue sums up the central elements of thought that were adopted in the PRG. Agnes knows Christ as her only beloved, who adorns her as his bride with golden robes and jewels that dwarf the gifts of the earthly bridegroom. As a sign of her fidelity she receives a ring from Christ, the expression *subarrhare annulo* coming from the Roman legal tradition for betrothal.[78] Christ also marks her with a sign on her forehead. In return, Agnes pledges service in fidelity and devotion. The love that underlies this union does not call into question her purity and virginity (in contrast to the physical desire of the prefect's son). On the contrary, her fidelity to Christ places her alongside the angels as servants of Christ and the celestials who pay homage to His beauty.

Resistance to the marriage proposal motivates the further action of the *Passio* (here reduced to the essential elements of interest in our context):[79] the prefect takes Agnes to court and gives her the choice between marriage to his son or a life as a vestal virgin. As Agnes continues to resist, she is stripped of her clothes as punishment and led to a brothel. Her hair, however, grows miraculously and

---

[77] 'Discede a me, quia ab alio iam amatore praevenata sum, qui mihi satis meliora te obtulit ornamenta, et *annulo fidei suae subarrhauit me,* longe te nobilior et genere et dignitate. Ornavit inaestimabili dextrochirio dexteram meam, et collum meum cinxit lapidibus pretiosis. Tradidit auribus meis inaestimabiles margaritas, et circumdedit me vernantibus atque coruscantibus gemmis. *Posuit signum suum super faciem meam, ut nullum praeter ipsum amatorem admittam. Induit me cyclade auro texta, et immensis monilibus ornavit me.* [...] *Cui Angeli seruiunt, cuius pulchritudinem sol et luna mirantur:* cuius odore reuiuiscunt mortui, cuius tactu foventur infirmi: cuius opes numquam deficiunt, cuius diuitiae non decrescunt. Ipsi soli servo fidem. Ipsi me tota devotione committo. Quem cum amavero, casta sum; cum tetigero, munda sum; cum accepero, virgo sum.': 'Passio sanctae Agnetis', ed. *PL* col. 814 and the working edition and English translation (which I quote) by Phillipps, *Cult of Saint Agnes*, pp. 217–20. The passages in italics are those used in the PRG.

[78] Metz, *La consécration des vierges*, pp. 211–12.

[79] 'Passio sanctae Agnetis', ed. *PL*, col. 815–21; and Phillips, *Cult of Saint Agnes*, pp. 220–38.

covers her naked body. Once in her cell, an angel appears to her and dresses her in an immaculate tunic. The prefect's son, who comes rushing with evil intentions, is slain by the angel, but then brought back to life by Agnes's prayer. This enrages the pagan priests, so that the prefect's vicar is forced to condemn Agnes to death. Her grave soon becomes a place of worship for the Christians. There she also appears to her parents accompanied by a little lamb and a retinue of heavenly virgins. The vision proves her status as *sponsa Christi*. In the final part, the *Passio* refers to Agnes's significance as a model of the female *vita religiosa*: Constantia, the daughter of Emperor Constantine, takes note of the vision, goes to the saint's tomb and is healed of ulcers. She has a basilica built over the saint's grave and from then on lives nearby in a community of virgins consecrated to God.

In the *Passio Matthei*, too, the virgin's earthly battle is portrayed primarily as a struggle against the courtship of earthly pretenders.[80] The motif of the martyr's agon is missing there. The apostle Matthew consecrates the Ethiopian princess Iphigenia and her companions as virgins at her request to protect herself from the courtship of Hirtacus. Hirtacus had succeeded Iphigenia's father Egippus on the Ethiopian throne and had promised Matthew half of the kingdom if he could win Iphigenia over to marry Hirtacus. Matthew then explains to him that the princess is already married to the Eternal King Christ. Accordingly, the consecration blessing also deals with the marriage to Christ and the fight against the devil as the 'defender of the wicked'. God may 'cover his servants with his shield'; He who has reserved for them 'the crown of virginity' and should prepare them for 'every single work of virtue and glory, adorned with [...] [His] wisdom', and give them the strength to triumph over the 'seductions of the flesh' and to reject an earthly marriage, so that they might thus merit 'indissoluble union with [...] [His] Son' Christ. From this follows Matthew's request to God to give the virgins those weapons that draw their strength from the 'virtue of the Spirit'. These 'weapons of virtue' are to serve the protection of the virgins' chastity ['castitas'], their modesty ['pudor'], their unquestionable hope placed in God ['spes certa'] and their mutual love ['caritas']. Their activity is realised in fasting, in the reading of the Holy Scriptures and in prayers as an expression of their 'effort for the grace of virginity'.[81]

---

[80] Fabricius, *Codex apocryphus*, pp. 654–62.
[81] 'Deus plasmator corporum, afflator animarum, qui nunc quam spernis aetatem, non sexum reprobas, non ullam conditionem gratia tua ducis indignam, sed omnium aequalis creator es et redemptor, tu has famulas tuas (has [...] tuas] hanc famulam tuam), quas (-s] -m) ex omni numero gregis bonus pastor eligere atque (atque) vacat PRG) ad conservandam coronam perpetuae virginitatis, castimoniam conservare animar dignatus es, tuae protectionis scuto circumtege, ut quas (ut quas] et) ad omne opus virtutis et gloriae, magistrante sapientia praeparasti (praeparasti] praepara, et (et] ut) vincentes

The idea of the *sponsa Christi* is not only expressed in the PRG in the hagiographical quotations from the *Passio Agnetis* and the *Passio Matthei*. It is precisely these quotations, however, that recall central elements of the ascetic and eschatological model of the virgin's bridehood to Christ in the context of her consecration. In the case of the blessing of consecration from the *Passio Matthei*, the origin of the text is mentioned, even though the title *Benedictio Matthei apostoli* emphasises less the hagiographical origin than the apostolic authority of the words, which is transferred to the bishop as the central liturgical agent of consecration. The virgin to be consecrated was sworn in, as it were, to her future status, and the norms and tasks associated with it with the words of the blessing, which to a certain extent have the character of a sermon. In the case of the antiphons inspired by the *Passio Agnetis*, the hagiographical reference is concealed by the transposition from the *Officium Agnetis* into the PRG. However, due to the prominence of the saint and the widespread distribution of the *Passio*,[82] the virgin to be consecrated as well as the other persons participating in the liturgy could well have been aware of this reference to the Agnes legend. Irrespective of this question, the antiphons made normative offers of identification detached from

---

(-es] -s) carnis illecebras, et licita connubia recusantes (-tes] -s), insolubilem filii tui Domini nostri Iesu Christi copulam mereantur (-antur] -atur). His (His] Huic) petimus, Domine, arma suggeras non carnalia, sed Spiritus virtute potentia, ut te muniente earum (earum] eius) sensus et membra, in earum (earum] eius) corpore (corpore] corpore et animo) non possit dominari peccatum atque sub tua gratia vivere cupientibus (-ibus] -i), nihil sibi defensor malorum, et inimicus bonorum, de his vasis (his vasis] hoc vase) iam tuo nomini consecrates (-is] -o) praevaleat vindicare. Omnem etiam genuinum calorem imber gratiae tuae caelestis extinguat, lumen vero perpetuae castitatis accendat. Facies scandalis pudica non pateat, nec incautis (-is] -e) occasionem praebeat (praebeat] tribuat) negligentia delinquendi, sitque in eis (-is] -a) casta virginitas, et ornata pariter, et armata fide integra, spe certa, et (et] vacat PRG) charitate sincera, ut praeparatis (-is] -o) animis (-is] -o) ad continentiam virtus tanta praestetur, quae superet diaboli universa figmenta, atque contemnendo praedentia, futura sectentur (-tentur] -tetur), ieiunia epulis carnalibus praeferant (-ant] -at), et lectiones sacras (sacras] sacras et orationes) conviviis et potationibus anteponant (-ant] -at), ut orationibus pastae (-ae] -a), et eruditionibus expletae (-ae] -a), inluminatae (-ae] -a) vigiliis, opus gratiae virginalis exerceant (-ant] -at). His virtutum armis has tuas (has tuas] hanc tuam famulam) interius exteriusque communiens, praesta inoffensum cursum virginitatis, ut hunc implore (ut [...] implore] implore), per ipsum Dominum nostrum Iesum Christum, redemptorem animarum nostrarum, valeant, cum quo est Deo Patri honor et gloria, in Spiritu Sancto, et nunc et semper, et per immortalia secula seculorum. (per [...] seculorum] Per.)': *Ibid.*, pp. 662–3; and *Le Pontifical*, vol. I, p. 45. The 'readings' of the PRG (that is of the edition) are given in brackets. They are limited to those to be found only in the PRG tradition, especially the grammatical changes which were necessary to address a single virgin, as the original blessing concerned Iphigena and her fellow virgins.

[82] Lanéry, *Ambroise de Milan hagiographe*, pp. 347–9.

the hagiographical *exemplum*. The virgin to be consecrated sang her own identification in the words of Agnes with which she defined and defended her status as *sponsa Christi* in the hagiographical narrative.

Against the background of these remarks on the hagiographical inspirations of the PRG, it is time to turn attention to liturgical elements of the second version of the *Vita Glodesindis* and the *Vita Liutrudis* and their formal, textual and intellectual connections to the PRG. It is hardly surprising that we find such connections in descriptions of liturgical procedures and comments by the authors as well as in passages of direct speech with prayers and blessings by the protagonists or other participants. Both texts focus in particular on the consecration of the protagonists as virgins.

Consecration of the Virgins in Hagiography

In the Glodesind narrative, the consecration occurs as a consequence of the saint's flight from a forced marriage by her father. Glodesind was born at the time of the Frankish king Childeric as the daughter of the *dux* Wintrio and his wife Godila. She escapes a first marriage to the nobleman Obolenus with the help of Christ, who, according to the author, proves to be the protector of her body and her spirit, since Glodesind has already 'consecrated her body and her spirit to the heavenly spouse'. Obolenus is arrested 'by divine providence' ['consilio utique divinitatis'] by the king and finally executed.[83] The father, however, tries to force her again to enter 'into the bridal chamber' ['ad thalamum']. She rejects the second husband just as she rejected the first. Glodesind's father therefore decides to send her to his sister Rothild, a religious woman in Trier. She is to make Glodesind compliant so that she no longer rejects 'her father's advice'.[84]

Glodesind avoids the journey to Trier by fleeing to the cathedral of Metz, called 'basilica beatissimi protomartyris Stephani' in the text. There she spends six days fasting and praying before the altar of the church. In recognition of her 'constant prayers' ['precibus assiduis'], however, she is granted, according to John of Saint-Arnoul, the 'food of the angels' ['angelica refectio'].[85] The wording anticipates

---

[83] 'Sed, quia sancta virgo caelesti Sponso jam corpus et animam suam consecraverat, eodem forte praedicto sponso, consilio utique divinitatis, jussu regio evocato, palatium juvenis sine mora contendit.': 'Vita Glodesindis secunda', col. 211.

[84] 'Erat patri soror memorandae sanctitatis, Rotlindis nomine, fama religionis Treveris opinatissima. Ad hanc eam secum abducere tentabat, ut saltem ejus suasu animus Puellae emollitus, paternis non recusaret obtemperare consiliis.': *Ibid.*, col. 211.

[85] 'Est in eadem urbe [i.e. Mediomatrica] basilica beatissimi protomartyris Stephani, quam multis saepe operatio divina miraculis illustravit. Hanc ancilla Christi, cum jam sibi res prope ad vim spectaret, ingressa, ibi intra altare et confessionem, ubi cum ejusdem martyris sanguine plurimorum continentur sanctorum reliquiae, se profugam collo-

later events, for on the seventh day, a Sunday, 'a man with an angelic countenance appears, accompanied by two exceedingly beautiful youths', visible to all bystanders. At the altar where Glodesind is praying, the man 'covers the Virgin's head with a veil, the sign of her holy way of life, visible to all'.[86] In this context, it is striking that the bishop of Metz and, in general, a priestly intervention at the consecration is not mentioned. However, the description of the angels performing the consecration has quite clear priestly features.

After this event, which breaks the parents' resistance to a religious life for their daughter, Glodesind is sent to live with her aforementioned aunt Rothild in Trier, who provides for her religious education before her niece returns to Metz and founds a 'monastery for virgins consecrated to God' ['monasterium puellarum Dei'].[87]

For the narration of the events, John of Saint-Arnoul essentially follows the *Vita prima* of Glodesind. The nuns of Sainte-Glossinde, who were mentioned as the patrons of the second version in the prologue as well as in the further course of the *Vita*, were obviously interested above all in the idea of the consecrated virgin's bridehood in Christ, which John develops and explains with greater detail and precision than the original in additions and longer passages with a special interest in the exemplary nature of his protagonist. It is therefore surprising that at the same time he deletes an allegorical poem in the prologue of the *Vita prima*, even though this refers to the Parable of the Wise and Foolish Virgins (Mt 25:1–13),[88]

---

cavit. [...] sex continuis diebus manens in ecclesia, non modo non egressa, sed et omni prorsus cibo abstinet et potu: verum qui dat escam omni carni, et replet omne animal benedictione, famulam suam humanis frustratam, divinis recreat alimentis, eamque precibus assiduis caelo intentam angelica dumtaxat probatur pavisse refectio.': *Ibid.*, col. 211.

[86] 'Instante namque jam septima die, quae Dominica erat, ecce, vir quidam vultu angelico, sequentibus pueris duobus pulcherrimis, sub omnium conspectu advenit, partemque altaris, qua virgo sacratissima pudorem tuendo celabatur, recta ingressus, velamine, sanctae specimen religionis cernentibus cunctis, beatae virginis caput obnubit.': *Ibid.*, col. 211.

[87] 'Parentibus deinceps in nullo impatiens, placidam se subdidisset, ad praedictam amitam suam Rothildam, magnae probitatis fama celebrem, quam in secundo actu de nuptiis, pudori metuens, non contumaci mente, refugerat, jam in gratia percepta non minimum gerens fiduciae, Treviros sponte contendit. Ibi, pro modo conversationis, tempore non multo exacto, cunctis jam bonorum studiis morum actuumque statu ad normam caelestis disciplinae, quidquid divinitus et humanitus aequo competit et honesto, plenissime informata, urbem sibi patrociniis divinis amicam Mettim repetiit. [...] Hunc sancta virgo divinis usibus dono dari sibi expostulans, nec mora, paratissima eorum liberalitate adeptum, monasterium puellarum Dei hodie usque insigne pulchro materialiter decore construxit, pulchriori nihilominus virtutum robore nobiliter gubernavit.': *Ibid.*, col. 212.

[88] 'Vita Glodesindis prima', col. 203.

which is a standard biblical reference for the theme of the bridehood of the virgin in Christ and features quite prominently in the PRG and the older liturgical tradition of the *Consecratio virginum*.[89]

We should not forget, however, that, especially in contexts of monastic erudition, several versions of a hagiographical narrative could be read and meditated upon in parallel. The critical and scholarly examination of the original text, especially with regard to the historical information on the characters of the narrative, is a recurring motif in the *Vita secunda* of Glodesind, an aspect which may also have interested the nuns of Sainte-Glossinde who had commissioned the *Vita secunda*. The discussion of aspects of the historical authenticity of the narrative confirmed the founding abbess as an exemplar of the *sponsa Christi*.

Central in this regard is John's commentary following the account of the *velatio* of Glodesind, in which he summarises essential elements of the consecrated virgins' special connection to God, the angels and Christ. Through allusions, his explanations are tied back to the example of Glodesind. However, she is not explicitly mentioned by name. In this way, his comments on the special qualities of the consecrated virgin – as in the case of the antiphons of the *Officium Agnetis* adapted to the PRG – are detached from the hagiographical *exemplum* and made available to the reader as universal norms.

The virgins learned from the example that 'nothing is dearer to God and more familiar to the angels' than 'the treasure of chastity'. From this follows for John also the special closeness of the virgin to Christ as his bride, 'who alone immaculately follows the immaculate Lamb'. For these reasons, 'his servant (i.e. Glodesind) was granted that inestimable grace' to be consecrated by an angel.[90] In the context of the presentation of the *velatio*, John had already emphasised that God and the angels supported Glodesind primarily because of her persistent prayer. He now elaborates on this with regard to the liturgical work of the virgin. Her 'praise of the Creator' as well as her 'hymnic singing' enabled the virgin to see and hear the heavenly sphere in the earthly context. With her 'gaze turned inward' ['cum occulos [...] in se dejectos'] on the invisible heavenly light and a special capacity to hear the divine voice, Glodesind had recognised the efficacy of her prayers and was thus able to behold the angel at her side who rejoiced with her and comforted her with the prospect of her future being with God.[91] Thus John

---

[89] See on this p. 48.

[90] 'Attendant hic virgines, et castitatis thesauro nihil Deo gratius vel angelis discant familiarius. [...] Haec sola immaculata agnum sequitur ubique immaculatum. [...] Ecce, quam praesto huic ancillae suae gratia illa inaestimabilis affuit.' Vita Glodesindis secunda', col. 212.

[91] 'Quo vero putas ore eam tunc in laudem sui erupisse creatoris, aut cujus genere vocis hymnum inaestimabili fudisse cum jubilo, cum oculos lucis illius invisibilis tam placide

describes the intervention of God and the angel in the consecration of Glodesind, in the end, as 'prophetic exultation' ['prophetica exultatione'], for in it her future status as 'heavenly bride' ['sponsa caelestis'] was already realised. Therefore, she could also say: 'Induit me Dominus vestimento salutis, et indumento justitiae circumdedit me' ['He hath clothed me with the garments of salvation, he hath covered me with the robe of righteousness']. Likewise, she could declare 'with the voice of the Church consisting of both sexes, joyfully giving thanks to the one Head (i.e. Christ)': 'Sicut sponso imposuit mihi mitram, et sicut sponsam ornavit me ornamento' ['As a bridegroom he decketh me with a mitre, and as a bride he adorneth me with jewels'].[92]

The two Latin passages of the *Vita* are two related quotations from Isaiah 61:10 in the *Vetus Latina* version, whose adoption by John of Saint-Arnoul is of some importance in our context. We have already seen that the same passage from the Book of Isaiah served as the basis for the antiphons ['Induit me Dominus ciclade auro texto'] and ['Annulo suo subarravit me'] in the *Officium Agnetis* and the PRG. The first passage quoted by John of Saint-Arnoul is indeed also found in the *Officium Agnetis*.[93] This is a rather striking textual interface between the *Vita secunda* of Glodesind and the PRG, although it cannot be ruled out that John sought inspiration directly in the Book of Isaiah or – independently of the PRG – in the *Officium* for Agnes.

However, clear parallels in motifs between the *Passio Agnetis* and the *Vita Glodesindis* speak for a direct adoption from the hagiographical tradition of the roman virgin. Like Agnes, Glodesind consecrated herself to God from childhood. Like Agnes, she rejects the earthly bridal adornment that is promised to her if she leaves Metz cathedral and thus agrees to marry the second bridegroom. The consecration of Glodesind with the veil that is placed on her head by an angel after her flight to the cathedral can perhaps be related to the episode of the *Passio Agnetis*, in which an angel also clothes the naked Agnes with a garment that is explicitly described as immaculate. It is therefore not surprising that Glodesind, from the point of view of John of Saint-Arnoul, was apparently able to intone an antiphon

---

in se dejectos, et aures illas secretissimas voci suae tam propere cognovit admotas, tamque facili via preces datas effectui, ut angelum sanctum sub ipsis mortalium oculis ad se laetificandum et consolandum praepotenti majestate advenisse gauderet?': Ibid., col. 212.

[92] 'Prophetica nimirum exultatione, jam sponsa caelestis effecta, uti poterat ac dicere: Induit me Dominus vestimento salutis, et indumento justitiae circumdedit me: itemque voce universalis ecclesiae ex utroque sexu collectae uni capiti suo gratulabunda proclamare: Sicut sponso imposuit mihi mitram, et sicut sponsam ornavit me ornamento': Ibid., col. 212.

[93] Albi, Bibliothèque municipale Rochegude, Ms. 44, fol. 73v; and Emerson (ed.), *Albi, Bibliothèque Municipale Rochegude, Manuscript 44*, p. 180, n. 470.

that came from the same tradition as the Agnes antiphons of the *Consecratio virginum* in the PRG.

The observations on the depiction of the *Consecratio virginum* in the *Life* of Liutrud coincide with René Metz's analysis of the description of the consecration of virgins in the *Vita* of Liutrud's sister Pusinna.[94] Both texts, as mentioned at the beginning, draw upon a lost prose version of the *Vita Liutrudis*. Liutrud's verse *Vita* emphasises that, in view of the special piety of Liutrud and her six sisters, their father Sigmar dedicated them at an early age to live as virgins consecrated to God and thus made a prospective vow for his daughters. As a result, they were instructed by Eugenius, a priest whom they befriended, in the knowledge of the Holy Scriptures and in the singing of psalms and hymns in a domestic context ['in domo propria'] and so they could perform daily praises to God ['dignas ei [i.e. Deo] laudes solvebant quotidie']. They underwent ten years of spiritual training, at which point Alpinus, the bishop of Châlons-sur-Marne, became aware of the seven daughters and their exemplary wisdom and sanctity. When he was on a tour of his diocese, the bishop followed the wish of both the father and his daughters and consecrated all seven sisters as virgins.[95]

The actual consecration is described as a three-part ritual. First, the bishop questioned the sisters in order to assure himself of their suitability and actual willingness to lead a life as a virgin consecrated to God. This was followed by the renewal of their vows and their confirmation by the bishop, who finally performed the actual consecration by placing the veil on each sister's head.[96]

---

[94] Metz, 'La consécration des vierges ... Pusinne', 38–45.

[95] '30. Ergo temporis processu / transeunte infantia // cum pater devotionem / filiarum cerneret, // curabat, ut pio voto / adesset scientia. 31. Sanctis siquidem scripturis / in domo tunc propria // mox ipsas per sacerdotem / instruxit Eugenium // psalmos atque spiritales / ipsas ympnos edocens. 32. Postquam nativitatem / transacto decennio // iuxta captum singularum / temporisque spatium // in sciencia librorum / perfecte enutrierant. 33. Nam psalmis simul et ympnis / sacratisque canticis // et deum plene laudare / iam instructe noverant // atque dignas ei laudes / solvebant cotidie. 34. Ea fuit tempestate / sanctitate pariter // et scientia librorum / divulgatus merito // Alpinus Cathalaunensis/ antistes ecclesie. 35. Hic cum suam circuiret / pastor parrochiam // atque confirmationis / gratiam imparciens // sive predicationis / documenta traderet, 36. Suis tunc votis Sigmarus / aptum tempus pervidens // sacerdoti consecrandas / septem tradens filias // has divino mancipari / petiit obsequio.': 'Vita sanctae Liutrudis', p. 158. I reproduce here the numbering of the stanzas given by Karl Strecker's edition in the *MGH*: 'Vita S. Liudtrudis', in *Die lateinischen Dichter des deutschen Mittelalters. Die Ottonenzeit*, MGH. Poetae Latini medii aevi (6 vols, Leipzig, 1937), vol. 5, 1.2, pp. 153–73.

[96] '37. Pontifex videns puellas / etsi adhuc teneras // tamen ad annos venisse / iam intelligibiles // ipsarum super hoc votum / sciscitandum credidit. 38. Que mox uno omnes ore / responderunt presuli // hoc sese non velle solum, / sed et multum poscere, // illis

For this part, Dietrich of Trier – probably following his model – switches to the mode of direct speech. He has Alpinus say a prayer of blessing for the consecration,[97] the beginning of which takes up the wording of the eucharistic prayer 'Deus castorum corporum benignus habitor' ['God, kind dweller in chaste bodies'] in the mass form for the consecration of virgins in the so-called *Sacramentarium leonianum*, accessible through the so-called *Sacramentarium Veronense*. It was probably written by Pope Leo I and was widespread in the Gaulish-Frankish context, especially the longer version to be found in the *Sacramentarium Gelasianum*, which added an allusion to the Parable of the Wise and Foolish Virgins.[98] Alpinus then asks God to bless and protect his 'servants' ['ancillas'] and to keep them 'chaste in spirit and body' ['castas et mente […] et corpore'].[99] The middle part of the prayer emphasises the importance of the veil as a symbol of the virgins' chastity and proof of their 'future glory' ['future glorie'] with God, but also as a sign of their 'permanent protection' ['perhennis defensio'] against the temptations of the devil.[100] The final part of the prayer could again be inspired by the tradition of the *Leonianum*, more precisely by the collect *Respice domine* ['Have regard, Lord']

---

in virginitate / fixum fore animum, 39. Se soli iam votis deo / dedicatis affore, // preter ipsum sese numquam / cognituras alium, // pro ipso et vitam ipsam / se daturas propere, 40. Eius benedictionem / ipsas solam poscere // quo actutum virginali / velate flaminio // divino consignarentur / ita ministerio. 41. Quod ut audivit sacerdos, / letus mox efficitur, // miratus devotionem / patri tantam affore, // ut deo offerret dicandas / septem simul filias.': *Ibid.*, p. 159.

[97] '43. Ergo collaudans beatum / virginum propositum // atque has virginitatis / consecrans velamine // istam benedictionem / super ipsas fuderat: 44. 'Deus benedictionum, / solus auctor omnium, // qui es castorum benignus / habitator corporum, // has modo tuas ancillas / benedic et protege': *Ibid.*, p. 159.

[98] Metz, 'Le consécration des vierges … Pusinne', 44. On the preface *Deus castorum corporum* see also Muschiol, *Famula Dei*, pp. 292–3, as well as Metz, 'Les consécration des vierges dans l'église franque', 108; Carolus Coebergh, 'Saint Léon le Grand auteur de la grande formule "Ad uirgines sacras" du Sacramentaire Léonien', *Sacris erudiri*, 6 (1954) 282–326; Jean Magne, 'La prière de la consécration des vierges 'Deus castorum corporum', *Ephemerides liturgicae*, 72 (1958), 245–67; Harrison, 'The Formulas Ad virgines sacros'; Gabriel Ramis Miquel, 'La oración "Deus castorum corporum". Teologiá sobre la virginidad consagrada', *Ephemerides liturgicae*, 100 (1986), 508–61; and *id.*, 'La consagración de las virigines en la liturgia galicana y ambrosiana', *Ephemerides liturgicae*, 105 (1991), 66–9.

[99] '45. Tu istas castas et mente / conserva et corpore, // quo virginitas suscepta, / et tuam illis gratiam // exemplumque te donante / subministret aliis': 'Vita sanctae Liutrudis', p. 159.

[100] '46. Sit hoc velamen ipsarum / capiti impositum // signum sumpte castitatis / et future glorie, // sit contra hostem antiquum / perhennis defensio.': *Ibid.*, p. 159.

that precedes the eucharistic prayer already mentioned.[101] Both prayers were taken over by the PRG from the older tradition of the mass form.[102]

The description of the consecration of Liutrud and her sisters by Alpinus seems to underline the authority of the bishop as the central actor of the *Consecratio virginum*. However, this is questioned by a second description of a woman taking the veil later in the narrative. On her way back from a pilgrimage to Rome accompanied by the priest Eugenius, Liutrud also arrives in Ravenna. In the hope of receiving help from her, the parents of a terminally ill girl invite Liutrud to their house. The mother vows on behalf of herself and her husband to consecrate the child to God if she is healed.[103] In the face of the dying girl, Liutrud addresses a prayer of supplication to God and Christ: she first speaks to God as the 'Creator [...] of all things' ['Plasmator [...] conctorum] and 'saviour of men' ['salvator hominum'], who possesses the 'power over life and death' ['vite et mortis potestatem'] and who leads the way 'into the underworld' ['ad inferos'] but also knows the way back from there.[104] In the second part, Liutrud turns to Christ and recalls – paraphrasing the Gospel of John (Ioh 11:39–41) – his raising of the dead Lazarus and his own resurrection.[105] In a third part, Liutrud formulates the actual request that Christ, through 'the hand of' his 'servant' ['par manum ancille'], may bring healing to the sick girl for the increase of his glory and the piety of the faithful, and give the parents back their only child.[106]

---

[101] 'Quatinus virginitatis / professe propositum, // sicut te nunc inspirante / devote susceperant, // sic et te has adiuvante / perpetim custodiant.': *Ibid.*, p. 159: 47. On the inspiration by the collect *Respice domine* see Metz, 'La consécration des vierges ... Pusinne', 45. On the tradition of the prayer see *id.*, 'Les consécration des vierges dans l'Église franque', 110–11.

[102] *Le Pontifical*, vol. I, pp. 42–3, nos 14 and 15. See Metz, *La consécration des vierges*, p. 202.

[103] '99. Obviam mater puelle / protinus cucurrerat // et suscipiens cum suis / virginem cum gaudio // egram supplex postulabat / visitare filiam. 100. 'Credo', ait, 'temet nostris / prestitam doloribus, // ut egra nostra iam membris / omnibus premortua // per te nunc restituatur / sanitati pristine [...] 102. Atque utinam daretur / forte nobis optio, // ipsi mortem subiremus / voto voluntario, // ut nobis deo volente / ipsa superviveret': 'Vita sanctae Liutrudis', p. 164.

[104] '106. Deinde virgo beata / accessit ad lectulum // et videns ipsam puellam / iam pene exanimem // sic de medela secura / dominum rogaverat: 107. 'Plasmator', inquit, 'cunctorum / et salvator hominum, // qui simul vite et mortis / potestatem retines, // qui ad inferos deducis / et reducis iterum': *Ibid.*, p. 165.

[105] '108. Christus, qui quatriduanum / iam fetentem Lazarum // reducem de monumento / redire preceperas // et nos resuscitaturus / terre es de pulvere': *Ibid.*, p. 165.

[106] '109. Tu et hanc, queso, puellam, / que morti nunc proxima // solo spiritu subsistit / membris iam premortuis, // per manum ancille tue / dignare erigere. 110. Quo per te nunc restituta / unica parentibus // nominis tui reverendi / crescat semper gloria // et fidelium tuorum / augescat devotio.': *Ibid.*, p. 165.

The girl is indeed healed. She immediately offers a prayer of thanksgiving to God, recalling above all her parents' vow and agreeing to live 'under the sign of virginity and the symbol of the veil' ['sub titulo virginitatis et signo velaminis']. She addresses Liutrud and asks her to 'put the holy veil on her head' ['suo sacrum velamen capiti'] and to be allowed to live by her side from then on.[107] Liutrud grants the first wish, but does not want to take her with her on her pilgrimage, as she cannot ensure her safety given the girl's beauty, and eloquently refers to the dangers within the world for the chastity of the consecrated virgin. She therefore suggests that the girl remain with her parents and serve God under their 'protection' ['custodia'].[108]

In contrast to the well-planned consecration of Liutrud and her sisters, Dietrich describes here a spontaneous *conversio* to life as a virgin consecrated to God, which is presented at the same time as a vow and sacrifice of thanksgiving of the parents for the healing of their daughter. Because of her fame and sanctity as an outstanding virgin, Liutrud is given the task of putting the veil on the girl, which brings the healing to its ritual conclusion, so to speak. The archbishop of Ravenna is not involved in these proceedings, nor is Eugenius, the priest who accompanied Liutrud.

It is also noteworthy that the wording at the beginning of the prayer with which Liutrud requests the girl's healing from God and Christ is similar to the beginning of the Apostle Matthew's consecration of the *Passio Matthei*, which – as already seen – was introduced in the PRG as part of the *Consecratio virginum*. In the *Passio Matthei*, God is invoked as 'plasmator corporum' ['creator of all bodies'] and 'afflator animarum' ['bringer of breath to all souls'].[109] Liutrud addresses God as 'plasmator cunctorum' ['creator of all things'] and 'salvator hominum' ['saviour of all men'].[110] In particular, the term *plasmator* for God as creator seems

---

[107] '114. Et cum parentum meorum / me salvatam gaudio // Ipsa votivam tuopte / dicarem servitio // Sub titulo virginitatis / et signo velaminis. 115. Ita confortata cibo / ex manu mox virginia // beatam supplex Liudtrudem / ipsa postulaverat, // ut suo sacrum velamen / capiti imponeret 116. Atque devotam assumens / vite sue comitem // cunctis se secum diebus / manere permitteret // in profectibus virtutum / et dei servicio.': *Ibid.*, p. 165.

[108] '117. Sed virgo satis prudenter / et prorsus utiliter // ipsius petitionis / effectum considerans // unum prompta concedebat, / alterum negaverat. [...] 122. Nolite, ait, molesti / inde mihi fieri; // quod ago, causa puelle / me sciat is agere, // ne libidini malorum / peregrina pateat. [...] 126. Proinde sit hec vobiscum / vestra modo filia, // istic deo famuletur / sub vestra custodia // nec magni pendat hanc meam / ad presens absentiam.': *Ibid.*, p. 166.

[109] See the quote on page 41.

[110] See the quote on page 49.

to be rarely used in the contemporary context of Liutrud's *Vita*.[111] The choice of words is therefore probably no coincidence.

A direct connection between the *Vita Liutrudis* and the PRG seems unlikely, since the same expression is found in the oldest version of the *Vita Pusinnae* and thus was probably also in the lost prose version of the *Vita Liutrudis*.[112] Nevertheless, the question arises as to what extent we may discern here in detail a general interest in this passage of the *Passio Matthei* and its use for the hagio-liturgical design and interpretation of the consecration of virgins. The hagiographical tradition of Liutrud, Pusinna and their sisters, as well as the associated relic translations and cult traditions, point to a broad late Carolingian and Ottonian communication network with a focus on the key regions of Lotharingia and Saxony.[113] The importance of Liutrud and Pusinna may have prepared and motivated the liturgical use of the *Passio Matthei* in the PRG.

Beyond such questions of textual history and the history of ideas, it seems remarkable that Dietrich of Trier – after all, archbishop of an important Ottonian metropolis – has his protagonist improvise a prayer that draws on the hagiographically transmitted words of an apostle. On a formal level, Liutrud's words are not a prayer of consecration but a prayer of supplication in the context of a healing miracle. However, since she is directly connected to this healing miracle, her prayer can certainly be understood as a consecration blessing in a figurative sense. The miracle brought the girl the hoped-for physical healing, which was permanently secured by the reception of the veil as a protective shield. In this point, too, Liutrud's *Vita* and the consecration blessing in the *Passio Matthei* (and thus also in the PRG) meet, since in both texts the consecration of the virgin is repeatedly interpreted as a ritual act of strengthening and protection. If Liutrud's prayer was indeed inspired by the wording of the *Benedictio Matthei apostoli*, then the *velatio* by Liutrud was covered by the aura of Apostolic authority.

---

[111] For the lemma *plasmator* the *Library of Latin Texts database* offers for the tenth century only two entries (in the *Glossae biblicae* of the manuscript Vatican, Biblioteca Apostolica Vaticana, Vat. Lat. 1469 and in the so-called *Passionarium Hispanicum*). In the fifteenth-century manuscript Münster, Universitäts- und Landesbibliothek, Ms. 348, which is the second volume of the so-called *Magnum Legendarium* of Böddeken, a scribe has replaced *plasmator* with *salvator* in the margin (fol. 206), see 'Vita sanctae Liutrudis', p. 165, n. 107.

[112] de Gaiffier, 'La plus ancienne Vie de sainte Pusinne', p. 221.

[113] See on this Röckelein, *Reliquientranslationen nach Sachsen*, pp. 190–224.

Conclusion

This observation leads to the final question of the overall picture that emerges from the *lecture croisée* of the PRG and the two selected *Vitae*. While this article focused primarily on the *ordo* of the *Consecratio virginum* in the PRG and related it to the two selected *Lives*, we will return to its relationship to the other *ordines* concerning women in the PRG, especially the *ordo* for the consecration of virgins living in a domestic context and the *ordo* for the consecration of widows.

Let us recall the observations made at the beginning: the manuscripts reflect very different points of view with regard to the question of the relationship of religious women to the reading and conveying of the Gospel text. A minority of the manuscripts excluded all religious women from the teaching and preaching of the Gospels and saw them solely as recipients of learning in the sense of pastoral care. From the perspective of these manuscripts, religious women were considered to be laity. The majority of manuscripts, however, did not make this restriction and thus indirectly assigned religious women the ability to teach and communicate the Gospels. However, a clear distinction was made between consecrated virgins and widows; the latter were merely taught the Gospel and their consecration was thus to take place after the Gospel reading.

At first glance, the majority of manuscripts attributed the same authority over the Gospel to those virgins who remained in the domestic context as to those living in community. The liturgical tradition of the PRG even highlights the special significance of this category of consecrated virgins, since, as already stressed, it was the first time that an *ordo* for the consecration of domestic virgins was ever recorded. We saw that this *ordo* is missing in only nine of the thirty-three manuscripts of the PRG collated by Parkes. This fits well with Eliana Magnani's observations on the survival of this form of religious life in the early Middle Ages.[114]

Behind this apparent appreciation, however, lies another strategy of distinction of the liturgy: the *lecture croisée* of the PRG and the *Lives* of Glodesind and Liutrud identified the motif of the *sponsa Christi* as the central normative reference of both hagiographies as well as of the consecration of virgins living in community in the PRG. For John of Saint-Arnoul, Dietrich of Trier and the liturgists of the PRG, the authority of the virgin modelled as *sponsa Christi* was based equally on her special closeness to the *sponsus* Christ, to the heavenly sphere and to the angels, as well as on her special wisdom, which – according to the two hagiographers – sprang from a thorough intellectual and religious training. The

---

[114] Eliana Magnani, 'Female House Ascetics from the Fourth to the Twelfth Century', in CHMM, pp. 213–31, in particular pp. 224–30.

recourse to hagiographical *exempla* and textual quotations helped to place this definition of the consecrated virgin as *sponsa Christi* in a venerable tradition. The *Passio* of Agnes of Rome, a bestseller of the Middle Ages, was obviously of central importance for this and was therefore a key model.

However, it is striking that in the PRG only the virgins living in community were urged to follow this hagiographically based normative model. In the *ordo* for the consecration of domestic virgins, the hagiographical references so crucial for the stylisation of the virgin as the bride of Christ are missing. Only one reference to the Parable of the Wise and Foolish Virgins in the prayer *Infra actionem* – taken over from the *Consecratio virginum* in the *Sacramentarium Gelasianum* – establishes a connection to the motif of bridal mysticism.[115] Neither a ring nor a crown as bridal symbols are handed over to the virgin.[116]

The liturgical tradition of the PRG thus used the motif of the *sponsa Christi*, which was central to the self-understanding of the consecrated virgins, as a means of differentiation and hierarchisation by tying it primarily to communally organised forms of life. As the influence of the responsible bishops could be more easily guaranteed for such communities, the *sponsa Christi* motif in the PRG might have been also a means of episcopal control of the spiritual authority of consecrated virgins. It is possible, however, that in many places, despite an *ordo* now available specifically for the consecration of domestic virgins, the older tradition of consecrating them according to the same liturgical forms as virgins living in community was retained.

This confirms the diversity in the manuscript tradition of the PRG emphasised earlier, as a sign of a broad discussion about the order and classification of the female *vita religiosa* around the year 1000. The *Vita Glodesindis* and the *Vita Liutrudis* represent a complementary medial framework of this discussion, which is perceptible in the sections dealing with the consecration of virgins and liturgical acts of the protagonists discussed here.

John of Saint-Arnoul describes an exemplary *sponsa Christi* on the basis of the life of Glodesind and provides corresponding theoretical reflections that generalise the *exemplum* and actualise it as a normative reference. Hagiographical traditions are in most cases invoked only implicitly. What is decisive is that the frame of action of the virgin – with prayer and the vision and meditation of God in its centre – remains limited to the inner-monastic context. John does not

---

[115] '[…], ut in numerum sanctarum virginum eam [i.e. virginem consecrandam] transire praecipias, quatenus tibi sponso suo venienti cum lampade inextinguibili possit occurrere atque intra regna caelestia gratias tibi referat, choris sanctarum virginum sociata, diesque.': *Le Pontifical*, vol. I, p. 53, c. XXIII. See on this Metz, *La consécration des vierges*, pp. 218–19.

[116] *Ibid.*, p. 220.

mention one single action of Glodesind as abbess that would have reached beyond the walls of her monastery. The work of the virgins in the convent as a mirror of the heavenly sphere is thus directed solely towards their future being with God and the *sponsus* Christ. The convent is not involved in the concerns of the world beyond the nuns' prayers.

However, other, less institutionalised forms of life appear at least peripherally in John's account in the form of Glodesind's aunt Rothild, who is concerned with the ascetic and spiritual education of her niece, for Rothild is described merely as living religiously in Trier. The transitions between the two forms of consecrated virginity, which are neatly separated in the PRG, could thus still be described as fluid in the tenth century, even if Glodesind's *Vita* formally looks back to Merovingian times.

That a strategy of distinction and control was hidden behind the differentiation between women living in community and those living in a domestic context in the PRG is confirmed by the portrait that Dietrich of Trier draws of his protagonist Liutrud, which conveys very different ideas. For Liutrud is anything but a consecrated virgin remaining in a monastic context. As in the case of Glodesind, Liutrud and her sisters were educated in their parents' home, by the priest Eugenius. In this context, the seven sisters formed a virginal community of prayer and life. The girl who was healed in Ravenna by God through Liutrud also remained with her parents as a consecrated virgin.

The death of their parents ended the community of the seven sisters. From then on, Liutrud lived with the priest Eugenius as a hermit on her hereditary estate, the *Mons Sigmari*. The relics obtained in Agaune on the way back from her pilgrimage served Liutrud as the basis for the foundation of a basilica on the same spot, which necessarily included a religious community, even if the *Vita* does not specifically emphasise this. Liutrud resumed her life there as a hermit, a constellation that anticipates the conditions of many *reclusae* of the central Middle Age, but which points at the same time to continuities with late antique and early medieval traditions of this form of life.[117]

Finally, Dietrich's descriptions of the *Consecratio virginum* are particularly remarkable. The consecration of Liutrud and her sisters by Bishop Alpinus gives the episcopal blessing to their domestic form of life. Liutrud's *velatio* of the girl in Ravenna is juxtaposed with this episcopal consecration as an equal form. In view of the possible textual transpositions from the consecration of Iphigenia and her

---

[117] On hermitism and reclusion see Kathryn Jasper and John Howe, 'Hermitism in the Eleventh and Twelfth Centuries', in CHMM, pp. 684–96; Paulette L'Hermite-Leclercq, 'Reclusion in the Middle Age', in CHMM, pp. 747–65.

fellow virgins by the Apostle Matthew in the *Passio Matthei* to Liutrud's prayers, her liturgical action even appears to be apostolically legitimised.

The fact that early medieval synodal legislation consistently demanded the bishop's sole authority in the consecration of virgins points to the continuing need for discussion on this matter, not least among the bishops themselves.[118] It was evidently not just a question of episcopal exclusivity. The consecration of a girl by an already consecrated virgin raised the general question of the position of religious women within the Church. The question of the teaching and preaching authority of consecrated virgins *vis-à-vis* the Gospel pointed in the same direction. The circles involved in the compilation and development of the *ordines* concerning women in the PRG were apparently at odds about the affiliation of religious women to the *sacri ordines*, as the term in the preamble to the *Consecratio virginum* puts it.[119] As archbishop, Dietrich of Trier, who also held important clerical functions in Mainz and was thus in a position central to the development of the liturgical tradition of the PRG, answered the question affirmatively in the *Vita Liutrudis*, while at the same time the text also describes a pragmatic compromise.

These elements of a debate on the ecclesiastical status of religious women confirm Gary Macy's observation that, for a large part of the early Middle Ages, the clerical status of men and women was essentially based on the claim and exercise of specific functions and responsibilities and not necessarily on a legalised and ritualised ordination. In other words, it was not necessarily a question of an assigned office but a question of daily routine and practice.[120] At the same time, however, it seems that the development around the year 1000 had the aura of change. This is at least suggested by the tangible discussion in the PRG and the selected *Vitae* about the question of how far-reaching the authority attributed to consecrated virgins by the *Consecratio virginum* should be. For some, the authority was primarily spiritual and eschatological in nature and limited to the interior of the monastic sphere; for others, it explicitly included involvement in ecclesiastical tasks.

How do these observations and hypotheses relate to the idea of reform, a research concept that has deliberately not been used as a means of description and analysis here? Recent research on the concept of monastic reform emphasises diversity and processuality in the period before the High Middle Ages. From a methodological point of view, this makes it necessary to focus primarily on the means of action of individuals and groups of individuals to shape reform

---

[118] See Magnani, 'Female House Ascetics', p. 222.
[119] See above, p. 33.
[120] Macy, *The Hidden History of Women's Ordination*, in particular chap. 2, 'What Did Ordination Mean?', pp. 23–88.

processes and to explore the relationship between local and overarching levels of discourse.[121]

This contribution aims to show that hagiography and liturgy and their significance as media representative of a normative discussion with regard to the female *vita religiosa* represent ideal objects of investigation, in so far as both text forms, and the practices and rituals associated with them, were permanently determined by both local and overarching contexts of tradition and innovation. Ultimately, however, this is not only a question of reform phenomena and reform processes, but also a general question of how monastic dynamics can be made tangible by examining the interplay of local and overarching contexts. It was precisely in this respect that my article responds to Michel Parisse's thesis of comparison, summarised earlier, and uses the example of the connections between hagiography and liturgy to direct attention to the local anchoring and overarching effect of textual networks.[122]

By examining the use of hagiographical traditions – especially the model of the *sponsa Christi* – and their use as normative arguments in the period around the year 1000, this article ultimately also addresses the question of how hagiography as a narrated norm made models of sanctity available for imitation and emulation and how the liturgy of the *Consecratio virginum* benefited from this dimension of narrated normativity by incorporating hagiographical references. *Imitatio* and *aemulatio* were indeed the two complementary key concepts that could permanently mediate between venerable saints of the past and the lifeworld of monks and nuns in the present. Those ecclesiastical authorities who wanted to provide a normative framework for this life-world were well aware of this. The analysis of dynamics of *imitatio* and *aemulatio* is therefore perhaps the best way to grasp what determined the core of the ascetic and monastic world and its dynamics.

---

[121] Vanderputten, 'Monastic Reform', pp. 615–16; and *id.*, *Monastic Reform as a Process. Realities and Representations in Medieval Flanders, 900–1100* (Ithaca, N.Y., 2013).

[122] See on the interplay between the local and the universal and its methodological implications also Franz J. Felten, 'Wozu treiben wir vergleichende Ordensgeschichte?', in Gert Melville and Anne Müller (eds), *Mittelalterliche Orden und Klöster im Vergleich. Methodische Ansätze und Perspektiven* (Berlin, 2007), pp. 1–51.

CHAPTER 3

Remakers of Reform: The Women Religious of Leominster and their Prayerbook

KATIE ANN-MARIE BUGYIS

THE *Rule* attributed to Benedict of Nursia (d. 547) was first brought to England at the end of the sixth century with the Roman mission led by Augustine, the first bishop of Canterbury (579–c. 509). Among the monastic communities that were founded in the ensuing three and a half centuries, however, adherence to the *Rule* was by no means universal or exclusive.[1] It was not until the tenth century, when concerted efforts were made to revive monasticism in England, that the imposition of the *Rule* as the sole guide to monastic life on communities of both men and women religious became a *desideratum*. These efforts culminated in a council convened by King Edgar (959–75) at Winchester in c. 973. Led by Dunstan, archbishop of Canterbury (960–78), Æthelwold, bishop of Winchester (963–84), and Oswald, both bishop of Worcester (961–92) and archbishop of York (971–92), the council promulgated an agreement that Æthelwold had crafted: the *Regularis concordia anglicae nationis monachorum sanctimonialiumque*.[2] Through this

---

[1] Sarah Foot, *Monastic Life in Anglo-Saxon England, c. 600–900* (Cambridge, 2006), pp. 48–60; Barbara Yorke, *Nunneries and the Anglo-Saxon Royal Houses* (London, 2002), pp. 4–5; and Jacob Riyeff (ed.), *The Old English Rule of Saint Benedict: With Related Old English Texts* (Collegeville, 2017), p. 7.

[2] See Thomas Symons's introduction to his edition of the *Regularis Concordia Anglicae Nationis Monachorum Sanctimonialiumque* (London, 1953) (henceforth *Concordia*); Thomas Symons, 'Sources of the Regularis Concordia', *Downside Review*, 59 (1941), 14–37, 143–70, 264–89; the contributions to David Parsons (ed.), *Tenth-Century Studies: Essays in Commemoration of the Millennium of the Council of Winchester and Regularis Concordia* (Chichester, 1975), especially Thomas Symons's essay, 'Regularis Concordia: History and Derivation', in David Parsons (ed.), *Tenth-Century Studies. Essays in*

agreement, the council sought to unify the practices of monastic communities across England by placing them under the protection of the king and queen, and by standardizing liturgical practice and other aspects of daily life. The Benedictine *Rule*, decrees from the councils summoned by Louis the Pious at Aachen (814–40) in 816 and 817, the customaries of Fleury, Ghent and other northern continental monasteries, and some native traditions informed the agreement's composition.

In its proem, the *Concordia* addresses both monks and nuns, and recalls that abbots and abbesses attended the council at Winchester.[3] Such explicit inclusivity of nuns in the text's opening moved Jean Leclercq to observe that 'one of the most charming' features of this reform effort was 'the part played by women at all levels'; in his estimation, it was the characteristic that 'distinguished the English reform from all others'.[4] Thomas Symons thought it likely that members of the women's monastic communities at Nunnaminster, Shaftesbury and Wilton were in attendance at the council.[5] Symons did not provide evidence to support his claim beyond citing the *Concordia*'s proem, but the geographical locations of these communities – all in Wessex – and the manner in which they were founded – all by members of the royal house of Wessex – probably encouraged him to draw this conclusion. Perhaps strengthening Symons's assertion is the account found in both Wulfstan's and Ælfric's *Lives of Æthelwold*, which credits the bishop with imposing the Benedictine *Rule* on Winchester's Nunnaminster soon after

---

Commemoration of the Millennium of the Council of Winchester (London, 1975), pp. 37–59; Michael Lapidge, 'Æthelwold as Scholar and Teacher', in Barbara Yorke (ed.), *Bishop Æthelwold: His Career and Influence* (Woodbridge, 1988), pp. 89–117; repr. *Anglo-Latin Literature 900–1066* (London, 1993), pp. 183–211; Lucia Kornexl (ed.), *Die 'Regularis Concordia' und ihre altenglische Interlinearversion. Mit Einleitung und Kommentar* (Munich, 1993); Lucia Kornexl, 'The "Regularis Concordia" and its Old English Gloss', *Anglo-Saxon England*, 24 (1995), 95–130; Catherine Cubitt, 'The Tenth-Century Benedictine Reform', *Early Medieval Europe*, 6 (1997), 77–94; Patrick Wormald, 'Æthelwold and his Continental Counterparts: Contact, Comparison, Contrast', in Stephen Baxter (ed.), *The Times of Bede: Studies in Early English Christian Society and its Historian* (Malden, 2006), pp. 169–206; Julia Barrow, 'The Chronology of the Benedictine Reform', in Donald Scragg (ed.), *Edgar, King of the English 959–975: New Interpretations* (Woodbridge, 2008), pp. 211–23; and Tracey-Anne Cooper, *Monk-Bishops and the English Benedictine Reform Movement: Reading London, BL, Cotton Tiberius A. iii in its Manuscript Context* (Toronto, 2015), esp. chap. 2.

[3] *Concordia*, pp. 1–9.

[4] Jean Leclercq, 'The Tenth-Century English Benedictine Reform as Seen from the Continent', *The Ampleforth Review*, 84 (1980), 8–23, at p. 19. Relatedly, Frank Merry Stenton conceded: 'It is possible that historians have undervalued the contribution made by women to the religious idealism behind the English monastic revival': *Anglo-Saxon England* (Oxford, 1947), p. 445.

[5] Symons, 'Regularis Concordia', p. 41.

he monasticised the city's two male religious communities, Old Minster and New Minster, in 964.[6] In Mechthild Gretsch's studies of the nine extant manuscript copies of the Old English Benedictine *Rule*, which all bear traces of deriving from a version made for nuns in its Latin and/or Old English texts, she concluded that Æthelwold was behind the original attempt to translate and adapt the *Rule* for nuns' use sometime in the 960s.[7] If Gretsch is correct, and if Wulfstan's and Ælfric's *Lives of Æthelwold* can be trusted, then it is possible that Nunnaminster and other women's monastic communities founded by and located proximate to the royal house of Wessex became followers of the Benedictine *Rule* through Æthelwold's intervention and, thus, were committed to furthering his efforts to standardise the observance of every English monastery by sending their members to participate in the council at Winchester that agreed to promulgate a single, shared consuetudinary.

Symons maintained that the *Concordia*'s influence on the observance of monasteries in England was 'far-reaching'.[8] He expected that women's communities, no less than men's, were reformed according to its dictates, but he had to concede that '[o]f reformed houses of women there is scant record'.[9] Lucia Kornexl, in her analysis of the extant witnesses to the *Concordia*'s circulation, commented

---

[6] Wulfstan of Winchester, *The Life of St Æthelwold*, eds and trans M. Lapidge and M. Winterbottom (Oxford, 1991), chap. 22, pp. 36-9; Appendix A: Ælfric's Vita S. Æthelwoldi, chap. 17, p. 76.

[7] Mechthild Gretsch, 'The Benedictine Rule in Old English: A Document of Bishop Æthelwold's Reform Politics', in M. Korhammer (ed.), *Words, Texts, and Manuscripts: Studies in Anglo-Saxon Culture Presented to Helmut Gneuss* (Cambridge, 1992), pp. 131-58, at p. 143. Gretsch's conclusions have been challenged by Rohini Jayatilaka and Julie Smith. Given that Æthelwold composed the *Regularis concordia* for both monks and nuns, Jayatilaka thought it likely that he would have kept his translation of the Benedictine *Rule* as close as possible to the original to ensure uniform monastic observance. Based on her analysis of the extant manuscripts, moreover, she did not think that the *Rule* was adapted for nuns until after Æthelwold's death in 984, either in the late tenth or early eleventh century. See Rohini Jayatilaka, 'The Old English Benedictine Rule: Writing for Women and Men', *Anglo-Saxon England*, 32 (2003), 147-87, esp. pp. 183, 185. Differently, Smith concluded that there is no evidence for the comprehensive adaptation of the *Old English Benedictine Rule* until the early twelfth century. She did concede, though, that there were at least three manuscripts of the Benedictine *Rule* with feminised text that date to the late tenth century on. These manuscripts raise interesting insights into nuns' literacies during this period, challenging assumptions about the poor education they received in their communities. See Julie Ann Smith, '"I Consider Translation Very Rational": A Vernacular Translation of the Benedictine Rule in the Tenth-Century Monastic Reforms', *American Benedictine Review*, 67 (2016), 58-80, esp. pp. 73, 78-9.

[8] *Concordia*, p. 41.

[9] *Ibid.*, p. xxiii.

on the difficulty of assessing the influence of the text given its poor survival rate. She thought that it 'must have been circulated to every reformed monastery in Anglo-Saxon England', but acknowledged that only two complete manuscript copies, produced nearly seventy-five years after the promulgation of the original, still survive.[10] Also extant are two fragmentary Old English prose translations, an Old English interlinear gloss to one of the two extant Latin copies, and the abbreviation of the text sent by Ælfric, a disciple of Æthelwold's, to the monks of Eynsham Abbey sometime after he became their abbot in 1005. These witnesses suggest attempts to incorporate the *Concordia* into the curriculum guiding the instruction of members of reformed monasteries.

Significantly, in regard to answering the question of the impact of the *Concordia* on women's monastic communities, one of the fragmentary Old English prose translations was partially adapted for female use. It can now be found in Cambridge, Corpus Christi College, MS 201 (henceforth CCCC 201), pp. 1–7 (Part A), an early eleventh-century manuscript of uncertain provenance.[11] It contains only the *Concordia*'s treatment of the Palm Sunday rituals through part of Good Friday, though it may have originally included a complete translation up to Good Friday.[12] Citing codicological and linguistic evidence, Joyce Hill argued that this partial copy of the *Concordia* ultimately derives from a complete translation of the text made not too long after its issue by a skilled translator in the ambit of Winchester who was very knowledgeable of the text, but in a form in which some of the practices had already been adapted.[13] Hill speculated that a copy of the complete translation was then acquired in the 980s or 990s by a community of women religious, likely at Nunnaminster or another West Saxon royal foundation located near the centre of reform, who then adapted it, rather unsystematically,

---

[10] Kornexl, 'The "Regularis Concordia"', 111, 117.

[11] Joyce Hill noted, but did not settle, the question of the manuscript's provenance. Various locations have been proposed, including Worcester, Canterbury, a London scribe working in York, the regions of Mercia, or the south of England more generally; Joyce Hill, 'The "Regularis Concordia" and its Latin and Old English Reflexes', *Revue Bénédictine*, 101 (1991), 299–315, at pp. 309–11. For an edition of this partial copy of the feminised *Concordia*, see Julius Zupitza (ed.), 'Ein weiteres Bruchstück der Regularis concordia in altenglischer Sprache', *Archiv für das Studium der neueren Sprachen und Literaturen*, 84 (1890), 1–24.

[12] Joyce Hill, 'Lexical Choices for Holy Week: Studies in Old English Ecclesiastical Vocabulary', in Christian Kay and Louise Sylvester (eds), *Lexis and Texts in Early English: Studies Presented to Jane Roberts* (Amsterdam, 2001), pp. 117–27, at p. 119.

[13] Hill, 'Lexical Choices', p. 119. See also Joyce Hill, 'The *Regularis Concordia* Glossed and Translated', in Patrizia Lendinara, Loredana Lazzari and Claudia Di Sciacca (eds), *Rethinking and Recontextualizing Glosses: New Perspectives in the Study of Late Anglo-Saxon Glossography* (Turnhout, 2011), pp. 249–68.

for their own use by occasional interlinear or marginal additions, which were then incorporated into the body of the text either by the scribe of CCCC 201 or by the scribe of its exemplar.[14] Such modifications to the *Concordia* would have been necessary to make the text usable by a women's monastic community because, even though the text's prologue addresses monks and nuns equally, 'the consuetudinary proper is written as if for a male community [...] Women are thus invisible within the main body of the text', as Hill observed.[15] The modifications to the *Concordia* preserved in CCCC 201, then, provide evidence that the consuetudinary did circulate to at least one women's monastic community, and that its members detected their absence in the text proper, wished to be included in it, and so adapted the ostensibly universal and unifying consuetudinary in the ways they deemed suitable to accommodate their particular local presence.

As suggestive as the witness of CCCC 201 is for women religious' participation in and creative adaptation of the tenth-century Benedictine reform, its implications should not be generalised to every women's monastic community in England, even to every West Saxon royal foundation, without corroborating evidence. Dagmar Schneider, Barbara Yorke, Catherine Cubitt and Sarah Foot all rightly questioned the degree to which women's monastic communities were 'Benedictinised' at this time.[16] In their analyses of the extant evidence, they found

---

[14] Hill, 'Lexical Choices', p. 119; Joyce Hill, 'Rending the Garment and Reading by the Rood: *Regularis Concordia* Rituals for Men and Women', in Helen Gittos and M. Bradford Bedingfield (eds), *The Liturgy of the Late Anglo-Saxon Church* (Cambridge, 2005), pp. 53–64, at p. 60; Joyce Hill, 'Making Women Visible: An Adaptation of the *Regularis Concordia* in Cambridge, Corpus Christi College MS 201', in Catherine Karkov (ed.), *Conversion and Colonization in Anglo-Saxon England* (Tempe, 2006), pp. 153–67, at p. 157.

[15] Hill, 'Making Women Visible', p. 154.

[16] Dagmar Schneider, 'Anglo-Saxon Women in the Religious Life: A Study of the Status and Position of Women in an Early Medieval Society' (unpublished Ph.D. dissertation, University of Cambridge, 1985), pp. 81, 196, 299–301; Barbara Yorke, '"Sisters under the Skin"? Anglo-Saxon Nuns and Nunneries in Southern England', *Reading Medieval Studies*, 15 (1989), 95–117, at pp. 109–10; Yorke, *Nunneries*, p. 72; Catherine Cubitt, 'Virginity and Misogyny in Tenth- and Eleventh-Century England', *Gender & History*, 12 (2000), 1–32, at pp. 1–2, 9–10; Sarah Foot, 'Remembering, Forgetting and Inventing: Attitudes to the Past in England at the End of the First Viking Age', *Transactions of the Royal Historical Society*, 9 (1999), 185–200, at p. 193; Sarah Foot, *Veiled Women: The Disappearance of Nuns from Anglo-Saxon England* (2 vols., Aldershot, 2000), vol. 1, pp. 12, 87–8, 91, 93, 95–6. It should be noted that these studies all made significant contributions to the scholarship on the tenth-century reforms. Earlier scholars had largely overlooked the question of the reforms' impact on women's monastic communities. See, for example, David Knowles, *The Monastic Order in England: A History of its Development from the Times of St Dunstan to the Fourth Lateran Council, 940–1216* (Cambridge, 1940; repr. 1950); and Stenton, *Anglo-Saxon England*.

a significant discrepancy between the rhetoric and the implementation of reform: the former was inclusive of women's communities, but the latter, for the most part, was not.[17] None of the leaders of the reform is known to have founded or even championed a women's community.[18] Even Æthelwold, Yorke emphasised, 'seems to have had limited objectives where nunneries were concerned'.[19] Thus, at many of the communities that scholars have long assumed played a role in the tenth-century monastic revival because of their close ties to the West Saxon royal house and their visibility in the surviving sources, such as Nunnaminster, Shaftesbury and Wilton, women religious continued earlier practices that contradicted the Benedictine *Rule*, including the retention of private wealth and members' ability to leave to get married.[20] Such assessments of the reform's implementation – or lack thereof – at women's communities accurately reflected the extant narrative and documentary sources from the period, limited though they are, but none of them took into consideration the surviving books produced and/or used by women religious in their liturgies and private devotions.[21] In the afterword to her *Veiled Women*, Sarah Foot recognised 'the need for further consideration of liturgical evidence' in order to assess fully the effect of the reform on women religious' observance, but she left it to other scholars to address the need.[22] This has been one of the primary aims of my research.[23]

Galba A.xiv: A Prayerbook by and for Women Religious

In this essay, I focus on one witness to the impact of the reform on women religious' practices: London, British Library, Cotton MS Galba A.xiv, an early eleventh-century prayerbook of disputed origin. It comprises 154 folios, preserving

---

[17] See especially Foot, *Veiled Women*, vol. 1, pp. 7–88.
[18] See especially Yorke, *Nunneries*, pp. 89, 93; and Cubitt, 'Virginity and Misogyny', 9.
[19] Yorke, '"Sisters under the Skin"?', 111.
[20] See especially Yorke, *Nunneries*, p. 193; and Cubitt, 'Virginity and Misogyny', 9.
[21] Dagmar Schneider did discuss three prayerbooks owned by women religious, including the one that is the subject of this essay, London, British Library, Cotton MS Galba A.xiv, but she studied them mainly for their insights into the literacies of women religious: Schneider, 'Anglo-Saxon Women', pp. 89, 95, 173–8.
[22] Foot, *Veiled Women*, vol. 1, p. 207.
[23] Katie Ann-Marie Bugyis, 'The Practice of Penance in Communities of Benedictine Women Religious in England', *Speculum*, 92 (2017), 36–84; Katie Ann-Marie Bugyis, *The Care of Nuns: The Ministries of Benedictine Women in England during the Central Middle Ages* (Oxford, 2019).

two computistical texts and approximately one hundred other identifiable texts of various types in both Latin and Old English – prayers, poems, hymns, two litanies, creeds, biblical florilegia and medical recipes – that, quite unusually, were copied in what was originally a blank book.[24] Bernard Muir used the terms 'prayerbook', 'collection of miscellaneous private devotions', and 'personal book of private devotion' to categorise Galba A.xiv.[25] Similarly, Ronald Banks called it a 'private collection of prayers, devotions and recipes',[26] and Rebecca Rushforth identified it as a 'personal prayerbook'.[27] Differently, Michael Lapidge thought that 'the book was kept as a sort of devotional commonplace by a monastic community',[28] and Joseph Hillaby echoed Lapidge's identification.[29] Muir resisted calling Galba A.xiv a 'commonplace book', because he thought that this term suggested that it was a formal liturgical book. He emphasised instead the informal and composite nature of the book, noting its lack of apparent structure in order to raise the possibility that it 'may have been used as an 'exercise' book by those being taught in the monastery'.[30] I favour identifying Galba A.xiv as a 'prayerbook' or 'collection of prayers, devotions, and recipes', but I question characterisations of its intended use as simply or exclusively 'private'. The book may have indeed been used by individuals on their own for devotional purposes, but the cooperative manner in which it was produced and the communal voice with which several of its texts were to be recited suggest a 'public' origin and use for the book, too.

There are only six prayerbooks among the extant manuscripts that predate the Norman Conquest; five, including Galba A.xiv, exhibit signs of ownership and/or use by women; and only two of these, again including Galba A.xiv, postdate the tenth-century reforms.[31] These statistics may indicate that the prayerbook was a

---

[24] Concerning the fact that it was originally a blank book, Bernard Muir noted that he had not discovered another early manuscript that was compiled in this way; Bernard Muir, 'The Early Insular Prayer Book Tradition and the Development of the Book of Hours', in Margaret Manion and Bernard Muir (eds), *The Art of the Book: Its Place in Medieval Worship* (Exeter, 1998), pp. 9–19, at p. 16.

[25] Bernard Muir (ed.), *A Pre-Conquest English Prayer-Book (BL MSS Cotton Galba A.xiv and Nero A.ii (ff. 3–13))* (Woodbridge, 1988), p. xxxiv; Muir, 'Early Insular Prayer Book Tradition', p. 16.

[26] Ronald Banks, 'Some Anglo-Saxon Prayers from British Museum MS. Cotton Galba A.xiv', *Notes & Queries* (1965), 207–13, at p. 207.

[27] Rebecca Rushforth (ed.), *Saints in English Kalendars before A.D. 1100* (London, 2008), p. 36.

[28] Michael Lapidge (ed.), *Anglo-Saxon Litanies of the Saints* (London, 1991), p. 70.

[29] Joe and Caroline Hillaby, *Leominster Minster, Priory and Borough, c. 660–1539* (Almeley, 2006), p. 25.

[30] Muir, *A Pre-Conquest English Prayer-Book*, p. xvii.

[31] Michelle P. Brown, 'Female Book-Ownership and Production in Anglo-Saxon England: The Evidence of the Ninth-Century Prayerbooks', in Christian Kay and Louise Sylvester

particularly female genre, as Michelle Brown and Barbara Raw both thought, but the possibility of coincidence cannot be ruled out given the chance survival of many of the manuscripts produced in England during the Middle Ages.[32] Galba A.xiv's history offers an excellent case in point. Little is known about it prior to its acquisition by the antiquarian Robert Cotton (1570/1–1631). It was badly burned and water damaged due to the fire that broke out at Ashburnham House, where Cotton's collection was kept, on 23 October 1731. The remains of the manuscript were subsequently mounted and rebound, thereby challenging any attempt to recover the physical structure of the book and the organisation of its folios. The manuscript's folios now measure approximately 14.5 x 11cm, and the ruled areas range 11.3–12.5 x 8–9cm in size, making it a small, portable book.[33] To make matters worse, many of its folios are now illegible, and some were placed out of order, reversed, or inverted by later conservators.[34] Considering these challenges, Julia Crick deemed it 'an enigmatic manuscript by any reckoning', and concluded that careful analysis of 'the distribution of the hands offers our only opportunity of gauging how and when the constituent parts of the manuscript were assembled'.[35]

A remarkably large number of scribes was responsible for copying the texts contained in Galba A.xiv. In her analysis of the manuscript's hands, Crick identified twelve or more, working in at least thirteen different stints.[36] She determined that there was not a significant time lag between the different writing stints, nor

---

(eds), *Lexis and Texts in Early English: Studies Presented to Jane Roberts* (Amsterdam, 2001), pp. 45–67; and Julia Crick, 'An Eleventh-Century Prayer-Book for Women? The Origins and History of the Galba Prayer-Book', in Rory Naismith and David A. Woodman (eds), *Writing, Kingship and Power in Anglo-Saxon England* (Cambridge, 2017), pp. 281–302, at pp. 281–2. The five prayerbooks owned and/or used by women include the following: London, British Library, Cotton MS Galba A.xiv, which is discussed at length in this essay; London, British Library, Cotton MSS Titus D.xxvi+xxvii (1023 x 1031); London, British Library, Harley MS 2965 (s. viii/ix or ix[1]); London, British Library, Harley MS 7653 (s. viii/ix or ix[in]), and London, British Library, Royal MS 2.A.xx (s. viii[2] or ix[1/4]). For the dates and provenances of these prayerbooks, see Helmut Gneuss and Michael Lapidge, *Anglo-Saxon Manuscripts: A Bibliographical Handlist of Manuscripts and Manuscript Fragments Written or Owned in England up to 1100* (Toronto, 2014), nos 333, 380, 432, 443 and 450, respectively.

[32] Brown, 'Female Book-Ownership'; Barbara Raw, 'Anglo-Saxon Prayerbooks', in Richard Gameson (ed.), *The Cambridge History of the Book in Britain I (c. 400–1100)* (Cambridge, 2012), pp. 460–7.

[33] Crick, 'An Eleventh-Century Prayer-Book', p. 295.

[34] According to Bernard Muir, the following folios were reversed (17, 19, 145, 148, 150), placed out of order (75, 86, 87, 88, 136), reversed and placed out of order (146, 147, 149), and inverted (73); *Prayer-Book*, p. xii.

[35] Crick, 'An Eleventh-Century Prayer-Book', pp. 282, 284.

[36] *Ibid.*, p. 293.

did she think that it was copied at more than one scriptorium; rather, she was 'incline[d] to the conclusion that Galba A.xiv was produced at a single centre within a single biological generation'.[37] On the basis of the information found in the book's computistical tables (fols 9r–10r) and the inclusion of an elsewhere unattested prayer for the soul of King Æthelred II (d. 1016) (fol. 89v), Bernard Muir set Galba A.xiv's production sometime between 1016 and 1029.[38] But contrary to the practice of many scribes working in this period, particularly in the ambit of Winchester, those responsible for copying the texts in Galba A.xiv did not maintain a clear-cut distinction between the Caroline and Insular minuscule alphabets; instead, many 'employed bizarre combinations of ostensibly outmoded usages', as Crick remarked.[39] Uncommon, too, was the attempt made by several scribes to write in a high-grade register of Caroline and Insular minuscule, perhaps in imitation of their exemplars.[40] Muir noted the presence of both highly trained and less well trained scribes at work in Galba A.xiv: 'at times the script is so poor and/or childishly large (especially fols 147r, lines 1–4 and 147v, lines 1–3), and so plagued by inaccuracies as to make it conceivable that the manuscript was once used as a beginner's or novice's exercise book'.[41] Such features may locate the production of the manuscript at a scriptorium 'without a coherent script style', as Peter Stokes suggested,[42] but they could indicate instead that 'these scribes were not simply ignorant of good scribal practice but were deliberately following unusual conventions', as Crick thought.[43]

In addition to paleographical analysis of Galba A.xiv's hands, internal textual evidence has been utilised to locate the manuscript. All of the scholars who have studied Galba A.xiv agreed that it was made for or by a monastic community given references in several prayers to 'this monastery' and to the 'work' of the Divine Office.[44] The intercessions offered to St Benedict in three of Galba A.xiv's prayers may also indicate that his *Rule* guided the community's practice in some

---

[37] *Ibid.*, p. 289.
[38] Muir, *A Pre-Conquest English Prayer-Book*, p. xv. Galba A.xiv's computistical tables were applicable to the years 1034–5, 1029 and 1040.
[39] Crick, 'An Eleventh-Century Prayer-Book', p. 287. Peter Stokes also described the hands in Galba A.xiv as 'old-fashioned' and noted that some of the scribes used vernacular minuscule for Latin texts; Peter Stokes, *English Vernacular Minuscule from Æthelred to Cnut, c. 900–c. 1035* (Woodbridge, 2014), p. 88.
[40] Crick, 'An Eleventh-Century Prayer-Book', p. 288. See, too, Rushforth, *Saints in English Kalendars*, p. 37.
[41] Muir, *A Pre-Conquest English Prayer-Book*, p. xiii.
[42] Stokes, *English Vernacular Minuscule*, p. 88.
[43] Crick, 'An Eleventh-Century Prayer-Book', p. 287.
[44] The following references seem to indicate a monastic origin for Galba A.xiv: 'ad opus Dei' (fol. 51r), 'de opere Dei' (fol. 52v), 'familiam huius sacri cenobii' (fol. 86r), 'hoc

way.[45] The inclusion of a number of prominent Winchester saints in the first litany (fols 76r–79v, 86r1) – Swithun, Machutus, Beornstan, Ælfheah, Grimbald, Hæddi and Æthelwold – as well as the additions of a collect for Ælfheah (fol. 73r), a prayer to Æthelwold (fol. 125r), a collect and hymn to Machutus (fols 125v–126r) and a collect that references Machutus (fol. 148v/r), encouraged many scholars to assign a Winchester origin to Galba A.xiv.[46] More specifically, these scholars located the original production and/or subsequent augmentation and adaptation of the prayerbook at Nunnaminster because of the presence of feminine grammatical forms for the supplicants in several of the prayers.[47] Yet, in many of the prayers in which the gender of the supplicant is made explicit, masculine grammatical forms are present.[48] Alexandra Barratt thought that the presence of these forms was the result of scribal inexperience:

> Possibly the Latin of most of the young women novices was not strong enough for them to attempt any more than transcription; a few, more ambitious, tried to adapt some of the texts for their own sex, perhaps as an educational exercise.[49]

---

monasterium' (fol. 89v), and *psalmodias* (fol. 100v). Galba A.xiv also contains a prayer with blessings for various buildings in a monastery (fols 118v, 119r/v, 130r–2v).

[45] Galba A.xiv, fols 86r/v, 80r, 89v.

[46] See Edmund Bishop, 'About an Old Prayer Book', in Edmund Bishop (ed.), *Liturgica Historica: Papers on the Liturgy and Religious Life of the Western Church* (Oxford, 1918), pp. 384–91, at p. 387; Neil Ripley Ker, *Catalogue of Manuscripts Containing Anglo-Saxon* (Oxford, 1957; reissued with supplement, 1990), p. 201; Banks, 'Some Anglo-Saxon Prayers', 208; Michael Lapidge, 'Some Latin Poems as Evidence for the Reign of Athelstan', *Anglo-Saxon England*, 9 (1981), 61–98, at pp. 84–5; Schneider, 'Anglo-Saxon Women', p. 178; Muir, *A Pre-Conquest English Prayer-Book*, pp. xiv–xv; David Dumville, 'On the Dating of Some Late Anglo-Saxon Liturgical Manuscripts', *Transactions of the Cambridge Bibliographical Society*, 10 (1991), 40–57, at pp. 46–7; Kate Thomas, 'The Meaning, Practice and Context of Private Prayer in Late Anglo-Saxon England' (unpublished Ph.D. dissertation, University of York, 2011), p. 96. A few of these scholars also cited the phrase 'unde cohors Þentana' (fol. 132) as further proof of the manuscript's Winchester origin; however, this folio was very badly damaged, so it is difficult to make out the lines surrounding this phrase. Consequently, concerning the significance of this phrase, Muir admitted, 'more cannot be made of it'; Muir, *A Pre-Conquest English Prayer-Book*, p. xiv.

[47] Ker was the only scholar who thought that Galba A.xiv was originally compiled for male use and subsequently adapted for a female audience; *Catalogue*, p. 201. Feminine grammatical forms were used for the supplicants of the prayers on fols 6, 53–7, 70, 74r, 86r, 85v–7, 89r, 98, 88, 99–102, 108r/v8, 125v/r.

[48] Masculine grammatical forms were used for the supplicants of the prayers on fols 24–7, 28v–36r, 38v, 45–9, 50–2, 58–62r, 75, 66–70r, 72v, 103, 104–5, 108r/v8, 110–4r, 118v, 127–9r, 130–2r.

[49] Barratt, 'Review of *A Pre-Conquest English Prayer-Book* by Bernard James Muir', *The Journal of Theological Studies*, 40 (1989), 655–7, at p. 657.

This explanation especially makes sense of the interlinear addition of feminine endings above the masculine grammatical forms in three prayers,[50] but it does not account for the interlinear addition of masculine endings above the feminine grammatical forms in two prayers,[51] or the alteration of the feminine grammatical forms in the main text of three prayers to masculine ones.[52] Muir interpreted these additions and alterations as evidence still supporting a Nunnaminster origin for the prayerbook, recalling that the community supported a certain number of chaplains and canons.[53] Lending further support to Muir's interpretation of Galba A.xiv as a prayerbook primarily intended for a women's monastic house, but also inclusive of ancillary male residents, are the contributions of one scribe, writing just over a third of the manuscript in its present state in a competent Insular minuscule. Two of the prayers this scribe copied clearly script a female monastic leader as their supplicant,[54] leading Dagmar Schneider to conclude that the scribe was an abbess.[55] Her conclusion is difficult to prove or disprove on the basis of evidence internal to Galba A.xiv alone. Her more general claim that the prayerbook 'confirms that women were still copying and adapting manuscripts for their

---

[50] The prayer programme for the veneration of the Cross on fols 110r–14r contains masculine singular grammatical forms in the main text, but they were glossed by a different hand with feminine singular endings. The blessings for a monastery on fols 130–2r contain masculine plural grammatical forms in the main text, but they were glossed by a different hand with feminine plural endings. The prayer of confession on fol. 108r/v8 contains a combination of masculine and feminine grammatical forms in the main text, and the masculine forms were later glossed with feminine endings. Notably, this prayer has no known analogues, which suggests that the prayer was an original composition, written by someone with an imperfect grasp of Latin grammar, whose errors had to be corrected.

[51] See the prayers on fols 53–7r and fols 70r/v, 74r. In the latter prayer, the feminine grammatical forms in the main text were glossed with masculine *and* feminine third-person singular pronouns.

[52] See the prayers on fols 20–1r, 39–45r, and 105v–7v.

[53] Muir, *A Pre-Conquest English Prayer-Book*, p. xiv.

[54] In the first prayer, an adaptation of the collect from the *Missa pro abbate et congregatione*, the female penitent, a 'miseram famulam', asks for the spirit of grace 'super cunctam congregationem mihi indignam commissam' (fol. 86r). The second prayer, a dialogical confession between a female monastic leader and the chapter, erroneously headed by the rubric *Incipit confessio* [sic] *inter presbiteros*, prompts its female penitent to admit: 'omnes familias domus mee correxi, sed luxuriosas et adulterias et fornicarias enutriui et non prohibui; dominicum diem ac sollemnitates sanctorum non digne nec dux uel acceptabile duxi nec custodiui, et nescientibus non adnuntiaui' (fol. 88v). For the analogues to both prayers, see Bugyis, *Care of Nuns*, pp. 267, 196, respectively. Notable, too, among the suffrages following the first litany is the reference to 'episcopum et abbatissam' (fol. 79r).

[55] Schneider, 'Anglo-Saxon Women', pp. 89, 95, 177.

own use' in the early eleventh century is more defensible given recent findings of women religious' scribal activities in England prior to the Conquest.[56]

Other scholars have disputed the assignment of Galba A.xiv's origin to Nunnaminster.[57] They viewed the references to Winchester and its principal saints not as clues to the prayerbook's origin, but as evidence of the city's 'far-reaching liturgical influence'.[58] They also observed that the liturgical calendar often thought to be a *membrum disiectum* of Galba A.xiv (now London, British Library, Cotton MS Nero A.ii, fols 3–13) contains only four of the sixteen major feasts celebrated at Winchester – Grimbald (8 July), the Translation of Birinus (but on 3 September, instead of on the 4th, the correct date), the Deposition of Birinus (3 December) and Judoc (13 December)[59] – and these four feasts are widely attested in other extant pre-Conquest calendars.[60] Comparison of the prayer *Defende quesumus Domine intercedente* as it was copied in Galba A.xiv (fol. 80r) to the version included in a prayerbook produced in the early eleventh century for Ælfwine, dean, then abbot, of New Minster in Winchester (1031–57) (now London, British Library, Cotton MSS Titus D.xxvi+xxvii), moreover, reveals that the latter invokes the confessors Judoc and Grimbald, while the former names only Benedict.[61] The discrepancies between the cults of saints promoted at Winchester and in Galba A.xiv, compounded by the significant differences between their scribal conventions,[62] undermine the assignment of a Winchester origin to the manuscript.

[56] *Ibid.*, p. 175. See Alexandra Barratt on this point, too; 'Review', 657. On women religious' scribal activities in England prior to the Conquest, see Bugyis, *Care of Nuns*, pp. 34–5, 68–76.

[57] Joseph Hillaby, 'Early Christian and Pre-Conquest Leominster: An Exploration of the Sources', *Transactions of the Woolhope Naturalists' Field Club*, 55 (1987), 557–685, at pp. 628, 646; Hillaby, *Leominster*, pp. 25–40; Rushforth, *Saints in English Kalendars*, p. 37; Crick, 'An Eleventh-Century Prayer-Book', pp. 292–3.

[58] Rushforth, *Saints in English Kalendars*, p. 37.

[59] Neil Ripley Ker, Bernard Muir, Rebecca Rushforth and Joseph Hillaby all thought that Galba A.xiv and Nero A.ii, fols 3–13 were once parts of the same volume; Ker, *Catalogue*, p. 201; Muir, *A Pre-Conquest English Prayer-Book*, pp. xi–xiii; Rushforth, *Saints in English Kalendars*, pp. 36–7; and Hillaby, 'Early Christian and Pre-Conquest Leominster', 628. Julia Crick has been supportive of their claims, noting that, at minimum, we can establish that the two manuscripts issued from the same scriptorium; Crick, 'An Eleventh-Century Prayer-Book', p. 295. For the bibliography on opposition to joining Galba A.xiv and Nero A.ii, see Crick, 'An Eleventh-Century Prayer-Book', p. 283, n. 11.

[60] See Rushforth, *Saints in English Kalendars*.

[61] London, British Library, Cotton MSS Titus D.xxvi, fol. 58v; Beate Günzel (ed.), *Ælfwine's Prayerbook (London, British Library, Cotton Titus D. xxvi+xxvii)* (London, 1993), pp. 76–8.

[62] Crick, 'An Eleventh-Century Prayer-Book', p. 293; Stokes, *English Vernacular Minuscule*, p. 51.

Joseph Hillaby has made a convincing argument for locating the origin of Galba A.xiv and Nero A.ii, fols 3–13 at Leominster, a community of women religious in the far west of England near the Welsh marches.[63] Most notable among the features he highlighted as evidence supporting his assignment are the inclusion of two prayers (one with no analogue) to St Peter, the dedicatee of Leominster's church (fols 37r–38v);[64] calendar and litany entries for Æthelmod, Hemma and Eadfrith, three saints uniquely venerated at Leominster;[65] a prayer to Hemma (fol. 152v); calendar entries for the feasts of Mildburh and Mildryth, two prayers to Mildburh (fol. 151r), and a litany entry for Mildgyth, all three daughters of Merewalh, the king of the Magonsætan, who was credited with supporting Leominster's foundation in the mid-to-late seventh century.[66] Rebecca Rushforth thought that Hillaby made 'a compelling argument' for a Leominster origin for Galba A.xiv, and Peter Stokes remarked that Hillaby presented 'the most feasible solution' to the question of the prayerbook's origin or at least its ownership.[67] Julia Crick agreed that Hillaby's assignment of origin to the manuscript 'remains

[63] Hillaby, 'Early Christian and Pre-Conquest Leominster', 628–54; Hillaby, *Leominster*, pp. 25–40.

[64] The incipits to these prayers are *Sanctus Petrus princeps* (fols 37r–38r) and *Sancte Petre apostole* (fol. 38v). No analogue has yet to be identified for the former prayer. In a footnote to his edition of the prayerbook, Bernard Muir remarked that this prayer is 'noteworthy for the peculiarities of its syntax'; *Prayer-Book*, p. 53, n. 1. Muir identified one close analogue to the latter prayer: the so-called Book of Cerne, a ninth-century Mercian prayerbook; *ibid.*, p. 55.

[65] Æthelmod, Hemma and Eadfrith do not appear in any other pre-Conquest calendar or litany. In Galba A.xiv's second litany, these three saints appear in this sequence in the list of confessors (fol. 93v). Æthelmod (9 January) was Leominster's foremost saint. His name appears in Leominster's relic list, but his identity is unknown; Gilbert Hunter Doble, 'The Leominster Relic-List', *Transactions of the Woolhope Naturalists' Field Club*, 31 (1942), 58–65, at p. 58. Hemma (25 May) was believed to have been Leominster's first abbot. Eadfrith (26 October) may have been the founder of Leominster. He was a Northumbrian monk who converted Merewalh, king of the Magonsætan, to Christianity in the mid-seventh century.

[66] The feast of Mildburh (23 February), who became the abbess of Wenlock in Shropshire, appears in only two other pre-Conquest calendars; Rushforth, *Saints in English Kalendars*, Table II. Leominster claimed to possess the saint's relics; Doble, 'Leominster Relic-List', 59. The feast of Mildryth (13 July), who became the abbess of Minster-in-Thanet in Kent, was observed in eleven of the twenty-seven extant pre-Conquest calendars; Rushforth, *Saints in English Kalendars*, Table VII. Significantly, Mildgyth does not appear in any other extant pre-Conquest litany. See Lapidge, *Anglo-Saxon Litanies*.

[67] Rushforth, *Saints in English Kalendars*, p. 37; Stokes, *English Vernacular Minuscule*, p. 51. John Blair and Pauline Stafford independently endorsed Hillaby's assignment of origin to Galba A.xiv. See Blair, 'A Handlist of Anglo-Saxon Saints', in Alan Thacker and Richard Sharpe (eds), *Local Saints and Local Churches in the Early Medieval West* (Oxford, 2002), pp. 495–565, at p. 507; and Pauline Stafford, '"Cherchez la femme":

viable' given how well it explains the paleographical and textual features detailed above, but she still thought that it 'requires from the paleographer a leap of faith', in view of Leominster's fragmentary history.[68] Even Hillaby cautioned that it cannot be known for certain whether the community he credited with Galba A.xiv's production was an old monastic foundation, dating back to the seventh century, or a new institution founded during or just before the tenth-century reforms.[69] Documentary evidence suggests that Leominster was flourishing c. 1000, about the time that Galba A.xiv was copied.[70] The fortunes of the community were imperilled in 1046 when its abbess, Eadgifu, was abducted by Swein (d. 1052), son of Earl Godwine of Wessex (d. 1053).[71] Eadgifu was eventually returned to Leominster when King Edward the Confessor (r. 1044–66) denied Swein's proposal of marriage. Remarkably, Eadgifu's abduction does not seem to have resulted in Leominster's dissolution. Domesday Book names the abbess of Leominster as the holder of a hide at Fencote in Herefordshire, and records the revenue of the manor of Leominster as '£60 besides the provision of the nuns'.[72] To Pauline Stafford this valuation suggested 'a significant if not sizable community in and after 1066'.[73] The manor of Leominster was actually held by Queen Edith (d. 1075) by at least 1066, at which time it passed to King William I (r. 1066–87), but the record of its revenue in Domesday may still reveal that Leominster's wealth was comparable to that of the abbeys founded by the West Saxon royal house, such as Wherwell, whose lands were also held for a time by the reigning Queen Ælfthryth (d. 999x1001), the consort of King Edgar.[74] Using Domesday's

---

Queens, Queens' Lands and Nunneries: Missing Links in the Foundation of Reading Abbey', *History*, 85 (2000), 4–27, at p. 9.

[68] Crick, 'An Eleventh-Century Prayer-Book', p. 296.
[69] Hillaby, 'Early Christian and Pre-Conquest Leominster', 625.
[70] Stafford, '"Cherchez la femme"', 9.
[71] Dorothy Whitelock, David C. Douglas and Susie I. Tucker (eds and trans), *The Anglo-Saxon Chronicle: A Revised Translation* (London, 1961), s.a. 1046 [text C]; Reginald R. Darlington and Patrick McGurk (eds) and Jennifer Bray and Patrick McGurk (trans), *The Chronicle of John of Worcester: The Annals from 450 to 1066* (2 vols, Oxford, 1995), vol. 2, pp. 548–9; and Thomas Hearne (ed.) *Hemingi Chartularium Ecclesiae Wigorniensis* (2 vols, Oxford, 1723), vol. 1, pp. 275–6.
[72] Frank and Caroline Thorn (eds), *Domesday Book, 17. Herefordshire* (Chichester, 1983), fol. 180ra (1, 10a–b), fol. 180rb (1, 14).
[73] Stafford, '"Cherchez la femme"', 9. See, too, Reginald V. Lennard, *Rural England, 1086–1135: A Study of Social and Agrarian Conditions* (Oxford, 1959), pp. 400–1.
[74] Stafford, '"Cherchez la femme"', 9, n. 30; Pauline Stafford, 'Queens, Nunneries and Reforming Churchmen: Gender, Religious Status and Reform in Tenth- and Eleventh-Century England', *Past and Present*, 163 (1999), 3–35, at p. 30. See, too, Marc Anthony Meyer, 'The Queen's Demesne', in Marc Anthony Meyer (ed.), *The Culture of Christendom: Essays in Medieval History in Commemoration of Denis L. T. Bethell*

valuations, Hillaby ranked Leominster third in wealth among women's monastic communities at the time of the Conquest, after Wilton and Shaftesbury.⁷⁵ By 1121, Leominster definitely ceased to support a community of nuns because its land, along with those of two other 'destroyed' communities, was used by King Henry I (r. 1100–35) to refound Reading Priory as a single male Cluniac house.⁷⁶ Despite the fragmentary and, perhaps, abbreviated nature of Leominster's history, and the seeming impossibility that a women's monastic community in the far west of England could have supported so many scribes, I am persuaded by Hillaby's arguments in favour of assigning a Leominster origin to Galba A.xiv. They make the best sense of the prayerbook's distinctive paleographical and textual features. If his assignment is correct, then Galba A.xiv offers a rare witness to the liturgical, devotional and scribal practices of a women's monastic community flourishing a generation or two after *Regularis concordia*'s promulgation, at a far remove from the main centre of reform – Winchester. Close examination of the prayerbook's contents reveals the degree to which the members of Leominster tried to adhere to, adapt, or depart from the *Concordia*'s dictates on proper monastic observance.

Galba A.xiv: A Witness to Monastic Reform?

Not prescribed by the *Concordia*, but indicative of the reformers' far-reaching influence, is the inclusion of reminders to pray for the souls of Dunstan, Oswald and Æthelwold in Galba A.xiv. They appear in this very order in the first litany near the end of the list of confessors, following the series of Winchester saints – Machutus, Beornstan, Ælfheah, Grimbald and Hæddi (fol. 77v) – but only Dunstan and Oswald were identified by their episcopal titles. Just Dunstan's feast day (19 May) was added to the prayerbook's calendar, but this observance was marked in nearly every other extant English calendar postdating his death.⁷⁷ More unique is the addition of two prayers for Dunstan and one prayer for Æthelwold to the prayerbook.⁷⁸ One of the prayers to Dunstan, *O inclite confessor*, now found

---

(London, 1993), pp. 75–113, at p. 89; and Patricia Halpin, 'Women Religious in Late Anglo-Saxon England', *The Haskins Society Journal*, 6 (1994), 97–110, at p. 103.

⁷⁵ Hillaby, 'Early Christian and Pre-Conquest Leominster', 665.
⁷⁶ Brian R. Kemp (ed.), *Reading Abbey Cartularies* (2 vols, London, 1986–7), vol. 1, p. 1.
⁷⁷ Rushforth, *Saints in English Kalendars*, Table V.
⁷⁸ The two prayers to Dunstan are *O inclite confessor* (N fol. 13r) and *Deus qui hodierna die sanctum pontificem Dunstanum* (G fols 150r–151r; n.b. fol. 150 was reversed). The former is without any analogue, and Bernard Muir identified the latter as a prayer for Matins on the saint's feast day on the basis of a close analogue to the prayer found in the late fourteenth-century missal from Westminster Abbey; Muir, *A Pre-Conquest English Prayer-Book*, p. 186, n. 1. For comparison, see J. Wickham Legg (ed.), *Missale ad usum ecclesie Westmonasteriensis* (3 vols, London, 1891–97), vol. 3, p. 1360. Muir

in the Nero portion of the prayerbook (fol. 13r), appears to be without analogue. Raising the possibility that it is an original composition are the peculiarities in its syntax.[79] The prayer was to be recited as a collective 'us [nos]' that was not explicitly gendered, and the interlinear addition of neumes suggests that it was to be sung. Different from the other prayer for Dunstan included in the prayerbook, *O inclite confessor* does not address Dunstan as a *pontifex*, but as a 'confessor of Christ', a 'candelabra and doctor of English-born people', a 'good shepherd', a 'caretaker of all Britain', and a 'healer of the diverse sick people visiting [his] tomb'.[80] Given these epithets, it is fitting that the supplicants ask Dunstan in the concluding line of the prayer to intercede to God to 'pluck out this country from enemies and free [them] from the binding of sin and lead [them] to eternal life'.[81] By the time this prayer was copied, England had already succumbed to Danish rule, but it communicates an enduring hope that God would still rescue the country from its enemies through the great saint of the English-born people – Dunstan.

Potentially more indicative of the *Concordia*'s influence on Galba A.xiv's production is the addition of the prayer programme for the veneration of the Cross (fols 110r–114r). It is identical to the one scripted in the *Concordia*.[82] This programme is composed of the seven Penitential Psalms, divided into three groups, with accompanying collects. First, the supplicant recites Psalms 6, 31 and 37 and a prayer of six *Adoro te* petitions to Christ that encourage the supplicant to reflect on his ascent on the cross, wounding on the cross, burial in the tomb, descent into hell, resurrection from the dead and ascent into heaven, and future return in judgment, and after each reflection, the supplicant beseeches Christ that his saving actions provide the soul with freedom from the persecution of the devil, healing,

---

found three near-contemporary analogues to the prayer to Æthelwold, *Deus qui preclari sideris sancti pontificis Aþelwoldi* (fol. 125r); according to these analogues, the prayer was recited at Vespers on the vigil of the saint's feast day; Muir, *A Pre-Conquest English Prayer-Book*, p. 159, n. 1.

[79] *Ibid.*, p. 22, n. 1.

[80] 'O inclite confessor Christi, O candelabra doctorque angligena gente, O bone pastor Dunstane, altorque totius Albionis, qui es sanator diuersorum debilium tuo tumulo uisitantium': Nero A.ii, fol. 13r.

[81] 'Ut hanc patriam ab hostibus eruat nosque a nexu criminis soluat atque ad eternam uitam perducat': *Ibid.*

[82] *Concordia*, pp. 43–4. For analyses of these petitions in Galba A.xiv and their correspondence to the *Concordia*, see Muir, *A Pre-Conquest English Prayer-Book*, p. 143, n. 1; Lilli Gjerløw, *Adoratio crucis: The Regularis Concordia and the Decreta Lanfranci: Manuscript Studies in the Early Medieval Church of Norway* (Oslo, 1961), pp. 24–5; and Thomas, 'The Meaning, Practice and Context', pp. 117–20. Other than the manuscript witnesses to the *Concordia* itself, the three collects for the veneration of the Cross as prescribed by the consuetudinary are found in only four manuscripts, including Galba A.xiv.

life, preservation from hell, mercy, and forgiveness of sins. In the second part, the supplicant says Psalms 50 and 101 and a prayer that prompts further meditation on the mystery of Christ's incarnation and death and pleas for his mercy and forgiveness. In the concluding line of the prayer, the supplicant even acknowledges the position of his/her body in prayer: 'prostrate before your [Christ's] adorable and most glorious Cross'.[83] Finally, in the third part, the supplicant offers Psalms 129 and 142, and a prayer that recalls Christ's saving death on the Cross and then asks for feeling and understanding of this saving action so that s/he may always have 'true repentance and good perseverance'.[84]

Galba A.xiv's prayer programme for the veneration of the Cross contains rubrics marking the second and third parts of the programme that are identical to those found in the *Concordia*. Additionally, the line above the incipit to the first Penitential Psalm was left blank, likely for a rubric akin to the one provided in the *Concordia* – *In prima quidem oratione* – to be added later.[85] The textual correspondences between the rubrics and prayers for the veneration of the Cross in the *Concordia* and in Galba A.xiv suggest that the scribe responsible for copying the programme in the prayerbook – whom Dagmar Schneider identified as the abbess of the community[86] – consulted either a copy of the *Concordia* or another liturgical or devotional book that contained a version of the prayer programme based on the *Concordia*'s instructions. The latter possibility is raised by three discrepancies between the versions of the programme in the *Concordia* and in Galba A.xiv. Differently from the *Concordia*, the scribe of the programme in Galba A.xiv provided the incipits to all seven Penitential Psalms as an *aide-mémoire* for the supplicant. She also included very close Old English translations of the three prayers following the groups of Penitential Psalms. Based on internal textual evidence, it is not clear whether the scribe copied these additions from her exemplar or composed them herself. There is only one other known version of the prayer program for the veneration of the Cross with an Old English translation of the *Adoro te* petitions.[87] In Galba A.xiv, each translation appears immediately after the corresponding Latin prayer. This placement suggests that the translations were to be used not in performance, but for educational purposes – to help the supplicant more fully comprehend the Latin text either before or after recitation.

---

[83] 'Exaudi me prostratum coram adoranda gloriosissima cruce tua': Galba A.xiv, fol. 112v. The masculine singular ending of the past participle *prostratum* was glossed with the feminine singular ending '-am' to accommodate a female supplicant.

[84] 'Mitte in me sensum et intellegentiam quomodo habeam ueram penitentiam et habeam bonam perseuerantiam omnibus diebus uite mee': Galba A.xiv, fols 113v–114r

[85] *Concordia*, p. 43.

[86] See n. 55 above.

[87] Gjerløw, *Adoratio crucis*, p. 25.

Bernard Muir stressed the significance of the vernacular translations included in Galba A.xiv, observing, 'Liturgical manuscripts from before the year 950 generally do not contain translations, and it may be that their sudden appearance in the last half of the tenth century is directly related to the Benedictine Revival'.[88] He discussed the importance of the vernacular for religious instruction in the reforms promoted by Dunstan, Æthelwold, Oswald and their followers, and so it is likely not coincidental that ten to fifteen per cent of the texts in Galba A.xiv were written in Old English.[89] Equally notable among the efforts made to render the prayers for venerating the Cross more accessible to different types of users is their subsequent adaptation for a female supplicant. In the interlinear space above the masculine grammatical forms for the supplicant in the main text of the prayers, a different scribe supplied feminine singular endings. This adaptation is not found in any of the other known versions of the prayer programme, but it clearly indicates that the women religious at Leominster could venerate the Cross in the exact same way that the monks imagined in the *Concordia* would have, with only minor grammatical alterations.[90] Such veneration would have been important at Leominster, not only because it was an essential observance within the Good Friday liturgy, but also because the community claimed to possess part 'of the Lord's tree' as a relic.[91]

Galba A.xiv contains another prayer programme based on the Penitential Psalms (fols 59, 58, 60–62r) that could have been added to the prayerbook in observance of the *Concordia*'s directives on communal daily prayer. According to Jonathan Black, an independent prayer programme was created for the Penitential Psalms in the early ninth century with related *capitula*, collects and prayers.[92] This programme circulated widely in manuscripts produced on the European continent and in England from the ninth to the eleventh centuries, and in many of the manuscripts, including Galba A.xiv, it is preceded by Alcuin's *Deus inestimabilis misericordie*, which was likely used as an opening prayer to the programme. Notably, this programme, minus the opening prayer, appears in another prayerbook adapted for women religious' use, likely in the early twelfth

---

[88] Muir, *A Pre-Conquest English Prayer-Book*, p. xxii.
[89] Ibid., p. xxiii. In most of the cases, the Old English texts in Galba A.xiv are either translations of the Latin texts that precede them, or independent texts whose syntax and vocabulary depend on Latin liturgical materials.
[90] Unfortunately, the fragment of the Old English translation/adaptation of the *Concordia* for women religious' use found in CCCC 201 stops before the directions for the veneration of the Cross on Good Friday.
[91] Doble, 'Leominster Relic-List', 59.
[92] Jonathan Black, 'Psalm Uses in Carolingian Prayerbooks: Alcuin and the Preface to *De psalmorum usu*', *Mediaeval Studies*, 64 (2002), 1–60, at p. 1.

century, at Nunnaminster: London, British Library, Cotton MSS Titus D. xxvi, fols 46v–50v.[93] But the programme as it appears in this prayerbook was expanded to include Psalm 85, with accompanying *capitula* and a collect.

The *Concordia* stipulates that the Penitential Psalms were to be a fixed feature in the Benedictine *cursus*, sung thrice daily: before Matins, within the *Trina oratio* said in honour of the Trinity; after Prime; and in the veneration of the Cross on Good Friday, as we have seen.[94] The pre-Matins form of the *Trina oratio* divides the Penitential Psalms into three groups of prayers, each one devoted to a different intention: Psalms 6, 31 and 37 for oneself; Psalms 50 and 101 for the king, queen and *familiares* (benefactors and other religious houses joined to the community in confraternity); and Psalms 129 and 142 for the faithful departed.[95] After each group, the community is to say a *Pater noster* and a specific collect: *Gratias tibi ago omnipotens Pater* for oneself; *Deus qui caritatis dona* for the king, queen and *familiares*; and *Inueniant quaesumus Domine* for the faithful departed. This devotional regimen is structured differently in Galba A.xiv. The *Kyrie* and *Pater noster* precede each Penitential Psalm, which is then followed by a collect. The texts of the seven collects emphasise the communal voice of the entire prayer. Though the first person singular was preserved in the Psalm verses that comprise the *capitula*, all of the collects teem with the first person plural. They are nothing but inclusive of the 'we' gathered in prayer and are preceded consistently by the hortatory 'let us pray'.[96] Only one grammatically defines the gender of the penitents: the opening of the collect following Psalm 101 reads, 'Exorable Lord, hear the prayer of your supplicants ['supplicum tuorum']'.[97] The gendering of the penitents as masculine with 'tuorum' likely owes to scribal oversight or to the fact that the daily recitation of the Psalms accustomed the women religious at Leominster and elsewhere to praying as a masculine gendered supplicant.[98]

---

[93] See n. 61 above.

[94] *Concordia*, pp. 12–13, 15 and 43–4, respectively. The *Concordia* adds Psalm 85, presumably between Psalms 50 and 101, to the Penitential Psalms said after Prime. For more on the *Concordia*'s prescription of the Penitential Psalms during the adoration of the Cross on Good Friday, see Gjerløw, *Adoratio crucis*, pp. 13–14, 24–8.

[95] *Concordia*, pp. 12–13. The *Concordia* also notes that the *Trina oratio* is recited before Terce in winter or Prime in summer and after Compline (*ibid.*, pp. 16, 23–4). The *Concordia* does not provide details for the former recitation, only for the latter, which draws on different Psalms and collects than the ones supplied for the pre-Matins *Trina oratio*.

[96] According to Jonathan Black's edition of this programme, the prefatory *oremus* before each collect only appears in Galba A.xiv; Black, 'Psalm Uses', 42–5, 47–9.

[97] 'Exorabilis Domine intende in o<rationem su>pplicum tuorum.': Galba A.xiv, fol. 60v.

[98] In the version of Penitential Psalms programme found in Ælfwine's prayerbook, the collect accompanying Psalm 101 is nearly identical to the one found in Galba A.xiv,

Two of the collects that were to be recited at the pre-Matins *Trina oratio* according to the *Concordia* were also included in Galba A.xiv by the same scribe who copied the prayer programme for the veneration of the Cross. *Deus qui caritatis dona* (fol. 80v), the second collect for the king, queen and *familiares*, appears in massbooks deriving from the Gregorian sacramentary tradition as the opening collect to the *Missa pro familiaribus*.[99] According to the *Concordia*, this collect was also recited after the *Psalmi familiares* said for the king, queen and other benefactors after Matins.[100] The third collect recited during the pre-Matins *Trina oratio* for the faithful departed, *Inueniant quaesumus domine* (fol. 81r), can be found in massbooks descended from the Old Gelasian and Gregorian types as the postcommunion of the *Missa plurimorum defunctorum*.[101] According to the *Concordia*, this collect was also said during the Psalm-pair offered for the self and departed members of the community, following Psalm 50 for the deceased.[102] Perhaps significantly, the prayer immediately preceding *Inueniant quaesumus domine* in Galba A.xiv is *Vre igne Sancti Spiritus* (fol. 81r), the first collect cited in the *Concordia* for the Psalm-pair offered for the self and departed brethren, after Psalm 37 against carnal temptation.[103] This prayer can also be found in massbooks stemming from the Gregorian sacramentary tradition as the collect to the *Missa contra tentatione carnis*.[104] The close arrangement of these two prayers in Galba A.xiv may indicate that the *Concordia* dictated their inclusion, but if this was the case, one might reasonably expect to find the incipits to Psalms 37 and 50 before their respective collects, too; however, these cues to the supplicant do not appear, perhaps because the order and texts of the collects were based on a different source.

The *Concordia* contains an analogue for another prayer found in Galba A.xiv: *Deus cui omne cor patet* (fols 86v–80r), the second collect in the post-Compline *Trina oratio*.[105] Its origins can ultimately be traced back to massbooks deriving from the Gregorian sacramentary tradition as the collect to the *Missa de cordis emundatione per Spiritum Sanctum postulanda*.[106] In the case of this prayer, it is again not clear whether Galba A.xiv's correspondence with the *Concordia* owes

---

except 'uel -arum' was later interlineated above 'tuorum', by the scribe who adapted the prayerbook for women religious' use; *Ælfwine's Prayerbook*, p. 177.

[99] For the analogues to this prayer, see Bugyis, *Care of Nuns*, Table 5.2.

[100] *Concordia*, p. 14.

[101] For the analogues to this prayer, see Bugyis, *Care of Nuns*, Table 5.2.

[102] *Concordia*, p. 15.

[103] *Ibid*.

[104] For the analogues to this prayer, see Bugyis, *Care of Nuns*, Table 5.2.

[105] *Concordia*, p. 24.

[106] For the analogues to this prayer, see Bugyis, *Care of Nuns*, Table 5.2.

to a concerted effort made by the scribe and her community to follow the consuetudinary's dictates or to coincidence. This prayer was copied by the same scribe who added the prayer programme for the veneration of the Cross and the three collects mentioned above. As the prayer's odd foliation indicates, it was misplaced by later conservators. Internal textual clues helped Bernard Muir to restore the prayer to its relative position in the prayerbook, between *Actiones nostras quesumus Domine* (fol. 86v) and *Defende quesumus Domine intercedente beato Benedicto* (fol. 80r), two collects not mentioned in the *Concordia*.[107] Thus, in Galba A.xiv, *Deus cui omne cor patet* is clearly not the second constitutive part of the *Concordia*'s post-Compline *Trina oratio*; rather, together with the three collects discussed above, it belongs to a long series of prayers gathered between the prayerbook's two litanies, probably to be used selectively after reciting one of them. Still, we cannot dismiss the possibility that the *Concordia* – even if only through an intermediate liturgical or devotional source – influenced the selection of these four collects for inclusion in Galba A.xiv, especially given the similarities between the prayerbook's and the consuetudinary's scripts for the veneration of the Cross. Not to be discounted, too, is the likelihood that the prayerbook as it presently exists is an incomplete or at least altered version of what it once was. Noting the conservators' error in the placement of the folios on which *Deus cui omne cor patet* was copied serves as a salutary reminder that we are working with a damaged manuscript. Many of the texts that may have been relevant to this study of the *Concordia*'s impact on women religious' practice are now illegible or lost.

Peculiar among the *Concordia*'s directives for monastic practice compared to earlier and contemporary continental consuetudinaries are the intercessory prayers offered daily on behalf of the king, queen and their family, including eighteen Psalms, twenty-three collects, and, usually, the morrow Mass.[108] Lucia Kornexl observed that these prayers for the royal house 'played a central role in the give-and-take relationship between monasticism and monarchy that constituted an essential prerequisite for the success of the Benedictine revival'.[109] Thus it may be revealing of Leominster's status as a 'reformed house' that Galba A.xiv contains several reminders to pray for various royal personages: a calendar entry (20 May), a poem, and a litany entry for the East Anglian king and martyr Æthelberht II

---

[107] Muir, *A Pre-Conquest English Prayer-Book*, pp. 101–3.
[108] Scholars of the tenth-century reforms in England frequently commented on the peculiarity of the *Concordia*'s prescriptions on prayers for the royal family. See, for example, Knowles, *Monastic Order*, p. 45; Stenton, *Anglo-Saxon England*, pp. 453–5; Eric John, 'The King and the Monks in the Tenth-Century Reformation', in Eric John (ed.), *Orbis Britanniae and Other Studies* (Leicester, 1966), pp. 154–80, at p. 177; *Concordia*, p. 44; and Kornexl, 'The "Regularis Concordia"', 102.
[109] *Ibid.*

(d. 794);[110] entries in both litanies and two prayers for the East Anglian king and martyr Edmund (d. 869);[111] a poem for King Athelstan (d. 939), who may have contributed a sizable portion of his relic collection to Leominster;[112] a litany entry and prayer for Queen Ælfgifu (d. 944), the first wife of King Edmund (d. 946) and a saint buried and venerated at Shaftesbury Abbey but whose relics were claimed, in part, by Leominster;[113] a prayer for King Edgar (d. 975), the convener of the Council of Winchester, which promulgated the *Concordia*;[114] a calendar entry (18 March), a litany entry, and a prayer for King Edward (d. 978), a martyr buried and venerated at Shaftesbury but whose relics were also claimed, in part, by Leominster;[115] and a prayer for King Æthelred II (d. 1016).[116] Significantly, no analogues have been found for the poem for Æthelberht II or the prayers for Ælfgifu and Æthelred II.[117] This fact, along with the lexical and syntactical irregularities riddling the texts, raises the possibility that they are original compositions. All of the prayers for royalty in Galba A.xiv may reflect a conscious desire among the members of Leominster to bring their intercessory practices in line with the *Concordia*'s dictates. Barbara Yorke and Joseph Hillaby, however, independently claimed that prayers for the king and the royal house were already a feature of women religious' practices prior to the reforms.[118] This may very well have been the case at Leominster.

Arguably, the most conflicting piece of evidence against identifying Galba A.xiv as a witness to the monastic reforms are the Old English prayers *ad horas* (fols 105v–107v), a devotional exercise that associated each hour of prayer with Christ's crucifixion. This prayer programme is based on a six-hour office (Prime, Terce, Sext, None, Vespers, and the Twelfth Hour), rather than the eight-hour office prescribed by the Benedictine *Rule* and by the *Concordia*. This discrepancy

[110] Nero A.ii, fols 5r (calendar entry), 13v (poem); Galba A.xiv, fol. 91v (entry in second litany).
[111] Galba A.xiv, fols 77r (entry in first litany), 90v (entry in second litany), 147r (prayer), 147r–50v (prayer).
[112] The poem to King Athelstan is now found in the Nero portion of the prayerbook (fols 10v–1v). Joseph Hillaby speculated about Athelstan's contributions to Leominster's relic collection; Hillaby, 'Early Christian and Pre-Conquest Leominster', 627.
[113] Galba A.xiv, fols 95v (entry in second litany), 151v (prayer). On Leominster's possession of a relic of Queen Ælfgifu, see Doble, 'Leominster Relic-List', 58.
[114] Galba A.xiv, fol. 153v.
[115] Nero A.ii, fol. 4r (calendar entry); Galba A.xiv, fol. 77r (entry in first litany), fol. 150v/r (prayer). On Leominster's possession of a relic of King Edward, see Doble, 'Leominster Relic-List', 58.
[116] Galba A.xiv, fol. 89v.
[117] Muir, *A Pre-Conquest English Prayer-Book*, pp. 23, n. 1, 122, n. 1, 189, n. 2.
[118] Yorke, *Nunneries*, p. 192; Hillaby, 'Early Christian and Pre-Conquest Leominster', 640–1.

led Hillaby to interpret the presence of this prayer programme in Galba A.xiv as proof that Leominster did not adopt the reforms of the tenth century.[119] Kate Thomas recognised that the prayers are 'generally good' translations of Latin prayers *ad horas* found in Carolingian *libelli precum*, which derive from the sacramentary tradition.[120] She also noticed that the prayers were originally written for the use of a woman and subsequently altered for the use of a man.[121] The prayer programme was copied by the same scribe who added the prayers for the veneration of the Cross and the four collects discussed earlier. It is possible that this scribe was responsible for translating both the Latin prayers for the veneration of the Cross and the Latin prayers *ad horas* into Old English. Interestingly, she copied the Latin texts of the former in Galba A.xiv, but not those of the latter, perhaps because they were intended to be used only for 'the private observance of the Hours', as Thomas thought, but they may have also been used for educational purposes.[122] Either use raises pressing questions about the nature of the Leominster women's observance, because it clearly was not strictly Benedictine.

In their studies of Galba A.xiv, Bernard Muir and Joseph Hillaby offer divergent answers to the question of whether this prayerbook was a product of the tenth-century Benedictine reforms. Muir unequivocally answered in the affirmative, highlighting a number of features from the prayer programme for the veneration of the Cross to the use of the vernacular.[123] And Hillaby unequivocally answered in the negative, citing the inclusion of the Old English prayers *ad horas*.[124] The truth, however, probably lies somewhere in between. Galba A.xiv was not the product of a rigorous implementation of the *Regularis concordia* or even of the Benedictine *Rule*. If that had been the case, we could have reasonably expected to find more textual correspondences between the prayerbook and these two regulative texts, perhaps the sequence of collects for the pre-Matins or post-Compline *Trina oratio* or at least indications of the community's observance of the eight-hour office. And yet the inclusion of some of Galba A.xiv's contents, especially the verbatim copy of the prayers for the veneration of the Cross and the remembrances of the three principal reformers – Dunstan, Oswald and Æthelwold – in prayer, do seem to owe to their far-reaching influence. That the effects of the tenth-century reforms should continue to be felt during the time of Galba A.xiv's production, likely sometime between 1016 and 1029, is not altogether surprising. As Tracey-Anne Cooper observed:

[119] Hillaby, 'Early Christian and Pre-Conquest Leominster', 624; Hillaby, *Leominster*, p. 29.
[120] Thomas, 'The Meaning, Practice and Context', pp. 82, 150.
[121] *Ibid.*, pp. 151–2.
[122] *Ibid.*, p. 83.
[123] Muir, 'The Early Insular Prayer Book Tradition', pp. 18–19.
[124] See n. 119 above.

The end of Æthelred's troubled reign and the beginning of Cnut's required a conservative reassertion of the values of the reform, and it is no coincidence that all of our copies of the *Regularis concordia* and the majority of the Anglo-Saxon copies of the Rule of Benedict date to this period.[125]

But the women religious at Leominster evidently were able to mitigate the effects of this reassertion of reform on their own observance by adopting or creatively adapting only those practices they found salutary to their way of life. Pauline Stafford rightly insisted that we take seriously the agency of the women religious to engage with the tenth-century reforms on their own terms, certainly within communities that possessed sufficient wealth and social status to maintain some degree of autonomy.[126] For Leominster, its distance from Winchester, the centre of reform, surely helped to insulate it from unwanted outside influence, too. From here, the women religious could and did remake the reforms after their own likeness.

---

[125] Cooper, *Monks-Bishops*, p. 88.
[126] Stafford, 'Queens, Nunneries, and Reforming Churchmen', 35.

CHAPTER 4

The Materiality of Female Religious Reform in Twelfth-Century Ireland: The Case of Co-located Religious Houses

TRACY COLLINS

Reform in Medieval Ireland: An Overview

REFORM in Ireland began in the early twelfth century with native Gaelic elites and clerics instigating processes to change the institutional arrangements of the church there.[1] It is difficult to pinpoint specific reforms in Ireland, as gaps remain in the historical evidence.[2] Despite these constraints, twelfth-century processes were a 'transformation' whereby episcopal authority was restructured along with dioceses, and religious renewal took the form of the introduction of continental religious orders, most notably the Cistercians.[3] It continued throughout the twelfth century with the incoming Anglo-Norman elite undertaking their own

---

[1] See, for example, Aubrey Gwynn, *The Twelfth-Century Reform. History of Irish Catholicism* (2 vols, Dublin, 1968), vol. 2; *Id.*, *The Irish Church in the Eleventh and Twelfth Centuries* (Dublin, 1992); Kathleen Hughes, *The Church in Early Irish Society* (London, 1966); John Anthony Watt, *The Church in Medieval Ireland*, 2nd edition (Dublin, 1998); Marie Therese Flanagan, 'The Reformation of the Irish Church in the Twelfth Century', in John R. Bartlett and Stuart D. Kinsella (eds), *Two Thousand Years of Christianity in Ireland* (Dublin, 2006), pp. 65–84; Donnchádh Ó Corráin, *The Irish Church, its Reform and the English Invasion* (Dublin, 2017).

[2] For recent background see, for example, Edel Bhreathnach, 'Communities and Their Landscapes', in Brendan Smith (ed.), *The Cambridge History of Ireland, 1: 600–1550* (Cambridge, 2018), pp. 15–46; Colmán Ó Clabaigh, 'The Church 1050–1460', in Brendan Smith (ed.), *The Cambridge History of Ireland. 1: 600–1550* (Cambridge, 2018), pp. 355–84; *Id.*, 'Monasticism, Colonisation and Ethnic Tension in later Medieval Ireland', in CHMM, pp. 901–21.

[3] Marie Therese Flanagan, *The Transformation of the Irish Church in the Twelfth Century* (Woodbridge, 2010), p. 1.

episcopal and monastic reforms.[4] A number of synods were held throughout the twelfth century, beginning around 1101, known through disparate sources, for example the *Irish Annals*,[5] the Pontigny manuscript, genealogical compilations, contemporary episcopal documents and seventeenth-century writings based on earlier records now lost.[6] These ecclesiastical reforms were linked to pan-European Gregorian reform. The synods were tasked with a re-organisation of the existing church structure and concerned issues such as delimiting parishes, regulating dioceses and bishops, renewing church structures, re-organising existing religious houses and the introduction of continental orders.[7] There is a popular view that it was the invading Anglo-Normans (of England and Wales) who introduced the new reform orders to Ireland, after 1169. While this group certainly patronised such religious houses in Ireland, the first establishments of Cistercian and Augustinian religious houses had already occurred in the twelfth century, some years earlier.[8] So the earlier twelfth-century nunneries under consideration were founded by Gaelic Irish patrons and only in the latter years of the twelfth century did Anglo-Norman patronage emerge.[9]

There are two key figures in Ireland who are directly associated with the twelfth-century reforms: Malachy[10] and Gille.[11] While the status of women reli-

---

[4] Martin Holland, 'Dublin and the Reform of the Irish Church in the Eleventh and Twelfth Centuries', *Peritia*, 14 (2000), 111–60. For background see Damian Bracken and Dagmar Ó Riain-Raedel (eds), *Ireland and Europe in the Twelfth Century: Renewal and Reform* (Dublin, 2006).

[5] The *Irish Annals* refer to a group of medieval Christian chronicles that were maintained in Ireland from about the fifth century to the late sixteenth century. Daniel P. Mc Carthy, *The Irish Annals: Their Genesis, Evolution and History* (Dublin, 2008).

[6] Flanagan, *Transformation*, pp. 1–33. Bracken and Ó Riain-Raedel, *Ireland and Europe*; Ó Corráin, *The Irish Church*.

[7] Flanagan, *Transformation*, pp. 34–168.

[8] Francis J. Byrne, 'Church and Politics c. 750–c. 1100', in Dáibhí Ó Cróinín (ed.), *A New History of Ireland: Vol. I, Prehistoric and Early Ireland* (Oxford, 2005), pp. 656–79; Roger Stalley, 'Ecclesiastical Architecture before 1169', in Dáibhí Ó Cróinín (ed.), *A New History of Ireland: Vol. I, Prehistoric and Early Ireland* (Oxford, 2005), pp. 714–43, at pp. 735–43.

[9] Christina Harrington, *Women in a Celtic Church: Ireland 450–1150* (Oxford, 2002); Diane Hall, *Women and the Church in Medieval Ireland c. 1140–1540* (Dublin, 2003).

[10] Marie Therese Flanagan, 'Saint Malachy and the Introduction of Cistercian Monasticism to the Irish Church', *Seanchas Ardmhacha*, 22 (2009), 8–24; Ead., 'Saint Malachy, Saint Bernard of Clairvaux and the Cistercian Order', *Archivium Hibernicum*, 68 (2015), 294–311; Holland, 'Dublin and the Reform'; Id., 'Malachy (Máel-Máedóic)', in Seán Duffy (ed.), *Medieval Ireland: An Encyclopedia* (London, 2005), pp. 312–14; Robert T. Meyer (trans.), *The Life and Death of Saint Malachy the Irishman by Bernard of Clairvaux* (Kalamazoo, 1978).

[11] John Fleming, *Gille of Limerick c.1070–1145: Architect of a Medieval Church* (Dublin,

gious had long been debated within the continental church, as, for example, the correspondence between Heloise and Abelard has attested,[12] there is yet no known female counterpart in Ireland for these male reformers. However, what is known of their lives has enabled historians to infer an outline of the status of women religious in twelfth-century Ireland. Gille, bishop of Limerick from 1106–40, wrote an important tract on the constitution of the reforming church, *De Statu Ecclesiae* [*Concerning Church Order*] dated to c. 1111, which may have been intended as a synodal discussion document.[13] The enactments of this synod, known as the synod of Ráith Bressail, initiated a new church structure, which was similar but not identical to that set out by Gille.[14] He outlined the structure of the church hierarchy in three grades: first was the universal church, the bishops, archbishops, patriarchs and prophets; second the local church or diocese which included seven grades of cleric headed by a priest;[15] and third was the laity, which was grouped into those who prayed, who ploughed and who fought.[16] This schema would have been easily understood in medieval society where everyone had a place in a rigid social order.[17] It is noteworthy that nuns were excluded from Gille's schema; he preferred to accommodate them with the laity. Marie Therese Flanagan's study of a twelfth-century manuscript copy of *De Statue Ecclesiae*[18] revealed that Gille wrote *moniales* between *canonicales* (clergy) and *universales* (laity), which suggested to her:

> that [Gille] was conscious of the omission of women religious and the difficulty of accommodating them [...] but that he nonetheless felt the need to take

---

2001), pp. 38, 98; Martin Holland, 'Gille (Gilbert) of Limerick', in Seán Duffy (ed.), *Medieval Ireland: An Encyclopedia* (New York, 2005), pp. 198–9; John Lucey, 'Gillebert of Limerick as an Irish Saint: A Case of Mistaken Identity', *North Munster Antiquarian Journal*, 50 (2010), 45–50; Watt, *The Church*, p. 10.

[12] Gary Macy, 'Heloise, Abelard and the Ordination of Abbesses', *Journal of Ecclesiastical History*, 57 (2006), 16–32.

[13] Flanagan, *Transformation*, p. 55; Tomás Ó Carragáin, *Churches in Early Medieval Ireland: Architecture, Ritual and Memory* (London, 2010), p. 12; John Lucey, 'Gillebert of Limerick: Theorist or Shallow Theologian?', *Eolas: The Journal of the American Society of Irish Medieval Studies*, 5 (2011), 130–45.

[14] Holland, 'Gille', p. 199.

[15] Canonists disagreed on the number of clerical grades in the local church, which varied from seven to nine; Fleming, *Gille*, p. 90. Lower clerical grades – for example, exorcists and acolytes – could be married; Flanagan, *Transformation*, p. 70.

[16] Fleming, *Gille*, p. 88.

[17] Roberta Gilchrist, *Medieval Life: Archaeology and the Life Course* (Woodbridge, 2012), pp. 169–72.

[18] There are three manuscript examples of Gille's writing extant. See Fleming, *Gille*, pp. 119–42; Flanagan, *Transformation*, p. 70; Ó Clabaigh, 'The Church'.

account of them [...] [he] therefore indubitably exhibited awareness of women religious in the guise of abbesses, dedicated virgins and vowed widows.[19]

In contrast to Gille, more is known of Malachy, thanks to Bernard of Clairvaux who wrote his *Life*.[20] Malachy followed a career in the church, holding several offices and being instrumental in the reforms from *c.* 1111, though papal approval of those reforms was not received until 1152 at the synod of Kells.[21] The traditional narrative is that Malachy facilitated the introduction of the continental religious orders to Ireland – first the Cistercians and then the Augustinians – as part of his overall reforms. *Fons Mellis* (Fount of Honey), Mellifont, Co. Louth, the first Cistercian house in Ireland, was founded in 1142.[22] The introduction of the Augustinian Order (of canons), specifically of Arroasian observance, occurred after Malachy's visit to Arrouaise in Flanders in 1140.[23] The introduction of this religious order was to provide cathedral chapters and assist the bishops to form a sub-diocesan administration.[24] Therefore, Malachy may have strategically introduced two orders to perform two different functions: 'Cistercians were monks, Augustinians were canons and as such one of the key differences was that Augustinians were ordained priests and therefore entitled to celebrate the Eucharist, whereas monks need not necessarily have been in sacerdotal orders'.[25]

---

[19] Flanagan, *Transformation*, p. 70.

[20] Meyer, *The Life and Death of Saint Malachy*.

[21] Malachy's reforms were considered unsatisfactory by not going far enough, which caused difficulties throughout his career. Katharine Simms, 'Frontiers in the Irish Church – Regional and Cultural', in Terence B. Barry, Robin Frame and Katharine Simms (eds), *Colony and Frontier in Medieval Ireland Essays Presented to J.F. Lydon* (London, 1995), pp. 177-200, at pp. 185-6.

[22] Marie Therese Flanagan, 'Irish Royal Charters and the Cistercian Order', in Marie Therese Flanagan and Judith A. Green (eds), *Charters and Charter Scholarship in Britain and Ireland* (Basingstoke, 2005), pp. 120-39; Flanagan, *Transformation*, p. 134; Roger Stalley, 'Mellifont Abbey: A study of its Architectural History', *Proceedings of the Royal Irish Academy*, 80 (1980), 263-354; Id., *The Cistercian Monasteries of Ireland. An Account of the History, Art and Architecture of the White Monks in Ireland from 1142 to 1540* (London, 1987).

[23] For a critique of this narrative, see Edel Bhreathnach, 'The Vita Apostolica and the Origin of the Augustinian Canons and Canonesses in Medieval Ireland', in Martin Browne and Colmán Ó Clabaigh (eds), *Households of God: The Regular Canons and Canonesses of St Augustine and of Prémontré in Medieval Ireland* (Dublin, 2019), pp. 1-27.

[24] Patrick J. Dunning, 'The Arroasian Order in Medieval Ireland', *Irish Historical Studies*, 4 (1945), 297-315, at pp. 300, 304; Marie Therese Flanagan, 'St Mary's Abbey, Louth, and the Introduction of the Arrouasian Observance into Ireland', *Clogher Record*, 10 (1980), 223-34, at p. 227; Ead., *Transformation*, p. 139.

[25] *Ibid.*, p. 137.

By introducing both orders Malachy was progressing his dual reform of the church's clerical and monastic structures.

Moreover, Malachy made provision for nuns – probably influenced during his visit to the monastery at Arrouaise,[26] whose abbot, Gervase, had made specific provision for women religious.[27] There is historical evidence in the *Vision of Tnugdal*,[28] a twelfth-century (1149) religious text written by an Irish monk in Germany reporting the visions of an Irish knight, that described Malachy as founder of fifty-four congregations which included *sanctimoniales*.[29] This reference might be interpreted negatively, as Malachy attempting to exert control over previously autonomous female communities. Indeed, this view is supported by a decree of the second Lateran Council in 1139, which denounced female groups self-styling themselves as *sanctimoniales* without affiliation to a particular order, a decree which Malachy, as papal legate, would have been well aware of.[30] Nevertheless, Flanagan has pointed out 'that Malachy might have been less fearful of women than some of his contemporaries may be suggested by circumstantial evidence for his willingness to experiment with co-located communities for men and women'.[31] Indeed, the pre-twelfth-century Irish church may have had a less misogynistic attitude and perhaps Malachy continued this tradition.[32] Therefore, although never explicitly described, a vague picture of religious women does emerge. Religious women were present before and at the onset of church reform. Gille included women in his proposed schema, albeit with some difficulty, as did Malachy on a more practical level. Women were part of the Augustinian order of Arrouaise, introduced into Ireland from the continent, and reform efforts may be seen in Malachy's putative influence on the establishment of several nunneries in twelfth-century Ireland.[33]

---

[26] Watt, *The Church*, p. 46; Flanagan, *Transformation*, p. 149.
[27] *Ibid.*, p. 151.
[28] Jean-Michel Picard and Yolande de Pontfarcy, *The Vision of Tnugdal* (Dublin, 1989).
[29] Tracy Collins, 'Transforming Women Religious? Church Reform and the Archaeology of Female Monasticism in Ireland', in Edel Bhreathnach, Malgorzata Krasnodębska-D'Aughton and Keith Smith (eds), *Monastic Europe. Medieval Communities, Landscapes, and Settlements* (Turnhout, 2019), pp. 277–301; Flanagan, *Transformation*, pp. 123, n. 32, 150. Traditionally the foundation date of these nunneries is thought to have been in 1144 and this is the date most cited; see Aubrey Gwynn and Richard Neville Hadcock, *Medieval Religious Houses: Ireland* (Dublin, 1970), p. 307.
[30] Flanagan, *Transformation*, p. 150.
[31] *Ibid.* For background see Flanagan, 'St Mary's Abbey, Louth'.
[32] Harrington, *Women in a Celtic Church*, pp. 267–89.
[33] Bhreathnach, 'The Vita Apostolica'.

Nuns and Co-location

What remains completely unknown is the role of women in these processes of ecclesiastic change in twelfth-century Ireland. No woman is named in relation to those reforms and none is known to have attended any synod. Even though the female religious voice is muted, over thirty nunneries were established in Ireland throughout the twelfth century, mirroring the fervour of male religious house establishment in the same period.[34] This relatively high number of foundations of nunneries suggests that religious women were intrinsic to monastic reform processes, but their contributions now only remain in material form in the archaeology of those monuments, rather than in documentary evidence. Considering female and indeed male monastic reform in Ireland is something of a challenge due to the relative lack of contemporary evidence; this is what gives archaeology all the more importance in the Irish context. This research draws greatly on the work of monastic historians[35] and archaeologists, particularly the seminal works of Roberta Gilchrist.[36] Female monasticism in the medieval British Isles was particularly fluid. Female monasticism in Ireland has elements in common with its counterparts in Britain and on the Continent, but there are also factors that appear distinct and peculiar to Ireland.[37] This article concentrates on a particular subgroup of nunneries founded in the twelfth century.

---

[34] Collins, 'Transforming Women Religious?', pp. 277–301; Tracy Collins, 'The Archaeology of Augustinian Nuns in Medieval Ireland', in Martin Browne and Colmán Ó Clabaigh (eds), *Households of God: The Regular Canons and Canonesses of St Augustine and of Prémontré in Medieval Ireland* (Dublin, 2019), pp. 87–102.

[35] Harrington, *Women in a Celtic Church*; Hall, *Women and the Church;* Janet Burton, *The Yorkshire Nunneries in the Twelfth and Thirteenth Centuries* (York, 1979); Ead., *Monastic and Religious Orders in Britain 1000–1300* (Cambridge, 1994); Janet Burton and Karen Stöber (eds), *Monastic Wales, New Approaches* (Cardiff, 2013); Eads. (eds), *Women in the Medieval Monastic World* (Turnhout, 2015); Leonie V. Hicks, *Religious Life in Normandy 1050–1300: Space, Gender and Social Pressure* (Woodbridge, 2007); Marilyn Oliva, *The Convent and the Community in Late Medieval England. Female Monasteries in the Diocese of Norwich 1359–1540* (Woodbridge, 1998); Karen Stöber, *Late Medieval Monasteries and their Patrons: England and Wales c. 1300–1540* (Woodbridge, 2007); Sally Thompson, *Women Religious: The Founding of English Nunneries after the Norman Conquest* (Oxford, 1991).

[36] Roberta Gilchrist, *Gender and Material Culture: The Archaeology of Religious Women* (London, 1994); Ead., *Contemplation and Action: The Other Monasticism* (London, 1995); Ead., *Gender and Archaeology Contesting the Past* (London, 1999); Ead., *Medieval Life*; Roberta Gilchrist and Barney Sloane, *Requiem: The Medieval Monastic Cemetery in Britain* (London, 2005).

[37] Tracy Collins, 'An Archaeological Perspective on Female Monasticism in the Middle Ages in Ireland', in Janet Burton and Karen Stöber (eds), *Women in the Medieval Monastic World* (Turnhout, 2015), pp. 229–51.

Flanagan has termed these 'co-located houses',[38] to refer to an arrangement in which religious men and women, usually canons and nuns affiliated to the Augustinian order and of Arroasian observance, were thought to have lived in close proximity. This affiliation is derived from secondary written sources as no primary sources are currently known from these nunneries.[39] They are considered distinct from the mixed religious communities of early medieval Ireland, such as at Kildare for example,[40] in that they followed a known rule. Co-located houses have also been seen to differ from double houses of the Gilbertine and Fontevraud orders, which were constructed with a double cloister arrangement whereby men and women lived at the same monastery, but were segregated. These orders were not established in Ireland.[41] These co-located communities in Ireland were likely monastic experiments inspired by reformist ideals.[42] These establishments may have been entirely new foundations, but may also have been an attempt to re-shape existing religious communities into reformed houses and could be considered as a distinctive regional Irish response to reform.[43] It would appear that, for medieval Ireland at least, this experiment ultimately failed as no co-located house established in the twelfth century appears to have survived long into the thirteenth century.[44]

---

[38] Flanagan, *Transformation*, p. 150.

[39] For background and historical evidence on Arroasian observance in Ireland see Flanagan, *Transformation*, pp. 150–61; especially pp. 152–154; Dunning, 'The Arroasian Order', 297–315. For Clonard, see J. Brady, 'The Nunnery at Clonard', *Ríocht na Mide*, 2 (1960), 4–7.

[40] John H. Andrews, *Irish Historic Towns Atlas no. 1 Kildare* (Dublin, 1986); Carol L. Neuman de Vegvar, 'Romanitas and Realpolitick in Cogitosus' Description of the Church of St Brigit Kildare', in Martin Carver (ed.), *The Cross Goes North: Processes of Conversion in Northern Europe, AD 300–1300* (York, 2003), pp. 153–70.

[41] William Henry St John Hope, 'The Ground Plan of Watton in the East Riding of Yorkshire', *Yorkshire Archaeological Journal*, 58 (1901), 1–34; Brian Golding, *Gilbert of Sempringham and the Gilbertine Order c. 1130–1300* (Oxford, 1995); Berenice Kerr, *Religious Life for Women c. 1100–c. 1350: Fontevraud in England* (Oxford, 1999); Alison Beach, *The Trauma of Reform: Community and Conflict in Twelfth-Century Germany* (Cambridge, 2017), pp. 73–92.

[42] Burton, *Monastic and Religious Orders*; Ead., 'Looking for Medieval Nuns', in Janet Burton and Karen Stöber (eds), *Monasteries and Society in the British Isles in the Later Middle Ages* (Woodbridge, 2008), pp. 113–23; Flanagan, *Transformation*, p. 150.

[43] For recent overviews of reforms on the continent, particularly in relation to female religious, see Steven Vanderputten, *Monastic Reform as Process: Realities and Representations in Medieval Flanders 900–1100* (London, 2013); Id., *Dark Age Nunneries: The Ambiguous Identity of Female Monasticism 800–1050* (London, 2018).

[44] For an excellent overview of double monasteries in all their variety see Alison Beach and Andra Juganaru, 'The Double Monastery as a Historiographical Problem (Fourth to Twelfth Century)', in CHMM, pp. 561–78.

Throughout the course of the twelfth century in Ireland, some thirty-three nunneries were established, all thought to have been of Augustinian/Arroasian observance.[45] This number represents just over 50 per cent of the total number of nunneries known for the entire later medieval period in Ireland, c. 1100–1540.[46] Many nunneries may have been entirely new foundations at new locations. However, a significant number may have already been early religious communities, perhaps mixed – female and male – which may have adopted the Augustinian Rule but may not have physically changed their settlements, continuing to use existing structural arrangements that did not include a cloister. Such communities may have had a sense of longevity in their community identity and a tangible connection to their place, not wishing to physically change their architectural setting. New female communities also re-used older ecclesiastical sites, which may have been abandoned, again not wishing to structurally change these sacred locations.[47] Re-use of earlier sites by Augustinian male foundations has been noted in Wales[48] and England.[49] Unfortunately, the dearth of information on the institutional arrangements of Arroasian female communities in medieval Ireland means we can only speculate on their specific arrangements.[50]

The subset of co-located dual-sex houses are locations where communities of both Augustinian nuns and canons were recorded in close proximity. Aubrey Gwynn and Richard Neville Hadcock were among the first to highlight these communities, identified mainly through secondary antiquarian sources.[51] They noted that at eight locations of Augustinian canons, founded in the twelfth century, corresponding communities of nuns were established at the same locations.

[45] Collins, 'The Archaeology of Augustinian Nuns'. For background see Hall, *Women and the Church*, pp. 161–3; Dunning, 'The Arroasian Order', 308. For Augustinianism see Richard Neville Hadcock, 'The Origin of the Augustinian Order in Meath', *Ríocht na Mide*, 3 (1964), 124–31; Gywnn and Hadcock, *Medieval Religious Houses Ireland*, pp. 146–52; Tadhg O'Keeffe, 'Augustinian Regular Canons in Twelfth- and Thirteenth-Century Ireland: History, Architecture and Identity', in Janet Burton and Karen Stöber (eds), *The Regular Canons in the Medieval British Isles* (Turnhout, 2011), pp. 469–84; Flanagan, 'St Mary's Abbey, Louth'.
[46] Collins, 'An Archaeological Perspective'.
[47] Geraldine Carville, *The Occupation of Celtic Sites in Medieval Ireland by the Canons Regular of St Augustine and the Cistercians* (Kalamazoo, 1982).
[48] Karen Stöber and David Austin, 'Culdees to Canons: The Augustinian Houses of North Wales', in Janet Burton and Karen Stöber (eds), *Monastic Wales, New Approaches* (Cardiff, 2013), pp. 41–54, at pp. 40–1.
[49] Andrew Abram, 'Augustinian Canons and The Survival of Cult Centres in Medieval England', in Janet Burton and Karen Stöber (eds), *The Regular Canons in the British Isles* (Turnhout, 2011), pp. 79–96.
[50] Flanagan, *Transformation*, p. 152.
[51] Gwynn and Hadcock, *Medieval Religious Houses: Ireland*.

'Churches dedicated to St Mary appear to have been jointly owned by regular canons and canonesses of Arrouaise at Duleek, Termonfeckin, Kells in [Co.] Meath, Durrow, Annaghdown, Clonfert, Roscommon and Derrane'.[52] At the time of writing the authors labelled these sites with the now somewhat ambiguous term, 'double monastery'.[53] Forty years later, Flanagan again drew attention to this discrete group of religious communities. She used the term 'co-located' to describe these communities of nuns and canons living adjacent to each other and perhaps sharing a church.[54] Using Flanagan's description, I have expanded the list of eight, to include three more locations where canons and nuns are recorded contemporaneously. Their distribution forms a broad band from east to west across the centre of the island, which may highlight the spread of the idea of co-located houses to neighbouring dioceses.

Co-located religious houses of the twelfth century were thus where a community of Augustinian canons and nuns/canonesses are thought to have lived in close proximity in a symbiotic relationship and may have shared facilities. They were founded by Gaelic kings, possibly under the influence of religious personages such as Malachy. In three cases the founder remains unknown. Traditionally it was accepted that Malachy was the prime instigator in the foundation of nunneries during the reform period; but Edel Bhreathnach has made a compelling argument for a much more nuanced and sophisticated approach, arguing that not all reform was due to the influence of Malachy.[55] As for female founders, they are rare in an Irish context in this period, with only a single woman associated with a twelfth-century nunnery: Derbforgaill (daughter of the king of Meath), and her 'completion' of the Nuns' Church at Clonmacnoise, Co. Offaly in 1167 (a community of nuns was in existence there since at least 1144 and likely earlier – there are remains of earlier structures nearby).[56]

---

[52] *Ibid.*, p. 150. There is no evidence for the veneration of John the Evangelist with Mary in nunneries in Ireland; it is a model noted elsewhere, see Fiona J. Griffiths, 'The Cross and the Cura Monialium: Robert of Arbrissel, John the Evangelist, and the Pastoral Care of Women in the Age of Reform', *Speculum*, 83 (2008), 303–30.

[53] Gwynn and Hadcock, *Medieval Religious Houses: Ireland*, p. 168.

[54] Flanagan, *Transformation*, pp. 150–1. Unlike Gwynn and Hadcock, Flanagan thinks it unlikely that the church was a shared facility between the communities.

[55] Bhreathnach, 'The Vita Apostolica'.

[56] Collins, 'The Archaeology of Augustinian Nuns'; Jenifer Ní Ghádaigh, '"But What Exactly Did She Give?": Derbforgaill and the Nuns' Church at Clonmacnoise', in Heather King (ed.), *Clonmacnoise Studies Volume 2* (Dublin, 2003), pp. 175–207. Temple Finghin is a likely second nunnery at Clonmacnoise, and this could be tentatively added to the list of co-located sites; Conleth Manning, 'Finghin MacCarthaigh, King of Desmond, and The Mystery of The Second Nunnery at Clonmacnoise', in David Edwards (ed.),

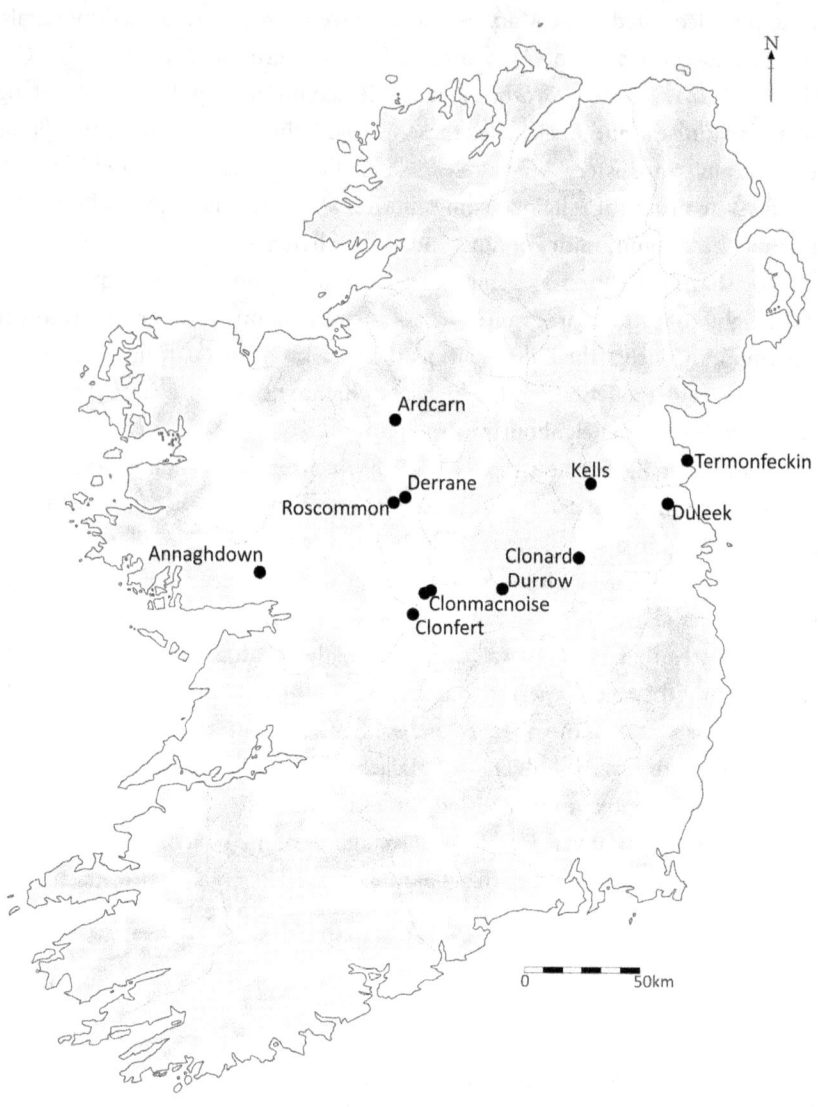

Map.4.1. Map showing locations of co-located religious houses in Ireland established by c. 1144 (by author).

Table 4.1. List of co-located religious houses in 12th-century Ireland, established by c. 1144.

Religious House	Modern County	Patron
Annaghdown	Galway	Tairrdelbach Mór Ua Conchobair, king of Connacht and High King of Ireland
Ardcarn	Roscommon	Unknown
Clonard	Meath	Murchad Ua Máelsechlainn, king of Meath,
Clonfert	Galway	Tairrdelbach Mór Ua Conchobair, king of Connacht, and High King of Ireland
Clonmacnoise: The Nuns' Church	Offaly	Murchad Ua Máelsechlainn, king of Meath, and later Derbforgaill (daughter)
Derrane	Roscommon	Tairrdelbach Mór Ua Conchobair, king of Connacht and High King of Ireland
Duleek	Meath	Unknown
Durrow	Offaly	Murchad Ua Máel Shechlainn, king of Meath (canons; nuns unknown)
Kells	Meath	Unknown
Roscommon	Roscommon	Tairrdelbach Mór Ua Conchobair, king of Connacht and High King of Ireland
Termonfeckin	Louth	Donnchad Ua Cerbaill, king of Airgialla

Co-located Houses in Ireland: Form and Function

But what was the purpose of co-located religious houses? First, co-location would have made practical sense, not least as a nunnery required a priest to celebrate Mass,[57] and second, if facilities were shared this would save costs for construction and maintenance.[58] Co-location likely originated from the early medieval Irish

---

Regions and Rulers in Ireland 1100–1650: Essays for Kenneth Nicholls (Dublin, 2004), pp. 20–6.

[57] Griffiths, 'The Cross and the Cura Monialium', pp. 316–27.
[58] Flanagan suggests that the church was not shared due to a prohibition of the Lateran Council in 1139 which forbade nuns and canons or monks coming together; Flanagan, *Transformation*, p. 151. However, in continental examples it has been shown that the male and female groups used the same church at different times to overcome this, for example at the Poor Clare house at Königsfelden, Switzerland; Carola Jäggi, 'Eastern Choir or Western Gallery? The Problem of the Place of the Nuns' Choir in Königsfelden and Other Early Mendicant Nunneries', *Gesta*, 40:1 (2001), 79–93, at p. 85; Matthias Untermann, 'The Place of the Choir in Churches of Female Convents in the Medieval German Kingdom', in Janet Burton and Karen Stöber (eds), *Women in the Medieval Monastic World* (Turnhout, 2015), pp. 327–53, at pp. 346–7.

tradition of monks and nuns living at the same site, which was then developed or renewed by adopting the Augustinian Rule or Arroasian observance.[59] Alternatively, they might have been experimental and intended as novel establishments formulated as co-located sites as a response to the enthusiasm for twelfth-century reforming ideals. The eleven co-located sites listed represent a third of all of the nunneries established in the twelfth century in Ireland and so it can be inferred that they were – at least at that time – a deliberate, accepted and legitimate form of religious foundation. Currently, little is known of the everyday interactions that were permitted between these adjacent female and male communities. The material and archaeological evidence for how any of these co-located sites may have looked and operated is sparse due to the lack of upstanding remains, and the reuse of the sites over time, which has completely obscured their original layout. It is likely that a variety of spatial and architectural responses was employed to enable canons and nuns to co-locate at these sites.

Termonfeckin, Co. Louth, believed to be the first co-located house, was founded by Donnchad Ua Cerbaill, king of Airgialla, an area stretching from the modern counties of Tyrone to Louth, under the influence of Malachy. Termonfeckin was established in the same diocese as the first Cistercian house at Mellifont, and the first Arroasian male house at Louth, both in 1142.[60] There was already an ecclesiastical community in Termonfeckin in the eleventh century, but it is unknown if this included female religious.[61] Ua Cerbaill's obituary stated he was responsible for the monastery of canons at Termonfeckin and the monastery of nuns and the great church of Termonfeckin and the church *lepadh Feichin* (a shrine church).[62] From this, it has been suggested that the canons and nuns had separate buildings and perhaps indicates that they did not share a church.[63] Termonfeckin has been identified as the co-located house in Airgialla that Gerald of Wales (*c.* 1146–1223) attacked in his *Speculum Ecclesiae*; he was particularly indignant regarding the

---

[59] For discussion of early medieval mixed communities in Ireland see Harrington, *Women in a Celtic Church*.

[60] Liam De Paor, 'Excavations at Mellifont Abbey, Co. Louth', *Proceedings of the Royal Irish Academy*, 68 (1969), 109–64; Roger Stalley, 'Decorating the Lavabo: Late Romanesque Sculpture from Mellifont Abbey', *Proceedings of the Royal Irish Academy*, 98C (1996), 37–64; Flanagan, 'St Mary's Abbey, Louth'.

[61] Victor Buckley, *Archaeological Inventory of County Louth* (Dublin, 1986), p. 80.

[62] John O'Donovan (ed.), *Annála Ríoghachta Éireann: Annals of the Kingdom of Ireland by the Four Masters from the Earliest Period to the Year 1616, Edited From Mss. in the Library of the Royal Irish Academy and of Trinity College, Dublin, with a Translation, and Copious Notes; 7 Volumes 2nd edition* (Dublin, 1856).

[63] Flanagan, *Transformation*, p. 151.

methods of segregating the two communities, which he described as thin and penetrable wooden fences and hedgerows with many deliberate gaps.[64]

Currently, nothing is known of the layout, architecture and archaeology of the co-located house at Termonfeckin. Its supposed site is currently under grassland and so has potential for future archaeological geophysical investigation to assist in outlining its layout. By 1196 Termonfeckin had come under the authority of Agnes, abbess of Clonard, Co. Meath, and there is no further mention of canons after this date. Clonard was by then the mother house of Arroasian nunneries in Ireland and had no less than thirteen daughter houses listed in a papal confirmation.[65] This reference has been interpreted as marking the end of co-location at Termonfeckin, and that the community had become exclusively female by that date. Although Clonard was once the premier mother house, remarkably no upstanding remains have survived. Geophysical surveys there have revealed features that are very suggestive of later medieval religious house buildings, some of which may relate to the nunnery.[66]

At several sites the precise location of either community remains unclear. For example, at Ardcarn, Co. Roscommon the location of the nunnery is identified as a small rectangular enclosure with at least two structures, but the location of the male community is unknown. Ardcarn was described in the sixteenth century as a church with two houses of stone, which may be interpreted as perhaps one each for nuns and canons.[67] Clonmacnoise, Co. Offaly, an important ecclesiastical complex from earliest times, had one and possibly two nunneries now represented by the Nun's Church and Temple Finghin. Temple Finghin is located close to the centre of the ecclesiastical complex, while the Nuns' Church is situated within its own enclosure beside a route known as the Pilgrim's Path to the north of the main complex. In this case, canons are thought to have been in residence at Clonmacnoise though their precise location remains conjecture; they may have been attached to the cathedral, but this is far from clear. At Annaghdown, Co. Galway the nuns' precise location is somewhat confused because Praemonstratensian canons later reused the complex, obscuring the

[64] Ibid., p. 153. John Brewer, James Dimock and George Warner (eds), *Giraldi Cambrensis Opera* (8 vols, London, 1861–91), vol. 4, pp. 182–3.
[65] Maurice P. Sheehy (ed.), *Pontificia Hibernica: Medieval Papal Chancery Documents Concerning Ireland 640–1261* (2 vols, Dublin, 1962–5), vol. 1, p. 84, no. 29.
[66] Paul J. Gibson and Dorothy M. George, 'Geophysical Investigation of the Site of the Former Monastic Settlement, Clonard, County Meath, Ireland', *Archaeological Prospection*, 13 (2006), 45–56. There were two houses of Augustinian canons at Clonard for a time, and it was the location of an important early medieval ecclesiastical complex also. Gwynn and Hadcock, *Medieval Religious Houses Ireland*, pp. 31, 63–4, 163–4.
[67] Mervyn Archdall, *Monasticon Hibernicum* (Dublin, 1786), p. 815, cited by Gwynn and Hadcock, *Medieval Religious Houses Ireland*, p. 312.

Fig. 4.1. View of the upstanding remains of the nunnery at Ardcarn, Co. Roscommon, noting extensive low earthworks in the background. Photo: author.

possible location used by the nuns. The religious buildings used by the Arroasian Augustinian canons are upstanding and lie almost 160 metres to the southwest of the presumed location of the nuns.

Several sites do not retain any upstanding trace of the nunneries, for example, Clonard, Kells and Duleek, Co. Meath, Durrow, Co. Offaly, and Roscommon. At Durrow, the location of the structures for neither the female or male communities is known, and neither geophysical survey nor archaeological investigations have revealed their outlines.[68] At Duleek and Roscommon there are some extant remains of the male Augustinian religious houses, though the location of the nuns is not known. At Kells, Co. Meath the location of the canons' religious house is known to have been to the west of the town, with a *Fratres Cruciferi* [Crutched Friars] house to the east,[69] though a later reference noted that the nuns 'dwelt in

[68] Heather King, 'St Columba's Monastery at Durrow: Some Additional Discoveries', in Peter Harbison and Valerie Hall (eds), *Carnival of Learning: Essays in Honour of George Cunningham* (Roscrea, 2012), pp. 125–32; Elizabeth O'Brien, 'Rediscovering Columba's Monastery at Durrow, Co. Offaly', in Peter Harbison and Valerie Hall (eds), *Carnival of Learning: Essays in Honour of George Cunningham* (Roscrea, 2012), pp. 111–24.

[69] Anngret Simms, *Irish Historic Towns Atlas, No. 4, Kells* (Dublin, 1990), p. 2. Gwynn

Fig. 4.2. View of the Nuns' Church, Clonmacnoise, Co. Offaly. Photo: author.

the town'.[70] Dianne Hall has suggested that the nuns at Kells were attached to the hospital of the *Fratres Cruciferi* and this is certainly possible.[71] Tomás Ó Carragáin has highlighted the double vaulted church at Kells as being the possible location of an anchorite,[72] and it is not unreasonable to suggest that a small community of nuns may have utilised these types of space within main ecclesiastical complexes. Other connections with nunneries and Augustinian male religious houses of the twelfth century are more tentative: for example, urban and ecclesiastical centres in Ireland sometimes had several religious houses within those complexes, as at Armagh where nuns' and canons' houses were physically close.[73] Clonfert, Co. Galway, established in the early medieval period, had a community of canons and nuns in the twelfth century. In this case, the nuns were located about 500 metres

---

and Hadcock, *Medieval Religious Houses Ireland*, p. 213. The Crutched Friars were a relatively small religious order running hospitals following a form of the Augustinian Rule, and nuns worked in those hospitals. See Gwynn and Hadcock, *Medieval Religious Houses Ireland*, pp. 208–9.

[70] Roger Dodsworth and William Dugdale, *Monasticon Anglicanum* (London, 1643), p. 1043.

[71] Hall, *Women and the Church*, p. 189.

[72] Ó Carragáin, *Churches in Early Medieval Ireland*, pp. 255–8, 263–8.

[73] Catharine McCullough and William H. Crawford, *Irish Historic Towns Atlas, No. 18, Armagh* (Dublin, 2007).

to the south of the centre of the main complex in an area known as Nunsacre, but it is unclear if the nuns shared any buildings. During works near this site, human remains were discovered at a location identified as the burial ground of the nunnery, though no structures were revealed.[74]

Co-located sites have been characterised as monastic experiments, perhaps representing groups of men and women, who adopted the Augustinian Rule without making radical structural changes to their religious lives prior to efforts by ecclesiastics to impose a unified reform upon their communities. These communities may well have been experimental, and a time-limited phenomenon, as several co-locations seem to have become single-sexed after a time, most becoming so by the end of the twelfth century or the beginning of the thirteenth century. For example, Termonfeckin became a female-only house, while Annaghdown became exclusively male. The precise cause of this shift remains unknown; it may have resulted through a stricter, later wave of reform; or may have been a more informal process. It has been postulated that the Annaghdown nuns moved to Inishmaine, Co. Mayo in the thirteenth century, which was originally an early medieval ecclesiastical site near the shore of Lough Mask.[75] The nuns from Durrow, Co. Offaly moved to the nunnery at Killeigh, Co. Offaly although there was also an Augustinian (and later Franciscan) male religious house there. Co-location is an occurrence that is noted elsewhere, for example the Cistercian foundation at Swine in Yorkshire, England, where a mixed female and male community lived for a time.[76] Another example of co-location is the Benedictine abbey at Bec in Normandy, France. Bec is of particular interest as its original foundation at Bonneville was located on the dower lands of Heloise, the founder's mother, who herself later retired to the monastery.[77]

Furthermore, co-location may not have been an exclusively twelfth-century phenomenon in Ireland.[78] Nuns are known to have been located at the male Cistercian monasteries of Inishlounaght, Co. Tipperary, Jerpoint, Co. Kilkenny

[74] Christy Cunniffe, 'The Canons and Canonesses of St Augustine at Clonfert', Martin Browne and Colmán Ó Clabaigh (eds), *Households of God: The Regular Canons and Canonesses of St Augustine and of Prémontré in Medieval Ireland* (Dublin, 2019), pp. 103–23.

[75] D. Healy, 'Two Royal Abbeys by the Western Lakes (Cong and Inishmaine)', *Journal of the Royal Society of Antiquaries of Ireland*, 35 (1905), 1–20; Gwynn and Hadcock, *Medieval Religious Houses: Ireland*, p. 318.

[76] Michael Carter, 'Silk Purse or Sow's Ear? The Art and Architecture of the Cistercian nunnery of Swine, Yorkshire', in Janet Burton and Karen Stöber (eds), *Women in the Medieval Monastic World* (Turnhout, 2015), pp. 253–78, at pp. 257–8.

[77] Hicks, *Religious Life in Normandy*, pp. 19–20, 136–9.

[78] See Beach and Juganaru, 'The Double Monastery as a Historiographical Problem (Fourth to Twelfth Century)', in CHMM, pp. 561–78.

and Mellifont, Co. Louth, because the English Cistercian, Stephen of Lexington, conducted a visitation to those monasteries in 1228, and objected strenuously to the proximity of female religious there.[79] Various suggestions have been made as to where the nuns were located at these sites.[80] It is likely that these thirteenth-century cases are different to the twelfth-century examples and resulted from more informal processes, such as small communities of nuns attached to an almonry or infirmary at a male monastery.

Conclusions

There is yet much to be learned of nunneries founded during the period of twelfth-century reform in Ireland, the precise nature of those reforms and how they might be reflected in the archaeological record.[81] Of these nunneries, there is a small but significant number, eleven, where nuns and canons appear to have been deliberately co-located. The reasons for this are not yet fully clear. Do they represent a continuity of early medieval religious sites, sites that already had mixed communities who adopted Augustinian or Arroasian Rules but without changing the buildings they were already using? Or were these brand-new establishments for canons and nuns living in proximity but separate in a symbiotic relationship, in a similar way – but not the *same* way – as the Gilbertines or the order of Fontevraud? It is likely that both scenarios existed. In many cases, as at Termonfeckin, co-location does not appear to have been ultimately successful, as by the end of the twelfth century it was a female-only nunnery. Co-location was not an exclusively Irish trait, as it has been identified in Britain and on the Continent. Further research must be undertaken to tease out the precise nature of these twelfth-century co-located houses; the discipline of archaeology is well-placed to further this research, especially at sites free of modern development such as Termonfeckin and Clonard, as they certainly have the potential to add to our understanding of the diversity and complexity of monasticism in medieval Ireland.

[79] Barry O'Dywer, *Stephen of Lexington: Letters from Ireland 1228–1229* (Kalamazoo, 1982).
[80] Stalley, *The Cistercian Monasteries of Ireland*, p. 6; Gilchrist, *Gender and Material Culture*, p. 68; Geraldine Carville, 'Cistercian Nuns in Medieval Ireland: Plary Abbey, Ballymore, Co. Westmeath', in John A. Nicols and Lillian T. Shank (eds), *Hidden Springs: Cistercian Monastic Women. Medieval Religious Women* (3 vols, Kalamazoo, 1995), vol. 1, pp. 62–84, at p. 62.
[81] See, for example, Bhreathnach, 'The Vita Apostolica'; Collins, 'Transforming Women Religious?'; Flanagan, *Transformation*; Hall, *Women and the Church*; Harrington, *Women in a Celtic Church*; Ó Corráin, *The Irish Church*. For an overview of the archaeology relating to nuns in Ireland see Tracy Collins, *Female Monasticism in Medieval Ireland: An Archaeology* (Cork, 2021).

CHAPTER 5

Women as Witnesses: Picturing Gender and Spiritual Identity in a Twelfth-Century Embroidered Fragment from Northern Germany

JULIE HOTCHIN AND VERA HENKELMANN

Furnishing the church with textiles to mark liturgical feasts performed various commemorative, representative and identity functions for religious communities and patrons.[1] Spiritually, they served as a metaphor for different kinds of spiritual adornment. Liturgical textiles dressed the church as *Ecclesia*, the bride of Christ, and provided visual imagery to focus and direct the meditation of the women and men who viewed them.[2] Women, in particular, commissioned, donated or made liturgical textiles to clothe priests and dress the altars of their church, through which they claimed a female presence in the celebration of the Christian liturgy.[3] From the tenth century women are also occasionally recorded

---

[1] Tanja Kohwagner-Nikolai, '*Per manus sororum*'...: *Niedersächsische Bildstickereien im Klosterstich (1300–1583)* (Munich, 2006), especially chap. 7, 'Funktion der Klosterstichbehänge', pp. 135–81. Stefanie Seeberg, *Textile Bildwerke im Kirchenraum: Leinenstickereien im Kontext mittelalterlicher Raumausstattungen aus dem Prämonstratenserinnenkloster Altenberg/Lahn* (Petersberg, 2014), pp. 98–103.

[2] Honorius Augustodunensis (d. 1140) described the embroidered hangings that adorned the walls of churches in allegorical terms as 'the miracles of Christ that are read in the Church' ['Pallia, quae in Ecclesia suspenduntur, sunt miracula Christi, quae in Ecclesia leguntur']. Honorius Augustodunensis, *Gemma animae*, c. 137, 'De palliis', PL, vol. 172, cols 541–733, here col. 587.

[3] Fiona J. Griffiths, '"Like the Sister of Aaron": Medieval Religious Women and Liturgical Textiles', in Gert Melville and Anne Müller (eds), *Female* vita religiosa *between Late Antiquity and the High Middle Ages: Structures, developments and spatial contexts* (Vienna, 2011), pp. 343–74; Stefanie Seeberg, 'Women as Makers of Church Decoration: Illustrated Textiles at the Monasteries of Altenberg/Lahn, Rupertsberg, and Heiningen

as picturing themselves – or being pictured – prominently in textile imagery and other media as participants in these stories of sacred history.[4] By projecting themselves into key scenes in sacred history, women expressed their relationship with Christ, chiefly at the Cross and the Tomb, and by extension with the men who supported their religious life.[5] Liturgical textiles can yield evidence of how male and female members of a community expressed collective identities and devotional concerns. Examining these textiles, therefore, offers an alternate perspective from which to consider questions of gender, women's spiritual roles and their relations with the men who were responsible for their spiritual care.

This chapter examines a fragment of figural embroidery, now preserved in the Kunstgewerbemuseum in Berlin (Inv. No. 1888,470), as evidence of how women and men in religious life imagined gender roles in northern Germany in the later twelfth century (Fig. 5.1).[6] The central scenes of the fragment depict two images of the Resurrection and Pentecost, with a border on two sides comprising figures of male saints and clerics. Female figures feature prominently in the textile's visual narrative of sacred history: three women are shown at the Tomb on Easter morning, the Virgin is seated among the apostles, and two nuns, arms outstretched in veneration, are embedded into the scenes of the Resurrection. Largely overlooked in the scholarly literature on this embroidered fragment, these

---

(13th–14th C.)', in Therese Martin (ed.), *Reassessing the Roles of Women as 'Makers' of Medieval Art and Architecture* (2 vols, Leiden, 2012), vol. 1, pp. 355–91; and Alexandra Gajewski and Stefanie Seeberg, 'Having her hand in it? Elite Women as "Makers" of Textile Art in the Middle Ages', *Journal of Medieval History*, 42:1 (2006), 26–50, at p. 46.

[4] Griffiths, 'Sister of Aaron', especially at pp. 355–65. Images of women as devotees were embedded in scenes of biblical events in manuscript illumination and other media such as metalwork from the twelfth century; for example, Edith of Wilton, who embroidered an alb in which she is reported to have depicted herself as Mary Magdalene at the foot of the cross, and Judith of Flanders, who was depicted embracing the foot of the cross in a frontispiece to a Gospel Book she donated to Weingarten abbey. See Andrea Worm, *Das Pariser Perikopenbuch. Bibliothèque nationale de France, Ms. lat. 17325 und die Anfänge der romanischen Buchmalerei an Rhein und Weser* (Berlin, 2008), pp. 155–9; and Christa Bertelsmeier-Kierst, 'Beten und Betrachten – Schreiben und Malen. Zisterzienserinnen und ihr Beitrag zum Buch im 13. Jahrhundert', in Anton Schwob and Karin Kranich-Hofbauer (eds), *Zisterziensisches Schreiben im Mittelalter – Das Skriptorium der Reiner Mönche* (Bern, 2005), pp. 163–77.

[5] Fiona J. Griffiths, *Nuns' Priests' Tales: Men and Salvation in Medieval Women's Monastic Life* (Philadelphia, 2018), pp. 182–97. Griffiths argues that liturgical textiles made by women 'hint at their claims to a gendered spiritual priority, even over and above their priests'; p. 194.

[6] Kunstgewerbemuseum der Staatlichen Museen zu Berlin – Preußischer Kulturbesitz, Inv. No. 1888,470. For a colour image and brief description, see http://www.smb-digital.de/eMuseumPlus?service=ExternalInterface&module=collection&objectId=1830386&viewType=detailView [accessed 12 April 2022].

embedded female devotional figures are one of the earliest, if not the earliest, examples of women religious depicted on an extant textile.[7] Positioned as witnesses to the events unfolding before them, these female figures make striking claims for women's presence in sacred history and in the celebration of the liturgy at the centre of this unknown community's life.

The twelfth century was characterised by an increasing diversity of forms of religious life for women, including new institutional models in which women worked for salvation alongside men.[8] The fragment's visual programme is a unique witness to the culture and self-understanding of women and men animated by reforming ideals, and how they were imagined within monastic settings. The textile's visual programme raises numerous devotional and contextual questions about how men and women in monastic life visualised their roles and relations. How are relations between religious women and men portrayed? What claims for male and female spiritual authority are expressed in the textile's imagery? What devotional concerns does the textile's visual programme convey and what do they suggest about the self-understanding of monastic men and women in the context of twelfth-century reform? In an endeavour to answer some of the questions raised by this embroidery, this chapter presents the first detailed critical study of the textile fragment's visual programme in its monastic, social and religious contexts. The textile fragment is well known in art historical scholarship as a rare example of figural embroidery from the late twelfth century. Since the foundational study of the fragment by art historian Renate Kroos in 1970, however, there has been little attempt to examine the fragment's monastic context, reception and layered meanings.[9] Broader questions of the nature of the religious landscape, especially

---

[7] The Rupertsberg antependium made c. 1220 also depicts the nuns and their provost and identifies them by name; Brussels, KBR, Inv. No. 1784. See Seeberg, 'Women as Makers', pp. 375–84 with reproductions at plate 13 and figure 8 at p. 376. See also the embroidery depicting the *Life* of St Elizabeth from Altenberg (second half of the thirteenth century) in which figures of a veiled woman and a woman in secular dress are shown at either side of St Elizabeth; Seeberg, 'Women as Makers', figure 3, p. 361 and pp. 365–6.

[8] Alison I. Beach, *The Trauma of Monastic Reform: Community and Conflict in Twelfth-Century Germany* (Cambridge, 2017), especially chap. 4, 'Women Among the Apostoles?', pp. 55–72; Giles Constable, 'Women and Religious Life in the Twelfth Century', *Studi medievali*, Series 3, 59.1 (2018) pp. 1–36; Julie Hotchin, 'Female Religious Life and the *Cura Monialium* in Hirsau Monasticism, 1080 to 1150', in Constant J. Mews (ed.), *Listen, Daughter: The Speculum Virginum and the Formation of Religious Women in the Middle Ages* (New York, 2001), pp. 59–83; and Eva Schlotheuber, 'Hildegard von Bingen und die konkurrierenden spirituellen Lebensentwürfe der *mulieres religiosae* im 12. und 13. Jahrhundert', in Rainer Berndt with Maura Zátonyi OSB, *Unversehrt und unverletzt. Hildegards von Bingen Menschenbild und Kirchenverständnis heute* (Münster, 2015), pp. 323–65.

[9] Renate Kroos, *Niedersächsische Bildstickereien des Mittelalters* (Berlin, 1970), pp. 26–8,

the context of male–female relations in monastic life, remained outside the scope of Kroos's study. Here, we address aspects that have to date received little attention in order to situate the fragment within the wider context of gender, monastic life and devotional concerns in northern Germany in the twelfth century. Closer examination of its imagery offers insight into how members of one community pictured their spiritual purpose as a shared mission of religious renewal, and highlights the ambivalences that informed gender relations in religious life.

'Scenes of the Life of Christ': The Embroidered Fragment in Berlin

The surviving fragment of figural embroidery, referred to as 'Scenes of the Life of Christ' because of its imagery, is worked in silk thread on linen in chain stitch and measures 118.5 cm in height by 120 cm wide.[10] Little is known about the provenance of this textile, although it is said to have circulated in the region around Halberstadt before coming onto the art market in the late nineteenth century.[11] On 5 September 1888 it was purchased for the collections of the

---

Catalogue no. 1, pp. 113–14. Lotem Pinchover appraises the textile in the context of new forms of iconography of the Resurrection in 'Re-Living the Resurrection in Medieval Saxony – The Development of New Imagery of the Resurrected Christ', in Hedwig Röckelein, Galit Noga-Banaj and Lotem Pinchover (eds), *Devotional Cross-Roads. Practicing Love of God in Medieval Jerusalem, Gaul and Saxony* (Göttingen, 2019), pp. 221–2. Fiona Griffiths compares the figures of a cleric and nuns with those depicted in a manuscript from Lamspringe, now Wolfenbüttel, HAB, Cod. Guelf. 475 Helmst., fol. 148v in 'Sister of Aaron', pp. 357–8; see also Fig. 5.5 and the discussion below. Andrea Worm also compares the textile's imagery with that in a Gospel Lectionary attributed to Lower Saxony in the 1130s/40s in *Das Pariser Perikopenbuch*, pp. 103–5, 125, n. 498, image 65 (noting differences with the lectionary).

[10] Sabine Thümmler and Lothar Lambacher (eds), *Details!: 100 Lieblingswerke im Kunstgewerbemuseum – 100 favorites from the Kunstgewerbemuseum* (Dresden, 2018), p. 54.

[11] Julius Lessing, *Wandteppiche und Decken des Mittelalters in Deutschland* (Berlin, nd [c. 1902]), p. 8, plate 8, where he refers to a personal communication of the seller. According to Schütte and Müller-Christensen, and Kroos, Lessing also claimed that the hanging could have originated from the Moritzkirche in Halberstadt (formerly the monastery of saints Boniface and Maurice), although this information is not mentioned in the publication. As Lessing, unlike Kroos, does not mention the date of acquisition of the fragment, Kroos appears to have obtained further details, which she did not cite. See Marie Schütte and Sigrid Müller-Christensen, *La Broderie* (Paris, 1963), p. 32, and Renate Kroos, 'Niedersächsische Bildstickereien des Mittelalters' (unpublished PhD Dissertation, University of Göttingen, 1957), p. 155. The acquisition records of the Kunstgewerbemuseum (Schlossmuseum) for the period before 1945 were destroyed during the war; the inventory entry in the surviving acquisition inventory has no record of any origin from Halberstadt. We thank Lothar Lambacher of

Fig. 5.1. Embroidered fragment with 'Scenes of the Life of Christ'. Berlin, Kunstgewerbemuseum, Inv. No. 1888,470. © Kunstgewerbemuseum, Staatliche Museen zu Berlin. Photo: Stephan Klonk.

Kunstgewerbemuseum in Berlin.[12] The fragment has undergone some restoration to recover its original colour.[13] A small fragment of the border was also acquired in the same transaction, but was destroyed in the fire at the Sophienhof in 1945.[14]

The central field comprises two registers, each depicting biblical scenes accompanied by an upper band with an inscription.[15] Here we describe the scenes from the lower left register to the upper right, according to the biblical sequence of events. The lower scenes portray the moment of the resurrection and the three women at the tomb. The inscription above links the two scenes: '. + · HIC · CO(N) SVRGIT · H(OM)O · QVE(M) · QUERV(N)T · I(N) · MONVM(EN)TO · + · ASCEND[IT...' ['+ Here rises the person whom they seek in the tomb + He has ascended']. The figure of Christ stepping out of the sarcophagus is flanked by two angels as the two guards sleep in the foreground. In the scene on the right, Mary Magdalene and two other women are shown at the empty tomb. Mary Magdalene holds a censer and the other two Marys carry ointment jars, while an angel hovers over the open sarcophagus.[16] A nun with her arms raised is depicted

---

the Kunstgewerbemuseum, Berlin, for his assistance in checking the extent inventory records of the museum.

[12] Formerly Inv. No. 88,470: Kroos, *Niedersächsische Bildstickereien*, p. 114. This is the entry in the acquisition inventory of the Kunstgewerbemuseum (Schlossmuseum), as advised by Lothar Lambacher. In 1921 the textile fragment was moved with the collections to the Schlossmuseum in the Berlin Palace from where it passed into the western part of the collection of the Kunstgewerbemuseum re-established in West Berlin after World War II. According to Lothar Lambacher, the inventory records that the fragment was sold by a certain R. Bernstein of Berlin, who may have been the antiquary Richard Bernstein (d. 1909) of Friedrichstraße 154, Berlin. The museum later acquired the Pritzwalker Silberfund (Inv. No. 1896,344) from the same dealer.

[13] For the post-war history of the larger fragment see Kroos, *Niedersächsische Bildstickereien*, p. 113. After restoration, the fragment was reported to have 'recovered its original coloured appearance, as one can see by the similarity of the front and rear'; *ibid.*, p. 26, n. 2 ['ist die ursprüngliche farbige Erscheinung – erwiesen durch die Gleichartigkeit von Vorder- und Rückseite – wiederhergestellt.']

[14] Kroos, *Niedersächsische Bildstickereien*, p. 114, Cat. No. 1 and Cat. No. 2.

[15] The script is an (early) Gothic majuscule in which round or uncial letters are used in parallel with upper case forms. See Mitarbeiter der Inschriftenkommissionen der Akademien der Wissenschaften in Berlin, Düsseldorf, Göttingen, Heidelberg, Leipzig, Mainz, München und der Österreichischen Akademie der Wissenschaften in Wien (eds), *Deutsche Inschriften. Terminologie zur Schriftbeschreibung* (Wiesbaden, 1999), pp. 31–45. We are indebted to Tanja Kohwagner-Nikolai (Munich) for assistance with identifying the style and deciphering features of the transcriptions.

[16] For the Marys at the tomb, understood in the medieval period to be Mary Magdalene, Mary of Cleophas and Mary Salome, see Katherine Ludwig Jansen, *The Making of the Magdalen: Preaching and Popular Devotion in the Later Middle Ages* (Princeton, 2000), pp. 18–46.

in the lower right corner of both scenes.[17] The women are clothed in brown robes and each wears a headdress of a fabric crown. Whether it is placed over their veil or hair is difficult to discern from the image, although the outline of the crown is visible against the blue cloth cap worn to support it. Unlike the male figures in the border, who are identified with inscriptions, the nuns embedded into the scenes of the Resurrection are not identified as individuals; rather, they embody a collective viewer. The end of the inscription reads 'ASCEND[IT]', which implies that the following scene was the Ascension.

The remaining full scene in the upper register illustrates the events of Pentecost, indicated by the inscription: '+ · HIC · CELOS · LINGVIS · EXORNAT · CEL …'.[18] ['Here he adorns the heavens with tongues of fire']. The Mother of God is shown enthroned and crowned, as the Holy Spirit in the form of a dove descends upon her. She is flanked on each side by four apostles, each of whom receives the tongue of flames upon the crown of his head. St Peter is distinguished by the large key he holds, which is clearly visible against the dark background. The four apostles holding books likely refer to the four evangelists; the beardless youth to the left of Mary is probably John. The figures are shown within the interior of a building, perhaps reflecting the account in Acts [1: 13–14] which mentions that the disciples gathered in an upper room with the 'women and Mary, Mother of Jesus', where the spirit is said to have descended onto them on the fiftieth day after Easter [Acts, 2: 1–13]. The series of buildings topped with domes and roofs extending above the ceiling likely indicate the heavenly Jerusalem.

The partial scene to the right depicts an apostle with hands outstretched standing on a dais, while a cleric with hands raised kneels before him. The features of the apostle are similar to those of the figure of St Peter holding the key in the Pentecost scene. This figure has been interpreted as St Peter healing the lame man Aeneas (Acts 9: 32–5).[19] This reading is plausible, and is based on a reading of the

---

[17] Kroos acknowledged the distinctive headdress of the nuns and their prominence as devotees in the narrative scenes. She did not further address their function within the visual programme; *Niedersächsische Bildstickereien*, p. 28. Pinchover identifies the figures as male (a monk or bishop); 'Re-Living Resurrection', p. 221.

[18] Leonie von Wilckens, 'Fragment eines Wandbehangs', in Jochen Luckhardt and Franz Niehoff (eds), *Heinrich der Löwe und seine Zeit. Herrschaft und Repräsentation der Welfen 1125–1235. Katalog der Ausstellung Braunschweig 1995. Vol. 1, Catalogue* (Munich, 1995), p. 228, Cat. No. D 46. The reading of 'CEL' here is uncertain: we read it as 'CEL[IS]', in agreement with the ablative 'LINGVIS'.

[19] This is the most common interpretation, cited for example by Heidi Blöcher in 'Fragment eines Wandbehangs', in Lothar Lambacher (ed.), *Schätze des Glaubens. Meisterwerke aus dem Dom-Museum Hildesheim und dem Kunstgewerbemuseum Berlin* (Regensburg, 2010), p. 84, Cat. No. 36 (with further literature); and Kroos *Niedersächsiche Bildstickereien*, p. 26.

initials above the kneeling clerics as 'AE[NEAS]'. However, a close examination of the characters embroidered above the kneeling figure reveal them to be AB, and not AE. This may be an allusion to 'AB[BAS]'.[20] If this is accurate, we propose an alternative interpretation of the scene as the sermon of St Peter, which, according to biblical accounts, took place immediately after the events of Pentecost (Acts 2: 14–36). The upper inscription extends across this partial scene, uniting it with the Pentecost scene just as the lower inscription extends across the scenes of the Resurrection and the Women at the Tomb. Moreover, the kneeling cleric appears to be positioned self-consciously within the events, as if among the audience of Peter's sermon. This position corresponds to the integration of the nuns in the scenes of the Resurrection and the Women at the Tomb below, although on this occasion it is not women depicted at the centre of salvation history but St Peter. An abbot identifying himself against the background of the apostolic succession in a particular manner with St Peter is hence plausible.[21]

The fragment is framed by a border comprising busts of clerics and saints with alternate floriate decoration. In the upper left corner a tonsured cleric holding a sceptre or staff of office is identified as 'HEIN/RIC/[VS]/ PAT(ER)/ MONAS/ TERI/I'[22] ['Henry, father of [this] monastery']. To the right is the protomartyr St Stephen, shown with halo and martyr's palm leaf: 'S(ANCTVS) ·/ S/T/E/P/H/ A/N/[VS]'.[23] Next to him is the saintly bishop Boniface, depicted with crosier,

[20] The reading is based on a comparison with the preceding upper case and round E and especially in the clearly recognisable closed, upper arch of the damaged second letter. We thank Tanja Kohwagner-Nikolai (Munich) for her assistance with identifying the transcription of AB[BAS] and for the suggested reading. Although Lessing, *Wandteppiche*, p. 8, also interpreted the scene as the healing of Aeneas, he read the two characters as 'AL'. If one compares the images he includes (plate 8) with the fragment's current condition, the second character is not necessarily read as an 'E'.

[21] It is difficult to determine whether the figure is a canon regular or a Benedictine monk on the basis of dress. Closer investigation is required to identify whether the garment is a dalmatic worn over an alb. Moreover, the colour of the robe is not a reliable criterion to distinguish a clear identity for the figure. One could assume that the robe was originally dark and that the dye used has faded (on this see Tanja Kohwagner-Nikolai, 'Inschriften auf Textilien, oder: Wie läuft der Faden? Versuch einer Annäherung an materialspezifische Eigenheiten', *Archiv für Diplomatik* 55 (2009), pp. 225–62, here at p. 228), which, however, is unlikely as the contours stitched in dark thread remain visible. The pale colour may also have been a deliberate choice to ensure the figure of the cleric stood out against the background. We thank Tanja Kohwagner-Nikolai and Katrin Kania for their advice and suggestions on these questions.

[22] Compare with the reading of 'HEINRIC(us) Pat(er) MONASTERII' by von Wilkens, 'Fragment', p. 228, Cat. No. D 46. This cannot be verified because of the quality of the available images.

[23] 'H' is outlined in uncial. This corrects the reading of 'S(anctus) STEFAN(us)' by von Wilkens, 'Fragment', p. 228, Cat. No. D 46.

mitre, book and halo: 'BO/NI/FA/CI/VS'.[24] On the left border, below the cleric Heinrich, two further figures are shown, each with crosier, mitre and halo. The upper is identified as St Benedict: '· S(ANCTVS) · BE/NE//DIC/TVS ·', and the lower as St Severus: 'S(ANCTVS) · SE//VE/RVS ·'. Below the image of St Severus the head of a tonsured cleric can just be made out, identified as 'SAM//SON'.

The lost border fragment (formerly Schlossmuseum Berlin, no Inv. No) measured 113 cm long and 26 cm wide and displayed the same alternating pattern of round and square shapes surrounding images of half-figures and foliate decoration (Fig. 5.2).[25] This piece certainly once formed part of the same textile, as it was worked in a corresponding technique and colour palette, and the figures and floriated decoration are arranged in an identical manner.[26] Three half-figures were depicted in this fragment: a cleric holding a book in the upper section, identified as a provost ['P[RE]/POSI/TVS'],[27] the bishop saint Servatius appears below him, with a crosier, mitre and halo: '· S(ANCTVS) · SER/VA//CI/VS ·'. The final figure is St Eustace ['· S(ANCTVS) · EV/STA//CHI/VS ·'] who holds a martyr's palm, crown and halo.

Dating, Style and Reconstruction

The study of the Berlin fragments by Renate Kroos remains foundational for any appraisal of the embroidery. Based on a stylistic analysis of Lower Saxon manuscript illumination, Kroos proposed that it was made in the last third of the twelfth century, probably *c.* 1160–70, in the region around Halberstadt.[28] This comparison was largely based on two liturgical manuscripts produced at the Benedictine abbey of St Michael in Hildesheim: the Ratmann Sacramentary, completed in 1159, and the Stammheim Missal, completed in the 1170s.[29] Of interest here is that

---

[24] Compare with the reading 'BONIFACIVS' by von Wilkens, 'Fragment', p. 228, Cat. No. D 46. This cannot be verified because of the quality of the available images.

[25] Kroos, *Niedersächsische Bildstickereien*, p. 114, Cat. No. 2.

[26] Ibid. A further, smaller fragment of a border (see *ibid.*, p. 114, Cat. No. 3 (formerly Schlossmuseum Berlin, without Inv. No.)), which is now lost, was also decorated with foliate ornament in a similar style to these two fragments, but it is not close enough stylistically to the larger fragment to be considered to have been part of the same work.

[27] Ibid., p. 114, Cat. No. 2 (lower case letters are given here, although as far as can be ascertained from the reproduction upper case letters are used).

[28] Kroos, *Niedersächsische Bildstickereien*, p. 28. For a later date of 1180–1200 see Schütte and Müller-Christensen, *La Broderie*, p. 32. Gertrud Schiller posits a date around 1200; *Iconography of Christian Art*, trans. Janet Seligman (2 vols, New York, 1971-2), vol. 2, pp. 32-4, image 206.

[29] For a brief introduction to the Ratmann Sacramentary (Hildesheim, Dombibliothek, Ms 37) and the Stammheim Missal (Los Angeles, J. Paul Getty Museum, Ms 64), see Elizabeth C. Teviotdale, *The Stammheim Missal* (Los Angeles, 2001).

Fig. 5.2. Fragment of embroidered border with *praepositus*. Formerly Berlin, Schlossmuseum (without Inv. No.; lost in 1945); image now Berlin, Kunstgewerbemuseum. © Kunstgewerbemuseum, Staatliche Museen zu Berlin. Photo: Archiv Kunstgewerbemuseum.

the iconography of the Resurrected Christ stepping out of the sarcophagus, such as we see in the lower left scene of the embroidered fragment, first appears in the Ratmann Sacramentary.[30] Moreover, the iconography of the Virgin surrounded by the apostles at Pentecost is also an early example of this imagery, which is prominent in manuscript illumination from the north of Germany produced for

[30] Hildesheim, Dombibliothek, Ms. 37, fol. 75r. Kroos, *Niedersächsische Bildstickereien*, p. 27, also mentions a similar image in a textile from Halberstadt around the same date, which is known from an eighteenth-century copy; n. 22. Pinchover outlines the emergence of this new iconographical form; 'Re-Living Resurrection', with a reproduction of the image from the Ratmann Sacramentary on p. 237, figure 4. See also Worm, *Das Pariser Perikopenbuch*, pp. 98–103.

female audiences from the early twelfth century.[31] The iconography of the textile fragment, therefore, incorporates elements of a new visual vocabulary to emphasise the human dimension of Christ and Marian devotion that emerged in Lower Saxony in the twelfth century.[32]

Kroos also identified stylistic similarities, in particular the draping of clothing and facial features, to manuscript illumination in a bible and Gospels executed in the last quarter of the twelfth century at the Augustinian monastery of Hamersleben, an influential centre of reform near Halberstadt.[33] Palaeographical analysis of these manuscripts by Aliza Cohen-Mushlin led her to conclude that they were executed between 1170 and 1178.[34] We therefore propose a slightly later date for the embroidery of *c.* 1160–80, possibly in the 1170s. Based on these stylistic comparisons, Kroos has posited that the embroidery's design may have been developed around Halberstadt, possibly in Hamersleben, and that it was worked in the Halberstadt region.[35] In the twelfth century the monastic community at Hamersleben comprised canons regular and a community of women, about which little is known.[36] The manuscripts produced at Hamersleben have been attributed

---

[31] Christa Bertelsmeier-Kierst, '*Audi filia et vide*. Frauenkonvente nach der monastischen Reform', in ead. (ed.), *Zwischen Vernunft und Gefühl: weibliche Religiosität von der Antike bis heute* (Frankfurt am Main, 2010), pp. 61–90, at p. 85. Worm, *Das Pariser Perikopenbuch*, pp. 103–5, 125. And see discussion below, p. 125–6.

[32] Leonie von Wilckens: 'Als eine um die Mitte des 12. Jahrhunderts neuartige Verbildlichung entsteigt Christus mit der Osterfahne in der Rechten dem offenen Sarkophag, vor dem zwei Wächter mit ihren Schilden schlafen; Christus belgeiten zwei akklamierende Engel [...] Neben der Auferstehung aus dem Grabe war auch die Darstellung des Pfingstgeschehens mit der in der Mitte der Apostel herausgehoben thronenden Muttergottes zu dieser Zeit eine ikonographisch neuartige Verbildlichung: beide lassen sich damals in Niedersachsen erstmals nachweisen', in 'Fragment', p. 228, Cat. No. D 46.

[33] Based on comparison with the illuminations in the so-called Hamersleben Bible (Halberstadt, Domschatz, Inv. No. 472) and the Gospels from Heiningen (London, British Library, Additional Ms 27926 and New York, The Morgan Library and Museum, Ms M565), which also is attributed to the Hamersleben workshop in the last quarter of the twelfth century.

[34] Aliza Cohen-Mushlin, *Scriptoria in Medieval Saxony. St Pancras in Hamersleben* (Wiesbaden, 2004), p. 110. Cohen-Mushlin dates the Hamersleben Bible to 1170–5 and the so-called Heiningen Gospels to 1178.

[35] Kroos, *Niedersächsische Bildstickereien*, p. 28: 'eine Lokalisierung des Entwurfs im Umkreis von Halberstadt, vielleicht in Hamersleben. Wo er ausgeführt wurde, entzieht sich unserem Urteil, jedoch wohl im Umkreis der Bischofsstadt.' For the dating see p. 27, 113. (Cat. Nos 1 and 2).

[36] Women religious are documented at Hamersleben from the early twelfth century. Günter Peters analyses the evidence for the female community in: 'Das Augustinerchorherrenstift Hamersleben. Entstehung und soziales Umfeld einer doppelklösterlichen Regularkanonikergemeinschaft im hochmittelalterlichen Ostsachsen',

to the canons; there is no evidence at present to indicate female involvement in manuscript production there.³⁷ Further contributing to the textile's likely localisation in the Halberstadt region is the fact that the Berlin fragment was also worked in the same technique and shares several similarities in iconography, style and colour palette to fragments of another textile embroidered at a slightly earlier date, which were acquired from the Benedictine abbey of Huysburg, north of Halberstadt, in the nineteenth century.³⁸

The prominent female imagery in the textile's visual programme raises questions about women's involvement in the design and production of the original embroidery. Women are documented as producing textiles from the early Middle Ages, although clear evidence for their involvement in the production of extant textiles only dates from the thirteenth century.³⁹ The iconography of the textile fragment depicts devotional themes expressive of male as well as female spiritual concerns. It offers no evidence, however, as to who was the 'maker' of the work, in the broader understanding of 'making' an artefact proposed by Therese Martin.⁴⁰ Although it is impossible to know who designed or produced the embroidery

---

Jahrbuch für die Geschichte Mittel- und Ostdeutschlands, 52 (2006), 1–53, at pp. 36–53; and *id.*, 'Skriptorium, Gottesdienst und Bauernhof: Die Regularkanoniker und Stiftsdamen von Hamersleben um 1200', in Dirk Martin Mütze (ed.), *Regular- und Säkularkanonikerstifte in Mitteldeutschland* (Dresden, 2011), pp. 83–102.

³⁷ Cohen-Mushlin does not mention the women at Hamersleben in her analysis. Peters speculates that women at Hamersleben may have undertaken some form of scribal activity on the basis of how the monastery's female founders are described in the *Stiftsurbar* (register of property donations). See Peters, 'Regularkanoniker und Stiftsdamen', p. 93. For Hamersleben canons instructing the Benedictine nuns at Lamspringe, see Cohen-Mushlin, *Scriptoria*, pp. 155–70 and p. 119 below.

³⁸ Kroos, *Niedersächsische Bildstickereien*, pp. 28–9, Cat. No. 77 a–c (London, Victoria and Albert Museum, Inv. No. 8713–1863, 1252–1864, 1252A–1864), 112 a–d (Wien, Museum für angewandte Kunst, Inv. No. T 771, T 772), 107 (Paris, Musée de Cluny, Inv. No. Cl. 3048); possibly also Cat. No. 3 (formerly Schlossmuseum Berlin, now lost), 109 (unknown private collection). The larger fragment depicts the apostles Bartholomew and Paul, with a partial figure of a third apostle; London, Victoria and Albert Museum, Inv. No. 8713–1863: https://collections.vam.ac.uk/item/O117830/textile-fragments-unknown/ [accessed 12 April 2022].

³⁹ Gajewski and Seeberg, 'Having her hand in it?', pp. 26–7; and Jane Tibbets Schulenberg, 'Holy Women and The Needle Arts: Piety, Devotion, And Stitching The Sacred, Ca. 500–1150', in Katherine Allen Smith and Scott Wells (eds), *Negotiating Community and Difference in Medieval Europe Gender, Power, Patronage and the Authority of Religion in Latin Christendom* (Leiden, 2009), pp. 83–110.

⁴⁰ This takes into account how the process of creating an object involves a variety of activities and skills, including conceiving, designing, financing and embroidering the textile, performed by different people over time, many of whom are unlikely to be identified by name. Therese Martin, 'The Margin to Act: A Framework of Investigation for Women's (and Men's) Medieval Art-making', *Journal of Medieval History*, 42:1 (2016), 1–25.

without further evidence, we cannot exclude the possibility that women were responsible or that the original textile was a collaboration between male and female members of the monastery about how to express their collective self-image.[41] Nuns in reforming circles associated with Hamersleben were accomplished designers and illuminators; it is also likely that they possessed the iconographic, theological and technical knowledge to design large figural embroideries such as wall hangings.[42] Alternatively, even if the textile was designed by men with no or limited female involvement, the visual programme with its emphasis on female presence within salvation history indicates how at least some men valued and chose to represent female spiritual privilege and men's relation to it.

The Berlin fragment was likely once part of an embroidered wall hanging. Kroos proposed a reconstruction of the original textile based on the size of the surviving image fields of the larger fragment, the assumption that the original scenes were arranged symmetrically, and on iconographical considerations. The original embroidery was thus perhaps 240 cm high by 200 cm wide, comprising four horizontal registers, surrounded by a border.[43] The reconstructed upright

---

[41] While Pinchover claims that the work was embroidered by women, Griffiths and Adolpho Cavallo leave open the question of the design of its visual programme and production as involving men and/or women as a collaborative enterprise. See Pinchover, 'Re-Living Resurrection', p. 221; Griffiths, 'Sister of Aaron', p. 357; and Adolpho Salvatore Cavallo, *Medieval Tapestries in The Metropolitan Museum of Art* (New York, 1993), p. 74: 'These large hangings [Halberstadt und Berlin] prove that ambitious weaving and embroidery projects were being executed in Germany by highly skilled needleworkers and weavers, during the twelfth and thirteenth centuries; but we have no evidence that these craftsmen and women functioned in the context of a highly capitalised and organised luxury industry like that which existed in the fourteenth to sixteenth centuries in southern Netherlands'.

[42] Female scribes, artists and intellectual activity at Lamspringe and Lippoldsberg are briefly discussed at p. 118–19 below. Women in the twelfth century are documented as 'making' and donating large scale figural embroideries to ecclesiastical institutions. In 1158 Rederich and Cunegund presented a 'great hanging' depicting the epistles of Paul to the cathedral in Minden. The textile contained an inscription identifying both women who 'fashioned' the work; see Charles Reginald Dodwell, *The Pictorial Arts of the West, 800–1200* (New Haven, 1993), p. 16.

[43] Kroos, *Niedersächsische Bildstickereien*, p. 26. This proposed reconstruction is persuasive, although it does not rule out other possibilities due to the loss of the other scenes. For discussion of the challenges of reconstructing a textile's iconographic programme, see Lothar Lambacher, 'Inkunabeln des *Opus teutonicum*. Die verlorenen romanischen Weißstickereien des Berliner Kunstgewerbemuseums', in Hans-Jürgen Beier and Thomas Weber (eds), *Altes und Neues – Vom Museum in den Landtag. Festschrift für Volker Schimpff zum sechzigsten Geburtstag* (Langenweißbach, 2014), pp. 111–13. Another, smaller fragment of a border, now lost (formerly Schlossmuseum Berlin, no Inv. No.: Kroos, *Niedersächsische Bildstickereien*, p. 114, Cat. No. 3), was also decorated

rectangular format as well as the size support the hypothesis that the fragment once formed part of a wall hanging. Wax flecks on the larger fragment have led scholars to suggest that it may have been used as an altar cloth,[44] although these may also indicate that the textile hung behind an altar[45] as it was common to use textile hangings in place of a retable.[46] Embroidered hangings were popular and are mentioned frequently as adorning monastic churches in contemporary records.[47] Although the precise context of the production and use of the original embroidery remains elusive, this surviving fragment nevertheless represents the kind of luxury object commonly commissioned and displayed in twelfth-century church interiors to communicate wealth, status and identity.

The Berlin Fragment's Monastic Origins

Based on stylistic features, iconography and technique, the embroidered fragment can be located to northern Germany, likely the Halberstadt region, in the third quarter of the twelfth century. The fragmentary state of the textile, however, makes it difficult to identify its possible origin with any certainty. Below we briefly review the evidence to identify the textile's origin in a female or dual-sex Benedictine community and then consider the wider implications of the monastic context in the Halberstadt region for interpreting the textile's visual design.

The clerics identified in the border of the fragment offer a point of departure to further localise the textile. Kroos's search for evidence of the combination of *Heinricus pater monasterii* (Fig. 5.3) and the unusual name Samson (Fig. 5.4) in documentary records for the diocese of Halberstadt identified connections with three female Benedictine monasteries.[48] The first is Drübeck, where a priest

---

with foliate ornament in a similar style to these two fragments, but it is not close enough stylistically to the larger fragment to be considered to have been part of the same work.
[44] Griffiths, 'Sister of Aaron', n. 61, proposes a temporary use at some time as an altar cloth.
[45] For this thesis, see von Wilckens, 'Fragment', p. 228, Cat. No. D 46. On the use of wall hangings behind altars see Alexandra Gajewski and Stefanie Seeberg, 'Art in Monastic Churches of Western Europe from the Twelfth to the Fourteenth Century', in CHMM, p. 1011, in particular the example of the Elisabeth hangings from the Premonstratensian convent of Altenberg (St Petersburg, The Hermitage, Inv. No. T-3728).
[46] For an example at Altenberg see Seeberg, *Textile Bildwerke*, pp. 99–100, 249.
[47] Franz Kirchweger, '"Nunc de vestibus altaris". Kirchentextilien in Schriftquellen des 11. und 12. Jahrhunderts', *Wiener Jahrbuch für Kunstgeschichte*, 50 (1997), 75–109.
[48] Kroos also identified possible associations with other churches in Halberstadt. However, based on the dress of the nuns and the ecclesiastical figures in the border, we have only considered further the evidence for a monastic origin for the textile here. Kroos also observes that, in the diocese of Halberstadt, the title *pater* was interchangeable with *praepositus* to refer to this office; *Niedersächsische Bildstickereien*, p. 28.

Fig. 5.3. *Pater Heinricus*. Detail from Berlin, Kunstgewerbemuseum, Inv. No. 1888,470. © Kunstgewerbemuseum, Staatliche Museen zu Berlin. Photo: Stephan Klonk.

Fig. 5.4. Samson and St Severus. Detail from Berlin, Kunstgewerbemuseum, Inv. No. 1888,470. © Kunstgewerbemuseum, Staatliche Museen zu Berlin. Photo: Stephan Klonk.

Samson and *praepositus* Heinrich are recorded in a charter in 1141.[49] Samson is also recorded as *praepositus* of the Benedictine convent at Hornburg/Holzzelle (*praepositus de Horenberg*) in 1159, which at the time was subject to Drübeck.[50] This Samson may have been the priest mentioned earlier at Drübeck. The third possibility is the female Benedictine monastery of Hadmersleben, where a *Heinricus* is recorded as *praepositus* between 1179 to 1202.[51] A 'priest Samson from Hadmersleben' [*sacerdos Samson de Hadmersleve*] is mentioned in a fragment of a necrology from the dual-sex Augustinian community of St John in Halberstadt.[52] This necrology is dated to after 1190, which would place Samson at Hadmersleben during Heinrich's tenure as provost there.[53] Hadmersleben was initially dedicated to the apostles Paul and Stephen, and later dedicated to the apostles Peter and Paul in 1145, after the Benedictine Rule was introduced.[54] These saints feature prominently in the design of the larger textile fragment, such as the prominence of St Peter in the Pentecost scene and the adjoining scene in which he is depicted preaching.

Another possible location is the dual-sex Benedictine monastery at Huysburg, although the evidence for this connection is more circumstantial. The figure of *pater Heinricus* may allude to Heinrich, abbot of Huysburg between 1194 and 1197.[55] To date no documentary reference to a Samson has been found for the monastery, leaving open the possibility of a priest of this name having a connection

---

[49] Gustav Schmidt (ed.), *Urkundenbuch des Hochstifts Halberstadt und seiner Bischöfe* (4 vols, Leipzig, 1883–9), vol. 1, no. 200, pp. 169–70. Heinricus is documented on only this occasion as *praepositus* at Drübeck. Heinricus was likely serving as provost prior to this. Karlotto Bogumil indicates 'before 1141'. See Karlotto Bogumil, *Das Bistum Halberstadt im 12. Jahrhundert; Studien zur Reichs und Reformpolitik des Bischofs Reinhard und zum Wirken der Augustiner-Chorherren* (Cologne, 1972), p. 129, n. 356. For a brief orientation to Drübeck, see Claudia Mohn, *Mittelalterliche Klosteranlagen der Zisterzienserinnen. Architektur der Frauenklöster im mitteldeutschen Raum* (Petersberg, 2006), pp. 389–90.

[50] Schmidt, *UB Hochstift Halberstadt*, no. 253, p. 220. For a brief orientation to Holzzelle/Hornburg, see Mohn, *Mittelalterliche Klosteranlagen*, p. 399.

[51] Schmidt, *UB Hochstift Halberstadt*, p. 599. For a brief orientation to Hadmersleben, see Mohn, *Mittelalterliche Klosteranlagen*, pp. 397–8.

[52] Otto von Heinemann, 'Bruchstück eines Nekrologiums des St. Johannisklosters zu Halberstadt', *Zeitschrift des Harz-Vereins für Altertumskunde und Geschichte*, 2 (1879), 1–14, at p. 2. For the monastery of St John (*Johanniskloster*) as dual-sex see below, p. 118..

[53] Patrizia Carmassi gives the *terminus ante quem* for the fragment of the necrology from St John as 1190. See 'Neue Ergebnisse aus der Katalogisierung der Halberstädter Handschriften. Aspekte der Fragmentenforschung', *Wolfenbüttler Notizen zur Buchgeschichte*, 35 (2010), 1–22, at p. 12, n. 45.

[54] For the dedication to St Stephen, see Bogumil, *Bistum Halberstadt*, p. 192. He also mentions that a parish church dedicated to the same saint was also incorporated into the monastery at Hadmersleben in 1189.

[55] Christof Römer, Alexander Dylong, Petrus Henke, Frank Högg, Antonius Pfeil, Wolfgang Milde and Ralf Lusiardi, 'Huysburg', in Christof Römer and Monika Lücke

with the abbey. On the other hand, an interpretation of the figure kneeling before St Peter identified by the letters Ab[as] would make sense as an abbot in this context. As mentioned, the Berlin fragment shares similarities in technique and style with embroidered fragments dated slightly earlier (*c.* 1150/60), acquired from Huysburg in the nineteenth century, although there is no evidence to indicate whether they were made at or for the community at Huysburg. Finally, it is possible that *Heinricus pater monasterii* and the *praepositus* on the separate border fragment may represent prelates from two different monasteries. This could be explained by close, even personal, contact between the two institutions. Thus, *Heinricus* could be honoured in the border as *pater monasterii*, together with *Samson* as priest and the unnamed *praepositus*, for his connection with the female monastery as a patron or for the provision of spiritual direction.

While the fragmentary survival of the textile makes it impossible to attribute it to any place with certainty, the iconographic and documentary evidence points to the original embroidery as a work made for or by a female or dual-sex Benedictine monastery in the region of Halberstadt.

Women, Men and Monastic Reform in the Diocese of Halberstadt

The monasteries with a possible connection to the fragment are representative of the transformations shaping religious life for women and men by the middle of the twelfth century. The images of the priest Samson, *pater Heinricus* and the unidentified *praepositus* in the textile fragments represent new institutional realities for monastic women in reformed communities in northern Germany. The female communities of Drübeck and Hadmersleben are illustrative of these wider changes. Both were founded as *Stifte* in the Ottonian period and, through the impetus of reform-minded bishops, had adopted a Benedictine observance and the office of provost by the mid-twelfth century.[56] The appointment of a provost, who, in northern Germany, was usually an Augustinian canon, bound female monasteries such as Drübeck and Hadmersleben with the circle of reform centred on Hamersleben. The bishops of Halberstadt favoured Augustinian canons to implement reform because of their pastoral and preaching roles, which extended to the governance and spiritual direction of women religious.[57] With responsibility for the spiritual direction of nuns and the monastery's external affairs, a provost

---

(eds), *Die Mönchsklöster der Benediktiner in Mecklenburg-Vorpommern, Sachsen-Anhalt, Thüringen und Sachsen* (St Ottilien, 2012), pp. 627–96, at p. 686.

[56] Bogumil, *Bistum Halberstadt*, pp. 132–5.

[57] *Ibid.*, pp. 181–203; Hedwig Röckelein, 'Die Auswirkung der Kanonikerreform des 12. Jahrhunderts auf Kanonissen, Augustinerchorfrauen und Benediktinerinnen', in Franz

could assume great significance in the context of an enclosed female community and greater limits upon female autonomy.[58] In Saxony, this ideal held such sway that by the mid-twelfth century almost all *Stifte*, or foundations of canonesses, had adopted this organisational change together with regular observance.

The reform of women's religious institutions in Saxony fundamentally reformulated ideals of religious life for women and their self-understanding. Among other things, reform ideology placed renewed emphasis on virginity, self-discipline and observance of a recognised rule.[59] The status of nuns within the ecclesiastical hierarchy was represented symbolically by the idea of their spiritual marriage to Christ. This privileged status was materialised in the nun's crown, which symbolised a nun's virginity and identity as a bride of Christ.[60] The object worn by the nuns in the lower scenes of the textile fragment closely resembles the form of an extant fabric crown dating from the twelfth century, now held in Riggisberg.[61] Nuns received their crown in the ritual of consecration (or coronation as it was known in Germany), which was performed as part of their transition into religious life. This ceremony was also an acknowledgement by the Church of nuns' status as virgins and brides of Christ. The symbolism of the crown and the ritual context in which it was received symbolically assimilated the wearer to the Virgin and likened her to

---

J. Felten, Annette Kehnel and Stefan Weinfurter (eds), *Institution und Charisma. Festschrift für Gert Melville* (Cologne, 2009), pp. 55–72.

[58] Hotchin, 'Female Religious Life', and Eva Schlotheuber, 'The "Freedom of their Own Rule" and the Role of the Provost in Women's Monasteries of the Twelfth and Thirteenth Centuries', in Fiona J. Griffiths and Julie Hotchin (eds), *Partners in Spirit: Women, Men, and Religious Life in Germany, 1100–1500* (Turnhout, 2014), pp. 109–44.

[59] Schlotheuber, 'Hildegard von Bingen und die konkurrierenden spirituellen Lebensentwürfe der *mulieres religiosae*'.

[60] Caroline Walker Bynum, '"Crowned with Many Crowns": Nuns and Their Statues in Late-Medieval Wienhausen', *The Catholic Historical Review*, 101:1 (2015), 18–40; Eva Schlotheuber, 'The Role of the *sponsa Christi*, the "Bride of the Highest King", in the Social and Sacral Hierarchy of Medieval Society. Assumptions, Potential and Reinterpretation', in Gert Melville and James D. Mixson (eds), *Virtuosos of Faith. Monks, Nuns, Canons, and Friars as Elites of Medieval Culture* (Wiesbaden 2020), pp. 171–94, and ead. 'Best Clothes and Everyday Attire of Late Medieval Nuns', in Regula Schorta and Rainer C. Schwinges (eds), *Fashion and Clothing in Late Medieval Europe / Mode und Kleidung im Europa des späten Mittelalters* (Riggisberg, 2010), pp. 139–54. An image of the crown is reproduced on p. 146.

[61] Riggisberg, Abegg-Stiftung, Inv. No. 5257. Philippe Cordez and Evelin Wetter, *Die Krone der Hildegard von Bingen* (Riggisberg, 2019). Evelin Wetter, 'Bortenkrone mit gestickten Medaillons (Nonnenkrone)', in Evelin Wetter (ed.), *Mittelalterliche Textilien. Vol. 3, Stickerei bis um 1500 und figürlich gewebte Borten* (Riggisberg, 2012), cat. No. 1, pp. 41–7; ead. 'Von Bräuten und Vikaren Christi. Zur Konstruktion von Ähnlichkeit im sakralen Initiationsakt', in Martin Gaier, Jeanette Kohl and Alberto Saviello (eds), *Similitudo: Konzepte der Ähnlichkeit in Mittelalter und Früher Neuzeit* (Munich, 2012), pp. 129–46.

Agnes, the virgin martyr who rejected a worldly suitor in favour of her heavenly spouse.[62] The embedded figures of nuns in this fragment are among the earliest images of nuns depicted wearing crowns, and are the earliest (to our knowledge) in an extant textile.[63] Descriptions and images of the nun's crown are recorded from the mid-twelfth century, illustrating how the reformulation of ideas about female religious life associated with religious reform emphasised a nun's identification with the Virgin and her status as a *sponsa Christi*.[64] This complex of ideas is also evident in a contemporary image from Lamspringe. A miniature illuminated by sister Ermengarde (Fig. 5.5) in the last quarter of the twelfth century portrays the convent's first abbess, Ricburg, wearing a crown, illustrating how this symbol of nun's status was integral to the (self-)image of religious women in northern Germany in the latter twelfth century.

Ideals of monastic life for women in reforming circles stressed their primary liturgical duty of intercessory prayer. As Christ's brides, nuns were understood to share a special intimacy with their heavenly groom, from which they were thought to receive privileged access to divine knowledge. Nuns' prayer and intercession were held to have great efficacy.[65] The images of nuns as devotees in the textile's design embodies their special status as intercessors between Christ and the world. Pictured at prayer and as if observing events unfolding before their eyes, these figures highlight the potency of female intercession, of which men, such as the clerics in the border, were among the intended beneficiaries.

---

[62] Eva Schlotheuber, *Klostereintritt und Bildung. Die Lebenswelt der Nonnen im späten Mittelalter. Mit einer Edition des 'Konventstagebuchs' einer Zisterzienserin von Heilig-Kreuz bei Braunschweig (1484–1507)* (Tübingen, 2004), pp. 156–74; Wetter, 'Von Bräuten und Vikaren Christi'. In this context, two images of the Virgin at the Nativity wearing a crown of a similar form to that worn by the nuns in the Berlin fragment are of particular interest: Ratmann Sacramentary, fol. 7r and the Stammheim Missal, fol. 92r. For the ritual of *consecratio virginum* and nuns' self-image in early medieval period, see Gordon Blennemann's chapter in this volume.

[63] Andrea Worm has observed that the incorporation of devotional figures into biblical scenes, such as we see in the Berlin fragment, was unusual for the twelfth century. The depiction of embedded devotional figures such as the nuns in the Berlin fragment became more popular from the eleventh century, reflecting the shifting devotional preference for affective forms of meditation, and to emphasise more personal devotional concerns. See Andrea Worm, *Das Pariser Perikopenbuch*, pp. 151–6.

[64] The contemporary practice of nuns wearing crowns also attracted criticism, such as the searching queries the Augustinian canoness Tenxwind of Andernach sent to Hildegard of Bingen. See Schlotheuber, 'Konkurrierenden spirituellen Lebensentwürfe', pp. 339–48. For the epistolary exchange between the two women c. 1148–50, see Letters 52 and 52r in *The Letters of Hildegard of Bingen*, trans. by Joseph L. Baird and Radd K. Ehrmann (3 vols, Oxford, 1994), vol. 1, pp. 127–30.

[65] Griffiths, *Nuns' Priests' Tales*, pp. 141–76.

Fig. 5.5. Martyrdom of St Andrew with *praepositus* Gerhard and nuns of Lamspringe. Wolfenbüttel, Herzog August Bibliothek, Cod. Guelf. 475 Helmst., fol. 148v, last quarter of the 12th century.

The reformulation of religious life for women also had implications for male religious. The appointment of a canon regular as provost connected female monasteries such as Drübeck and Hadmersleben with the circles of Augustinian reform centred on Halberstadt. Canons such as those from Hamersleben assumed influential positions in regional networks, including through their involvement with monastic women as their provosts and priests. As we have mentioned, the community at Hamersleben comprised women as well as canons during the twelfth century, suggesting that the spiritual care of women religious was an attribute of the canons' spiritual outlook.[66] We know little about the organisation, development or nature of the female community at Hamersleben. Nevertheless, the collective image of a community of 'canons and sisters' at Hamersleben [*canonicorum sororumque*] expressed this monastery's corporate identity as one of spiritual equality between the sexes.[67]

[66] Günter Peters, 'Augustinerchorherrenstift Hamersleben', pp. 36–45.
[67] The monastery is referred to as 'venerabilis conventus regularium canonicorum sororumque ecclesie sancti Pancratii in Hameresleve' by a donor in a charter recording a grant of land dated 23 June 1220. See Walter Zöllner (ed.), *Die Urkunden und Besitzaufzeichnungen des Stifts Hamersleben (1108–1462)* (Leipzig, 1979), no. 39, p. 154. Bishop Ludolph of Halberstadt directed the canons to no longer admit female members into the community at Hamersleben in 1238. See *Ibid.*, no. 45, p. 162 and Peters, 'Augustinerchorherrenstift Hamersleben', p. 35.

Bonds of shared spiritual endeavour also fostered connections between several male and female monastic communities in the Halberstadt region. Fragments of two necrologies from the Augustinian community of St John in Halberstadt (*Johanniskloster*) permit a glimpse into the ties linking monastic women and the men who provided their spiritual care. Sources from the late twelfth century document exchanges of personnel between communities and obligations to pray for female and male members of this network, including women and men from Drübeck, Hadmersleben, Hamersleben and Huysburg.[68] These fragmentary commemorative records document a collective self-image of women alongside men in religious life, creating an 'imagined community' that extended beyond the walls of the cloister to encompass both sexes in a shared spiritual mission.[69]

The connections between canons of Hamersleben and Benedictine female monasteries in Lower Saxony suggest how involvement in women's religious life, for some men, was integral to their spiritual mission and self-understanding. The imagery of nuns with a priest, *pater* and provost in the Berlin fragment adds to the scant visual evidence of how monastic men and women in this monastic network pictured their collective identities and devotional concerns. Portrayals of provosts or male prelates alongside nuns appear in contemporary manuscript illumination, especially from double monasteries, but are rarely depicted in extant textiles.[70] The scant visual evidence of men and women in monastic life surviving for this region portrays Hamersleben canons in contexts that highlight their involvement in the educational and intellectual lives of nuns in Benedictine communities.[71] The dedication image in the Lippoldsberg Gospels commemorates the shared endeavour of canon and provost Gunther (1139–61) and prioress

---

[68] Otto von Heinemann, 'Bruchstück', 1–14; and Klaus Nass, 'Ein neues Nekrolog-Fragment aus dem Stift St. Johann in Halberstadt', *Harz-Zeitschrift*, 71 (2019), 90–4.

[69] Alison I. Beach conceptualises the necrology of Petershausen as an 'imagined community' based on an analysis of how the names of men and women were arranged spatially. See *Trauma of Monastic Reform*, pp. 89–90.

[70] Susan Marti, 'Double Monasteries in Images?: Observations on Book Illumination from Women's Communities in the Southwestern Empire', in Griffiths and Hotchin (eds), *Partners in Spirit*, pp. 75–107. For later medieval examples of the representation of nuns and their provost in relation to textiles, see the chapter by Katharina Mersch in this volume.

[71] Julie Hotchin, 'Women's Reading and Monastic Reform in Twelfth-Century Germany: The Library of the Nuns of Lippoldsberg', in Alison I. Beach (ed.), *Manuscripts and Monastic Culture. Reform and Renewal in Twelfth-Century Germany* (Turnhout, 2007), pp. 139–90; and Eva Schlotheuber, 'Die gelehrten Bräute Christi. Geistesleben und Bücher der Nonnen im Hochmittelalter', in Helwig Schmidt-Glintzer (ed.), *Die gelehrten Bräute Christi. Geistesleben und Bücher der Nonnen im Hochmittelalter* (Wiesbaden, 2008), pp. 39–82.

Margaret to foster the convent's culture of learning and the monastery's library.[72] Gerhard, provost at Lamspringe (1178–1205/10) and brother of prior Hermann of Hamersleben (fl. c. 1186), similarly worked with the prioress Jutta (c. 1178–1205) to extend the nuns' library, and he may also have directed the training of Lamspringe nuns in scribal production.[73] A miniature painted by sister Ermengarde from Lamspringe expresses the corporate identity of this community (fig. 5.5). Provost Gerhard is depicted clasping the cross of St Andrew as the martyred saint gives his final sermon, while the nuns are shown observing to the right of the scene. While the image presents interpretive challenges, the suggestion that it commemorates provost Gerhard's assertion of the monastery's interests shortly after he assumed office is persuasive.[74] The visual evidence of Hamersleben canons' involvement in women's religious lives is emblematic of the dynamic of collaboration in which the original embroidered hanging was made.

Women as Witnesses to the Resurrection

The three surviving intact scenes present a potent image of women's presence in salvation history. These scenes originally formed the upper left section of the embroidered hanging, and appear to have been excised and then preserved together.[75] These scenes of the Resurrection, Women at the Tomb and the Virgin at

---

[72] Hotchin, 'Women's Reading and Monastic Reform', pp. 139–40. C. Stephen Jaeger interprets the gesture between prioress Margaret and provost Gunther as the *iunctio dextrarum*, associated with marriage ceremonies; 'Men and Women in the Life of the Schools', in Micol Long, Tjamke Snijders and Steven Vanderputten (eds.), *Horizontal Learning in the High Middle Ages* (Amsterdam, 2019), pp. 166–7.

[73] Schlotheuber, 'Die gelehrten Bräute Christi', pp. 39–82. The paleographical analysis of manuscripts copied and illuminated by sister Ermengarde reveals that she was following scribal and stylistic models from Hamersleben; see Helmar Härtel (ed.), *Geschrieben und gemalt: gelehrte Bücher aus Frauenhand. Eine Klosterbibliothek sächsischer Benediktinerinnen des 12. Jahrhunderts* (Wiesbaden, 2006), p. 20; Cohen-Muslin, *Scriptoria*, pp. 155–70.

[74] Christa Bertelsmeier-Kierst argues for an interpretation of the image in the context of Gerhard assuming office as provost and obtaining papal confirmation of the monastery's property and privileges shortly afterwards; 'Handschriften für Frauen und von Frauen. Buchkultur aus norddeutschen Frauenklöstern im 13. Jahrhundert', in Schmidt-Glintzer (ed.), *Die Gelehrten Bräute Christi*, pp. 83–122, at pp. 94–102.

[75] The right edge of the fragment has been cut along the frame of the scene of the Women at the Tomb, which has resulted in dividing the scene of the apostle above. In the nineteenth century it was common to cut scenes from textile to circulate as iconographic models, for study and to sell to decorative art museums. For one of the leading practitioners of this form of 'curation', canon Franz Bock from Aachen, see Birgitt Borkopp-Restle, *Der Aachener Kanonikus Franz Bock und seine Textilsammlungen: ein Beitrag zur Geschichte der Kunstgewerbe im 19. Jahrhundert* (Riggisberg, 2008).

Pentecost comprise a compelling visual unity that emphasises the roles of biblical and contemporary religious women. In the absence of the remainder of the original textile, however, we cannot identify whether women's presence in these scenes was characteristic of the overall visual programme. The female presence within these scenes and their relationship to one another has largely evaded scholarly attention, no doubt because of their fragmentary nature and because medieval textiles have been undervalued as 'minor' or 'applied' arts.[76] In the following, we examine how the embedded figures of nuns and the cleric function in the scenes appraise the significance and meanings of the iconography, and consider how the scenes interact with the remaining imagery of the border. We aim to show that the visual programme of this fragment renders women's spiritual authority and claims to teach explicit through visual means.

The two scenes in the lower section of the fragment are unusual in depicting the Resurrection in complementary images, juxtaposing the contemporary imagery of the figure of Christ with the canonical iconography of the women at the tomb to portray the Easter message. The inscription above the first scene draws attention to the moment when the Resurrected Christ steps out of the sarcophagus: 'Here rises that man whom they seek in the tomb' ['Hic consurgit hominem quem querunt in monumento']. The demonstrative 'Hic' stresses the action while the verb 'consurgit', placed above the figure of Christ as he rises from the sarcophagus, emphasises the movement and symbolism of Christ's victory over death. He steps out of the sarcophagus with his left leg, his left hand raised in blessing and his right hand grasping the pole of a vexillum, a symbol of Christ's victory over death. Two angels look on, hands raised in acclamation, and two guards sleep at the bottom of the image. At the base of the scene a figure of a nun is located opposite the two sleeping guards, her wakefulness a counterpoint to their slumber in a metaphor of her spiritual insight.

The Resurrection is not described in the Gospel accounts, which simply record that the earliest reports of this event are known from the testimony of the women present at the empty tomb. Until the thirteenth century, the customary image of the Easter message in the western Church was the depiction of the three Marys at the tomb, as in the scene to the right.[77] Images of the Resurrection depicted by the human figure of Christ rising out of the sarcophagus do not appear, with

---

[76] For general observations about the nature and scope of art historical research into medieval textiles, see Gajewski and Seeberg, 'Elite Women as "Makers" of Textile Art', pp. 27–8, and Jeffrey. F. Hamburger, 'The Art and Architecture of Female Monasticism', in Conrad Rudolph (ed.), *A Companion to Medieval Art: Romanesque and Gothic in Northern Europe* (2nd edn, Chichester, 2019), pp. 823–56, at p. 829.

[77] Worm, *Das Pariser Perikopenbuch*, p. 98.

Fig. 5.6. Scenes of the Resurrection with figures of nuns. Detail from Berlin, Kunstgewerbemuseum, Inv. No. 1888,470. © Kunstgewerbemuseum, Staatliche Museen zu Berlin. Photo: Stephan Klonk.

one tenth-century exception, until the twelfth century.[78] This composition accentuates the dynamism of Christ's movement as he steps out of the sarcophagus, emphasising his physical presence and the glory of the Resurrection. By depicting Christ frontally, the image encourages the viewer to experience the glory of the Resurrection directly, thus enhancing the sense of immediacy implied between the Resurrected Christ and the nun with arms outstretched.

The nun's desire to participate in the miracle of the Resurrection is enhanced by hand gestures that mimic those of the angel above her, as if the two respond to the image of Christ before them in the same manner (Fig. 5.6). The gesture suggests acclamation or rejoicing, perhaps an allusion to the Easter Psalm: 'Arise, my glory, arise, psaltery and harp!' ['Exurge gloria mea, exurge, psalterium et citherum' [Psalm 56, 8], traditionally sung on Saturday night as the tomb was opened to commence the *Elevatio Crucis* ritual.[79] The shared gestures of the nun and the angel signal the co-existence of earthly and heavenly choirs in which the nun joins voice in the song of the angelic choirs. According to the *Rule* of Benedict,

---

[78] *Ibid.*, p. 101. The exception is an image of Christ standing in a sarcophagus in a manuscript of the Gospels from Reichenau (*c.* 1020); Munich, Bayerische Staatsbibliothek, Clm, 4454, fol. 86v. As Worm notes, earlier examples of the resurrected Christ illustrate psalm texts, although they do not show Christ in the act of stepping out of a sarcophagus.

[79] Judith Oliver, *Singing with Angels: Liturgy, Music, and Art in the Gradual of Gisela von Kerssenbrock* (Turnhout, 2007), pp. 141–2.

monks and nuns were understood to be in the presence of the angels as they sang the psalms with them. The mirrored gestures of the nuns and angel demonstrate *conformitas* between human and divine, earthly and heavenly beings.[80] Picturing nuns rejoicing in *jubilatio* as if as one with the angels at the Resurrection was, as Judith Oliver has observed, 'an empowering affirmation of their state as consecrated virgins', which highlighted nuns' intercessory role and made a compelling claim for its efficacy.[81]

The nun's rejoicing also echoes the eleventh-century sequence *Victime paschali laudes* sung at Mass on Easter Day to celebrate Christ's victory over death. One verse dramatises Mary Magdalene's encounter with the angel in the tomb and her dialogue with the apostles:

Tell us, Mary, what did you see on the way?
'I saw the tomb of the living Christ and the glory of the risen one.
The angelic witnesses, the shroud and the clothes.'[82]

The nun's presence in this scene draws parallels to Mary Magdalene, who, according to gospel accounts, was the first to see the Resurrected Christ and to announce the news to the apostles. Mary's encounter with the apostles, dramatised in the Easter liturgy, made an assertive claim for her role as first messenger of the Church, the *apostola apostolorum*.[83] The parallel between the embedded figure of the nun and Mary Magdalen is drawn more sharply in the next scene.

The second Resurrection scene depicts the three Marys who went to the tomb on Easter morning with ointment and incense to prepare Christ's body for burial. Instead of finding the body of Christ, the women discover an empty sarcophagus at which they were greeted by an angel. The scene illustrates the moment of the women's encounter with the angel, the empty sarcophagus underlining the angel's

---

[80] Worm, *Das Pariser Perikopenbuch*, pp. 152, with reference to Frank O. Büttner, *Imitatio pietatis: Motive der christlichen Ikonographie als Modelle zur Verähnlichung* (Berlin, 1983).

[81] Oliver, *Singing with Angels*, p. 109.

[82] 'Dic nobis Maria, Quid visti in via? / Sepulchrum Christi viventis, et gloriam vidi resurgentis: / Angelicos testes, suadarium et vestes'. The sequence is usually attributed to Wipo of St Gall or Nottker. See Elizabeth Monroe, 'Mary Magdalene as a Model of Devotion, Penitence and Authority in the Gospels of Henry the Lion and Mathilda', in Peter V. Loewen and Robin Waugh, *Mary Magdalene in Medieval Culture. Conflicted Roles* (New York, 2014), pp. 99–115, at p. 100.

[83] Jansen examines the development of Mary Magdalene as the *apostola apostolorum* in *Making of the Magdalen*, pp. 266–75; Griffiths explores the significance of this understanding of the Magdalene in the context of clerical relations with women religious and male spirituality in *Nuns' Priests' Tales*, pp. 66–8.

response that 'He is not here'.[84] The empty sarcophagus coupled with the commanding figure of the angel contrasts with the prominence of Christ in the previous scene. The women's encounter with the angel is observed by an embedded figure of a nun at prayer in the lower right corner, whose gaze is directed towards Mary Magdalene and her companions as if she envisions the scene through her prayer. The nuns embedded in these scenes express religious women's special relationship with Christ and identify women as the first to witness and comprehend the meaning of the Resurrection. The juxtaposition of the dynamic imagery of the Resurrected Christ with the traditional scene of the Women at the Tomb evokes the understanding of Christ as man and God, through bodily and spiritual means. On the left, the nun rejoices at the human form of Christ as he steps out of the sarcophagus, while on the right, the nun joins with the three Marys as she comes to understand His divinity. The figures of nuns, therefore, bear witness to the dual human and divine nature of Christ.[85]

Women's presence at the drama unfolding on Easter morning was amplified in the liturgy. The search for Christ's body by the three Marys is emphasised in the second half of the inscription above the scene: 'whom they seek in the tomb' ['hominem quem querunt in monumento']. The inscription alludes to the Easter trope *Quem queritis*, sung at Mass on Easter day.[86] The text re-enacted the dialogue between Christ and Mary Magdalene, when, after leaving the empty tomb, Mary encountered a man in the garden. He asks her: 'Whom do you seek?' ['Quem queritis?'], after which she recognised the man as Christ. Mary Magdalene is thus the first to learn of the Resurrection, and is directed – by the angels in some accounts, or by Christ himself according to John – to announce the miracle to the apostles.[87]

The women's dramatic encounter with the angel in the tomb received greater liturgical elaboration in the eleventh century, when the *Quem queritis* trope was incorporated into the *Visitatio sepulchri*, which was a liturgical re-enactment of

[84] This composition of this scene is closest to the account of events in the gospel of Mark, in which the evangelist records that the three women called Mary arrive at the tomb on Easter morning where they are informed by an angel that Jesus has risen ['Surrexit, non est hic'; Mark 16: 1–6]. See Jansen, *Making of the Magdalene*, pp. 21–3.

[85] Elizabeth Carrasco develops this idea in relation to the St Albans Psalter. See Elizabeth Carrasco, 'The Imagery of the Magdalene in Christina of Markyate's Psalter (St Albans Psalter)', *Gesta*, 38 (1999), 67–80.

[86] David A. Bjork, 'On the Dissemination of *Quem quaeritis* and the *Visitatio sepulchri* and the Chronology of their Early Sources', *Comparative Drama*, 14:1 (1980), 46–69.

[87] John 20: 1–18; Jansen discusses the Gospel accounts in *Making of the Magdalen*, pp. 21–4. The theological context for Mary Magdalene as the first witness to the resurrection was well established by the twelfth century, although visual representations were unusual until this time. See Monroe, 'Mary Magdalene', p. 100.

the events at the tomb on Easter morning.[88] The expansion and development of the *Visitatio* from the eleventh century reflects the greater importance afforded to women's role as witness to the Resurrection, especially for female monastic communities.[89] The Gospel accounts present one of the central moments in Christian history as an event at which women are the sole human actors. The re-enactment of the events of Easter granted women religious in many monasteries an opportunity to perform the roles of the faithful women and thereby to present a vivid reminder to an audience, which would have included priests and churchmen, as well as other nuns, of women's spiritual privilege as the first human to encounter the risen Christ.[90]

The imagery of the grief-stricken Mary Magdalene searching for Christ at Easter bore deeper resonances for consecrated nuns. From the third century, Mary's search for Christ was likened to the bride of the Song of Songs seeking her bridegroom. Mary thus came to symbolise the desire of the soul for union with Christ. Although the soul's desire for spiritual union was relevant for men and women, the identification of Mary with the soul created deeply gendered associations.[91] If Mary Magdalene was implicitly understood as a bride, therefore, it was not difficult to identify her as a spiritual exemplar for nuns, whose self-image as brides was shaped by their spiritual betrothal to Christ and symbolised by the crowns they wore.

The Resurrection scenes depict women as privileged human actors in salvation history, in events from which men were excluded. The prominent female presence and emphasis on Mary Magdalene in this imagery draws attention to what Katherine Jansen has referred to as Mary being 'doubly blessed', as the first to witness the Resurrection and entrusted with the privilege of announcing it. The

---

[88] Bjork, 'Dissemination'. The *Visitatio* was performed at the end of the Holy Saturday vigil as the dawn of Easter day approached.

[89] The earliest text of the *Visitatio* in northern Germany is preserved in a twelfth- to-thirteenth-century breviary from the Augustinian convent of Marienberg in Helmstedt. It also includes the sequence *Victime paschali*, further underscoring Mary's role in announcing the resurrection to the apostles; HAB, Cod. Guelf. 309 Noviss. 8°. See Walther Lipphardt (ed.), *Lateinische Osterfeiern und Osterspiele* (8 vols, Berlin, 1976), vol. 5, pp. 1548–51, No. 791.

[90] For the performance of the *Visitatio sepulchri* at Essen in the fourteenth century, see Jürgen Bärsch, *Die Feier des Osterfestkreises im Stift Essen nach dem Zeugnis des Liber Ordinarius* (Münster, 1997), pp. 230–3. He notes that in some monasteries clerics could perform these female roles (at p. 230, n. 178). See also Katharina Ulrike Mersch, *Soziale Dimension visueller Kommunikation in hoch- und spätmittelalterlichen Frauenkommunitäten. Stifte, Chorfrauenstifte und Klöster im Vergleich* (Göttingen, 2012), pp. 65–75; and for Barking Abbey see Anne Bagnall Yardley, *Performing Piety. Musical Culture in Medieval English Nunneries* (New York, 2006), pp. 146–55.

[91] Griffiths, *Nuns' Priests' Tales*, pp. 70–1; and Monroe, 'Mary Magdalene', pp. 105, 108.

location of the figures of nuns within the lower scenes suggests parallels with the Women at the Tomb, thus enhancing their status as witnesses and their claims to enjoy intimate knowledge of divine mysteries. The composition implies the validation of female speech. As Jansen has observed, 'as women were the first to announce the Resurrection, men should not disdain women's words.'[92]

Female Teaching: The Virgin at Pentecost

Themes of women and teaching receive further elaboration in the Pentecost scene. The depiction of the Virgin as the central figure in the events at Pentecost was an iconographic novelty that gained popularity from the early twelfth century. The dominant visual tradition placed Peter at the centre of the gathered apostles, in recognition of his role as the founder of the earthly church through his preaching after the death and resurrection of Christ. Locating Mary at the centre of the apostles, on the other hand, highlighted her ecclesiological role as *Ecclesia*, the Bride of Christ, and her role in the establishment of the Church at Pentecost.[93] Images of Mary at Pentecost appear in early medieval imagery; however, the popularity of this iconography in the twelfth century has been attributed to the influence of St Bernard's writings about the church as bride.[94] Mary's figure also indicates the presence of historical women among the first Christian communities that formed in response to the preaching of the apostles.[95]

The image of the Virgin at Pentecost in the Berlin fragment is among the earliest known examples of this iconography in the twelfth century. The Virgin appears in the midst of the apostles in manuscript illumination produced from the early twelfth century, notably in manuscripts intended for female readers.[96] In each of

---

[92] Jansen, *Making of the Magdalene*, p. 270.

[93] Claudine A. Chavannes-Mazel, 'Paradise and Pentecost', in Mariële Hageman and Marco Mostert (eds), *Reading images and Texts: Medieval images and Texts as Forms of Communication* (Turnhout, 2005), pp. 121–60, at pp. 134–6.

[94] Chavannes-Mazel, 'Paradise and Pentecost', p. 134; and Worm, *Das Pariser Perikopenbuch*, pp. 121–6. In his second sermon on Pentecost, for example, Bernard praises Mary as the 'focal point of the universe'; Oliver, *Singing with Angels*, p. 183.

[95] For the importance to contemporary men and women of women's historical presence among the apostles, see Griffiths, *Nuns' Priest's Tale*, pp. 56–60, and Beach, *Trauma of Monastic Reform*, pp. 73–92.

[96] Examples include the St Alban's Psalter (c. 1120–40), thought to have been made for Christina of Markyate; Hildesheim, Cathedral Library, St Godehard 1, fol. 55. See Kristen Collins, Peter Kidd and Nancy Turner, *The St. Albans Psalter: Painting and Prayer in Medieval England* (Los Angeles, 2013). The Gospels of Henry the Lion and Mathilda (1160s); HAB, Cod. Guelf. 105 Noviss. 2°, fol. 171r; and in two early thirteenth-century liturgical manuscripts associated with Cistercian female communities: a psalter from Wöltingerode (near Goslar); HAB, Cod. Guelf. 521 Helmst, fol. 108v. See

these illuminations the Virgin is portrayed as a static figure, in a frontal pose with her gaze directed towards the viewer.[97] In contrast, in the Berlin fragment, Mary is depicted as interactive and dynamic; she turns towards an apostle seated to her left, who is likely John, as both figures raise their hands in a gesture indicating speech. As the Virgin alone receives the grace of the spirit in the form of a dove directly above her head, the image suggests that she is privileged to receive and communicate the words of the Holy Spirit to the apostles. This interactive composition echoes Rupert of Deutz's [c. 1075/80–1130] praise of Mary as the *magistra magistorum*, the 'mistress of masters'. In his Commentary on the Song of Songs, the theologian and Benedictine abbot Rupert stressed Mary's leadership role in the nascent Christian community, noting how she taught the apostles through her maternal and nurturing role.[98] In the context of male spiritual care for women in religious life, it is particularly apt that the Virgin is shown here in dialogue with John, as he was the apostle to whom Christ entrusted the care of his mother when on the cross. Fiona Griffiths has drawn attention to the importance of John's care of Mary as a model for and legitimation of many men charged with spiritual direction of women religious. It is possible that John's spiritual responsibility for the Virgin provided a similar model for emulation and self-understanding for the ordained men associated with the original embroidery.[99]

This dynamic composition adapts the iconographical motif of the Virgin and the apostles to project female spiritual leadership. As the Holy Spirit descends upon the Virgin, it suggests that she is filled with the Spirit and shares her spiritual knowledge with John. The image implies that she – and by extension other women – has authority to speak and a role in the establishment of the Christian church. The seated figure of Mary is positioned directly above the column that divides the two scenes of the resurrection below, linking the women's role as witness to the Resurrection with Mary's speech in the Pentecost scene. These three scenes of women's involvement represent what Barbara Newman has described as 'feminine exempla for the apostolic role'. As Newman observes, however, the women

---

Bertelsmeier-Kierst, 'Audi filia', p. 85; and the so-called Gisela Codex, a gradual copied and illuminated by Gisela von Kerssenbrock (d.1300) perhaps for the convent at Rülle (near Osnabrück); see Oliver, *Singing with Angels*, plate 35 (fol. 86v).

[97] The image in the Gospels of Henry and Mathilda depict the Virgin facing the viewer, as John, to her left, leans towards her with a hand raised to indicate speech.

[98] Bertelsmeier-Kierst, 'Audi filia', p. 85, and Peter Gittins, '*Magistra Apostolorum* in the Writings of Rupert of Deutz' (PhD Dissertation, University of Dayton, 1996), pp. 89–90, published as *Magistra Apostolorum: Mary in the Mariology of Rupert of Deutz* (Scholar's Press, 2013).

[99] John 19: 25–7. See Fiona Griffiths, 'The Cross and the Cura Monialium: Robert of Arbrissel, John the Evangelist, and the Pastoral Care of Women in the Age of Reform', *Speculum* 83 (2008), 303–30.

'represent the prophetic or didactic rather than the sacramental role of the clergy.'[100] The visual programme boldly claims a central role for religious women, alongside men, as teachers within Christian communities based on their privileged relationship to Christ.

Clerical (Self-)Image: Preaching and the Care of Nuns

While the surviving intact scenes present claims for women's spiritual knowledge based on their spiritual intimacy with Christ as his bride, the partial scene and figures in the border are peopled with male ecclesiastical figures that embody the Church by virtue of their preaching and sacramental roles. Any interpretation of how the remaining sections of the border interact with the surviving biblical scenes will necessarily be inconclusive. Yet, closer attention to the male figures depicted in the border and their relationship to the remaining scenes offers some clues as to how male spiritual identity was shaped by their relations with religious women, and how their respective claims to spiritual authority were imagined.

The final, partial scene of the original embroidery depicts St Peter giving a sermon after Pentecost, as discussed above. Of interest here is the male figure with outstretched arms kneeling at the feet of Peter. As a devout witness to the apostle's sermon, this figure offers a point of identification for canons regular and priests whose responsibilities also entailed preaching and pastoral ministry in the service of reform. The kneeling cleric also shares close parallels with an image of provost Gerhard of Lamspringe, who, as we have seen, is identified with the preaching of St Andrew as he clasps the cross during the apostle's martyrdom (Fig. 5.5).[101] The composition of these scenes illustrates how canons active in monastic reform

---

[100] Barbara Newman, *Sister of Wisdom. St. Hildegard's Theology of the Feminine* (Berkeley, 1987), p. 83. In the thirteenth century Thomas Aquinas elaborated his position in relation to Church doctrine and women teaching, stating that as women were endowed with the gift of prophecy they were entitled to instruct in theological truths, albeit only in 'private' or in small groups (such as a prioress or *magistra* and her nuns) and not 'publicly', as they were held to lack the wisdom to be entrusted with theological debate. See Eva Schlotheuber, 'Intellectual Horizons', in Jeffrey F. Hamburger, Eva Schlotheuber, Susan Marti and Margot Fassler (eds.), *Liturgical Life and Latin Learning at Paradies bei Soest, 1300–1425* (2 vols, Münster, 2016), vol. 1, pp. 43–90, at pp. 52–3.

[101] The manuscript containing this scene of the martyrdom of St Andrew, copied and illuminated by Ermengarde of Lamspringe, also contains a copy of the Pseudo-Clementine *Recognitions*, at the time attributed to Clement of Rome; see Härtel, *Geschrieben und Gemalt*, p. 44. It was highly regarded by canons regular for its emphasis on preaching and pastoral care as a model of religious activity in emulation of the first Christian communities; see Bertelsmeier-Kierst, 'Handschriften für Frauen', pp. 94–6.

conceived their role as evangelical and missionary, in which the spiritual direction of women religious formed an integral responsibility.

Apostolic themes are developed further through what remains of the textile's border, in which the priest Samson, *pater* Heinricus and a provost are depicted among holy figures who preached and were venerated for their missionary zeal. The figures depicted in the border also hint at a clerical self-image informed by male involvement with religious women. Four of the saints shown (Stephen, Boniface, Eustace and Servatius) are identified with the diocese of Halberstadt, and, in the case of Benedict, with monastic life. Two of these, saints Stephen and Boniface, offer striking parallels for men associated with a female or dual-sex religious community animated by religious renewal and reform. St Stephen was the patron of the diocese of Halberstadt and was also known for his spiritual care of women. According to Acts [6: 1–5], Stephen was one of seven deacons charged with the care of women in early apostolic community. His public ministry included a ministry to widows, an activity which it was thought may have contributed to his condemnation and martyrdom by stoning.[102] St Boniface, situated in what was originally the centre of the upper margin,[103] was patron of several churches in the diocese.[104] Boniface was best known as a missionary bishop who left England to evangelise in Europe. Several women were active in the missionary circles around Boniface, performing pastoral and educational activities and corresponding with the bishop as spiritual equals.[105] Stephen and Boniface presented exemplars of shared spiritual endeavour between religious men and women in promoting spiritual renewal. The imagery in the border depicts recognisable clerical individuals alongside apostolic and missionary figures who also engaged with women religious. It provides a compelling model of validation and justification for contemporary churchmen who also ministered to women as an aspect of the mission for spiritual renewal as in the first Christian communities. Although only a fragment of the original visual programme survives, nevertheless women are presented as central, not marginal, figures in relation to the self-image of male religious.

---

[102] Griffiths, *Nuns' Priests' Tales'*, p. 57.
[103] Following the reconstruction by Kroos, *Niedersächsische Bildstickereien*, p. 114.
[104] For example, the church of St Maurice and Boniface in Halberstadt, dedicated in 1034.
[105] For an important critical reappraisal of the intellectual abilities and contribution of these women, see Felice Lifshitz, 'Women in the Anglo-Saxon Missionary Circles', in Michel Aaij and Shannon Godlove (eds), *A Companion to Boniface* (Leiden, 2020), pp. 68–96.

Conclusion

The surviving visual programme in the embroidered fragment preserved in Berlin is a unique witness to how the respective roles of monastic women and men were imagined as a shared spiritual mission in the latter half of the twelfth century. Although the origins of the original hanging cannot now be established firmly, the style, iconography and technique point to its production within the networks of monastic reform in the diocese of Halberstadt, in which the Augustinian canons of Hamersleben were influential. Although there is insufficient evidence to connect the embroidery's design or production with the canons (or women) of Hamersleben, nevertheless elements of its design and technique identify the embroidered fragment as a product of the artistic, intellectual and religious culture of the monastic networks associated with this community. Questions remain about to what extent the imagery can be said to reflect women's concerns. We also lack tangible evidence to indicate how or even whether women were involved in the design or 'making' of the original embroidery. Nevertheless, the remaining imagery of the textile is evidence of a culture of collaboration that we also find in contemporary manuscript illumination by and for female communities associated with Hamersleben canons. The fragment's imagery portrays the collective identity and devotional concerns of one community within this *milieu*, demonstrating how ideas about gendered spiritual authority were visualised.

Without further evidence to identify the origin of the embroidered hanging more closely, it is not possible to know for whom or for what purpose it was made, or the circumstances that prompted a community of women and men to commission the original textile. Precious silk hangings such as this fragment were displayed, among other reasons, to assert identity, to promote the spiritual efficacy of the community's prayer, or to legitimise the model of religious life of a community, especially in a period of uncertainty, challenge or criticism.[106] The embroidery was likely made in the 1170s, around two decades or so after female Benedictine monasteries such as Drübeck and Hadmersleben had adopted reform. The surviving visual design may therefore be read as a self-assertion of gendered spiritual roles in the context of debates about how to realise an authentic monastic life. Depicting the spiritual potency of nuns as brides of Christ and the efficacy of their prayer, alongside the authority of canons who emulated apostolic models through their preaching, the remaining imagery makes a compelling statement about the spiritual merits of a monastic community moulded by reform.

---

[106] Tanja Kohwagner-Nikolai discusses the range of functions of wall hangings in 'Patrons, Saints and Benefactresses: The Use of Tapestries to Create Corporate Identity in Late Medieval Nunneries', in Evelin Wetter (ed.), *Iconography of Liturgical Textile in the Middle Ages* (Riggisberg, 2010), pp. 141–52.

Another aspect of the political and religious climate in which the textile was created that merits consideration is the growing criticism towards forms of male involvement in women's religious life by the second half of the twelfth century.[107] In the diocese of Halberstadt, anxieties about the presence of the female communities near to those of men evidently motivated efforts to prohibit the practice. In 1156 Pope Hadrian IV directed the *moniales* that had recently settled near the monastery at Huysburg to be removed.[108] The nuns at Huysburg, however, also had their supporters, and this attempt to relocate them evidently was unsuccessful, as a female donor makes a gift for the *fratres et sorores* there in 1185.[109] The women at Hamersleben, too, attracted increasing criticism in the early thirteenth century, until in 1238 the canons were directed to accept no further female entrants.[110] Is it possible that a visual programme that eloquently validated the co-existence of women religious alongside men could have been produced in response, even if in part, to criticism of this model of monastic life?

The imagery in the Berlin fragment illustrates how medieval gender discourses informed ideas about women's role in the Church and reflects aspects of the institutional realities that shaped religious women's lives. Yet the claims to ecclesiastical power projected in what remains of the border are troubled by how female presence and spiritual privilege are foregrounded in the central scenes. Careful attention to the textile's visual programme yields insight into the inherent tensions and ambiguities that characterised relations between men and women in monastic life.[111] Women religious were respected for their intercessory power and privileged relationship with Christ, but remained subject to the authority of their priests. Nuns were understood as brides of Christ by virtue of their spiritual proximity and intimacy to their bridegroom, which was thought to give their prayers greater power. This in turn afforded men who ministered to women the potential for privileged access to divine mysteries and closeness to Christ as a

---

[107] Marti, 'Double Monasteries in Images?'; Fiona J. Griffiths, 'Women and Reform in the Central Middle Ages', in Judith M. Bennett and Ruth. M. Karras (eds), *The Oxford Handbook of Women and Gender in Medieval Europe* (Oxford, 2013), pp. 447–63.

[108] UB Hochstift Halberstadt, no. 248, pp. 215–16: 'moniales vero iuxta Hugsborg, iuxta monachos, sicut nobis dicitur, circa eandem ecclesiam noviter habitantes, te volumus, si ita est, religiosorum consilio a monachis amovere.' The direction to relocate the nuns was one of several decrees in the same bull concerning the governance of women's monastic houses.

[109] *UB Hochstift Halberstadt*, no. 311, p. 280.

[110] Zollner (ed), *Urkunden Hamersleben*, no. 45, pp. 162–3, 25 April 1238. See Peters, 'Augustinerchorherrenstift Hamersleben', pp. 34–5, 42.

[111] These observations about how the design of the Berlin fragment engages with gendered ambivalences in religious life are indebted to the discussion by Griffiths in *Nuns' Priests' Tales*, pp. 197–8.

servant of his bride. Men ministered the sacraments and controlled the central symbol of the Eucharist, but they nevertheless recognised women as participants in and witnesses to key moments of salvation history, through which women claimed a place in the formation of Christian communities. Examined within its wider monastic and religious context, therefore, the imagery of this embroidered fragment can be read as a response to debates between women and men about forms of spiritual knowledge, authority and gender, and how to realise them within a monastic community.

CHAPTER 6

Mulieres religiose and Cistercian Nuns in Northern Italy in the Thirteenth Century: A Choice of 'Order'

ELENA VANELLI

THIS chapter investigates the dynamics of institutional reform in northern Italy at the beginning of the thirteenth century.[1] It focuses on how religious women influenced and shaped the processes of institutionalisation that affected their way of life. By examining two exemplary case studies from the northern region of Lombardy, I will explore how these *mulieres religiose* were gradually consolidated into monastic institutions through a long-term and negotiated process. Close attention to how these processes unfolded highlights how religious communities were shaped by their local social, religious and political circumstances. The roles of papal, episcopal and monastic authorities, local benefactors and stakeholders in the affected communities and, above all, the women themselves, are key to understanding the contingent processes through which *mulieres religiose* became Cistercian nuns.

The case studies in this chapter are from the northern Italian cities of Cremona and Pavia. The individual communities shared similar features, such as their location in an urban environment, strong local support and relation to episcopal authority, although the processes of institutionalisation unfolded along very different trajectories contingent upon specific local circumstances. This analysis allows us to examine the motives of various actors involved; it also gives an insight into how very different processes of institutional change

---

[1] This article is based on the findings of my dissertation '*Mulieres religiose* und Zisterzienserinnen. Zur Institutionalisierung weiblichen Religiosentums im Hochmittelalter', which was completed in 2021 at the University of Hamburg.

nevertheless produced similar results in transforming the organisational structures of women's religious communities.

Religious Women and the Cistercian Order in Lombardy

Women's religious communities could be associated with the Cistercian Order in varying ways. Some female monasteries were officially incorporated into the Order by the General Chapter, although this juridical status did not necessarily guarantee the provision of spiritual care by the Cistercians. In contrast, many female communities were granted Cistercian privileges and the right to follow the Cistercian *Institutiones* by the pope, and were recognised as Cistercian by the Curia without any involvement by the General Chapter. Further, various monastic patrons, such as episcopal or secular founders, also favoured the Cistercian way of life and initiated processes to gain recognition and incorporation of their foundations with the General Chapter, as much as they could. The women concerned also endeavoured to live a religious life influenced by Cistercian ideals, adopting Cistercian customs and acquiring the benefits of their associated legal privileges, although they remained outside the formal structures of the General Chapter.[2]

The links between female communities and the Cistercian Order were diverse, and the exact nature of this institutional relationship has been widely debated.[3] Earlier scholarship emphasised a perceived reluctance by the General Chapter to incorporate houses of Cistercian nuns, and thereby assume responsibility for provision of their pastoral care. On the other hand, Brigitte Degler-Spengler's research in the 1980s demonstrated the fundamental willingness of Cistercians to provide spiritual care for female communities, through which they were integrated into the Cistercian network by the thirteenth century.[4] Focusing her

---

[2] For an overview of current scholarship about Cistercian nuns in Europe see, for example, Emilia Jamroziak, *The Cistercian Order in Medieval Europe 1090–1500* (London, 2013), pp. 124–55.

[3] Guido Cariboni, 'Il monachesimo femminile cistercense. Ipotesi per la lettura di una complessa realtà istituzionale', in Cosimo Damiano Fonseca (ed.), *Il monachesimo femminile tra Puglia e Basilicata. Atti del Convegno di studi promosso dall'Abbazia benedettina barese di Santa Scolastica (Bari, 3–5 dicembre 2005)* (Bari, 2008), pp. 61–74, at pp. 65–8.

[4] Brigitte Degler-Spengler, 'Zisterzienserorden und Frauenklöster. Anmerkungen zur Forschungsproblematik', in Kaspar Elm and Peter Joerißen (eds), *Die Zisterzienser. Ordensleben zwischen Ideal und Wirklichkeit, 2. Ergänzungsband: Vorträge und Berichte des 5. Forschungskolloquiums des Projektschwerpunktes 'Vergleichende Ordensforschung'* (Köln, 1982), pp. 213–20; Franz J. Felten, 'Der Zisterzienserorden und die Frauen', in

research on regional studies, Degler-Spengler argued that individual Cistercian abbots accommodated women seeking a Cistercian way of life at a local level.[5] Recent studies, such as those by Constance Berman and Anne Lester, which concentrate on France, reinforce the impression that in some regions Cistercian men were more willing to assume the spiritual care of religious women in conjunction with the institutionalisation of quasi-religious women's communities.[6]

Although the position of the General Chapter regarding women religious is one important factor, Guido Cariboni's research into female Cistercian monasteries in the regions of Lombardy and Emilia offers an exemplary case study of how local arrangements were more important for understanding women's ties to the order than a focus on the standpoint of the General Chapter. His depiction of the female religious panorama of northern Italy from the beginning of the thirteenth century highlights the specific institutional links of female communities to the Cistercian Order in this region, which he interprets as the starting point for the construction of their religious identity.[7] One of his central findings is that the official incorporation of female communities into the Cistercian Order by the General Chapter played little role in the region examined in this chapter, Lombardy.[8] Rather, the designation of a community as Cistercian in papal sources as well as the bestowal of papal privileges were central to identifying this relationship. He argues that it is indeed legitimate to speak of Cistercian nunneries in this region, as these female communities were first addressed as *Cistercensis Ordinis* – usually in papal records from the beginning of the thirteenth century – for instance when important privileges such as the *Religiosam vitam eligentibus* were granted.[9] Female religious communities could be directly inserted into the Order's *ius proprium*

Harald Schwillus and Andreas Hölscher (eds), *Weltverachtung und Dynamik* (Berlin, 2000), pp. 34–135.

[5] Degler-Spengler, 'Zisterzienserorden und Frauenklöster', p. 215.

[6] Constance Hoffman Berman, *The White Nuns. Cistercian Abbey for Women in Medieval France* (Philadelphia, 2018); Anne E. Lester, *Creating Cistercian Nuns. The Women's Religious Movement and Its Reform in Thirteenth-Century Champagne* (Ithaca, 2011).

[7] Guido Cariboni, 'Cistercian Nuns in Northern Italy: Variety of Foundations and Construction of an Identity', in Janet Burton and Karen Stöber (eds), *Women in the Medieval Monastic World* (Turnhout, 2015), pp. 53–74, at pp. 54–63.

[8] Guido Cariboni, 'Il monachesimo cistercense femminile in Lombardia e in Emilia nel XIII secolo. Una anomalia giuridico istituzionale', in Rinaldo Comba (ed.), *Il monastero di Rifreddo e il monachesimo cistercense femminile nell'Italia occidentale (secoli XII-XIV). Atti del Convegno: Staffarda-Rifreddo, 18–19 maggio 1999* (Turin, 1999), pp. 37–56, at pp. 39–41.

[9] The *Religiosam vitam eligentibus* is a papal privilege for Cistercian female religious communities. It includes different conditions according to the particular community to which it was granted: Michael Tangl, *Die päpstliche Kanzleiordnungen von 1200-1500* (Innsbruck, 1894), pp. 229–32.

through papal intervention[10], thus bypassing the official procedure for incorporation.[11] In certain situations, this offered the female communities the opportunity to avoid episcopal oversight, to varying degrees, a privilege that could be granted to Cistercian houses.[12] Another important element which shaped the development of the Cistercian identity of female communities was the visitation by a member of a Cistercian monastery, which female communities often requested themselves. Women could thus secure an important requirement for the female religious life, the *cura monialium*, through the mechanism of monastic visitation.[13] It is also worth noting that these characteristics are not interpreted here as the result of processes of institutionalisation, but rather as elements contributing to the formation of a Cistercian identity.[14]

The foregoing analysis provides context for understanding the institutional identity of female Cistercian communities in northern Italy. Before proceeding, however, it is also necessary to locate an institution's relationship to the papacy and religious order within a network of human actors. In order to evaluate the importance of institutional connections and structures for a community, we need to recognise that they are not the sole factor contributing to the identity of these communities. These institutional connections represent only one stage of the evolving process through which a community was transformed or reformed, as Steven Vanderputten's studies show.[15] The central questions are how and under what circumstances an institution's characteristics came about. Therefore, the relation between institutional developments and the respective social, religious, political and economic constellations in which women and their communities were embedded is central to my analysis.[16]

This study explores how women's religious communities were institutionalised in the context of religious reform in the thirteenth century. The regularisation of lay religious communities in the first half of the thirteenth century was part

---

[10] In this manner a female Cistercian community could obtain the same canonical privileges and treatment as if they were a member of the Cistercian Order.

[11] As occurred in the case of S. Cristoforo in Pavia, discussed below. Cariboni, 'Il monachesimo cistercense femminile', pp. 48–51; Cariboni, 'Cistercian Nuns in Northern Italy', pp. 62–3.

[12] Guido Cariboni, *Il nostro ordine è carità. Cistercensi nei secoli XII e XIII* (Milan, 2011), pp. 127–39.

[13] Cariboni, 'Il monachesimo cistercense femminile', pp. 45–7; *Id.*, 'Cistercian Nuns in Northern Italy', pp. 63–4.

[14] *Ibid.*, pp. 65–9.

[15] Steven Vanderputten, *Monastic Reform as Process. Realities and Representations in Medieval Flanders 900-1100* (Ithaca, 2013), pp. 8–13.

[16] Steven Vanderputten, *Reform, Conflict and the Shaping of Corporate Identities. Collected Studies on Benedictine Monasticism 1050-1150* (Berlin, 2013), pp. xxi–xxvii.

of a wider ecclesiastic effort to direct expressions of religious life into acceptable models, often within a context of wider church reform. In this context the generic term 'reform' lacks specificity and fails to account for the multiple factors that shaped the development of female devotional communities. By adopting an actor-focused approach to question institutional processes and dynamics at the local level, we can highlight the complexity, contingency and unpredictability of the institutional transformation of female religious communities, and at the same time emphasise the independent character of these religious transformations.[17]

Female Cistercian monasteries that originated as lay religious communities offer particularly rich case studies to examine how historical contingency influenced processes of institutionalisation. The emergence of various religious movements across western Europe in the twelfth century transformed the religious landscape in the thirteenth century. The laity played an increasingly important role in this religious transformation. In particular, new forms of female spirituality flourished as greater numbers of women sought to lead a religious life, leading to the emergence of new *modi vivendi*. As a result, the question of women's spiritual direction acquired greater urgency.[18] In 1215, the Fourth Lateran Council attempted to bring this spiritual efflorescence under control. Canon 13 directed that new foundations were to be based on existing monastic rules. Therefore, ecclesiastical efforts to order the burgeoning forms of religious life resulted in a process of regularisation and institutionalisation, as religious communities had to adopt a recognised rule to guide their lives. This process was itself diverse, as communities adopted varied institutional structures contingent upon their specific circumstances.[19] In addition to traditional Benedictine monasticism, new rival concepts of religious life such as the Cistercians or the mendicant orders

---

[17] Sherri Franks Johnson, *Monastic Women and Religious Orders in Late Medieval Bologna* (Cambridge, 2014), pp. 16–18, pp. 61–8; Alison More, *Fictive Orders and Feminine Religious Identities, 1200–1600* (Oxford, 2018), pp. 41–62.

[18] Herbert Grundmann, *Religiöse Bewegungen im Mittelalter. Untersuchungen über die geschichtlichen Zusammenhänge zwischen der Ketzerei, den Bettelorden und der religiösen Frauenbewegung im 12. und 13. Jahrhundert und über die geschichtliche Grundlage der deutschen Mystik* (Berlin, 1935).

[19] More, *Fictive Orders*, pp. 41–62; Maria Pia Alberzoni, 'Il concilio dopo il concilio. Gli interventi normativi nella vita religiosa fino al pontificato di Gregorio IX', in Gert Melville and Johannes Helmrath (eds), *The Fourth Lateran Council. Institutional Reform and Spiritual Renewal: Proceedings of the Conference Marking the Eight Hundredth Anniversary of the Council organized by the Pontificio Comitato di Scienze Storiche (Rome, 15–17 October 2015)* (Affalterbach, 2017), pp. 289–318; Michele Maccarrone, 'Le costituzioni del IV concilio Lateranense sui religiosi', in Michele Maccarrone and Roberto Lambertini (eds), *Nuovi studi su Innocenzo III*, Nuovi studi storici, 25 (Rome, 1995), pp. 1–45.

now offered attractive spiritual care from the perspective of a female community. This environment, therefore, offered what we might call a 'market of religious offerings'.[20] Moreover, as a community acquired a monastic status, the choice of religious identity may not have been motivated primarily by spiritual affinity, but prompted by the need for protection or the wishes of a patron. Attention to how local circumstances shaped the process of institutionalisation enables us to examine the contingencies that otherwise are obscured when scholars focus on the resulting institutional identity alone.

The following analysis is based on two case studies from Lombardy, S. Giovanni della Pipia in Cremona and S. Cristoforo in Pavia. Both communities are representative of the dynamics of institutionalisation of lay religious communities in this region. Each community shared similar attributes, although their different local circumstances and political contexts resulted in these processes of transformation taking very different paths. These examples also illustrate the diverse circumstances that led to the formation of female Cistercian monasteries in the first half of the thirteenth century, the period of greatest expansion of female monasteries associated with the Order. The sources for these houses are fragmentary and scarce, especially in comparison with other regions and periods. The following analysis is primarily based on legal and economic records such as charters. The evidence of who issued the charters makes it clear that local bishops, the pope and the latter's representatives were decisive figures in the reorganisation of the communities concerned. In this context, we may interpret the scope of their intervention in these two female communities as an exercise of clerical authority to reform religious life according to the decrees of Lateran IV. The church's legal apparatus strengthened significantly during this period and enabled both the bishops and the pope to intervene more strongly in the ecclesiastical landscape.[21] Nevertheless, these sources enable us to reverse the perspective of our investigation, and examine the transformations of female communities from 'bottom-up'. This approach emphasises the strategies women and their communities developed and adopted in exchange with the local actors who influenced their immediate environment. Therefore, the relation between institutional developments and the respective social, religious, political and economic constellations in which they were embedded is central to my analysis here. My aim is to make religious women visible as empowered actors within their urban and regional networks.

---

[20] Christoph Dartmann, *Die Benediktiner. Von den Anfängen bis zum Ende des Mittelalters* (Stuttgart, 2018), p. 108.
[21] *Ibid.*, pp. 108–13.

Cistercian Nuns as Players in a Multifaceted Reform Process: S. Giovanni della Pipia in Cremona

At the beginning of the thirteenth century the female Benedictine monastery of S. Giovanni della Pipia was reformed through the introduction of a new female Cistercian community.[22] The process of institutional reform at S. Giovanni della Pipia is particularly significant as it illustrates how this change reflected wider political rivalries within the city. The office of abbess was crucial to this transformation. Competing claims to control the monastery centred on the abbatial succession, highlighting the contingent and contested nature of institutional change and women's participation in it.

Sometime between 1217 and 1220 there was a change of leadership at S. Giovanni della Pipia when Imelda de Giroldis assumed office as abbess from Lucia de Bezanis, who had directed the monastery between 1212 and 1217. A disciplinary incident may have afforded the opportunity for this change, as is suggested by the record of a later process conducted by two Dominican visitors and Lucia's later excommunication.[23] This change of leadership had broader political ramifications within the city of Cremona. Since the end of the twelfth century, Cremona had been torn apart by internal struggles between rival social groups: the *Popolus* and the *Milites*, as was common in other northern Italian cities at that time. The *Popolus*, comprising wealthy merchant families, increasingly claimed more influence in the political scene, then controlled by the old noble families of the *Milites*.[24] The elevation of Imelda de Giroldis to abbess of

---

[22] S. Giovanni della Pipia was founded by Count Bernardo of Sospiro and his wife Berta on 28 October 1079. This Benedictine convent evolved from their proprietary church on the banks of the river Pipia, in the northeast of Cremona. See Elena Vanelli, '"Libertas" e monachesimo femminile: l'interazione tra papa e vescovo a livello locale', in Nicolangelo D'Acunto and Elisabetta Filippini (eds), *Libertas. Secoli X–XIII* (Milan, 2019), pp. 323–34, at pp. 323–7.

[23] In 1220 Imelda de Giroldis is recorded as abbess, while Lucia is mentioned as 'quondam' ['former'] abbess; ASMi, Pergamene per fondi, cart. 150, 24 January 1220. From this later process it is evident that Lucia probably was accused of a disciplinary offence, but it is never explicitly mentioned in the source. At the same time, Lucia's problematic status, her membership of several institutions, was resolved by Bishop Omobono of Cremona, who in 1222 confirmed her as the head of the hospital of S. Sisto. A few years later the hospital was converted into a convent by the same bishop, according to the guidelines of the Fourth Lateran Council, as 'sorores vellate' ['veiled sisters'] were already there. Lucia is recorded as abbess of S. Sisto until 1240.

[24] Giancarlo Andenna, Art. 'Cremona', in Ortensio Zecchino and Maria Paola Arena (eds), *Federico II: Enciclopedia fridericiana*, 2 vols (Rome, 2006) vol. 1, pp. 393–8; François Menant, 'Il lungo Duecento (1183–1311). Il Comune fra maturità istituzionale e lotte di parte', in Giancarlo Andenna (ed.), *Storia di Cremona. Dall'alto medioevo all'età comunale* (8 vols, Cremona, 2004), vol. 2, pp. 282–363, at pp. 282–300.

S. Giovanni della Pipia marked a turning point in control over the abbey. The mercantile *Popolus* group, to which the former abbess Lucia and her family de Bezanis belonged, lost their influence on the monastery to the old and anti-papal *Milites* family of Imelda de Giroldis.

Although Imelda apparently governed S. Giovanni della Pipia until at least 1234, later papal letters from 1235 and 1236 record the monastery's spiritual and economic decline in the preceding years, that is, the later years of her abbacy. The papal narrative alleges that some nuns even bore children, although they sought to cover up these 'misdeeds'.[25] The pope, Gregory IX, therefore requested Stephan, Provincial of the Dominicans, and Bishop Omobono of Cremona to intervene.[26] It is worth mentioning that Gregory IX uses the language of the Lateran decree, *correctio* and *reformatio*, to describe the mandate granted to the Dominican Provincial and the bishop. However, behind the rhetoric of spiritual and economic decline we see here a clear papal intervention to liberate S. Giovanni della Pipia from the long-standing influence of the anti-papal and *Milites* family of de Giroldis.

As one of their first attempts to reform the community, Stephan and Bishop Omobono appointed a new abbess, a woman known as Castellana, in January 1234.[27] In the previous year, Castellana was recorded as abbess of the church of S. Maria del Boschetto and its *conventus* and *fraternitas*.[28] This community had probably only formed recently and settled at the city walls near the river Cremonella. As the mention of a *fraternitas* suggests, religious men were also involved in this settlement. This vague designation and the lack of further

---

[25] ASMi, Pergamene per fondi, cart. 172, 28 September 1235: 'Tu vero in executione mandati procedens, prout ex litteris tuis accepimus, recepisti a singulis eiusdem monasterii monialibus de veritate dicenda corporaliter iuramentum, et quamquam per assertionem ipsarum nichil de nefandis earum actis penitus invenisses, cum ea etiam que manifesta erant et publica negavissent, presertim cum ante paucos dies quedam ipsarum que credebantur virgines matres essent, earum tantum infamiam fama publica manifesta', edition in: Guido Cariboni, 'Comunità religiose femminili legate ai Cistercensi a Piacenza e in Lombardia tra i pontificati di Innocenzo III e Alessandro IV' (unpublished Ph.D. dissertation, Università Cattolica del Sacro Cuore di Milano, 1998), ASMi, Pergamene per fondi, cart. 172, 12 July 1235 und 2 June 1236.

[26] ASMi, Pergamene per fondi, cart. 172, 12 July 1235: 'Gregorius episcopus servus servorum Dei, dilecto filio Stephano priori provinciali fratrum Predicatorum in Lombardia, salutem et apostolicam benedictionem. Cum corectionem et reformationem monasterii monialium Sancti Iohannis de Pipia Cremonensis venerabili fratri nostro episcopo Cremonensi et tibi duxerimus comitendam.', edition in: Cariboni, 'Comunità religiose femminili legate ai Cistercensi a Piacenza e in Lombardia'.

[27] ASMi, Pergamene per fondi, cart. 172, 31 January 1234.

[28] *Ibid.*, 7 July 1233.

information also suggests that it involved a religious group of men and women who had not yet adopted a particular rule.

As later sources show,[29] the ancient *Milites* family of de Giroldis, represented by Giovannibuono de Giroldis, resisted the change of abbess to such an extent that Castellana could only effectively act as abbess of S. Giovanni della Pipia in the early months of 1234.[30] Giovannibuono was also a canon in the Cathedral Chapter and played an influential role in diocesan administration. Moreover, from 1249 to 1266 he assumed the episcopal administration with the support of the city during the political exile of the bishop, a papal loyalist. In the disputes between pope and emperor, Cremona was mainly an imperial city that rarely recognised the bishops designated only by the pope.[31] Due to Giovannibuono's influence, his relative Imelda de Giroldis was reappointed abbess of the monastery in November of the same year, 1234.[32] In addition, numerous interactions between S. Giovanni della Pipia and the family de Giroldis are testified, as family members are recorded as witnesses in economic documents concerning monastic goods. Furthermore, the monastery could also wield extensive political influence, as the abbess had the right to appoint the *Potestaria* of the *curtis* Pescarolo, the official responsible for the administration of this community. This office was still occupied by the de Giroldis family in the 1250s.[33] These events show the strong connections between the noble *Milites* families and the urban society despite papal attempts to remove the monastery from the family's influence.

Another failed attempt to reform S. Giovanni della Pipia is also documented. Evidence shows that from June 1235 Margherita Casanova was the new abbess of this monastery.[34] However, her administration was unsuccessful in freeing S. Giovanni della Pipia from de Giroldis control, because the resistance of Giovannibuono de Giroldis strengthened.[35] In fact, the papal letters indicate

---

[29] *Ibid.*, 12 July 1235.

[30] *Ibid.*, 1 February 1234; 2 February 1234.

[31] Giancarlo Andenna, 'Episcopato cremonese, capitolo cattedrale, papato e impero nel XIII secolo', in Carla Bertinelli Spotti (ed.), *Cremona città imperiale, Atti del convegno internazionale di Studi (Cremona 27-28 ottobre 1995)* (Cremona, 1999), pp. 161-83, at pp. 179-80.

[32] ASMi, Pergamene per fondi, cart. 172, 23 November 1234.

[33] ASMi, Pergamene per fondi, cart. 172, 13 March 1230, 21 April 1254, 13 August 1260.

[34] Unfortunately, we have few details about Margherita Casanova. Prior to being recorded as abbess she is not mentioned among the nuns of S. Giovanni della Pipia. Her family name, however, identifies her as a member of the Casanova family. In 1247 this family, together with others, was thanked by Pope Innocent IV for its loyalty and support: Lorenzo Astegiano (ed.), *Codex diplomaticus Cremonae 715-1334* (2 vols, Turin, 1896), vol. 2, p. 301.

[35] ASMi, Pergamene per fondi, cart. 172, 12 July 1235.

that in July 1235 another strategy was planned, to entrust S. Giovanni della Pipia directly to the Dominicans.[36] The friars supported the reform process of the monastery and, although they were recognised as faithful executors of papal orders, on this occasion their involvement appears to have faltered, for reasons unknown. It is possible, too, that the nuns of S. Giovanni della Pipia objected to the transfer of their monastery to Dominican oversight.[37]

After the failure of these numerous and varied attempts to intervene in the control of the monastery, Pope Gregory IX again entrusted Stephan, the Provincial of the Dominicans, with a reorganization of S. Giovanni della Pipia by transferring the monastery to the Cistercian Order.[38] This act highlights the complex politics of institutional reform within the city, and the leading role played by the Dominican Provincial in repeated attempts to secure institutional change. The transfer of the monastery did not occur until the following year, in March 1236, when Stephan managed to reinstate Castellana as abbess. This time, however, she did not come alone, as she was accompanied by 20 *sorores*, who for the first time were named as Cistercian, and who were transferred from the monastery of S. Maria del Boschetto, also in Cremona, where Castellana was then abbess.[39] During the period between Castellana's initial deposition until her later reappointment to S. Giovanni della Pipia (that is, early 1234 to 1236), the church and *fraternitas* of S. Maria del Boschetto had been restructured into a Cistercian female monastery, with some lay brothers, under Castellana's leadership and probably with the support of the Dominican Provincial, who directed the institutional reform of S. Giovanni della Pipia.[40] The timing of this transformation, only two years after Castellana's return to S. Maria del Boschetto, together with the influential presence of Dominican friars at both S. Giovanni della Pipia and S. Maria del Boschetto, suggests that the adoption of a monastic rule by the original *conventus* and *fraternitas* of S. Maria del Boschetto may have been initiated

---

[36] *Ibid.*, 28 September 1235.

[37] The Dominicans had recently settled in the city, and since 1228 they had theoretically no longer been allowed to provide spiritual care for women. However, the papal report on this failed reform attempt only indicates the lack of progress, without explaining the exact reason: 'Gregorius episcopus servus servorum Dei, dilecto filio [...] priori provinciali fratrum Predicatorum in Lombardia, salutem et apostolicam benedictionem. Olim miserabili statu monasterii Sancti Iohannis de Pipia Cremonensis diocesis intellecto, correctionem et reformationem ipsius primo quibusdam fratribus tui ordinis ac demum, eis non proficientibus [...]': ASMi, Pergamene per fondi, cart. 172, 28 September 1235, edition in: Cariboni, 'Comunità religiose femminili legate ai Cistercensi a Piacenza e in Lombardia'.

[38] ASMi, Pergamene per fondi, cart. 172, 28 September 1235.

[39] *Ibid.*, 18 March 1236.

[40] *Ibid.*, 20 March 1235.

with the intent to later transform the status of S. Giovanni della Pipia. Further suggestive evidence of these intentions is the fact that part of the community remained in S. Maria del Boschetto and developed in quite a different direction. In later sources the community that remained in S. Maria del Boschetto appears as 'congregatio fratrum et sororum professorum et professarum commorantium'.[41] This implies that only twenty *sorores* decided to maintain Cistercian customs and to transfer to S. Giovanni della Pipia, while the rest of the community was able to decide to evolve in another form of religious life. These turbulent years for the women and men at S. Maria del Boschetto highlight the fluidity of institutional forms of religious life at this time. According to papal sources, another reason for the relocation of some members of S. Maria del Boschetto was their unfavourable location and the community's great poverty.[42] In contrast, those members of this new religious community who moved to S. Giovanni della Pipia secured a better location and endowment to sustain their religious life, through which they could become established and improve their status in the city.

In comparison with the previous attempts by the pope to intervene in the observance of the nuns of S. Giovanni della Pipia, the arrival of the sisters from S. Maria del Boschetto proved decisive for an internal rearrangement of the community. Many of the nuns who originally belonged to S. Giovanni della Pipia chose to accept the Cistercian observance of the new nuns. Others preferred to leave to join other Benedictine communities. The nun Vittoria of S. Giovanni della Pipia was sent to a Benedictine convent in Pavia called S. Maria Teodota,[43] while Agnese de Bezanis joined her relative Lucia in the Benedictine monastery of S. Sisto, where she became the next abbess.[44] Others, however, did not want to reform or join another Benedictine monastery and left the monastery, although where they went is unknown.[45]

Although Bishop Omobono so far had supported this transformation, he now opposed the new Cistercian community and excommunicated the religious women of S. Giovanni della Pipia, because its new status threatened to reduce episcopal income. The monastery had papal protection by virtue of belonging to the patrimony of *Sancti Petri*.[46] Although it was subject to episcopal jurisdiction, the monastery had been partially exempt from paying episcopal dues since its

[41] *Ibid.*, 9 January 1249.
[42] *Ibid.*, 2 June 1236.
[43] *Ibid.*, 10 April 1237.
[44] ASMi, Pergamene per fondi, cart. 150, 24 September 1240.
[45] ASMi, Pergamene per fondi, cart. 172, 2 June 1236.
[46] The monasteries that belonged to the patrimony of *Sancti Petri* were under the special protection of the pope: Michele Maccarrone, 'Primato romano e monasteri dal principio del secolo XII ad Innocenzo III', in *Istituzioni monastiche e istituzioni canonicali in*

foundation.⁴⁷ The sources refer to these contributions as 'indebitae exactiones' or 'iacturae et iniurae', so we may assume that these taxes refer to the episcopal 'potestas ordinis', that is, the various consecration actions of the bishop such as the consecration of nuns, altars and oil.⁴⁸ In effect, these dues were probably paid by the monastery in the early part of the thirteenth century through the influence of the powerful canon Giovannibuono de Giroldis and the control of his family over S. Giovanni della Pipia.⁴⁹ The adoption of Cistercian status, whereby the monastery was exempt from episcopal taxation but remained under episcopal jurisdiction, ended this custom. The bishop's strong reaction by excommunicating the nuns of S. Giovanni della Pipia might also suggest that not only did Castellana not want to pay the customary, albeit unjust fee for her ordination as abbess, but also that she did not want to be consecrated by the bishop, although it was his prerogative. Because of this escalation in 1237 Pope Gregory IX asked the abbot of the Cistercian Abbey of S. Maria della Cava in Cremona, twice within ten days, to intervene in order to abolish the unjust levy and free the women religious from the bishop's excommunication.⁵⁰

The nuns of S. Giovanni della Pipia defended their position.⁵¹ In June 1238 the nuns were granted, at their request, the privilege of papal protection to confirm their Cistercian status and to reaffirm their relations with the bishop in this new constellation of power.⁵² In October 1244 the nuns requested further papal support against episcopal usurpation of their monastic rights, through a petition by the lay brother Girardo Berençanus on their behalf.⁵³ Perhaps in response to the nuns' petition, in the following year S. Giovanni della Pipia was granted the right to receive the visitation from the Cistercian monastery of S. Maria della Colomba in Piacenza, which had some experience in the spiritual care of nuns.⁵⁴ The papal confirmation of the monastery's rights and the visitation by the Cistercian monastery of S. Maria della Colomba in Piacenza can both be interpreted as papal

---

    Occidente 1123-1215, Milano 1980 (Atti della settima Settimana internazionale di studi medioevali, Mendola 28 agosto-3 settembre 1977) (Milan, 1980), pp. 49–132, at pp. 49–56.
⁴⁷ Vanelli, '"Libertas" e monachesimo femminile', pp. 323–7.
⁴⁸ Georg Schreiber, *Kurie und Kloster im 12. Jahrhundert. Studien zur Privilegierung, Verfassung und besonders zum Eigenkirchenwesen der vorfranziskanischen Orden vornehmlich auf Grund der Papsturkunden von Paschalis II. bis auf Lucius III. (1099-1181)* (2 vols, Stuttgart, 1910) vol. 1, p. 232.
⁴⁹ *Ibid.*, pp. 329–32.
⁵⁰ ASMi, Bolle e Brevi, cart. 7, n. 50 [A], 20 May 1237; ASMi, Bolle e Brevi, cart. 7, n. 52 [A], 30 May 1237.
⁵¹ Vanelli, '"Libertas" e monachesimo femminile', pp. 332–4.
⁵² ASMi, Bolle e Brevi, cart. 7, n. 55 [A], 25 June 1238.
⁵³ ASMi, Pergamene per fondi, cart. 172, 21 October 1244.
⁵⁴ Cariboni, 'Cistercian Nuns in Northern Italy', p. 61.

responses to the request for support of the female community in the conflict with the bishop and the cathedral chapter.[55]

As the conflict with the bishop and cathedral chapter remained unresolved, the community turned to the secular authorities to defend their privileges. Particularly important in this regard are the letters that the community requested from Emperor Frederick II in 1246 and later from the imperial vicar Uberto Pellavicino in 1256 to obtain the tax exemption to which they were entitled.[56] In this example, which illustrates what the pope referred to as a spiritual and financial reform of a female Benedictine monastery by introducing a new Cistercian female community, there was an attempt to release the monastery from the unjust economic exactions to the bishop and his supporters.

Although sources that explicitly record the voices of these women are scarce, their support or resistance to the changes in the monastery are evident in their actions. While Imelda de Giroldis embodied her family's insistence on controlling S. Giovanni della Pipia, Castellana, who accompanied the introduction of the new Cistercian Observance into the old Benedictine convent, can be considered a promoter of reform. The community also defended its own interests, for example through envoys to appeal to ecclesiastical and political authorities to intercede in their conflict with the bishop. A similar agency of religious women to pursue their political, spiritual and economic interests can also be observed in the next case study.

Translatio as Reform Process: Creating and Relocating Cistercian Nuns

I now focus on the female community at the Church of S. Cristoforo, the process through which it was transformed into a Cistercian nunnery and its relocation to the premises of the *Iesu Christi* monastery in the city of Pavia at the beginning of the thirteenth century. Lying behind this institutional and spatial transformation was a longstanding and continuing contest between competing actors such as the communal ruling classes, the bishop and the Cistercian Order, each of whom claimed the monastic property of what was originally the male religious foundation *Iesu Christi*. This case study examines both the scope for the women's community of S. Cristoforo to pursue their own interests, and why we can speak of this transformation as a reform process, although this term is not used explicitly in papal or monastic sources. After sketching the initial stages of the community

---

[55] Vanelli, '"Libertas" e monachesimo femminile', p. 332.
[56] Astegiano (ed.), *Codex diplomaticus Cremonae*, vol. 2, n. 552, 8 April 1246, p. 276; ASMi, Pergamene per fondi, cart. 178, [A], 23 November 1256.

of S. Cristoforo, I deal with the complicated, contingent and idiosyncratic reform process itself and its resulting conflicts.

A group of religious women at S. Cristoforo's church is mentioned in written records three times over a period of ten years. In 1209, the *sorores collegii Sancti Christofori* bought, with the assistance of a clerical intermediary, all the properties of the church of S. Cristoforo from the Hospital della Carità.[57] S. Cristoforo was located just outside the city wall near the city gate, Porta Laudense. The women's acquisition of this property, at the location where they had already settled, shows their willingness to create the conditions necessary to lead an independent religious life. Their financial means, however, were probably not extensive, as the *sorores* paid the purchase price in six instalments. Particularly striking is the support of Bishop Bernardo of Pavia and the advocate of the vendor, the Hospital della Carità, Guidone Bottigella, who was at that time also a member of the civic government. From the outset, therefore, the establishment and continued existence of this community was bound with ecclesiastic and political authority.

Despite the limited sources, we gain a glimpse into the spiritual role this community performed from the early days of its formation. In 1218, the *ministra et rectrix* Ottabona is recorded acting on behalf of the *mansio Sancti Christofori* in a transaction concerning the late Lanfranco de Santa Mustiola.[58] The deceased's mother sought to clarify matters of his inheritance, which included a house in Pavia, and also to ensure provision for the family's *memoria*. It was agreed that an annual commemoration for Lanfranco and his parents should be held at the church of S. Cristoforo.[59] This legacy is, therefore, associated with memorial practices already attributed to this community in its early stages of development. The document offers a further hint of the community's spiritual profile. The religious women are referred to as *Capuccine*, alluding to their appearance, as the women wore a robe with a hood, perhaps as a marker of penitence.[60] Although other communities with this designation have been documented, this community of S. Cristoforo is the only one known to have become a Cistercian community.

Shortly after these events, in November 1218 the religious women at S. Cristoforo were transformed into a Cistercian nunnery at the direction of the new bishop of Pavia, Folco Scotti.[61] Bishop Folco seems to have acted on his own

---

[57] Pavia, Biblioteca Civica 'Bonetta', Pergamene Bottigella, n. 4, 3 November 1209.
[58] ASMi, Pergamene per fondi, cart. 632, 29 October 1218.
[59] Ibid.
[60] The name probably refers to the penitential character of their way of life and only appears in another case in Monza: Renato Mambretti, 'Prime ricerche per una storia delle case religiose di Monza. La *domus caputiarum de Piro* (sec. XIV)', *Aevum. Rassegna di Scienze storiche e linguistiche e filologiche*, 61 (1987), pp. 398–407.
[61] ASMi, Fondo Religione, cart. 5718, 13 November 1218, ed. in: Cariboni, 'Il monachesimo

initiative, perhaps seeking to replicate the model from the neighbouring town of Piacenza, where he had already supported the establishment of female Cistercian monasteries. Bishop Folco's patronage of these female monastic communities was part of a wider pattern in northern Italy, and indeed elsewhere in Europe, of bishops extending their authority by sponsoring female Cistercian monasteries.[62] Moreover, the influence of the Fourth Lateran Council as a motivation to institutionalise and reform communities should not be underestimated. The bishop describes the *sorores* as *commorantes*, as inhabitants of the church of S. Cristoforo, and stresses that this church rightly belonged to his diocese. He also imposed regular life upon the community, so that the women henceforth would live according to the *Rule* of St Benedict and the *Institutiones* of the Cistercian order, wearing the white robe to signal their shift in religious status. Their abbess could be elected within the community by the nuns themselves or appointed from another community of the Cistercian order. The abbess would be ordained, however, by the bishop of Pavia. In addition, the bishop consented to an annual visitation by the Cistercian Order.[63]

In this case, it should be noted that the bishop asserted his claims to the church and what was now the Cistercian nunnery of S. Cristoforo. The abbess was obliged to act to ensure that the bishop's rights in the church and monastery were preserved, and that no claims were made upon the church during the visitation by the Cistercian order, which was exclusively responsible for the sisters' spiritual care. Here we see that the institutionalisation of the community did not infringe upon episcopal rights. Rather, the institutional transformation was a means to secure the bishop's claims to the property of this church, which also ensured that the newly established female religious community received adequate material provision.

Of particular interest here is the reference to the white robe that the nuns were required to wear. Like the nickname *Capuccine*, the appearance of the white religious habit was an important status symbol to distinguish a certain religious way of life. However, such a transformation could not be carried out quickly. A source from 1220, a decade later, still speaks of a *collegium commorante* at the monastery of S. Cristoforo, suggesting that the identity of the community was still in flux. It is interesting, however, that the woman Ottabona, who was called *ministra* and *rectrix* a few years prior, is now recorded as abbess of the nunnery

---

cistercense femminile', p. 53.

[62] Cariboni, 'Cistercian Nuns in Northern Italy', pp. 54–5; Jamroziak, *The Cistercian Order in Medieval Europe*, pp. 130–1.

[63] ASMi, Fondo Religione, cart. 5718, 13 November 1218, ed. in: Cariboni, 'Il monachesimo cistercense femminile', p. 53.

of S. Cristoforo.⁶⁴ The institutional change was thus underway, although not yet fully implemented, as the name *collegium* was reminiscent of the somewhat loose associative character of the original organisation. In the same source from 1220, abbess Ottabona is referred to as *humilis*. This term might allude to her modest familial origins and/or her spiritual demeanour. Significantly, no family connections between members of this community and the city's influential families have been identified to date.

The new Cistercian nuns of S. Cristoforo were relocated shortly after their formation. In the spring of 1221, bishop Folco Scotti provided them with the Church of *Iesu Christi* together with its estates, where Cistercian monks had lived until the first two decades of the thirteenth century, but where now 'hardly any traces of the Cistercian Order could be found'.⁶⁵ The male Cistercian community here had shrunk to just two monks and a lay brother. This episcopal initiative was confirmed in the same year by the papal legate Ugo of Ostia, the future Pope Gregory IX. At the same time, at the request of the sisters, Ugo granted papal protection to the *sorores*, as *regularem vita professe*, and their present and future properties.⁶⁶ A few months later this move was described as a *translatio* and endorsed by Pope Honorius III. The move was approved because the buildings of S. Cristoforo were inadequate for the new Cistercian nuns, who could live comfortably (*comode*) in the monastery of *Iesu Christi*.⁶⁷ The former location seemed to be unsuitable for the implementation of new monastic requirements, while the adjective *comode* to refer to the new location might allude to a greater monastic endowment that enabled improved living conditions.

At first glance the resettlement of the community of S. Cristoforo appears to be a measure to better provide for the female religious community, both materially and spiritually, through the existing buildings of *Iesu Christi*. It can be argued that the transfer of S. Cristoforo represented a further attempt to rescue or reform two declining and dilapidated monasteries, which had been united for exactly the same reason. Moreover, the bishop wanted to assert his rights of administration and jurisdiction on the monastic complex of *Iesu Christi*, which he had lost to Cistercian control while the monks directed the affairs of *Iesu Christi*. The first monks at *Iesu Christi* came from the remote Cistercian abbey della Barona, which had officially belonged to *Iesu Christi* since 1210. This *translatio*, documented

---

⁶⁴ ASMi, Pergamene per fondi, cart. 632, 26 July 1220.
⁶⁵ 'Sane referentibus vobis didicimus quod cum monasterium vestrum in quo mares fuerant ad eum statum pervenerit ut nulla pene ibi vestigia sui videlicet Cisterciensis ordinis remansissent, duobus tantum monachis et uno converso commorantibus in eodem [...]': ASMi, Bolle e Brevi, cart. 6, n. 48 [A], 5 July 1221
⁶⁶ ASMi, Pergamene per fondi, cart. 632, 7 May 1221.
⁶⁷ ASMi, Bolle e Brevi, cart. 6, n. 48 [A], 5 July 1221.

in the year 1210, was carried out with the approval of the General Chapter and was intended on the one hand to reform, namely to improve *Iesu Christi*'s management of the estates, and on the other hand to expand and consolidate the young and then marginalised Cistercian abbey della Barona.[68] In 1219, just a few years before the arrival of the nuns of S. Cristoforo, the General Chapter of the Cistercians sought to address the dire situation of the abbey della Barona, which was described as 'pauper et oppressum pondere debitorum', that is, 'poor and burdened by debt'. The aim of the *translatio* thus failed.[69] Bishop Folco was now in a position to assert his rights, because he could profit from the spiritual and economic decay as a justification for the *translatio* and intended reform, and because the other competitor, the civic commune, was currently weakened by internal struggles. Indeed, Folco was appointed as *rector communis Papie* in 1220 by Emperor Frederick II and was thus also responsible for the political order in the city.[70] The commune had the right to claim *Iesu Christi* because, when it was founded in 1187, the responsibility for its administration was transferred from its founder, a citizen of the commune, to both the bishop and the commune.[71]

The removal of the Cistercian monks in 1227 from *Iesu Christi* caused tensions for the nuns with the French mother abbey of the Cistercian evacuees, La Ferté. La Ferté appealed to the pope and, after negotiations involving the pope, the bishop of Pavia and the Cistercian General Chapter, La Ferté eventually had to yield, although the monastery received a payment in respect of its original foundation at della Barona.[72] Already in 1228, the nuns of *Iesu Christi* received papal confirmation of their possession of *Iesu Christi* from Gregory IX, who had been involved from the beginning, probably working for this verdict.[73] It is interesting to note that the pope does not address the nuns as Cistercian, compared to those recognised by the Order, but referred to them by their original name and corresponding nickname: 'conventus de domo Iesu Christi, que Capitine dicitur'.[74] An

---

[68] On the union of the abbey della Barona and Iesu Christi: Guido Cariboni, 'Monasteri cistercensi maschili a Pavia tra XII e XIII secolo', *Rivista di storia della chiesa in Italia*, 50 (1996), 350–98, 372–86.

[69] Ibid., 386.

[70] Giovanni Forzatti Golia, 'Folco Scotti "Episcopus et rector communis papie" (1216–1229)', in: Ettore Cau and Angelo Settia (eds), *'Speciales fideles imperii'. Pavia nell'età di Federico II. Atti della giornata di studi (Pavia, 19 maggio 1994* (Pavia, 1995), pp. 61–96.

[71] On the foundation of *Iesu Christi*: Cariboni, 'Monasteri cistercensi maschili a Pavia', 366–72.

[72] ASMi, Pergamene per fondi, cart. 632, 8 November 1227; Cariboni, 'Monasteri cistercensi maschili a Pavia', p. 391.

[73] ASMi, Fondo Religione, cart. 5718, 17 February 1228.

[74] In the sources there are both textual variants: *Capitine* and *Capuccine*.

explicit connection between these nuns and the Cistercian Order would likely have strengthened the claim of La Ferté to the complex of *Iesu Christi*.

The importance of location for monastic life is brought into relief through the nuns' *translatio*. Only about six years after the move, the nuns complained that the location of *Iesu Christi* was isolated and far from the city, unlike S. Cristoforo, which was close to the city wall. For this reason, the nuns claimed they were constantly subjected to robbery and assaults that made it impossible for women to lead their sincere religious lives, 'sine gravi despendio et infamia' ['without serious damage and shame']. The women religious may have emphasized the negative aspects of the location of *Iesu Christi* to persuade the pope of the necessity to relocate them. Soon afterwards they received permission from Gregory IX to return to S. Cristoforo. The prerequisite for the return was the construction of a *claustrum* so that the enclosure could be upheld, as was expected of Cistercian nuns.[75]

Despite the papal confirmation of their relocation, the first mention of the women at S. Cristoforo does not appear in the convent's archive until 1245.[76] Presumably, there was a transitional period during which both sites were used. For example, in 1230, abbess Ottabona, together with the whole community of nine women religious, appointed a procurator in the parlour of S. Cristoforo to request further documents in Rome concerning their forthcoming resettlement and the spatial restructuring of the Church of S. Cristoforo.[77] When in 1237 Gregory IX renewed the papal protection of the community, *Iesu Christi* was still recorded as the monastery's base and the church of S. Cristoforo, with all its possessions, appeared among its other estates.[78] The bishop of Pavia could perhaps have modified the premises of S. Cristoforo for the nuns from the beginning, but he preferred at the time to relocate the female community to *Iesu Christi* to fulfil other political and economic aims and requirements. In particular, Bishop Folco of Pavia intended to secure the recovery and improved management of *Iesu Christi*'s property through an institutional reform in which the male community was replaced with the women of S. Cristoforo. Pope Gregory IX consistently supported the bishop's agenda regarding women religious and ensured that their new, monastic way of life was safeguarded through enclosure and the community received adequate material provision.

Another important concern for S. Cristoforo's Cistercian nuns was to secure the right to receive visitation from a representative of the Cistercian Order.[79] The

---

[75] ASMi, Brevi e Bolle, cart. 7, n. 8 [A], 20 October 1227.
[76] *Ibid.*, cart. 8, n. 61 [B], 1 June 1245.
[77] ASMi, Pergamene per fondi, cart. 632, 24 August 1230.
[78] *Ibid.*, [B], 9 April 1237.
[79] *Ibid.*, 24 August 1230.

disputes with La Ferté were probably still too fresh to consider a closer relation with this Cistercian community to provide spiritual care. Evidently, the nuns not only needed to secure suitable material endowment, but also wanted to receive spiritual care from the Cistercians, which had been promised to them from the outset. Nevertheless, the nuns of S. Cristoforo remained under episcopal supervision until the 1260s, when the first traces of contact with Cistercians are recorded in their archive.[80] The nuns themselves were, in fact, only able to assert their own wishes within a long-term process, in relation to the location of their community and who would conduct their visitation.

In this case, Ottabona's role seems to have been central to the institutional transformation of S. Cristoforo. She was both head of the former religious community and abbess of the new Cistercian nuns. In order to maintain the leadership of this religious group during the process of transformation, Ottabona must have received special recognition and support from the bishop of Pavia. Her leadership must also have played an important role in the transformation and relocation of the community, as she may have been able to motivate the religious women to take such steps and maintain communal functioning. Even without a more precise identification of her social background, Ottabona's implicit actions within the women's community appear to indicate that she favoured the implementation of the changes in the community. Finally, the office of abbess and the person who held it is crucial for creating unity within the community and for mediating relations with external actors.[81]

Conclusion

My purpose here has been to examine institutional sources from a perspective that focuses on the actors involved in the dynamics of reform and therefore to bring a critical approach to the concept of 'institution'. By analysing the processes through which lay women's religious communities became Cistercian nuns from a 'bottom-up' perspective, my aim has been to foreground the actions of these religious women within their social environment. The sources for these case studies offer little insight into the spiritual experiences or inner worlds of the women concerned. They do, however, hint at women's institutional identities and the choices they made in negotiating the changes affecting their communities. This approach emphasises the strategies women and their communities developed and adopted in exchange with the local social, religious, political and economic actors

---

[80] *Ibid.*, cart. 633, 28 February 1266.
[81] On the direct influence that the person of the abbess and abbot could exert on reforms, see Steven Vanderputten (ed.), *Abbots and Abbesses as a Human Resource in the Ninth- to Twelfth-Century West* (Berlin, 2018).

who influenced their immediate environment. These dynamics of institutional transformation are not about abstract institutions, but rather concern particular female communities that wanted to lead a religious life and had to navigate a path in a specific political and social environment.

The large number of actors entangled with the communities in these two case studies is particularly striking. My analysis shows how reform was a negotiated process with various actors, each with their own diverse religious, political and economic interests. The interaction of these elements contributes to the complexity of these processes, which depend upon the respective social and ecclesiastical circumstances within and outside the respective cities. Planning a reform process, therefore, would have been difficult for all parties, highlighting the contingent character of these events. In the Cremonese example of S. Giovanni della Pipia, the bishop seemed at first to accommodate the nunnery's reform, but later resisted when his interests were threatened. The same applies to the de Giroldis family, who did not want to lose control of S. Giovanni della Pipia. The Cistercians gained prominence only after the introduction of the new female Cistercian community of S. Maria del Boschetto, part of an attempt by the female community of S. Giovanni della Pipia to defend themselves against episcopal intervention. The reform at S. Giovanni della Pipia also triggered the parallel reorganisation and institutionalisation of the other female community of S. Maria del Boschetto, which may have benefited from greater economic stability as a result.

In the case of S. Cristoforo in Pavia, the decisive role of Bishop Folco Scotti in collaboration with the papacy is particularly striking. Moreover, Pope Gregory's support to this community is fully in line with his wider strategy for the regularisation of religious communities. On the one hand, Bishop Folco appears to promote and assert the Cistercian *Institutiones* for female religiosity; on the other hand, this institutionalisation process also enabled him to replace the original male community in order to assert his interests over episcopal property. The Cistercians were thus pressed to yield a male community and accept the establishment of a new, female, one, along with the loss of the associated property. Both case studies thus illustrate how an intervention to reform a religious community or institution was often motivated by economic imperatives, couched in the rhetoric of purported spiritual or economic decay.

The religious women and their communities proved to be neither only resistors nor completely oppressed puppets of male authorities. They appear as fully-fledged actors who were able, within their context, to represent, negotiate and achieve their own interests. The abbesses and other members, as well as supporters acting on behalf of the female community, promoted the women's cause. The Cistercian nuns of S. Cristoforo asserted their interests within a long-term process, for example in relation to the community's location. Women of both communities did not hesitate to pursue their interests with the Curia. The nuns of S. Giovanni della Pipia sent envoys to petition against episcopal taxation, whereas the envoys for S. Cristoforo petitioned against the removal of the nuns from their original location. When ecclesiastical authorities or the Cistercians could not guarantee sufficient protection of the community's interests, religious women also turned to secular powers for support, even if (or precisely because) the secular authority may also have supported the nuns' adversary. For example, S. Giovanni della Pipia received a privilege of protection from Emperor Frederick II, which was later renewed by the imperial vicar Uberto Pellavicino, while S. Cristoforo in Pavia repeatedly countered the opposition of the commune. In both cases, we see how the actions of religious women were marked by a certain pragmatism in order to advance their own interests in dynamic situations.

In the absence of personal testimonies or manuscript evidence which could provide information about the spiritual preferences of these women in these moments of upheaval, the links they sought with the Cistercian Order through privileges or the spiritual care they often fought for are not sufficient to suggest that Cistercian spirituality was the sole motivation for the nuns' actions. Family affiliation and political strategies also played an important role in shaping a woman's religious identity and sense of belonging, as we saw in the contest over the abbacy of S. Giovanni della Pipia. Religious women's adoption of an institutional religious identity may have been prompted more by the need for protection or legitimisation than by spiritual affinity or a desire for affiliation with a particular order. Of course an institutional identity may have provided stability and legitimacy for women, but it also came with 'trade-offs' about freedom to move in the world and the ability to continue a life of active charity.[82] In the case of S. Giovanni della Pipia, however, the transformation into Cistercian nuns offered the possibility of liberation from episcopal economic demands. The women religious were, after all, subject to a new institutional order, one that indeed was too distant to represent a new form of oppression.

I argue that the adoption of Cistercian customs and identity in the cases analysed here also represented a similar means to provide the necessary and protected

---

[82] This observation is inspired by an aspect of the concept of 'fictive orders' argued by Alison More. On one hand, More argues that clerics who supported women's lay communities moulded them into adopting various institutional structures to grant them legitimacy and protection in an environment in which lay religious life was increasingly regarded critically (More, *Fictive Orders*, Chap. 2). On the other hand, her analysis of later medieval narratives shows how clerical and mendicant authors created 'fictive histories' of female religious life through which clerics sought to impose regular identities upon lay religious women and claim their association with their orders (*Ibid.*, Chap. 3).

framework for the women to lead a religious life after the Fourth Lateran Council. The institutional status of the Cistercians, moreover, offered these female communities patronage that protected them from the suspicion of heresy, provided legal means such as privileges for the defence of community rights and possessions, and gave guidance in the form of spiritual care. Furthermore, episcopal actions to institutionalise the community of S. Cristoforo can also be interpreted as an effort to contain and manage these lay religious communities within a recognisable and legitimate canonical framework. According to these considerations, the connection to the Cistercians in the examples examined here could be seen as a choice of 'order' – at least initially – that religious women negotiated in interaction or conflict with the other actors involved, or adopted accepting the pope's or bishop's suggestion. In the course of the thirteenth century, female communities were intertwined in negotiated processes with various local actors in order to find the most suitable religious provider who could offer the conditions for the realisation of their own religious life within a 'market of religious offerings'.

Against this background, it is easier to understand why new Cistercian nuns were addressed with their old names, as for example in the privilege of protection granted to S. Cristoforo by Gregory IX in 1228.[83] In contrast to S. Giovanni della Pipia, where the name *Cistercensis ordinis* was intended to avert the bishop's monetary claims, S. Cristoforo's Cistercian connection had to be concealed in order to preserve the new property of *Iesu Christi*. Therefore, an affiliation with a religious order could be omitted intentionally if mentioning it was potentially counterproductive to achieving a certain outcome, or to stress another aspect that would be more beneficial to the cause. At the same time, there was the flexibility to alter the affiliation to an existing order, as soon as the conditions for religious life described above could no longer be guaranteed. Based on these examples, the fluidity of female monasticism in the first half of the thirteenth century was premised on how religious women in the transitional stages of institutional change (or formation) sought to take advantage of the multiple aspects of their identities to promote their spiritual, economic and legal interests.

---

[83] ASMi, Fondo Religione, cart. 5718, 17 February 1228.

CHAPTER 7

Circulation of Books and Reform Ideas between Female Monasteries in Medieval Castile: From Twelfth-Century Cistercians to the Observant Reform

MERCEDES PÉREZ VIDAL

Processes of Reform in Female Monasteries in Medieval Castile: A World of Diversitas

THE revision of the traditional rhetoric of religious reform by recent scholarship has acknowledged the lack of a clear definition.[1] Indeed, there were many reform movements, all of them distinct from one another and closely related through the contingencies of time and space.[2] Thus, we must analyse the peculiarities of each of these reforms, avoiding preconceived ideas about the uniformity of these movements which have shaped modern scholarship's vision of reform.[3] As Steven Vanderputten has argued, reforms of individual institutions have to be

---

[1] Much of this essay was written with the support of a Clarín-Cofund grant, co-funded by the 7th WP of the European Union, Marie Skłodowska Curie Actions, grant agreement n. 600196. Image rights were acquired with the support of the Government of the Principality of Asturias through the FICYT (Fundación para el Fomento en Asturias de la Investigación Científica Aplicada y la Tecnología) project SVPA–21–AYUD/2021/57166.

[2] See Steven Vanderputten, *Monastic Reform as Process: Realities and Representations in Medieval Flanders, 900–1100* (Ithaca, 2013); Michael Vargas, *Taming a Brood of Vipers: Conflict and Change in Fourteenth-Century Dominican Convents* (Leiden, 2011), pp. 16–22; and also Michael A. Vargas, 'Administrative change in the 14th century Dominican Order. A Case Study in Partial Reforms and Incomplete Theories', in Christopher M. Bellitto and David Zachariah Flanagin (eds), *Reassessing Reform. A Historical Investigation into Church Renewal* (Washington, 2012), pp. 84–104.

[3] Vanderputten, *Monastic Reform*, pp. 3 and 11.

analysed and understood as processes, rather than as 'flashpoint events'.[4] Hence, they should not be seen as a result of the agency of a charismatic reformer, nor as the simple implementation of a reformist programme. On the contrary, reform was normally a long-term process, with different phases, and in which the tension between structure and agency, and between the institution's past and present, were a constant.[5] It was a negotiated, collective endeavour, which evolved through time, in response to changing circumstances. Claire Taylor Jones has reached similar conclusions in analysing the specific case of the Observant reform of the German Dominican Order, and in particular of Dominican nuns. She proved how the traditional narrative presenting the Golden Age at the order's founding in the thirteenth century, the decline in the fourteenth century and renewal by Dominican 'Observants' was a preconceived scheme that does not reflect reality.[6]

Every reform movement can only properly be understood in a broader and comparative framework. At present this comparative approach is hampered by the imbalance in the state of research into different territories, religious orders and timeframes. Whereas a high number of studies have focused on Central and Northern Europe, as well as on Italian convents,[7] research into reform processes for the Iberian Peninsula, and particularly in Castile, has remained fairly underdeveloped.[8] Moreover, in Castile, traditional historiography has approached these questions from the perspective of the 'official' reformers, offering a vision of false homogeneity. For instance, regarding the Observant reform, the majority of studies have focused on the late period coinciding with the reign of the Catholic

---

[4] *Ibid.*, p. 9
[5] *Ibid.*, pp. 8–13.
[6] Claire Taylor Jones, *Ruling the Spirit. Women, Liturgy, and Dominican Reform in Late Medieval Germany* (Philadelphia, 2017).
[7] Anne Winston-Allen, *Convent Chronicles. Women Writing About Women and Reform in the Late Middle Ages* (University Park, 2004); Alison I. Beach, *Manuscripts and Monastic Culture: Reform and Renewal in Twelfth Century Germany* (Turnhout, 2007); Fiona J. Griffiths, *The Garden of Delights: Reform and Renaissance for Women in the Twelfth Century* (Philadelphia, 2007); *Id.*, 'Women and Reform in the Central Middle Ages', in Judith M. Bennett and Ruth Mazo Karras (eds), *Oxford Handbook of Women and Gender in Medieval Europe* (Oxford, 2013), pp. 447–63; Jones, *Ruling the Spirit*. On Italian female monasteries: Sylvie Duval, *'Comme des anges sur terre': Les moniales dominicaines et les débuts de la Réforme observante* (Rome, 2015).
[8] In Portugal, the subject of women and Observant reform has been only recently approached. Paula Cardoso, 'Unveiling Female Observance: Reform, Regulation and the Rise of Dominican Nunneries in Late Medieval Portugal', *Journal of Medieval Iberian Studies* (2020), 365–82. In 2021 an international conference approached these matters in a broader context: *Political and Ecclesiastical Agents in the Reform(s) of the Religious Orders in Europe during the Late Middle Ages (c. 1250–1500)*, Complutense University of Madrid, November 24–6, 2021.

Monarchs, Ferdinand and Isabella (r. 1475–1516).[9] Nevertheless, although their role cannot be denied, the monarchs were not the only agents of reform and, as we will see later, they acted only in the later phase of a long-term reform process.

In fact, during the last quarter of the fourteenth century and the first half of the fifteenth century, both nuns and female patrons actively promoted the introduction of Observant reform in Castilian female monasteries. However, as we will see and in contrast to what we normally would expect, these women kept some privileges and the control over these religious foundations, which may have been a strong reason for them to promote these ideals, and at the same time to avoid subjection to male reformers. This makes evident the necessity of a gendered perspective, revising women's role as agents in these processes of reform long before the reign of the Catholic Monarchs, to offer a more nuanced panorama.[10] In doing so, our analysis should consider the concept of 'intersectionality': that is to say, gender's relationship with other markers of difference, such as religious order, social class, race or place.[11] This relates to Judith Butler's concept of 'gender performativity', which explains that gender identities were constructed in performance, they were in constant change, thus, they cannot be understood separately from the cultural intersections that produced and maintained gender.[12] Status and place were both important markers for most of the women considered in this article. Unlike the majority of their northern European counterparts, Spanish royal and aristocratic women kept rights over their family inheritance during the high and late Middle Ages. They had access to and control over important goods, including female monasteries, which, in Castile, worked as platforms for the power of the nobility. This close connection between female monasteries and aristocratic women implied a heterodox adoption of reformist ideas, creating distinct differences to the Italian or German Observant monasteries.

---

[9] The early foundational studies were mainly by members of religious orders, such as Vicente Beltrán de Heredia, *Historia de la Reforma de la Provincia de España (1450–1550)* (Rome, 1939), for the Order of Preachers, to the more recent scholarship: Guillermo Nieva Ocampo, 'La creación de la observancia regular en el convento de San Esteban de Salamanca durante el reinado de los Reyes Católicos', *Cuadernos de Historia de España*, 80 (2006), 91–126.

[10] The complexity of these processes has been clarified in the case of Observant Dominican nunneries in North and Central Italy. Duval, *'Comme des anges sur terre'*.

[11] A concept introduced by feminists of colour, who fought hard to displace hegemonic and reductive discourses supporting the equation women = gender. The term is commonly attributed to Kimberle Crenshaw, 'Demarginalizing the Intersection of Race and Sex: A Black Feminist Critique of Antidiscrimination Doctrine, Feminist Theory and Antiracist Politics', *University of Chicago Legal Forum*, 1 (1989), 139–67.

[12] Judith Butler, *Gender Trouble: Feminism and the Subversion of Identity* (New York, 1990), pp. 6–7.

Furthermore, although it is necessary to reassess women's roles in these reform processes, we must avoid interpretations that disregard how they intervened with other agents. Recent studies, in the Iberian Peninsula and elsewhere, have shown the prominent role of women as agents in reform processes, but they have also shown that they did not act alone but collaborated with other agents: the bishops, the regular clergy, the nobility, the monarchs and other lay patrons.[13] As the agents involved in these intersections were different from one nunnery to another, the consequences in all aspects of monastic life varied also from place to place, and from one reform process to another, showing the complexity of these processes, and also the diversity of gendered responses.

In late medieval Castile, we can distinguish two major turning points for reform processes. The second half of the twelfth century and the turn of the thirteenth century coincided with a renewal of monastic life throughout the kingdoms of Christian Spain. This period saw the appearance of new religious orders: notably the Cistercians, the mendicants, the Military and Hospitaller orders, and the foundation of female communities associated with them. One of the more remarkable aspects of this moment was the progressive orientation of 'family monasteries', which were monastic seigneuries, properties of lay aristocratic families, towards Benedictine monasticism, until their disappearance at the turn of the thirteenth century.[14] This was the third and last stage of this evolving process of monastic family institutions and, as well as being Benedictine, patrons also favoured the adoption of the reformed practices of the Cistercian Order.[15] The second turning point was the so-called Observant reform that, between the end of the fourteenth century and the turn of the sixteenth century, brought about significant changes

---

[13] Diana Lucía Gómez-Chacón, 'Reinas y Predicadores: el Monasterio de Santa María la Real de Nieva en tiempos de Catalina de Lancaster y María de Aragón (1390–1445)', in María Dolores Teijeira Pablos, María Victoria Herráez Ortega and María Concepción Cosmen (eds), *Reyes y prelados: la creación artística en los reinos de León y Castilla (1050–1500)* (Madrid, 2014), pp. 325–40; *Id.*, 'Religiosidad femenina y reforma dominicana: el sepulcro de Beatriz de Portugal en el monasterio del Sancti Spiritus de Toro', *Anuario de Estudios Medievales*, 47:2 (2017), 607–45; Duval, '*Comme des anges sur terre*'. See as well the papers presented at the conference *Political and Ecclesiastical Agents in the Reform(s) of the Religious Orders in Europe during the Late Middle Ages (c. 1250–1500)*, Complutense University of Madrid, November 24–6, 2021.

[14] Pascual Martínez Sopena, 'Aristocracia, monacato y reformas en los siglos XI y XII', in *El monacato en los reinos de León y Castilla (siglos VII–XIII), X Congreso de Estudios Medievales 2005* (Ávila, 2007), pp. 67–100, at p. 92.

[15] Gregoria Cavero Domínguez, 'Spanish Female Monasticism: "Family" Monasteries and Their Transformation (Eleventh to Twelfth Centuries)', in Janet Burton and Karen Stöber (eds), *Women in the Medieval Monastic World* (Turnhout, 2015), pp. 15–52, at pp. 26 and 46.

in devotional, liturgical and religious life. Despite the significant differences between these two processes, they shared some elements that constituted the vehicles and threads through which reform advanced, namely liturgical books and female aristocratic networks. Unfortunately, women's active role in liturgy as well as in the commission and circulation of liturgical books remains an understudied topic for the Iberian Peninsula, one which is only now being addressed.[16] Thus, studies on reform for the Iberian region have mainly considered written official documents, overlooking, with some exceptions, other types of written sources, such as liturgical and devotional books, as well as material sources, like images, artworks and other artifacts.[17]

In this paper I will focus on the circulation of liturgical sources as a prism through which reform processes in female monasteries in late medieval Castile can be analysed. As mentioned, this was a common feature shared by the two major reform processes. Books were crucial for the shaping of these new Cistercian communities in the second half of the twelfth century and well beyond the turn of the thirteenth century, as well as for the spread of Observant reform ideas and practices. Thus, a broader comparative framework will allow us a better understanding of the key role of these sources, of the continuities and changes in their use over time, and of women's role in promoting liturgical and religious reform. We can pose many questions: who promoted these book transmissions and exchanges between communities and how did this operate in the reform in female monasteries in Castile? How do these books allow an analysis of these networks of monasticism and patronage? What was their function? I will try to answer some of these in the following pages, although, due to the emerging state of the research, and the limited number of examples here studied, only partial conclusions can be drawn. Finally, I will also consider other sources that at some point had a liturgical use and can be linked to processes of monastic renewal, such as the *Book of Devotions and Offices* [*Libro de Devociones y Oficios*] by Constanza de Castilla, and two illuminated copies of the *Commentary on the Apocalypse* by

---

[16] In particular, I'd like to mention the project of Pablo Acosta WiMPACT. *Late Medieval Visionary Women's Impact in Early Modern Castilian Spiritual Tradition*, hosted at the University of Düsseldorf (2019–2021), as well as Mercedes Pérez Vidal, 'La liturgia en la encrucijada de la reforma religiosa en los monasterios femeninos castellanos', paper presented at the conference *Political and Ecclesiastical Agents*.

[17] The importance of reform movements in relation to art and architecture has not been taken into consideration for Iberia until recently. See for instance Diana Lucía Gómez-Chacón, *El Monasterio de Santa María la Real de Nieva: reinas y predicadores en tiempo de reforma (1392–1445)* (Segovia, 2016); the project *Arte y reformas religiosas en la España medieval* (HAR2012-38037) at the Complutense University of Madrid; and, more recently, Mercedes Pérez Vidal, *Arte y liturgia en los monasterios de Dominicas en Castilla. Desde los orígenes hasta la reforma observante (1218–1506)* (Gijón, 2021).

Beatus of Liébana – the Las Huelgas Beatus and the Lorvão Beatus.[18] Although the stylistic and iconographic features of these Beatuses have been widely researched, neither their use in nuns' liturgy in this context of reform, nor the role played by women in this reform, have hitherto been analysed.

Books and Networks in Cistercian Renewal

As stated, Cistercian foundations were the most popular at this moment of renewal during the second half of the twelfth century. The first monastery of Cistercian nuns in the Iberian Peninsula was Santa María de La Caridad (Tulebras), established in 1147, which in turn was the impetus for founding several other Cistercian nunneries in the second half of the twelfth century: Perales (near Palencia, 1160), Gradefes (near León, 1169), Cañas (in La Rioja, 1170), Vallbona (near Lleida, 1173), Trasobares (near Zaragoza, 1182) and Las Huelgas (Burgos, 1187).[19] However, we should remember that during the twelfth century, when the Cistercian Order, in the current sense of the term, was still taking shape, the reference to the *Ordo cisterciensis* when founding female communities was a way to adopt certain practices and to claim a particular religious identity, but did not necessarily imply an institutional relationship with Cistercians. This was the situation before 1213 when, with the aim to centralise administrative control, the General Chapter assumed responsibility for the admission of female communities.[20]

Circulation of books was considered fundamental in these foundational processes, and was something that had been established since the origins of the Cistercian Order to assure liturgical uniformity. Indeed, the Cistercian General Chapter Statutes [*Instituta Generalis Capituli*] determined which liturgical books should be carried to a new foundation, and this remained in the *Statuta Capitulorum* at least until 1400: 'Missals, book of the epistles, rules and customaries, psalters, hymnaries, collectaries, antiphonaries, lectionaries and graduals' ['Missali, Epistolari, Textu Regula libro usum, Psalterio, Hymnario, Collectaneo, Antiphonario, Lectionario, Graduali'].[21] However, this was the theoretical and ideal situation; reality was frequently very different, and this desired uniformity

---

[18] See further, pp. 162–8.
[19] Raquel Alonso Álvarez, 'Promotores de la Orden del Císter en los reinos de Castilla y León: familias aristocráticas y damas nobles', *Anuario de Estudios Medievales*, 37:2 (2007), 653–710.
[20] Ghislain Baury, *Les religieuses de Castille: Patronage aristocratique et ordre cistercien (XIIe-XIIIe siècles)* (Rennes, 2012), pp. 117–26.
[21] A.R.P.D. Juliano, Solesmis, E. Typographeo (ed.), *Instituta Capituli Generalis Ordinis Cisterciensis Nomasticon Cisterciense, seu Antiquiores ordinis Cisterciensis constitutions* (Sancti Petri, 1892), p. 215.

was not achieved in many cases.[22] In twelfth-century Castile, convents were thinly populated and their members came from the local aristocracy who, as stated, controlled these institutions. The small size of the convents might have been expected to hamper the circulation of books, as well as nuns, from one monastery to a new foundation.[23] As we will see, it is indeed very likely that such exchanges did not occur only through the network of the Cistercian Order.[24] Hence, we must consider other networks operating at a local, national and international level: aristocratic networks, female networks and those based on kinship. An overlapping interaction of networks was not only frequent, but indeed the historical norm.[25] The study of this interplay will illustrate the multidirectional interactions generated by institutional reform, and the liturgical, cultural and artistic exchanges linked to them.

We can easily see how this complex interaction between different networks operates in the case of the monastery of Las Huelgas in Burgos. The books preserved from this foundation circulated through different networks: that of the Cistercian Order, operating at different levels, and with different centres (not only Cîteaux, but in our case also the male Cistercian monastery of Alcobaça, in Portugal); and the aristocratic networks created by some noble women or nuns. Some of these books had a foreign origin and underwent a long journey before reaching the monastic institution which now holds them, in this case, Las Huelgas.[26] A known example is the manuscript now known as Martyrology I, which was actually a *Liber Capituli* that made its way to Burgos from Cîteaux.[27]

The late twelfth-century antiphonary (now Las Huelgas Ms. 10) also had a provenance outside of Las Huelgas, and it, too, probably circulated through

---

[22] Catarina Fernandes Barreira, 'Um missal alcobacense dos micios do séc. XIV (Alc. 26)', in Gerardo Boto Varela, Xavier Barral Altet and Alessandra Bilotta (eds), *Medieval Europe in Motion: The Circulation of Artists, Images, Patterns and Ideas from the Mediterranean to the Atlantic Coast (6th–15th centuries)* (Palermo, 2018), pp. 151–68.

[23] Baury, *Les religieuses de Castille*, p. 123.

[24] Studied by the projects *Cistercian Horizons* (PTDC/ART-HIS/29522/2017), or *Aragonia Cisterciensis* (HAR2015- 63772-P).

[25] Caroline Levine, *Forms. Whole, Rhythm, Hierarchy, Network* (Princeton, 2015), p. 113.

[26] On the books from Las Huelgas see Ana Suárez González, 'Entre renglones y al margen (de libros y monjas cistercienses en los siglos XII-XIII)', in Daniele Arciello, Jesús Paniagua Pérez and Nuria María Rosa Salazar Simarro (eds), *Desde el clamoroso silencio. Estudios del monacato femenino en América, Portugal y España de los orígenes a la actualidad* (Berlin, 2021), pp. 69–104, at pp. 84–91.

[27] Ana Suárez determined that it was made between 1236 and 1247 for Cîteaux, where it was used, as marginal notes show. Later, the book travelled to Burgos, sometime between 1240 and 1287, probably during the abbatiate of the abbess Eva (1261-2): Ana Suárez González, 'Un ex libris y algunas respuestas sobre el "MS.1" de las Huelgas de Burgos', *Cistercium*, 245 (2006), 587-614.

networks created by aristocratic women involved in religious reform. Despite other previous interpretations, more recent studies have shown how the musical notation of this manuscript was modelled on that of Clairvaux whereas its artistic features point to the male Cistercian monastery of Alcobaça in Portugal as its probable origin.[28] How did it come to Las Huelgas? We have no evidence, although its illumination shows affinities with other Portuguese manuscripts from female Cistercian monasteries, namely two antiphonaries from Arouca and a gradual from Lorvão.[29] All of them are examples of a regional interpretation of the so-called '1200 style'.[30] Due to their stylistic affinities, these manuscripts seem to have been produced in Alcobaça, from whence they would have been disseminated to the Cistercian female foundations of Lorvão and Arouca.[31] Although all three monasteries were incorporated into the Cistercian Order in the second or third decade of the thirteenth century,[32] the agents or promoters of this circulation seem to have been different women of the Portuguese royal house who had a close relationship with these monasteries, as well as with the kingdoms of León and Castile. They were the *infanta* Mafalda, her sister, the *infanta* Teresa, and Branca de Portugal. Mafalda (*c.* 1195–1256), introduced Cistercian observance in the previously Benedictine foundation of Arouca.[33] She left bequests of books in

---

[28] Manuel Pedro Ferreira, 'Early Cistercian Polyphony: A Newly-Discovered Source', *Lusitania Sacra*, 2a série, 13–14 (2001–2), 267–313.

[29] Arouca, Museu de Arte Sacra, Antiphonary temporale, Ms. MASSAM 21, and Antiphonary santorale, Ms. MASSAM 25; Lisboa, Arquivo Nacional da Torre do Tombo, Gradual, PT-TT-MSML-B-15. Luís Correia da Sousa and Adelaide Miranda, 'Confluências artísticas em torno de 1200: manuscritos iluminados cistercienses – Alcobaça e Las Huelgas Reales de Burgos', in Marta Poza Yagüe and Diana Olivares Martínez (eds), *Alfonso VIII y Leonor de Inglaterra. Confluencias artísticas en el entorno de 1200* (Madrid, 2017), pp. 423–43.

[30] The term '1200 style' was coined by the exhibition of the Metropolitan Museum of Art, New York, in 1970, 'The Year 1200', to distinguish the uniqueness of the art produced during the decades around this year, between 1180 and 1230. This innovative style was characterised by a stylistic proximity with the works of Antiquity combined with the use of Byzantine motifs. See Willibald Sauerländer, 'Entre le roman et le gothique: style de transition, Alternativgotik et "style 1200"', *Perspective*, 4 (2008), 756–61.

[31] Fernando Galván Freile, 'El proceso de internacionalización de la miniatura en torno al año 1200 en la Península Ibérica: el antifonario de Las Huelgas Reales de Burgos', in Juan Ignacio Ruiz de la Peña Solar (ed.), *El monacato en los reinos de León y Castilla (siglos VII–XIII)* (Ávila, 2007), pp. 437–56.

[32] Alfonso VIII placed Las Huelgas in the direct filiation of Cîteaux in 1199: Baury, *Les religieuses de Castille*, pp. 145–9.

[33] Arouca was incorporated into the Order by the General Chapter in the 1220s. Luís Rêpas, 'As abadessas cistercienses na Idade Média: identificação, caracterização e estudo de trajectórias individuais ou familiares', *Lusitania Sacra*, 2a série. 17 (2005), 63–91, at p. 65.

her will: she ordered the return of a portable bible (Bibliotheca Nacional de Portugal, Alc, 458), to the monks of Alcobaça, from whom she had borrowed it; she donated a psalter to Arouca and a Book of Hours to her sister, Doña Urraca Sanches.[34] Her sister, the *infanta* Teresa Sanches (c. 1176–1250), was patron of the Benedictine male monastery of São Mamede de Lorvão. In 1206, the Benedictine monks were forced to leave, and they were replaced by a community of nuns who were officially recognised as Cistercian by papal decree in 1211.[35] Finally, at a later date, the *infanta* Branca de Portugal (1259–1321) became *senhora* of Lorvão in 1277 and later of Las Huelgas (from 1295 to her death in 1321).[36] We have no additional evidence, but this connection suggests that Branca may have donated the aforementioned antiphonary to Las Huelgas.[37] Thus, this network of female kinship overlapped the Cistercian network, or it was even more important, reinforcing it or creating new relationships, bonds and intersections. Also, as we have seen, and we will see in further examples, these networks extended to the neighbouring kingdom of Castile.

Together with liturgical books, we must also consider sources not specifically liturgical, but used at some point in the liturgy, for example some hagiographical or exegetical texts that were also commissioned by and for women and can be linked to the implementation of reform.[38] A good example of this category of source are the several copies of the illuminated *Commentary on the Apocalypse*, by Beatus of Liébana, that were produced between the end of the twelfth century and the beginning of the thirteenth century, mainly in or for royally favoured monasteries of Cistercian nuns.[39] These manuscripts seem to have been related to a movement based on renewal in Cistercian nunneries; however, neither the meaning of the

---

[34] Correia da Sousa and Miranda, 'Confluências artísticas em torno de 1200', p. 430.
[35] Rêpas, 'As abadesas cistercienses', p. 65.
[36] Luis Rêpas, 'Esposas de Cristo: as comunidades cistercienses femininas na Idade Média' (unpublished Ph.D. thesis, Universidade de Coimbra, 2021), vol. 1, pp. 280 and 396; Araceli Castro Garrido, *Documentación del Monasterio de las Huelgas de Burgos (1307-1321)* (Burgos: 1987), pp. 322–33.
[37] Ferreira, 'Early Cistercian Polyphony', 269; Galván Freile, 'El proceso de internacionalización', pp. 449–50.
[38] On exegesis among Cistercians monks and nuns in the Iberian Peninsula see Ghislain Baury, 'Singuli in singulis libris legentes. Exégèse et lectio divina dans les cloîtres cisterciens ibériques, XIIe–XVe siècle', *Mélanges de la Casa de Velázquez*, 49-1 (2019), 85–106 (Online: http://journals.openedition.org/mcv/10298; DOI: https://doi.org/10.4000/mcv.10298 [both accessed 7 May 2022].
[39] The Cistercian monks of Alcobaça, and those of Poblet, also had copies of the Beatus. Lisboa, Biblioteca Nacional de Portugal, Ms. 247, and Universidad de Salamanca, Ms. 2632. As pointed out by Ghislain Baury, the significant presence of Commentaries on the Apocalypse by Beatus of Liébana was an Iberian peculiarity. Ghislain Baury, 'Singuli in singulis libris legentes', 85–106.

circulation of these copies and their use in nuns' liturgy in this context of reform, nor the role of women in all this, have hitherto been examined. I will focus here on two of these copies: the so-called Las Huelgas Beatus and the Lorvão Beatus.

The Lorvão Beatus, now in the Archivo Nacional da Torre do Tombo, was illuminated by Egeas and finished in 1189, according to the colophon. Although the colophon did not mention the origin, a comparison with other manuscripts produced in Lorvão's scriptorium around this time makes it clear that the Beatus was also copied there, when it was still a Benedictine monastery. Stylistically and iconographically it followed a much older, unknown version of the Beatus's commentary, making it unique.[40]

Although belonging to a different group or *stemma* in the Beatus family, the so called Beatus of Las Huelgas, now in the Morgan Library (Ms. 429) and completed in 1220, was also inspired by an older version, namely the Beatus of Tábara, finished in 970 in a mixed community (including monks and nuns).[41] We know that this Beatus was in Las Huelgas in the eighteenth century when it was studied by Enrique Flórez.[42] However, the question of where it was produced has not been settled.[43] According to David Raizman, this copy may have been commissioned for a political-dynastical purpose by Queen Berenguela (1180-1246), daughter of the founders of Las Huelgas, Alfonso VIII and Leonor Plantagenet. Berenguela lived in the monastery after the dissolution of her marriage with Alfonso IX of León in 1204.[44] However, this attribution lacks strong arguments. Berenguela is not mentioned in the colophon or anywhere else in the manuscript, and this is difficult to explain if she had commissioned it. On the other hand, Raizman himself has considered that the characteristics and style of the miniature and the script of the manuscript point towards an origin in Toledo.[45] At this point, a cross checked analysis with monastic inventories could help to establish its origin. The female Benedictine monastery of San Clemente de Toledo was another monastery generously supported by the founder of Las Huelgas. In 1175 Alfonso VIII placed

---

[40] Anne de Egry, *Um estudo de o Apocalipse de Lorvão e a sua relaçao com as ilustraçoes medievais do Apocalipse* (Lisbon, 1972), p. 21.

[41] Madrid, Archivo Histórico Nacional, Cod. 1097B.

[42] Enrique Flórez (ed.), *Sancti Beati Presbyteri Hispani Liebanensis in Apocalypsin Ac Plurimas Utriusque Foederis Paginas Commentaria* (Madrid, 1770), p. xxxviii.

[43] John Williams and Therese Martin, 'Women's Spaces – Real and Imagined – in the Illustrated Beatus Commentaries', *Arenal*, 25:2 (2018), 357-96.

[44] David Raizman, 'Prayer, Patronage, and Piety at Las Huelgas: New Observations on the Later Morgan Beatus (M. 429)', in Therese Martin and Julie A. Harris (eds), *Church, State, Vellum, and Stone. Essays on Medieval Spain in Honor of John Williams* (Leiden, 2005), p. 242.

[45] Ibid., p. 256.

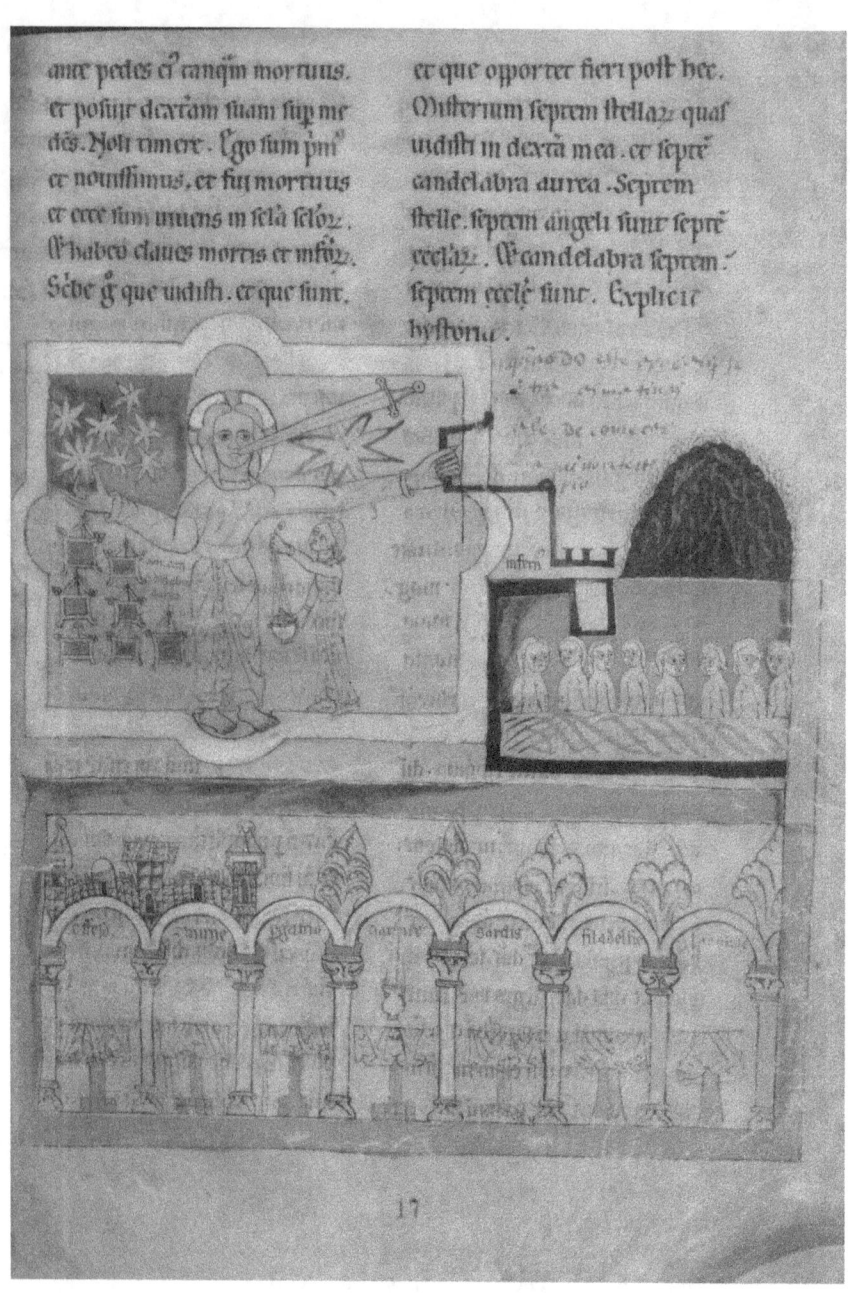

Fig. 7.1. The Lorvão Beatus. São Mamede de Lorvão, codex 44, PT/TT/MSML/B/44, f. 17r. 'Quando este apocalypse entra as matinas a se de começar aqui no Refeitorio'. © Arquivo Nacional da Torre do Tombo, Lisboa.

this monastery symbolically under the authority of the abbot of Cîteaux.[46] One of the earliest inventories preserved from female monasteries in the whole Iberian Peninsula comes from San Clemente. It was made in 1331 by the 'caput scholae cantorum',[47] Urraca López, and it lists sixty-four books and fifteen individual quires that were kept in different places: in the enclosure area, in the nuns' choir and in the refectory.[48] Among the latter, we find a volume of the Apocalypse: 'un libro que dicen Apocalipsi' ['a book called Apocalypse']. Although it has been recognised as the *Expositio in Apocalypsim* by Joachim of Fiore (m. 1201-2),[49] I would like to suggest a possible identification with the Las Huelgas Beatus. This last was sold to the Morgan Library in 1910 by the nuns of San Clemente de Toledo.[50] Could it have been in San Clemente de Toledo at least in 1331, being subsequently moved to Las Huelgas and later returned to Toledo? We would need more evidence to confirm this suggestive hypothesis, but, as we have seen, the circulation of books between Cistercian foundations was common, even more so between two important female houses both under royal protection.

Regarding the function of these Beatus manuscripts, we should not forget that the particular use of a book cannot always be safely inferred from the text alone, but we should consider other material evidences of the manuscripts: additions, annotations of scribes, ex libris, etc. Some marginal notes, added at a later moment in both Beatus manuscripts, provide interesting information regarding this point. First Anne de Egry and then Peter Klein have pointed out that, at least by the later Middle Ages, each copy had been adapted to be read in the refectory

---

[46] Baury, *Les religieuses de Castille*, p. 131
[47] The monastic *cantrix* was the nun who supervised all aspects of music-making and liturgical performance. She was also in charge of the library in the absence of a librarian. About this office in female monasteries in medieval England see Katie Ann-Marie Bugyis, 'Female Monastic Cantors and Sacristans in Central Medieval England: Four Sketches', in Katie Ann-Marie Bugyis, A. B. Kraebel and Margot. E. Fassler (eds), *Medieval Cantors and their Craft, Music, Liturgy and the Shaping of History, 800–1500* (York, 2017), pp. 151–71.
[48] Ramón Fernández Pousa, 'Catálogo de una biblioteca española del año 1331: el monasterio de San Clemente, de Toledo', *Revista de bibliografía nacional*, 1 (1940), 48–50. Nevertheless, the original inventory has not been preserved but this was copied in a Cartulary from 1753 from this monastery, and then in a manuscript by the Jesuit Andrés Marcos Burriel (Madrid, Biblioteca Nacional de España, Ms. 13058, fols 158–9 and fols 2–3).
[49] Pedro M. Cátedra, 'Lectura femenina en el claustro (España, siglos XIV–XVI)', in Dominique de Courcelles and Carmen Val Julian (eds), *Des femmes et des livres: France et Espagne, XIVe–XVIIe siècle* (Paris, 1999), pp. 7–54, at pp. 19–20.
[50] John Williams, *Visions of the End in Medieval Spain: Catalogue of Illustrated Beatus Commentaries on the Apocalypse and Study of the Geneva Beatus* (Amsterdam, 2017), p. 135.

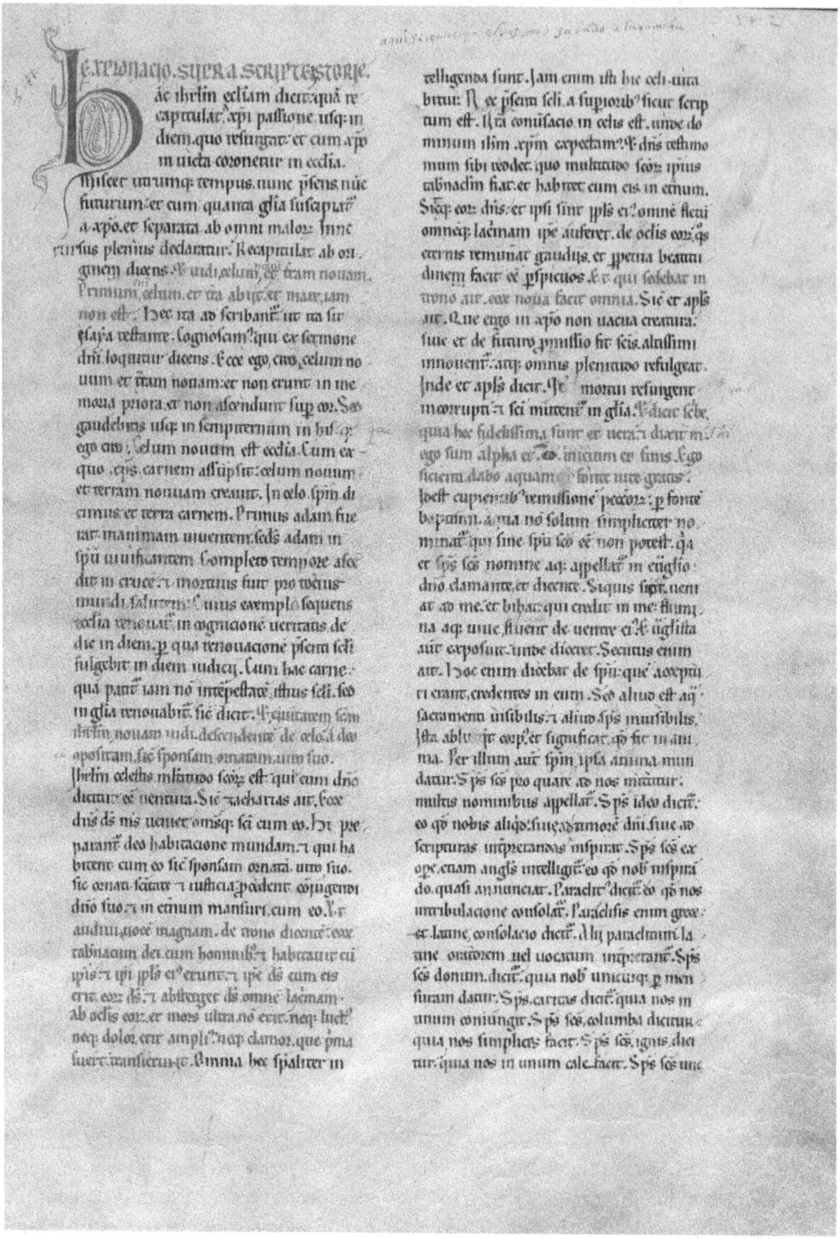

Fig. 7.2. Beatus, Saint, Presbyter of Liébana, Commentary on the Apocalypse. Spain, probably Toledo, *c.* 1220; Las Huelgas. The Morgan Library & Museum. MS M.429. Purchased by J. Pierpont Morgan (1837–1913) in 1910, f. 142r. Photo: The Morgan Library & Museum, New York.

at the respective Cistercian nunnery.[51] The Lorvão Beatus has marginal notations on folios 12 and 17, made at the end of the fifteenth century or the beginning of the sixteenth century, which prove not only that this manuscript was still in use, but also that is was to be read in the refectory at matins: 'Quando este apocalypse entra as matinas a se de começar aqui no Refeitorio', that is to say: 'when the Beatus was read at Matins the reading should start here in the refectory'.[52] Klein interpreted a marginal note in the Las Huelgas Beatus (fol. 142r) in the same way.[53]

When did this liturgical practice commence, and what was its meaning for these religious communities? The reading of the Vulgate Apocalypse in the church had already been established at a very early date in the Visigothic Kingdom. The Fourth Council of Toledo (633) ordered that this would take place during the Mass, from Easter to Pentecost: 'aut a Pascha usque ad Pentecosten missarum tempore in ecclesia'.[54] Furthermore, the reading of the Apocalypse (and we assume that this includes also the Commentaries on the Apocalypse), was a common practice, attested by a number of *Libri ordinarii* and customaries from Rome, Cluny and other abbeys and cathedrals in Central Europe.[55] Subsequently, due to the impossibility of carrying out all these readings in the church, they were read in the refectory.[56] We do not know from what date this practice was curent in these Cistercian female monasteries (Lorvão, and either Las Huelgas in Burgos, or San Clemente de Toledo), but the date of the mentioned additions suggests a possible relationship with the introduction of the Observant reform. Why the Apocalypse or its Commentaries were important for the Observant agenda is a question that deserves further analysis. In any case, we know that these texts

---

[51] An example of an alternative purpose can be found in the glossed Apocalypse that is listed in the inventory from St Mary in Lemgo, compiled fifty-five years later (1386). It was listed among the schoolbooks, so apparently had an educational rather than liturgical purpose. Jeffrey F. Hamburger, Eva Schlotheuber, Susan Marti and Margot Fassler (eds), *Liturgical Life and Latin Learning at Paradies bei Soest, 1300–1425* (2 vols, Münster, 2016), vol. 2, Appendix B, n. 60. See also vol. 1, p. 84.

[52] Egry, *Um estudo de o Apocalipse de Lorvão*, p. 30.

[53] 'Aquí se comiença el postrer sábado a la comida': Peter Klein, *Beato de Liébana. La ilustración de los manuscritos de Beato y el Apocalpsis de Lorvão* (Valencia, 2004), p. 48.

[54] José Vives, *Concilios visigóticos e hispano-romanos* (Barcelona, 1963), p. 198.

[55] Peter Klein, 'Circulation, Popularity and Function of Illustrated Apocalypses from the Late Antiquity to High Medieval Europe', in Alicia Miguélez Cavero and Fernando Villaseñor Sebastián (eds), *Medieval Europe in Motion: La Circulación de Manuscritos Iluminados en la Península Ibérica* (Madrid, 2018), pp. 201–14, at p. 205.

[56] This is clear already in some eleventh- and twelfth-century customaries. Teresa Webber, *Reading in the Refectory. Monastic Practice in England, ca. 1000–ca. 1300* (London, 2010), p. 22.

were still very popular in 1572, judging by the numerous copies that Ambrosio de Morales saw on his trip through León, Galicia and Asturias in 1572.[57]

As we have seen, readings in the refectory were also part of the liturgy and, indeed, were to be performed with the same solemnity as the Divine Office in the choir. Reformers insisted on that point, as we can read for instance in the treatise that Hernando de Talavera (1428–1507) wrote at the end of the fifteenth century to Cistercian nuns in Ávila: 'de vagar, bien entonada, bien pausada y pronunciada, como se dice en el choro quando más sollennemente cantáis los maytines' ['Well-toned, well measured and pronounced, as it is said in the choir when you sing more solemnly matins'].[58] Talavera's work was one of the few texts written specifically to guide a community of nuns. However, it had a much wider dissemination, beyond Ávila and the Cistercian Order. For instance, one of its preserved copies is included in a miscellaneous volume from Sancti Spiritus in Salamanca, a female foundation of the Spanish Order of St Jacques, together with the *Rule* of St Augustine, the constitutions of the order of St Jacques, a report on the reform of the monastery and some regulations on liturgical celebrations.[59] This literature of formation circulated widely among communities inspired by religious reform at the end of the fifteenth century. Although more examples would be needed to draw solid conclusions about the specific meaning and function these manuscripts had for religious communities, the examples here discussed have shown that liturgical and other books with a liturgical function or use circulated broadly among Cistercian nuns in Castile. Female royal patronage was often an important (but not exclusive) vector in the circulation of these manuscripts. As several of these manuscripts can also be linked with the late twelfth- and thirteenth-century reform movement in Castile, they show a network of female kinship coinciding with a Cistercian network in spreading reformist ideals. Furthermore, as the Beatus manuscripts have shown, there are also clear indications that these manuscripts equally influenced women's adoption of later reform movements, like the Observant reform. The following section will explore this further to better understand the pioneering role of women as promotors of religious change.

---

[57] Ambrosio de Morales, in Enrique Flórez (ed.), *Viage de Ambrosio de Morales por Orden del Rei D. Felipe II a los reinos de León y Galicia y Principado de Asturias* (Madrid, 1765).

[58] Cécile Codet (ed.), 'Suma y breve compilación de cómo han de bivir y conversar las religiosas de Sant Bernardo que biven en los monasterios de la cibdad de Ávila de Hernando de Talavera (Biblioteca del Escorial, ms. a.IV-29)', *Memorabilia*, 14 (2012), 1–57, at p. 34.

[59] Salamanca, Library of the University of Salamanca, Ms. 2236.

Women as Pioneers of the Observant Reform

In Talavera's list of books to be read in the refectory we find St Jerome's works: the *Epistola ad Eustochium de virginitate servanda*, the *Life, death and miracles* [*Vida, muerte y Milagros*] and his *Regula sanctimonialium*. The influence of St Jerome, through his letters, on the Observant movement's conception of female monasticism is undeniable.[60] In particular, copies of the *Epistola ad Eustochium* were common in reformed monasteries.[61] Indeed, the Observant movement took Paula and Eustochium as a model for nuns, and we find for instance nuns with these names in the reformed community of Santo Domingo de Toledo at the end of the fifteenth century.[62]

Some scholars have recently pointed out the necessity of reconsidering the active role of women in the implementation of Observant reform in Castile as well as the relationship between some queens, other members of the household of the queen, and certain royal monasteries in promoting the ideals of religious reform.[63] But what were these ideals? The movement for monastic renewal known as the 'Observance' promoted the return to a fundamental monastic value: obedience. In the case of the female monasteries, the application of this precept had a series of implications including strict enclosure, common life, the presence of friars-vicars,[64] or the liturgical uniformity within a religious order.[65] In the

---

[60] Duval, '*Comme des anges sur terre*', p. 51

[61] For instance, a vernacular translation of the *Epistola ad Eustochio* was copied in an interesting miscellaneous codex from the Benedictine nunnery Santa Maria di Porciglia in Padua, together with the episcopal act of visitation in 1487: Padua, Biblioteca Civica of Padua, 893.

[62] Mercedes Pérez Vidal, 'La Reforma de los monasterios de dominicas en Castilla. Agentes, etapas y consecuencias', *Archivo Dominicano*, 36 (2015), 197–237, at pp. 214–17; Pérez Vidal, *Arte y liturgia*, p. 80.

[63] Felipe Pereda, 'Liturgy as Women's Language: Two Noble Patrons Prepare for the End in Fifteenth-Century Spain', in Therese Martin (ed.), *Reassessing the Roles of Women as 'Makers' of Medieval Art and Architecture* (2 vols, Leiden, 2012), vol. 2, pp. 937–88; María del Mar Graña Cid, 'Favoritas de la corona? Los amores del rey y la promoción de la orden de Santa Clara en Castilla (ss. XIII–XIV)', *Anuario de Estudios Medievales*, 44:1 (2014), 179–213; Pérez Vidal, 'La Reforma de los monasterios'; Juan Antonio Prieto Sayagués, 'El mecenazgo femenino en los monasterios y conventos de Castilla (1350–1474): poder y espiritualidad', in Miguel García-Fernández and Sylvia Cernadas Martínez (eds), *Reginae Iberiae. El poder femenino en los reinos medievales peninsulares* (Santiago de Compostela, 2015), pp. 193–211; Lucía, 'Religiosidad femenina y reforma'; García Herrero, María del Carmen and Ángela Muñoz Fernández,'Reginalidad y fundaciones monásticas en las Coronas de Castilla y de Aragón', *Edad Media: revista de historia*, 18 (2017), 16-48.

[64] Duval, '*Comme des anges sur terre*', pp. 572–3.

[65] Jürgen Bärsch, 'Liturgy and Reform: Northern German Convents in the Late Middle

following, I will analyse some of the early efforts to introduce Observant ideas promoted by certain prioresses and patrons in mendicant monasteries in Castile, both Poor Clares and Dominican nunneries.

Bert Roest distinguished at least six or seven Observant reform movements among Franciscan nuns, of which the first was the Castilian Congregation of Tordesillas, started in 1380 at the eponymous monastery, and that constituted a network of monasteries under the control of a permanent visitator.[66] Significantly, however, both Maria de Padilla (c. 1334–61) and her daughter Beatriz earlier had used the expression 'regularis observantia' in the documents addressed to their respective monasteries of Poor Clares in Astudillo and Tordesillas.[67] Queen Juana Manuel promoted the reform in this last, between 1376 and her death in 1381. She did it not alone but in collaboration with other women (her sister-in-law, her niece, the abbess and the nuns), as well as friar Pedro Fernández Pecha, founder of the Order of St Jerome.[68]

Although less well known, some Dominican nuns, both prioresses and patrons, also fostered reform in their nunneries at an earlier time.[69] Catherine of Lancaster (1373–1418) had a strong devotion to the Order of Preachers. She founded the female monastery of San Pedro Mártir in Mayorga de Campos (1394) and the male convent of Santa María la Real de Nieva (1392). She was also protector of Santo Domingo de Toledo, to which she made generous donations, as she also did to Santa Cruz la Real in Segovia. She was stepsister of Philippa of Lancaster (1387–1415), queen of Portugal, where the first Observant Dominican foundations were established at the end of the fourteenth century: São Salvador of Lisbon (1391) and São Domingo of Benfica (1399). As Diana Lucía has pointed out, this relationship may have contributed to an earlier introduction of Observant reform in Castile, even before the Council of Constance (1414–18).[70] Although these are convincing indications that Queen Catherine was strongly devoted to the Order of the Preachers, we should, however, be cautious to brand her as the initiator of Observant Dominican life in Castile. Lucía has asserted that San Pedro Mártir in Mayorga de Campos, founded by Queen Catharine, was the first Observant Dominican female foundation in Castile,

---

Ages', in Elizabeth Andersen, Henrike Lähnemann and Anne Simon (eds), *A Companion to Mysticism and Devotion in Northern Germany in the Late Middle Ages* (Leiden, 2013), pp. 21–46, at pp. 22–3.

[66] Bert Roest, 'Observances "féminines" dans la famille franciscaine: phénomènes bouleversants, pluralistes et multipolaires', *Mélanges de l'École française de Rome Moyen Âge*, 130:2 (2018) (https://doi.org/10.4000/mefrm.4250) [accessed 10 December 2022].

[67] Graña Cid, 'Favoritas de la corona?', p. 198.

[68] Cynthia Robinson, 'La Orden Jerónima y el Convento de Clarisas de Santa María la Real de Tordesillas', *Reales sitios: revista del Patrimonio Nacional*, 169 (2006), 13–33.

[69] On the Observant reform in Dominican female monasteries in Castile, see Pérez Vidal, *Arte y liturgia*, pp. 71–84.

[70] Lucía, *El Monasterio de Santa María la Real de Nieva*, pp. 57–8.

describing her as the promoter of the Observance in Castile.[71] However tantalising, this claim might go too far, as none of the original foundational documents have been preserved. Moreover, the alleged influence exerted by friar Álvaro de Córdoba on the reformist ideas of Queen Catherine of Lancaster, and thus his role in the foundation of San Pedro Mártir de Mayorga de Campos, is not clear.[72] Although it is true that this Dominican reformer was also a royal confessor, he held this office at later dates, between 1418 and 1422. It is a reminder to always take the complexity of reform initiatives and dynamics into mind.

Another example brings us to Sancti Spiritus de Toro. The *Libro Becerro* of this community states that Leonor Sánchez de Castilla, the illegitimate daughter of the *infante* Sancho de Castilla, prioress of Santi Spiritus de Toro (from c. 1411 to 1444) reformed the spiritual life of this Dominican monastery.[73] According to Lucía, this prioress was arguably one of the designers of the iconographic programme of Queen Beatriz of Portugal's tomb, together with the former queen herself. The sepulchre's decoration includes one of the first depictions of St Catherine of Siena in Castile, with the stigmata, which may imply an earlier devotion to St Catherine in those territories than hitherto considered, probably through the circulation of manuscripts containing her *vita*.[74] Although this has been considered unlikely,[75] it is the only way to explain the iconography of the sepulchre.[76] I would add that, though medieval documents attesting to Leonor's role as reformer have not survived, we have an interesting miscellaneous volume, whose contents can be only explained in an Observant context.[77] This includes several texts, among which are the translation of Guillaume Perrault's *De eruditione religiosorum libri VI* (c. 1260–5) by Pablo de Santa María, bishop of Burgos, made in 1421 and dedicated to this prioress, and a translation of Chapter XX of the *Summa de virtutibus et*

---

[71] Lucía, 'Reinas y Predicadores', pp. 325–40.
[72] *Ibid.*, pp. 334–7.
[73] Madrid, Archivo Histórico Nacional, Clero, Libros, 18314, Libro de Becerro para este Real Convento de Sancti Spiritus de Toro. Compuesto por el Padre Fray Vicente Velásquez de Figueroa, A.1775.
[74] Lucía, 'Religiosidad femenina y reforma dominicana', pp. 629–30 and pp. 634–6.
[75] Jeffrey Hamburger and Gabriela Signori (eds), *Catherine of Siena: The Creation of a Cult* (Turnhout, 2013), pp. 7, 11.
[76] As pointed out by Pablo Acosta, we still need a systematic study about any early dissemination of 'mystical' literature in either secular or religious contexts in Castile before the printed editions promoted by Cardinal Cisneros: Pablo Acosta García, 'On Manuscripts, Prints and Blessed Transformations: Caterina da Siena's *Legenda maior* as a Model of Sainthood in Premodern Castile', *Religions*, 11:1 (2020), 33.
[77] Madrid, Biblioteca Nacional de España, Ms. 21626. A description of the contents in Juan Carlos Conde, 'De nuevo sobre una traducción desconocida de Pablo de Santa María (y su parentela)', *Quaderns de Filología, Estudis Literaris*, 8 (2003), 171–88. I am grateful to Silvia Bara Bancel for bringing this book to my attention.

Fig. 7.3. Sancti Spiritus de Toro. Beatriz de Portugal's tomb, first quarter of the 15th century, detail of Saint Catherine of Siena. Alabaster (155 x 229 x 71cm). © Diana Lucía Gómez-Chacón.

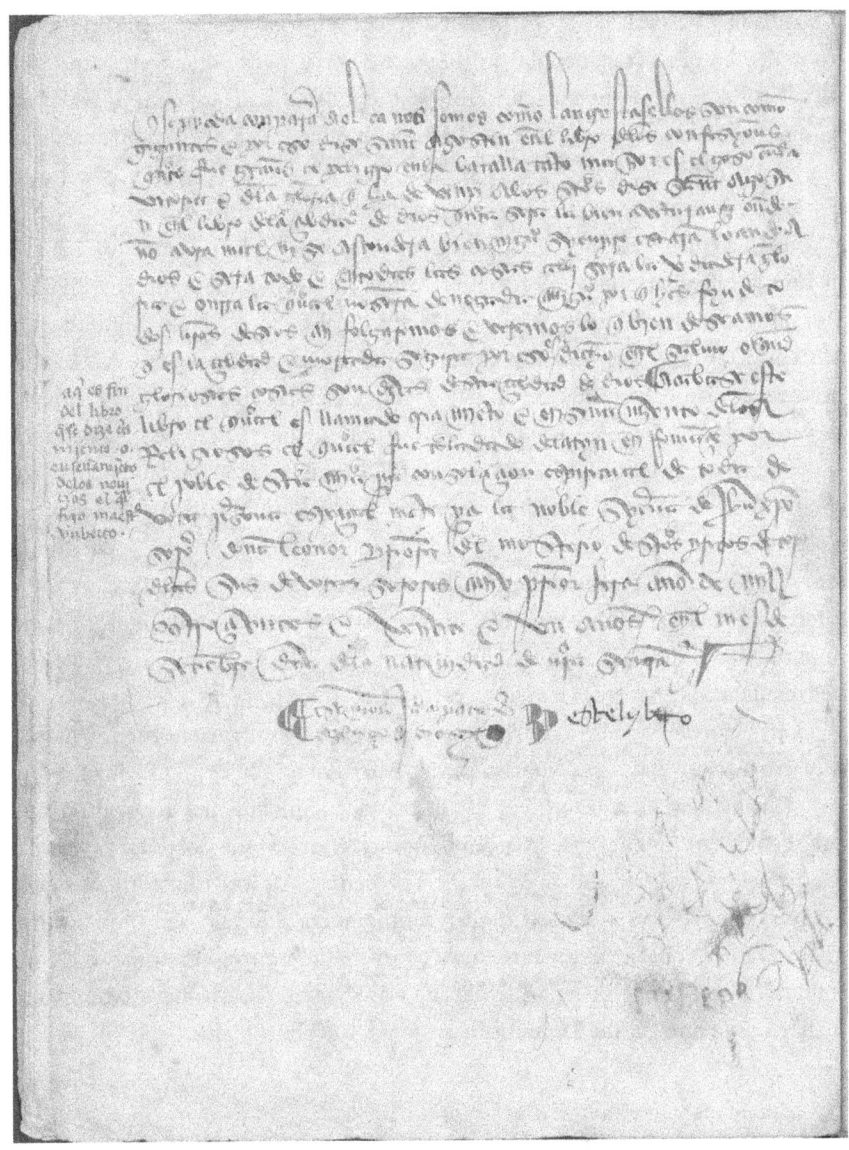

Fig. 7.4. Miscellaneous volume, Guillaume Perrault, *Libro del criamjento e enseñamiento de los religiosos*, translated by Pablo de Santa María in 1421, and dedicated to 'soror doña Leonor priora del mosterio [sic] de santosprtos [sic] de toro', Biblioteca Nacional de España, Madrid, MSS/21626, fol. 100v. © Biblioteca Nacional de España, Madrid.

vitiis, also by Perrault. Both works had a great diffusion both in manuscripts and printed exemplars (incunabula) in the Late Middle Ages. They were also quite successful among Observants, and the first was listed by Hernando de Talavera among the books to be read by nuns after compline.[78] The volume includes also the *Horologium Sapientiae* by Heinrich Seuse (1295–1366), whose devotional works were widely transmitted in communities of Observant nuns.[79]

In 1418, Queen Eleanor of Alburquerque, stepsister of the prioress Leonor of Sancti Spiritus de Toro, donated buildings she owned that adjoined another Dominican nunnery, Santa Maria in Medina del Campo, to this monastery.[80] Moreover, around this time she wrote a letter to her cousin, María de Castilla, prioress of Santo Domingo in Toledo, with a request to borrow an Ordinary in vernacular to make a copy. This copy was most likely intended as a gift for Santa María in Medina del Campo.[81] The Ordinary was a fundamental book, as any modification in it had to be approved by a General Chapter, like the Constitutions, so as to ensure the liturgical uniformity of the Order.[82] We do not know if this Ordinary was copied by the nuns themselves, but what is clear is the interest of the queen in maintaining uniformity with the Dominican liturgy, and in particular with the liturgy of Santo Domingo de Toledo, a monastery ruled by her relative.

Constanza de Castilla (d. 1478), prioress of Santo Domingo el Real de Madrid, was also a relative of these women, through her grandfather King Pedro I (1334–69). During her long priorate she undertook a fundamental renovation and enlargement of the monastery, rebuilding the refectory, the dormitory, perhaps the principal cloister, and the church. The main apse was transformed into a funerary chapel for King Pedro I and other members of her lineage, the Castilla.[83] The powerful Constanza was certainly a charismatic prioress and somewhat contradictory, since notwithstanding that she was characterised by her devotion and by her observance of the Dominican customs, she also obtained special licences

---

[78] Codet, 'Suma y breve compilación', p. 34.

[79] Jones, *Ruling the Spirit*, pp. 27–8.

[80] She kept for herself some dependencies in which she lived for five years, until she professed as nun: Juan López, *Tercera parte de la Historia de Sancto Domingo y de su Orden de Predicadores* (Valladolid, 1613, ed. Facsímile; Valladolid, 2003), fol. 28.

[81] Mercedes Pérez Vidal, 'The Art, Visual Culture and Liturgy of Dominican Nuns in Late Medieval and Early Modern Castile', in Sheila Barker and Luciano Cinelli (eds), *Artiste nel Chiostro. Produzione artistica nei monasteri femminili in età moderna* (Firenze, 2015), pp. 225–42, and 328–31, at p. 230.

[82] Raymond Creytens, 'L'ordinaire des Frères prêcheurs au Moyen Âge', *Archivum Fratrum Praedicatorum*, 24 (1954), 108–88.

[83] José María Eguren, *Memoria histórico-descriptiva del Monasterio de Santo Domingo el Real de Madrid* (Madrid, 1850), p. 21

from prelates of the Order to conduct a life that had more in common with the influential *señoras* than that of an Observant nun.[84] Apart from this renovation of the building, she had also an active role in the liturgy. She personally compiled her *Book of Devotions and Offices* [*Libro de Devociones y Oficios*][85] and she identified herself as the author of the content, which includes original elements in Latin and vernacular.[86] At least some parts of this book, in particular the bilingual *Office of the Nails* [*Oficio de los Clavos*], was not intended for her personal devotion but to be performed in the nuns' choir, with the dispensation of the pope and the Master General of the Order.[87] In 1451, the provincial Esteban de Sotelo (1449-54) authorised the nuns of Mater Dei to recite the Divine Office on feast days in the way that Constanza had directed.[88] Mater Dei was a new nunnery 'sub regulari observantia', whose foundation had been entrusted to Constanza by Pope Nicholas V between 1449 and 1451.[89] These concessions prove Constanza's reputation as Observant of the Dominican way of life among Dominican superiors and the pope, who at the same time recognised her authority in shaping the liturgical life of these communities to reflect her spiritual preferences.

In apparent contrast with Observant ideals, Constanza was permitted to live separately from the community, in her own lodgings around a secondary cloister, and she was allowed to leave the nunnery, when necessary, in order to visit her relatives or to address personal issues at the royal court.[90] This was not the only

---

[84] The *señoras* were traditionally linked to the Cistercian monastery of Las Huelgas, but recent scholarship has found more examples in other Cistercian, as well as in mendicant, monasteries. They oversaw the administration, having great power over the abbess, they acted as intermediaries, and they were in charge of keeping their lineage's memory. For a further discussion see Baury, *Les religieuses de Castille*, pp. 46-7 and 59-72.

[85] Madrid, Biblioteca Nacional de España, Ms. 7495.

[86] A complete modern edition of this text in: Constanza de Castilla, *Book of Devotions - Libro de devociones y oficios*, ed. Constance L. Wilkins (Exeter, 1998).

[87] Ronald. E. Surtz, 'Las oras de los clavos de Constanza de Castilla', in Liliana Von Der Walde Moreno, Concepción Company and Aurelio González (eds), *Caballeros, monjas y maestros en la Edad Media. Actas de las V Jornadas Medievales* (México, 1996), pp. 157-67.

[88] Madrid, Archivo Histórico Nacional, Clero, Libros, 7296, Libro de las licencias y gracias que los sumos pontífices y los Maestros Generales de la Orden de Predicadores concedieron a la Serenísima Señora Doña Constanza Nieta del Rey Don Pero y al Monasterio de Santo Domingo el Real de Madrid donde fue priora 38 años.

[89] The pope issued two bulls, the first on the 5 July 1449 and the second on 18 May 1451: Madrid, Archivo Histórico Nacional, Clero, Pergaminos, 1365/15, doc. n° 1713. Bull issued by Nicholas V on the 18 May 1451.

[90] All these privileges were collected in the aforementioned book: Archivo Histórico Nacional, Clero, Libros, 7296, Libro de las licencias y gracias.

case, as we find many other examples in Castile, starting with the aforementioned Queen Juana Manuel, and her sister-in-law, Leonor de Castro, who retired to Santa Clara de Tordesillas where they lived in her own lodgings outside the enclosure but connected to it.[91] Beatriz de Manrique (1405–71), wife of Pedro Fernández de Velasco, count of Haro, both of whom were promoters of Franciscan observance in Castile,[92] retired after her widowhood to the Poor Clares nunnery of Medina del Pomar. There, she built a house in the orchard to lodge some laywomen who came with her, as well as other pious women who could live at the nunnery without taking the vows.[93] Thus, as all these examples prove, there was no contradiction between promoting Observant ideals and aristocratic women living in their own lodgings in a convent. On the contrary, this custom was explicitly authorised in some cases and it had a continuity even after the Council of Trent, as did nuns' involvement in the secular world.[94]

The Dominican Provincial of Spain, Luis de Valladolid (1419–13), who granted Constanza de Castilla the aforementioned and other privileges, also encouraged reformist aims. On 5 February 1418, Martin V authorised him to create six male Dominican convents and four nunneries, although apparently only one of these, the foundation of Scala Coeli by Álvaro de Córdoba, was completed. All these attempts of reform were a consequence of the Council of Constance, in which all the aforementioned prelates – Álvaro de Córdoba, Luis de Valladolid and Martin V, who was elected pope by the Council – participated. However, the process of reform of the Order of Preachers in Castile was interrupted after the deaths of its main proponents Álvaro de Córdoba and Luis de Valladolid in the 1430s, and only resumed in the 1460s by Juan de Torquemada, albeit with a clearly different accent, in which the tradition inspired by Thomas Aquinas's theological thought had a significant weight.[95] The Congregation of the Observance was

---

[91] Leonor de Castro received authorisation by the pope, Gregory IX, in 1376, whereas the queen was authorised two years later by Urban VI. Robinson, 'La orden Jerónima y el convento de Clarisas', 26–7.

[92] Adeline Rucquoi, 'Los franciscanos en el reino de Castilla', in José Ignacio de la Iglesia Duarte, Francisco Javier García Turza and José Angel García de Cortázar y Ruiz de Aguirre (eds), *VI Semana de Estudios Medievales: Nájera, 31 de Julio al 4 de agosto* (Logroño, 1996), pp. 65–86, at p. 79.

[93] Will of Beatriz Manrique (given on 6 September 1471): Madrid, Archive Histórico Nacional, Sección Nobleza, Frías 598/38/fol. 5r; cited in Pereda, 'Liturgy as women's language', pp. 974–88.

[94] Elizabeth A. Lehfeldt, *Religious Women in Golden Age Spain: The Permeable Cloister* (Aldershot, 2005), pp. 105–6.

[95] Luciano Cinelli, 'Juan de Torquemada', in F. Troncarelli (ed.), *La città degli angeli, Catalogo de la Mostra* (Firenze, 2003), pp. 74–9.

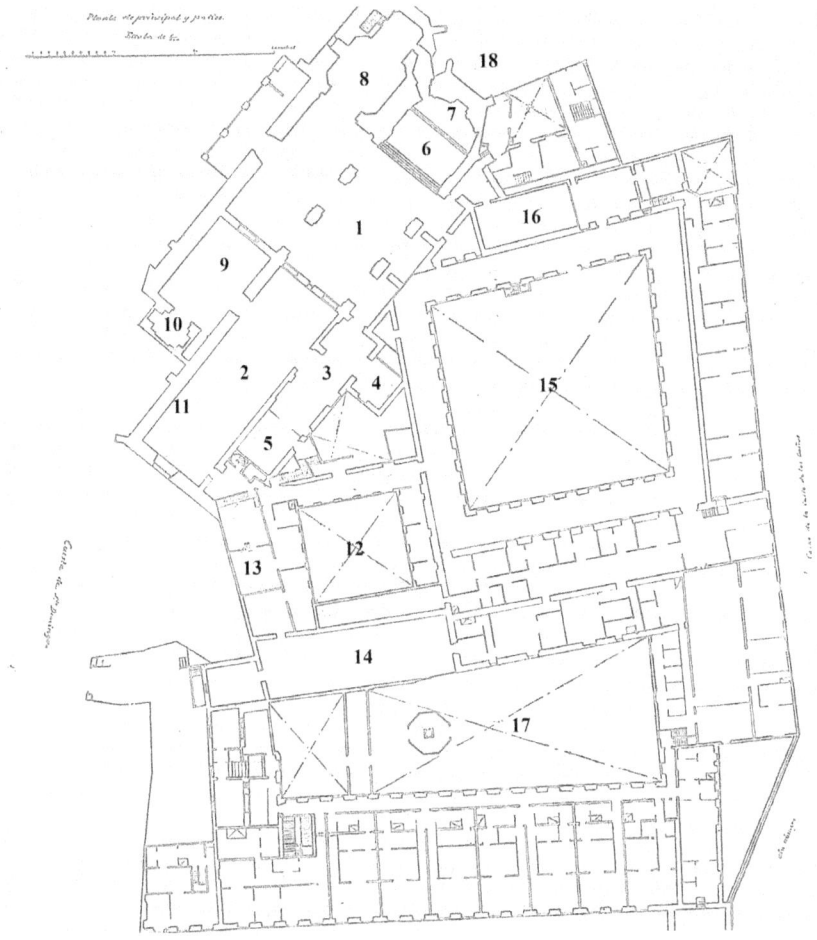

Fig. 7.5. Ground plan of Santo Domingo el Real de Madrid, hypothetical reconstruction of the state of the monastery in the mid-16th century with lodgings of Constanza de Castilla. Source: Author's reconstruction based on the ground plan of 1869. Ayuntamiento de Madrid, Museo de Historia de Madrid, Inv. No. 2695.

1. Church. 2. Nuns' choir. 3. Antechoir. 4. Chapel of St Dominic. 5. Chapel of St John the Baptist. 6. Chapel of Pedro I. 7. Sacristy. 8. Chapel of Alonso de Castilla. 9. Chapel of St Thomas Aquinas. 10. Chapel of St John the Evangelist. 11. Tomb of Constanza de Castilla. 12. Cloister of Constanza de Castilla. 13. Lodgings of Constanza. 14. Refectory. 15. Large Cloister. 16. Chapter house. 17. Cloister of St Dominic. 18. House of chaplains.

established in 1467 with the approval of the General Master, and its first chapter was held at San Pablo de Valladolid in 1477.[96]

The next big step in the implementation of Observant Dominican reform was taken in 1493, when Alexander VI granted wide powers to the Catholic Monarchs to guide the implementation of the reform through the bull *Exposuerunt nobis*. This led to the appointment of a series of reformers for the female monasteries of Castile. Friar Pascual de Ampudia, former vicar of the Congregation of Observance (1487–90), was in charge of the reform of the Dominican nuns.[97] However, as we have seen, although these events remain the better-known moment or phase in the Observant reform movement, they were only the last step in a long-term process that started much earlier, in which women's agency was fundamental. Furthermore, and to conclude, some of these communities of women religious offered a strong opposition to the reformers sent by the Catholic Monarchs. Although these instances were frequently silenced in the chronicles, they are known through other documents, such as the case of the Dominican nunneries of Caleruega and Quejana.[98] These conflicts are also well documented in some male convents, like San Esteban de Salamanca, and they have been studied by Guillermo Nieva Ocampo,[99] but in the case of female monasteries they still deserve further research.

Conclusion

When approaching the different processes of reform of female monasteries in late medieval Castile, traditional historiography offered a vision of false homogeneity. Women's agency in these reformist attempts, acting in collaboration with other agents, has often been overlooked, as women's activities were seen as isolated endeavours, carried out in a particular monastery, and not systematically, at the level of a religious order or of a kingdom.

However, as this critical revision has showed, paying close attention to other kinds of sources, often overlooked, such as liturgical books or books with a liturgical use, can reshape our vision and amend previous assumptions about these

---

[96] Beltrán de Heredia, *Historia de la Reforma*, p. 160. For a deeper analysis of the Observant reform among Dominicans in Castile see Guillermo Nieva Ocampo, 'Reformatio in membris: conventualidad y resistencia a la reforma entre los dominicos de Castilla en el siglo XV', *En la España medieval*, 32 (2009), 297–341. As for the Dominican nuns, Pérez Vidal, 'La reforma de los monasterios'.

[97] Ramón Hernández Martín, 'Actas de la Congregación de la Reforma de la Provincia de España (I)', *Archivo Dominicano*, 1 (1980), 7–140.

[98] Mercedes Pérez Vidal, 'La Reforma de los monasterios', 208–12

[99] Nieva Ocampo, 'La creación de la Observancia'.

processes. The gender perspective adopted here has shown that many of these books were commissioned by aristocratic women, both patrons and nuns, who also promoted their exchange between different monasteries. The comparative approach here proposed has shown similar dynamics in the circulation of books between female monasteries in the two major reform movements in late medieval Castile. In both cases, women did not act alone but through different networks, involving a diversity of agents. Women thus acted not only through networks constituted by the respective religious order, but also through those based on kinship and the legitimisation of lineage. Castilian aristocratic women used these books to convey religious ideals of reform, and to bond, at the same time, their monastic foundations with others controlled by their female relatives. The shifting nature of books' functionality has been also proven by some examples, like the two Beatus copies, that were used in the two major moments of reform studied here, showing how familiar texts were adapted to new circumstances and with reimagined goals.

CHAPTER 8

Women, Men and Local Monasticism in Late Medieval Bologna

SHERRI FRANKS JOHNSON

IN her magisterial work on women's monasticism from early Christianity to modernity, Jo Ann McNamara offered this contrast between men's and women's religious life:

> Scholars have easily perceived men who have served the Catholic Church in their orderly ranks as monks and secular clergy, distributed according to their specialized vocations. Women religious have been torn between lay and clerical status, between episcopal and monastic jurisdictions, between active and contemplative vocations defined by male authorities. Thus, despite the variety of their activities, women's experience of religious life, as it came to be called, had profoundly different lineaments from men's.[1]

This assessment of the differences in orderliness between men's and women's monastic communities is characteristic of continuing assumptions about high and late medieval monasticism. We have tended to associate men's monasticism with well-defined and centralised monastic orders such as the Cistercians, Dominicans and Franciscans. Participation in these orders involved exemption from the jurisdiction of the local bishop and clear connection to the order's governing structure. By contrast, we have seen women's communities as more local, with more tenuous connections to the governing structures that defined these monastic orders.[2]

---

[1] Jo Ann Kay McNamara, *Sisters in Arms: Catholic Nuns through Two Millennia* (Cambridge, 1996), p. 2.
[2] Early, influential work of Herbert Grundmann on religious women emphasised the

While important research since McNamara's work has demonstrated that some women's communities were more integrated into large monastic orders than had been previously believed, scholars of women's monasticism are aware that many communities of religious women remained under the local bishop, following the *Rule* of Saint Benedict or Saint Augustine.[3] A remaining problem in efforts to compare men's and women's monasticism is that we have thought of the continuing existence of individual monastic houses under the jurisdiction of the bishop as a phenomenon that primarily applied to women's houses due to the difficulty of gaining incorporation into male-centred, centralised monastic orders. Nevertheless, many men's communities remained outside of strong, organising networks.

In this chapter, I will look at continuing efforts by church leaders to organise both men's and women's monastic communities, connecting them to existing or new monastic networks in order to define and regulate individual, local monasteries. In earlier research on religious women in late medieval Bologna, I investigated the fluctuations in rule and affiliation that were part of the experience of some women's monastic communities.[4] I found that changes in local monasteries in the

---

difficulty they faced in gaining recognition from the governing institutions of centralised monastic orders: Herbert Grundmann, *Religious Movements in the Middle Ages: The Historical Links between Heresy, the Mendicant Orders, and the Women's Religious Movement in the Twelfth and Thirteenth Century with the Historical Foundations of German Mysticism*, trans. Steven Rowan (Notre Dame, 1995); this work was first published in 1935: id., *Religiöse Bewegungen im Mittelalter. Untersuchungen über die geschichtlichen Zusammenhänge zwischen der Ketzerei, den Bettelorden und der religiösen Frauenbewegung im 12. und 13. Jahrhundert und über die geschichtliche Grundlage der deutschen Mystik* (Berlin, 1935). Clifford Hugh Lawrence takes a similar approach, focusing on the 'subordinate role of women in the monastic revival' of the High Middle Ages and suggesting that the convents that did gain affiliation with monastic orders were exceptional: Clifford Hugh Lawrence, *Medieval Monasticism Forms of Religious Life in Western Europe in the Middle Ages*, 3rd edition (Harlow, 2001 [1984]), pp. 219–20. Jo Ann McNamara describes the role of the papacy in affiliating women's communities with monastic orders over the objections of monks and friars and the continuing foundation of new convents that were under the bishop's jurisdiction and not affiliated with a centralised order. This is a much more nuanced description, but still places a lot of weight regarding the status of religious women on whether they were accepted by male-centred religious orders: McNamara, *Sisters in Arms*, especially pp. 295–317.

[3] Studies that show better integration of women's communities into monastic orders include Constance Hoffmann Berman, *The White Nuns: Cistercian Abbeys for Women in Medieval France* (Philadelphia, 2018); Lezlie Knox, *Creating Clare of Assisi: Female Franciscan Identities in Later Medieval Italy* (Leiden, 2008).

[4] Sherri Franks Johnson, *Monastic Women and Religious Orders in Late Medieval Bologna* (Cambridge, 2014), especially pp. 201–36.

fifteenth century represented continuing efforts to organise monastic life in line with programmes that had begun in the high Middle Ages. In research on men's religious communities in this era, I have found that church leaders and monastic reformers were also engaged in efforts to incorporate individual and local men's monastic communities by connecting them to larger monastic governing structures.[5] It is certainly true that conditions for religious women – particularly limitations on their mobility and their exclusion from participation in the governing organizations of large, centralised religious orders – led to significant differences in their monastic experience compared to their male counterparts. I argue, however, that some of the contrasts that scholars have tended to draw between men's and women's monasticism are a product of a lack of recognition of the extent to which monasteries of both men and women did not conform to the ideals of institutional organisation that emerged in the high Middle Ages. We pay attention to ways in which women's communities do not fit the model of well-organised monastic orders. We do not pay attention to the large number of men's communities that remained outside of centralised organising structures.

To look at the continuation of local monasticism for men and women and also continuing efforts by church leaders to organise these communities into more cohesive monastic organisations, I will focus on efforts to reform and revive struggling monastic houses in fifteenth-century Bologna. First, I will show that scholarly emphasis on monasteries that are tied to large religious orders leaves out a substantial portion of the monastic community in the late Middle Ages in a way that may skew our sense of how orderly either men's or women's monasticism really was. Though monastic communities belonging to the mendicant orders and large reformed Benedictine orders were important, there were many monasteries that were either under the local bishop's jurisdiction or part of small, looser monastic congregations. Next, I will examine two struggling local monastic houses in Bologna – the Augustinian canons of San Giovanni in Monte and the Augustinian nuns of Sant'Orsolina (sometimes known as San Lorenzo after a move to a new monastery). These are not the only Bolognese monasteries that were affected by efforts to reorganise local monastic communities in the fifteenth century, but they will serve as case studies for monastic reform and revival in this era in Bologna. Finally, I will connect the changes that take place in these monasteries to the emergence of new congregations in this era. The two congregations

---

[5] Scholarship that informs this ongoing research on the collection of local men's monasteries into new congregations includes Nicola Widloecher, *La Congregazione dei Canonici Regolari Lateranensi: Periodo di Formazione, 1402–1483* (Gubbio, 1929); Gabriella Zarri, 'I canonici Renani (secoli XV–XVI)', in Gianna Del Bono (ed.), *Congregazione dei Canonici Regolari del SS. Salvatore* (Vatican City, 2018), pp. 21–72.

that were relevant to the case studies in this chapter – the canonesses of Santa Annunziata of Pavia and the Lateran Canons – were among a number of new congregations that emerged in this era in response to efforts from ecclesiastical leaders, patrons and the papacy to regulate seemingly disparate monastic communities. These new institutions developed in response to perceived widespread problems in local monasteries, including the low numbers of inhabitants in these houses and concerns about lax observance in both men's and women's houses. Studying efforts to revive, reform and connect monastic communities that were not part of large orders will contribute to gaining a better understanding of the spectrum of monastic life in the later Middle Ages, from local monasteries to those that were part of regional networks and those that were integrated into large, centralised orders. We can also see that this is an ongoing effort involving both men's and women's monastic communities, indicating that religious life for monks and canons was subject to the same kinds of fluctuation in observance and institutional status that we have tended to associate with women's monastic life.

Monastic Orders: Centralised, Local and In-Between

In order to understand different tendencies in monastic affiliations among men's and women's religious communities, it is necessary to get a good overview of the variation in kinds of association that linked one monastery to another. I will look at three different ways that monasteries were connected to similar houses and to their local diocese: centralised orders, local monasteries, and congregations.

As mentioned above, the study of monasticism in the high and late Middle Ages has focused on the development of large monastic orders such as the Cistercians in the twelfth century and the Dominicans and Franciscans in the thirteenth century, which I describe as centralised orders.[6] These orders covered a wide geographic scope and developed governing institutions that defined which monasteries were incorporated into the order. They also provided oversight of member

---

[6] For example, two important surveys of medieval monasticism follow a narrative of increasing centralisation, with the emergence of the Cistercians and their centralised governing institutions, followed by the emergence of the Mendicant Orders. See Lawrence, *Medieval Monasticism*; Gert Melville, *The World of Medieval Monasticism: Its History and its Forms of Life*, trans. James Mixson (Collegeville, 2016). Steven Vanderputten's recent survey of monasticism calls for greater recognition of the continuing variations in monastic life. He introduces the concepts of 'nebulas' to express the idea that there were many monasteries that were not fully integrated into larger orders but that were influenced by them, and also that there were groupings and affiliations that were not as well-defined as those in the orders that have received the most focus in monastic scholarship: Steven Vanderputten, *Medieval Monasticisms: Forms and Experiences of the Monastic Life in the Latin West* (Berlin, 2020), especially pp. 97–101 and 205–10.

houses and of individuals that had professed into the order. These organisations and their member houses often had privileges that provided exemptions from the local bishop's authority. In her work on Cistercians, Constance Berman described the transition from the understanding of *ordo* as 'way of life', describing general practices (as in the *ordo monasticus* or *ordo canonicus*), to one in which it could designate a sense of belonging to a particular monastic group (*ordo Cisterciensis*).[7] This shift in the understanding of the term *ordo* correlates with the emergence of the Cistercians and others as an organisation that has some ability to define and regulate its membership. These orders are mostly centred around men's monastic life, but women's communities participated in them as well. Although earlier research on women's monasticism assumed that convents had minimal connection to these orders, more recent scholars who have looked deeper into the workings of individual women's communities and their relationship to the monastic orders with which they identified has demonstrated that many women's communities had strong and enduring ties to these orders.[8]

These arrangements contrast with another category of monastic life, in which monasteries followed a widely-used rule – such as the *Rule* of Saint Benedict – but were not part of these larger organizing networks. I will describe these communities as local monasteries. Though some local monasteries managed to obtain privileges that placed them directly under papal authority, most were under the bishop's jurisdiction. Before monastic houses began to develop into regional congregations and larger monastic orders beginning in the tenth century, this was the dominant form of monastic life. In part due to the emphasis on studying the development of centralised orders in the high Middle Ages, we have not recognised the extent to which local monasticism remained an important phenomenon for both men's and women's monastic life in the later Middle Ages. We have been aware that many convents did not integrate into centralised orders and that there continued to be new women's communities following a basic rule and subject to the local bishop, but we have tended to assume that the failure to integrate into new, centralised order was due to the marginalisation of religious women in the later Middle Ages. Though the Fourth Lateran Council decreed in 1215 that all orders should hold regional General Chapters at least every three years

---

[7] Constance Hoffmann Berman, *The Cistercian Evolution: The Invention of a Religious Order in Twelfth-Century Europe* (Philadelphia, 1999), pp. 68–72.

[8] On Cistercian women, see Berman, *The White Nuns*, especially pp. 18–30; and Anne E. Lester, *Creating Cistercian Nuns: The Women's Religious Movement and its Reform in Thirteenth-Century Champagne* (Ithaca, 2011), especially pp. 78–116. On Franciscan women, see Knox, *Creating Clare of Assisi*, especially pp. 57–86 and 123–56; and on Dominican women, see Getrude Jaron Lewis, *By Women, for Women, about Women: The Sister-Books of Fourteenth-Century Germany* (Toronto, 1996), pp. 10–31.

and should choose officials to visit and correct monasteries in their order and region, many monasteries – both men's and women's communities – continued to be local houses that did not develop or participate in these kinds of governing activities.[9]

In addition to centralised orders and local monasteries, there was an intermediate category, for which I will use the term 'congregation'. In general, 'congregation' denotes a group of monasteries that follow a widely-accepted rule such as that of Saint Benedict or Saint Augustine but who define their specific practice of the rule with additional customs or statutes. Examples of these networks include the Camaldolese and Vallombrosan Benedictine reform movements, which included both cenobitic and eremitic ways of life. The Augustinian monasteries of Santa Maria in Porto in Ravenna and Santa Croce in Mortara (Lombardy) developed their own congregations in the twelfth century.[10]

In some cases, these monasteries exercised authority over subject monasteries and other religious institutions, but other communities that followed their practices did not have formal ties. For example, the Bolognese canons of Santa Maria di Reno and San Vittore adopted the customs of Santa Maria in Porto for their own small network of monasteries and churches but were not subject to the main house in Ravenna.[11] These several monastic houses, sometimes with some geographical distance, shared customs or statutes in addition to their basic rule or had some level of formal connection. While some monastic groups such as the Cistercians and the Mendicant Orders developed more centralised governing institutions and the church hierarchy held this up as a model for other monastic groups to emulate, many smaller, regional networks continued with their older organising practices.

Though usages of terms such as *congregatio* and *ordo* were far from consistent,

---

[9] James G. Clark notes that adopting the practice of holding provincial chapters was uneven. In England, there were regular chapters of black monks as early as 1218. Continental observance was spottier, with no clear evidence of German chapters until the fifteenth century and little observance of these mandates in Italy and France: James G. Clark, *The Benedictines in the Middle Ages* (Woodbridge, 2011), pp. 289–90.

[10] On the Camaldolese congregation, see Giuseppe Vedovato, *Camaldoli e la sua congregazione dale origini al 1184* (Cesena, 1994). On the Vallombrosans, see Francesco Salvestrini, *Disciplina caritatis: Il monachesimo vallombrosano tra medioevo e prima età moderna* (Rome, 2008), particularly pp. 181–244, see especially the discussion of Vallombrosan development from a *fraternitas* to a *congregatio* at pp. 209–12. For the Congregation of Santa Croce, see Cristina Andenna, *Mortariensis Ecclesia: Una congregazione di canonici regolari in Italia settentrionale tra XI e XII secolo* (Berlin, 2007), especially pp. 372–90, in which she also touches on the congregation of Santa Maria in Porto.

[11] Zarri, 'I canonici Renani', p. 22.

we can see some tendencies. In practice, congregations could in some cases be described as an order in their own right – for example, the Cistercians might fit this description as a Benedictine group with their own specific practices, but perhaps because of its size and centralised organisation it is described as an order. The network of houses dependent on or influenced by Cluny were sometimes described as a congregation, and the customs written down under Abbot Peter the Venerable use both the terms '*congregatio*' and '*ordo*' to describe Cluniac houses.[12] In general, monastic networks in the category of 'congregation' differed from large, centralised orders in that the boundaries that defined the group were less well-defined than those in centralised orders, or in that they were smaller and more regional than their more prominent counterparts. Earlier examples also differed from their more centralised contemporaries in that the ties among houses could be much looser, and the governing institutions were not as well-developed. Congregations such as the Olivetans and the Celestines that emerged in the later Middle Ages remained smaller than large orders, but emulated their governing institutions and oversight of member houses.[13] Though these groups have received much less scholarly attention than their larger counterparts, they represented an important element of local and regional monasticism life.

Though most of these congregations were male-centred, some of them included many communities of religious women. For example, Santa Cristina della Fondazza in Bologna was a significant convent in the Camaldolese Congregation, and there were at least two other Camaldolese convents in the city during the high Middle Ages. Congregations centred entirely on women were rare. In addition to the Annunziate, there was a congregation of Benedictine nuns founded by Santuccia Carabotti of Gubbio, whose first foundation in Perugia in the 1260s was the beginning of a congregation that included over twenty communities by her

---

[12] Twelfth-century statutes for Cluny compiled under Peter the Venerable mostly refer to institutes, monasteries and brothers with the adjective 'Cluniac': 'Ab hac institutione Cluniacensis [...] Statutum est, ut universi Fratres Cluniacenses [...]'. The authors tend to use *congregatio* to refer to a group of individuals or monasteries: 'Statutum est, ut omnium Monachorum Cluniacensium defuctorum anniversario dies ab universis Congregationis nostrae Fratribus vigilia sancti Michaelis Archangelei, more anniversariorum solemnium fiat, & vigilia conversionis sancti Pauli aliud eodem modo anniversarium, pro omnibus utriusque sexus parentibus universorum Fratrum Congregationis nostrae.' The term *ordo* tends to be used regarding practices: 'Hanc Regulam Apostoli ipsi sequuti sunt, hanc eorum successores Apostolici Pontifici, [...] hanc & precedentes Cluniacensis ordinis magni & egregi Fundatores.': L. Holstenius (ed.), *Codex Regularum Monasticorum et Canonicorum* (Graz, 1957), vol. 2, pp. 177–9.

[13] On Celestines and Olivetans, both founded in the late thirteenth and early fourteenth centuries, see Melville, *The World of Medieval Monasticism*, pp. 271–4.

death in 1305.[14] Her congregation included a Bolognese house, S. Elisabetta delle Santucce. The variety of these congregations and their diverse origins demonstrates the continuing vitality of religious life for both men and women in the later Middle Ages.

Men, Women and Monastic Organisations in Bologna

An overview of monastic affiliations for men and women's monasteries in late medieval Bologna illustrates the spectrum of religious life. Given impressions of women's monasticism as more local and less integrated into centralised orders, we might not be surprised to find that a tally of monastic communities would show that a large percentage of these houses remained local. What might be more surprising is the discovery that many men's communities were also local monasteries under a bishop's jurisdiction. An analysis of monastic communities in Bologna provides an example of the variation in the degrees of centralisation among monastic communities as late as the beginning of the fifteenth century.

In Bologna, fewer than half of the monasteries were affiliated with centrally organised monastic orders. The majority were either under the bishop's jurisdiction or part of looser congregations. Table 8.1 shows the distribution of monasteries in Bologna and the surrounding area around 1400. For women, monasteries with ties to these monastic orders represent only nine of the twenty-three monasteries extant in the early fifteenth century (three Cistercian convents, along with two Clarissan and four Dominican communities). In some case, founders made clear their intention to connect the convent to a particular order. Other communities had developed ties to centralised orders over time. The remainder were Benedictine or Augustinian communities under the bishop's jurisdiction (three and eight respectively), along with three houses that were part of reform Benedictine congregations with looser organisation than their Cistercian counterparts.

We might expect that men's communities would be more likely to be integrated into centralised monastic orders. Evidence from Bologna does not support this assumption. For men, seven out of twenty-three monasteries were part of centrally-organised monastic orders, all mendicant orders. In addition to the main Dominican and Franciscan communities, there were five houses associated with smaller mendicant orders (the Augustinian Hermits, the Servites, Carmelites

---

[14] Katherine Gill, 'Scandala: Controversies Concerning Clausura and Women's Religious Communities in Late Medieval Italy', in Scott L. Waugh and Peter Diehl (eds), *Christendom and its Discontents: Exclusion, Persecution, and Rebellion, 1000–1500* (Cambridge, 2002), pp. 177–203, especially pp. 187–91.

and Gesuati).[15] This leaves ten Benedictine houses that were either black monks (following the *Rule* of Saint Benedict without belonging to a more specific congregation or order) or members of looser Benedictine congregations such as the Vallumbrosans or Camaldolese. Augustinian communities – either local or in small, loose congregations – account for the remaining six monasteries in and near Bologna.

In Bologna, men's monastic houses affiliated with the mendicant orders exerted great influence. But so, too, did Benedictine monasteries such as Santo Stefano and San Procolo and houses of Augustinian canons such as Santissimo Salvatore, Santa Maria di Reno and San Giovanni in Monte.[16]

Two Bolognese Cases

In the fifteenth century, church reformers developed new regional monastic congregations that gained permission to send members of existing houses in the congregation to revive struggling local monasteries. After periods of decline and disruption, these communities became dependent on the leading monasteries in the congregations or were brought in as equal members through union with the congregation. Two examples in Bologna – the canons of San Giovanni in Monte and the nuns of Sant'Orsolina – will illustrate the path by which local monasteries came to be integrated into new monastic congregations.

AUGUSTINIAN CANONS: SAN GIOVANNI IN MONTE AND SAN VITTORE

As prominent examples of local monasteries, San Giovanni in Monte and San Vittore were, respectively, urban and suburban houses of canons that had been linked since the twelfth century. There is evidence that San Giovanni in Monte was subject to the Benedictine community of Santo Stefano in the early Middle Ages, but became home to regular canons in the early twelfth century.[17] San Vittore may have begun as an oratory in the eleventh century, becoming consecrated as a church in 1178. By the thirteenth century, the combined communities (especially the urban San Giovanni in Monte) were flourishing, producing several bishops of Bologna.[18]

---

[15] Paolo Foschi, 'Gli Ordini Religiosi Medievali a Bologna e nel suo territorio', in Paolo Prodi (ed.), *Storia della Chiesa di Bologna* (2 vols, Bergamo, 1997), vol. 2, pp. 463–99.

[16] For San Procolo and Santo Stefano, see Foschi, *Monasteri benedettini*, pp. 192–5 and 203–12; for San Salvatore/Santa Maria di Reno, see Zarri, 'I canonici Renani', pp. 21–2. For San Giovanni in Monte, see Widloecher, *La Congregazione*, pp. 45–50.

[17] Foschi, 'Gli ordini religiosi', pp. 472–3.

[18] Widloecher, *La Congregazione*, p. 46.

Table 8.1. Monasteries in Bologna in 1400.[i]

	Ben.	Aug.	Ben. Cong.[ii]	Cist.	Fran./Claris.	Dom.	Other Mend.[iii]	total
F	3	8	3	3	2	4	0	23
M	3	6	7	0	1	1	5	23

Notes
[i] Information for this table is drawn from Foschi, 'Ordini Religiosi'; Paola Foschi, *Monasteri benedettini nella diocesi di Bologna (secoli VII–XV)* (Bologna, 2017); Gabriella Zarri, 'I monasterii femminili a Bologna tra il XIII e il XVII secolo', *Atti e memorie della Deputazaione di storia patira per le province di Romagna*, 24 (1971), 133–224; and Johnson, *Monastic Women*, p. 94. For specific monasteries that fit in each category, see Appendices I and II on pp. 000–000.
[ii] This category includes small congregations from the high Middle Ages such as the Vallumbrosans and the Camaldolese, as well as more recent congregations such as the Celestines and Olivetans, which were founded in the fourteenth century.
[iii] Besides the Dominicans and Franciscans, other mendicant orders such as the Carmelites, the Augustinian Hermits and the Servites also established monasteries in Bologna. See Frances Andrews, *The Other Friars: Carmelite, Augustinian, Sack and Pied Friars in the Middle Ages* (Woodbridge, 2006).

By the early fifteenth century, however, San Vittore was uninhabited. San Giovanni was nearing the same fate: in two charters from the first decade of the fifteenth century that recorded property transactions, only the prior and three canons were present at the chapter meeting to approve the actions.[19]

The intervention of canons from Santa Maria in Fregionaia in Lucca led to a revival of San Giovanni in Monte and San Vittore. Santa Maria in Fregionaia had itself been uninhabited at the turn of the fifteenth century until reforming canons from Venice, Milan and Rome gained the rights to the monastery and established a new community there, with the goal of living a rigorous ascetic life. Though the early inhabitants were all from outside of the city, the group found favour among donors in Lucca, who provided them with significant endowments. In 1404, the group reformed another sparsely populated community, this time the Veronese monastery of San Leonardo. At first, the monasteries at Lucca and Verona followed the same practices but did not have a clear articulation of their institutional connection.[20] This changed when they sent some of their members to Bologna to revive San Giovanni in Monte and San Vittore. In 1415, it is clear that canons from Verona were living at San Giovanni in Monte. By 1417, Bishop Niccolò Albergati of Bologna had negotiated with the bishops of

[19] Bologna, Archivio di Stato di Bologna, Fondo Demaniale (henceforth ASB Dem) 22/1362, n. 20 and n. 33.
[20] Widloecher, *La Congregazione*, pp. 40–1.

Lucca and Verona to enact a formal union of the four monastic communities.[21] As part of this union, the bishops exempted the new Congregation of Santa Maria in Fregionaia from episcopal authority.[22]

SANT'ORSOLINA

The Augustinian convent of Sant'Orsolina was founded in the mid-thirteenth century and was located just outside Bologna's walls on the eastern side of the city. There is not much documentation about the house until the early fifteenth century. In a document regarding a long-term lease from 1404, there are six nuns, including the prioress, present to approve the agreement.[23] The lack of documentation makes it difficult to determine whether the small population of the community represents a decrease from previous eras or whether it had always been relatively small.

An unusual number of transfers of nuns from Sant'Orsolina to other communities and from other communities into Sant'Orsolina seems to have drawn episcopal scrutiny. On 25 January 1424, prioress Lasia Roncastaldi accepted a group of six women into the monastery.[24] They did so in front of Roderigo 'de Falconis', vicar of Bishop Niccolò Albergati. At least one of them, Tomasia di Tordi, had been a member of another Augustinian house, Santa Maria Nova, though the origins of the other women are unclear before their arrival at Sant'Orsolina.[25]

The new professions of nuns were followed by the departure of the prioress and at least two other inhabitants. On 30 January, a bishop's vicar named Lorenzo confirmed the acceptance of the new professions into Sant'Orsolina. On the same day, Lorenzo and Rodrigo together deposed Lasia from the office of prioress and ordered the nuns of Sant'Orsolina 'to elect for prioress or as prioress [...] one who will be of better life and character'.[26] Lasia and two other women who are described as belonging to other monasteries but living in the Monastery of the Virgins (Sant'Orsolina was also sometimes known as Santa Maria delle Vergini) were transferred to Santa Maria Maddalena delle Convertite, a Dominican convent.[27]

This set of events would bring Sant'Orsolina into a new congregation led by the Augustinian nuns of Santa Annunziata in Pavia. In 1426, the nuns elected a new prioress, Sister Caterina, who came from the mother house in Pavia. A

---

[21] ASB Dem 23/1363, n. 24.
[22] See more on the Congregation of Santa Maria in Fregionaia below.
[23] ASB Dem 6/3374, n. 16, 25 April 1404
[24] ASB Dem 8/3376, n. 10, 25 January 1425.
[25] ASB Dem 8/3376, n. 9, 11 August 1423. Documentation of Santa Maria Nova is sparse, and I have not been able to find evidence of the other women in that convent.
[26] 'Unam aliam que melioris vite et honestate foret [...] in priorissam et ut priorissam elligi mandaverunt.': ASB Dem 8/3376, no. 10.
[27] ASB Dem 8/3376, no. 15, 30 January 1425.

bull from Pope Martin V addressed to the abbot of the Benedictine monastery of Santo Stefano in Bologna asks him to confirm the election of a new prioress for Sant'Orsolina. The bull relates that the sisters of Sant'Orsolina had chosen to accept Caterina as prioress on the advice of the bishop of Bologna, Niccolò Albergati, who lauded the virtuous lives of the nuns of Santa Maria Annunziata.[28] Accepting Caterina as their prioress in this case also involved becoming subject to the authority of the monastery in Pavia from which she came.

By 1431, the nuns of Sant'Orsolina had left their monastery after it was damaged in war. After spending a brief time in secular housing, they put forth a successful petition to be allowed to unite with the Augustinian house of San Lorenzo in the southeastern part of the walled city.[29] Though the nuns in San Lorenzo (probably about three or four) were also Augustinian, they decided not to remain there, but rather moved across the street to become members of the Cistercian convent of Santa Maria del Cestello.[30] Sant'Orsolina/San Lorenzo did continue to grow substantially, and by 1473 there were sixty nuns in that convent. In March of that year, Pope Sixtus IV approved a request from the nuns – his letter states that bishop Niccolò Albergati of good memory had persuaded them to elect a prioress from Santa Maria Annunziata in Pavia and to accept the habit of that monastery, but with her death the nuns asked to be allowed to go back to their old habit that they might worship God with the brothers who had been providing their care. This is followed by another letter to the canons of Bologna at San Giovanni in Monte entrusting the nuns of San Lorenzo to the care of their congregation. Though the canons of San Giovanni in Monte petitioned to be absolved from the care of Sant'Orsolina, Pope Sixtus IV rejected their request and confirmed the affiliation.[31]

New Congregations

The situations of San Giovanni in Monte and Sant'Orsolina were not uncommon in Italian city-states in the era after the Black Death. One of the ways that monastic and secular church leaders endeavoured to repopulate and reform struggling monastic houses was to foster the growth of new monastic congregations that would link previously local monasteries. The difference between belonging to a centralised religious order and one that was not part of strong governing networks could have significant material effects, especially considering the loss of

---

[28] ASB Dem 9/3377, no. 3.
[29] ASB Dem 9/3377, no. 21, 12 June 1431.
[30] ASB Dem 9/3377, no. 25, 20 December 1431.
[31] Johnson, *Monastic Women*, pp. 118–19.

life associated with the Black Death in the fourteenth and fifteenth centuries. Orders such as the Dominicans and Franciscans could manage member houses by moving people around when necessary.[32] Less centralised orders or congregations could not do this as effectively, and local monasteries that were not connected formally to other similar communities could dwindle away.

While some of these local monasteries continued to thrive, others struggled. In the early years of the fifteenth century, monastic reformers and ecclesiastical leaders began to consider ways to revive depopulated monastic houses. In time, this involved fostering new networks to connect previously local monasteries into new congregations with governing features that resembled those of centralised monastic orders. In the first decade of the fifteenth century, a few monasteries were sites of successful revival and their inhabitants gained a reputation for religious rigour. Ecclesiastical or secular leaders enlisted the inhabitants of these growing communities to bring new people and renewed observance to monasteries in other cities. Popes hoping to end the schism and restore church authority and prestige after the resolution of the schism saw the promise that these new monastic networks held for aiding in this revival.[33]

Monasteries in Bologna were early members of these new religious networks. This situation is perhaps due to its importance as a city and also to the role of Bishop Niccolò Albergati, who served as bishop of Bologna before becoming a cardinal and supporter of monastic reform movements. He made efforts to connect struggling Bolognese monasteries to new monastic networks. Such intervention by reforming prelates was an important part of the spread of these new monastic networks. Both the Lateran Canons and the Canonesses of Santa Maria Annunziata developed presences in Bologna during his episcopate.

LATERAN CANONS

The congregation that would come to be known as the Lateran Canons began when Bartolomeo da Roma, an itinerant preacher who was well-connected with reforming monastic and ecclesiastical leaders, joined forces with canons who

---

[32] On the Observant Reform movement, see James Mixson, *Poverty's Proprietors: Ownership and Mortal Sin at the Origins of the Observant Movement* (Leiden, 2009).

[33] The Venetian reformer Ludovico Barbo, nephew of Pope Gregory XII, was instrumental in forming two new congregations that would influence the rise of many others. He founded S. Giorgio in Alga, a community of secular canons whose members would later become bishops, cardinals and even one pope, Eugenius IV. Then he became abbot of the venerable Paduan monastery S. Giustina, which would become the leader of congregation of reformed Benedictine monks. See Ildefonso Tassi, *Ludovico Barbo (1381–1443)* (Rome, 1952), pp. 12–72. On Gabriele Condulmer (Eugenius IV) and reform, see Joseph Gill, *Eugenius IV: Pope of Christian Union* (Westminster, 1961), pp. 15–37.

were dissatisfied with life at the Pavian monastery of San Pietro in Ciel d'Oro, an important community in the Congregation of Santa Croce in Mortara. San Pietro in Ciel d'Oro was unusual in that it was home to two separate monastic communities. Though the Augustinian canons had been present at that location since the previous century, in 1327 Pope John XXII decided to establish a separate community of Augustinian Friars at the church so that both canons and friars could be involved in caring for the relics of Augustine of Hippo housed at the church. The presence of the two communities led to conflict over schedules of masses and distribution of alms, and perhaps was among the factors that led a few inhabitants to leave San Pietro in order to establish a new, reformed community of canons.[34]

In 1402, Pope Boniface IX appointed Leone Gherardini da Carate, a former Cistercian monk, as the new prior of San Pietro in Ciel d'Oro. Leone had for some years been a proctor for the canons' affairs before becoming a member of the community.[35] Though it is difficult to determine the reason, Leone did not remain in San Pietro for very long. Leone and another canon from his monastery joined Bartolomeo da Roma to set up a new monastic community. Though existing documents do not permit us to see the process by which this happened, the group was given the abandoned monastery of Santa Maria in Fregionaia in Lucca.

It is likely that Bartolomeo da Roma had ties to other religious reformers in Lucca that helped him to settle in that spot. The early canons there were aided by the Gesuati and the Carthusians in Lucca. They quickly found local favour, as attested to by generous early donations and bequests to the monastery.[36] Pope Gregory XII provided them with a privilege placing the community directly under papal authority, and as the community grew, it began to send its members to other monasteries to re-establish or reinvigorate monasteries that were empty or nearly so.

On his way towards a potential meeting, Gregory spent some time in Lucca. Around this time, he asked one of the canons of Santa Maria in Fregionaia to lead a group that would reform the monastery of San Leonardo in Verona. San Leonardo had been dependent on San Marco of Mantua, but Gregory removed them from San Marco's authority. In 1408, he clarified the relationship between the canons of Lucca and Verona – individuals could move between the two houses, and they would share any privileges they might receive.[37]

The reputation of the canons grew such that others would appeal to them to repopulate and reform houses over which they had authority. As we have seen,

[34] Sharon Dale, 'A house divided: San Pietro in Ciel d'Oro in Pavia and the politics of Pope John XXII', *Journal of Medieval History*, 27 (2001) 55–77.
[35] Archivio di Stato Milano, Fondo Religione (henceforth ASM Religione) 6129, fols 151v–153r.
[36] Isabella Gagliardi, *Li trofei della Croce: L'Esperienza Gesuata e la societa Lucchese tra medioevo ed eta moderna* (Rome, 2005), pp. 97–9.
[37] Widloecher, *La Congregazione*, pp. 40–1.

the newly elected bishop of Bologna, Niccolò Albergati, gave them two previously connected Bolognese communities – the rural San Vittore and the urban San Giovanni in Monte. Between 1415 and 1417, Albergati communicated with the bishops of Lucca and Verona to arrange a formal union between the two Bolognese monasteries and those of Santa Maria in Fregionaia and San Leonardo.[38] The result was an agreement in 1418 that the four monasteries would unite into one institution, referred to as the Congregation of Santa Maria in Fregionaia.

This group continued to collect monasteries from older congregations. For example, in 1418 the canons in Verona reformed a Venetian monastery, Santa Maria della Carità, that had been under the authority of Santa Maria in Porto in Ravenna. The problem came to a head when the monastery in Ravenna had become so dysfunctional that it could not even approve the election of new priors for subordinate houses. So they called in the canons of Verona (and incidentally, the meeting in which they agreed to seek papal approval to ask for San Leonardo of Verona's help to reform the monastery happened in Padua at Santa Giustina – the monastery of the Venatian reformer and nephew of Pope Gregory XII, Ludovico Barbo – showing that these Benedictine and Augustinian reform movements remained connected).[39] Two years later, the *signore* of Ravenna, Obazine da Polenta, called in the canons of Fregionaia to reform Santa Maria in Porto as well.[40] Through networks of ecclesiastical and lay leaders, the congregation continued to grow. In 1421 under Martin V, they drew up a constitution and received approval for it. This included the holding of an annual General Chapter under a rector general, and one-year terms for priors (who could be re-elected). New canons professed into the congregation, not into an individual house, enabling the leaders of congregations to move them as needed.[41] Over the course of the fifteenth century, the congregation of the Lateran Canons would encompass more than fifty monastic communities in Italy. Pope Eugenius IV brought them to the papal basilica of San Giovanni in Laterano to regularise the canons there, leading to the change of name from the Congregation of Santa Maria in Fregionaia to the Congregation of Canons Regular of the Lateran. Though they would finally leave the Lateran when Pope Callistus III decided that the canons there should be secular canons, they were allowed to keep the name by which they had come to be known.[42]

---

[38] Gabriele Pennotto, *Generalis Totius Sacri Ordinis Clericorum Canonicorum Tripartita* (Rome, 1624), pp. 601–4.
[39] Venice, Archivio di Stato Venezia, Santa Maria della Carità, Ser I:36, no. 802.
[40] Widloecher, *La Congregazione*, pp. 55–60.
[41] Canons Regular of the Lateran, *Bullarium Lateranense* (Rome, 1727), pp. 154–7.
[42] Widloecher, *La Congregazione*, pp. 73–92 and 163–7.

THE ANNUNZIATE OF PAVIA

While most of the new congregations centred around men, at least one that formed in this era was specifically for women. In the first few years of the fifteenth century, a group of devout women coalesced in Lombardy. A network of women from communities in Milan, Pavia and Como would develop a religious association and work out the parameters of their religious goals, liturgy, and place in the church as an institution. By the late 1420s, these monasteries and others that had become affiliated with them would become the Congregation of Santa Maria Annunziata of Pavia, also known as the Annunziate. This group reflects the reform programme of religious individuals in this era as well as attempts for church leaders to find congregations that could organise formerly independent communities.

The nucleus of the group was centred around two communities: Santa Marta in Milan, a community that had begun in the fourteenth century as a house of penitent women, and Santa Maria Annunziata of Pavia, a new foundation in the early fifteenth century. Santa Marta began in 1345 as the 'Consorzio delle donne religiose di S. Marta'.[43] This group was comprised of wealthy women – mostly widows – who had decided to dedicate their lives to prayer and charity.

The transition of the group from a house of penitent women to an Augustinian convent occurred in the early years of the fifteenth century. We have a glimpse of the changes at Santa Marta and the development of a congregation of Augustinian nuns through the legal documents and letters of Margherita Lambertenghi, a wealthy widow who participated in the leadership of the congregation from its beginnings until well into the 1430s. In the course of establishing the congregation's rights to property in her hometown of Como, she recounted her own early involvement with the penitent group, providing an account of the congregation's growth.

Margherita recounts her decision following the death of her husband to turn away from worldly things. Along with three other widows and a servant, she lived in a house near the church of San Marco until 1403, when war broke out in Como. At this point she decided to go to Milan to live at Santa Marta. According to Margherita, 'in 1408, the order was given that two of the ladies from the house would go to Pavia to establish the order of the Annunziata'.[44] The Augustinian

---

[43] Lucia Sebastiani, 'Da bizzocche a monache', in Gabriella Zarri (ed.), *Il monachesimo femminile in Italia dall'alto medioevo al secolo XVII: a confront con l'oggi* (Verona, 1997), p. 197; Rita Bacchiddu, 'Una donna carismatica e i suoi critici: Paola Antonia Negri (1508-1555) ei primi Barnabiti' (unpublished Ph.D. dissertation, Collegio San Carlo di Modena, 2003), p. 27. Both Sebastiani and Bacchiddu describe the women who resided at Santa Marta as either beguines or as women associated with the *Humiliati* movement.

[44] 'Eyo Margarita' 'in mcccviii fu metuto ordine che doe dele sorelle de caxa andassene a

canons of San Pietro in Ciel d'Oro in Pavia (which incidentally held the remains of Augustine in their church, which they shared uneasily with a community of Augustinian Hermits) originally gave them the church and hospital of San Giorgio in Broglio in Pavia around 1407, but they then built their own monastery and named it Santa Maria Annunziata.[45]

What is clear, from Margherita's writings related to her claim to the house of San Marco in Como and from her correspondence with her counterpart at Santa Maria Annunziata, Elisabetta of Pavia, is that the women of the community had a strong sense of how they wanted to shape their religious life. They accepted the *Rule* of Saint Augustine, but wanted to retain autonomy from other Augustinian congregations.

The Annunziate then either united with existing communities or established new ones in Tortona, Piacenza, Como, Cremona and Rimini.[46] In the records of Santa Marta in Milan, there are letters from the 1440s between the prioress Elisabetta of the convent in Pavia of and Margherita Lambertenghi of Santa Marta in Milan regarding their efforts to get permission for their desired form of life, which involved exemption from the authority of the bishop and the ability to govern their own congregation.[47] They proved to be able to resist challenges to their way of life. In 1445, a group of Franciscan friars attempted to have the nuns of Santa Marta in Milan and San Marco in Como excommunicated as false nuns. Margherita Lambertenghi was able to obtain a bull from Eugenius IV confirming the union of Santa Marta and San Marco, demonstrating papal authorisation for their communities and their way of life.[48]

---

papia per acomenzare lo ordene de lannuntiata [sic].': ASM Religione 2146, no. 4.

[45] Balbino Rano, 'Annunziate di Lombardia', in Guerrino Pelliccia and Giancarlo Rocca (eds), *Dizionario degli Istituti di Perfezione* (10 vols, Rome, 1974), vol. 1, pp. 664–7.

[46] Luigi Torelli, *Secoli agostiniani overo historia generale del sacro ordine eremitano del gran dottore di santa chiesa S. Aurelio Agostino vescovo d'Hippona, divisa in tredeci secoli* (7 vols, Bologna, 1659–82), vol. 6, pp. 408–9.

[47] 'E parlando sopra questa fazenda de tore privilegio ne piaxeva molto de tore la regula de S. Agustino [...] ma non vorevemo per nessuno modo essere obligate de dire l'officio grande; e anche erano molto contente de essere exempte dal vescho e anche vorevano per ogni modo mantenere bassissima povertate. Si che non havevano voluntate de fare mutazion alcuna ma de esser confirmate in quello grado e in quello stato che nuy eramo perché la vitaera così bona che non bisognava fare mutatione nessuna.' Transcription of letter from Margherita Lambertenghi to prioress Elisabetta in Bacchiddu, 'Una donna carismatica', pp. 30–1, n. 96.

[48] Sebastiani, 'Da bizzocchi a Monache', pp. 216–18.

Monastic Reorganisation in Bologna

San Giovanni in Monte and Sant'Orsolina are examples of monasteries in Bologna whose struggles led to interventions in which they were connected to other monastic orders or congregations in the fifteenth century. Just as San Giovanni in Monte was an early part of the formation of the congregation that emerged from Santa Maria in Fregionaia and that would later become the Lateran Canons, the Bolognese canons of S. Salvatore were the nucleus of another congregation. In this case, former Augustinian Friars had left a monastery of S. Salvatore in Lecceto near Siena in 1408. In that community, a small group had convinced the Augustinian Friars to become canons, but the majority had decided to return to their former observance. This led to the departure of those who had preferred to live as canons and who wanted to seek a location in which to establish a new community. Through the intervention of Pope Gregory XII and the *condottiere* Guidantonio di Montefeltro in Urbino, they were given the depopulated monastery of Sant'Ambrogio in Gubbio in 1414.[49] While they were seeking a new monastery, they spent time in Bologna. The prior of S. Salvatore in Bologna invited canons from Gubbio to come to Bologna in order to revive his monastery, which had few remaining members. In 1418, Bishop Niccolò Albergati of Bologna united San Salvatore with Sant'Ambrogio, forming the Congregation of San Salvatore. Over the course of the fifteenth century, the congregation grew to include around thirty monasteries, including S. Salvador in Venice and S. Pietro in Vincoli in Rome.[50] In addition to these two houses of canons that were important parts of the foundation of new congregations, a venerable Benedictine monastery, San Procolo, was incorporated into the Congregation of Santa Giustina in 1431 under Eugenius IV.[51]

Where women's monasteries were concerned, Sant'Orsolina/San Lorenzo was somewhat unusual in its integration into two successive new congregations. A more common strategy for organising local women's communities was incorporating them into a large order. The combined community of Santa Maria del Monte della Guardia and San Mattia had long been associated with the Dominican Order, and was incorporated into that order under Pope Alexander VI in the late fifteenth century. Another phenomenon that coincided with the desire of church leaders to manage monastic personnel and property was a series of unions between convents within and across orders, usually initiated by one or both parties to the

---

[49] While he was staying in the city of Urbino, Pope Gregory XII played a role in connecting the canons of Lecceto with the *condottiere* Guidantonio di Montefeltro, *signore* of Urbino, who gave Sant'Ambrogio to the canons. Zarri, 'I canonici Renani', pp. 21–37.
[50] *Ibid.*, pp. 23–37
[51] ASB Dem 271/5489, n. 40.

union. Though these unions could result in significant strife and could require some religious women to change their rule or order, bishops and papal officials seemed to favour these unions as a practical strategy for economic stability and governance.[52] An example of this was San Lorenzo's union with the Cistercian convent of Santa Maria del Cestello. The sixty nuns of San Lorenzo petitioned to unite with the Cistercian community across the street, which housed only eight nuns, and to connect the two monasteries with a subterranean tunnel. Though the Cistercian nuns tried to resist the union, they were not successful.[53] This set of administrative actions in the fifteenth century is in line with church efforts to connect local monasteries to larger organizing monastic structures and to manage property and personnel in religious communities. Monastic communities that wanted to acquire new property from underpopulated houses also used the language of reform in their petitions.

Conclusion

S. Giovanni in Monte and Sant'Orsolina are examples of local monasteries that were unified into new monastic congregations in the fifteenth century, demonstrating the continuing dynamic nature of monasticism outside of large religious orders. Scholarship on men's monasticism in the high and late Middle Ages has tended to concentrate on the origins and institutional development of centralised religious orders and to the spiritual, intellectual, cultural and social influence of their members. This focus on centralised orders in men's monasticism leaves us with the impression that men's communities are consistently characterised by their clearer organisational affiliations. This ignores the large percentage of communities that do not fit this model – maybe they are part of regional congregations with looser ties, or even under the jurisdiction of the local bishop, following the *Rule* of Saint Augustine or of Saint Benedict but without strong connections to other monasteries. This kind of monastic life remained even after the model of centralised monasticism represented by the Cistercian order was held up as a desired norm at the Fourth Lateran Council in 1215.

Older scholarship on religious women's life has tended to focus on women's marginalisation, and in recent years we have come to understand that some convents were more clearly integrated into large, centralised monastic orders than we had previously thought. What we have not paid attention to is local men's monasticism. This has led to a situation in which, while there is much that remains unexplored and so many questions left to pursue regarding religious women, we

---

[52] Johnson, *Monastic Women*, pp. 201–34.
[53] *Ibid.*, pp. 212–15.

have a sense of the spectrum of women's monasticism but only a part of men's monasticism. We have had a tendency to explain messiness in women's monasticism as being related to their lack of integration into centralised monastic orders and their consequent marginal and local nature. Looking at both centralised and local men's monasticism (as well as continuing efforts to strengthen monastic governing organisations even after the thirteenth century) we will gain a fuller understanding of the dynamic and changing nature of monasticism in general.

Appendix I: Women's Religious Communities in 1400.

Benedictine	Augustinian	Ben. Cong.	Cistercian	Fran./Clarissan	Dominican	Other Mendicant
S. Margherita	S. Caterina di Quarto	S. Cristina della Fondazza	S. Maria della Misericordia	S. Francesco	S. Agnese	
SS. Gervasio e Protasio	S. Giovanni Battista	S. Anna	S. Maria del Cestello	SS. Ludovico e Alessio	S. Pietro Martire	
SS. Vitale e Agricola	S. Lorenzo	S. Elisabetta delle Santuccie	S. Guglielmo		S. Maria Nuova	
	S. Maria Maddalena di Valdipietra				S. Maria Maddalena delle Convertite	
	S. Maria delle Repentite					
	S. Maria del Monte della Guardia/S. Mattia					
	S. Orsolina					
	S. Maria delle Pugliole					
3	8	3	3	2	4	0

For more information on these communities, see Zarri, 'I monasteri femminili a Bologna', 293–55. S. Anna and S. Caterina della Fondazza were both Camaldolese communities; S. Elisabetta delle Santucce was part of the Benedictine congregation founded by Santuccia Carrabotti. This congregation consisted entirely of women's houses and included about twenty-five convents.

Appendix II: Men's Religious Communities in 1400.

Benedictine	Augustinian	Ben. Cong.	Cistercian	Fran./Clarissan	Dominican	Other Mendicants
S. Bartolomeo	S. Giovanni in Monte	S. Cecilia della Croara		S. Francesco	S. Domenico	S. Eustachio dei Gesuati
S. Procolo	S. Maria degli Angeli	SS. Cosma e Damiano				S. Giacomo Maggiore
S. Stefano	S. Maria di Monteveglio	S. Giovanni Battista dei Celestini				S. Girolamo
	S. Maria di Reno	S. Maria di Camaldoli				S. Maria della Grazie
	S. Salvatore	S. Maria di Monte Armato				S. Maria dei Servi
	S. Vittore	S. Michele in Bosco				
		SS. Naborre e Felice				
3	6	7	0	1	1	5

For more information on these communities, see Foschi, *Monasteri benedettini*; Id., 'Gli ordini religiosi medievali', pp. 463–93. Among the Benedictine congregations, SS. Cosma e Damiano, S. Maria di Camaldoli and SS. Naborre e Felice were Camaldolese; S. Cecilia della Croara and S. Maria di Monte Armato were Vallumbrosan; S. Michele in Bosco was Olivetan, and S. Giovanni Battista dei Celestini was Celestine. For the smaller mendicant orders, S. Maria dei Servi was Servite; S. Giacomo Maggiore was a community of Augustinian Hermits; S. Martino and S. Maria della Grazie were Carmelite; S. Eustachio was a community of Gesuati; and San Girolamo was Carthusian.

CHAPTER 9

Building Community: Material Concerns in the Fifteenth-Century Monastic Reform

JENNIFER EDWARDS

WHILE the long twelfth and the sixteenth centuries have most captivated scholars interested in monastic reform, the vivacity of monastic life in the fifteenth century has attracted a growing number of scholars who are uncovering a period vibrant with new forms of religious expression, including new religious movements and enthusiasm for religious reform.[1] Much of this interest has focused on movements such as the Modern Devotion, the establishment

---

[1] This article grew out of a conference paper presented at the International Medieval Congress at Leeds in 2019. I would like to thank the presenters for their invigorating and inspiring papers and the organisers, Jirki Thibaut and Julie Hotchin, for bringing us together, and for their patience.

The literature on monastic reform is vast. For orientation to key themes spanning the mid-to-late Middle Ages, see the chapters by Steven Vanderputten, John van Engen, Christina Andenna and Bert Roest in *Medieval Monasticism in the Latin West: The High and Late Middle Ages*; Alison I. Beach and Isabelle Cochelin (eds) (2 vols, Cambridge, 2020); and Carlos M. N. Eire, *Reformations: The Early Modern World, 1450–1650* (New Haven, 2016). For the reform of female monasteries in particular, see Fiona J. Griffiths, *The Garden of Delights: Reform and Renaissance for Women in the Twelfth Century* (Philadelphia, 2007); Sherri Franks Johnson, *Monastic Women and Religious Orders in Late Medieval Bologna* (Cambridge, 2014); Elizabeth A. Lehfeldt, *Religious Women in Golden Age Spain: The Permeable Cloister* (Aldershot, 2005); June L. Mecham, *Sacred Communities, Shared Devotions: Gender, Material Culture, and Monasticism in Late Medieval Germany* (Turnhout, 2014); Annalena Müller, 'From Charismatic Congregation to Institutional Monasticism: The Case of Fontevraud', *The American Benedictine Review*, 65:4 (2013), 428–44; and Anne Winston-Allen, *Convent Chronicles: Women Writing about Women and Reform in the Late Middle Ages* (University Park, 2004). For France, this story is told most comprehensively by Jean-Marie Le Gall, *Les moines au temps des réformes* (Paris, 2001).

of new orders, or the incorporation of holy women on the margins, such as the beguines.² Studies of reform, like monastic scholarship in general, tend to focus on an order, house or region, which allows for detailed studies but obscures a broad view of commonalities in reform and monastic experience across institutions.³ Examining the variety of reforming efforts in a long fifteenth century as a Europe-wide phenomenon, as Kaspar Elm, Bert Roest and James Mixson have suggested, provides a more expansive framework for contextualising fifteenth-century reform efforts, ideals, practices and resistance.⁴ While reform was not a coherent movement, organised and implemented across Europe as part of a consistent, centrally driven programme, it was made up of similarly intended local conversations with shared goals, methods, purposes and contextually contingent impacts that deserve more systematic study. Even as James Mixson and Bert Roest have highlighted the significance of the Observant reform as a web connecting reformers and institutions in Germany, the Low Countries, Italy and Spain, the vibrant reforms wrapping themselves around monastic life in Western France still need weaving into this web. This is especially true since even the Observant reform of the Franciscans in France, which shared similar ideals with the larger movement, worked separately from it, with French Vicar Generals and Provincial Masters overseeing reforms there, and Colette of Corbie (1381–1447), the influential French Franciscan abbess, complicating reform by founding the Colettine Poor Clares in the early fifteenth century.⁵

---

2 John Van Engen, *Sisters and Brothers of the Common Life: The Devotio Moderna and the World of the Late Middle Ages* (Philadelphia, 2008); Walter Simons, *Cities of Ladies: Beguine Communities in the Medieval Low Countries, 1200–1565* (Philadelphia, 2001); Bert Roest, *Order and Disorder: The Poor Clares between Foundation and Reform* (Leiden, 2013); Dennis D. Martin, *Fifteenth Century Carthusian Reform: The World of Nicholas Kempf* (Leiden, 1992).

3 Janet Burton and Karen Stöber, 'Introduction', in Janet Burton and Karen Stöber (eds), *Women in the Medieval Monastic World* (Turnhout, 2015), p. 8; Claire Taylor Jones, *Ruling the Spirit: Women, Liturgy, and Dominican Reform in Late Medieval Germany* (Philadelphia, 2018); Mecham, *Sacred Communities, Shared Devotions*.

4 James D. Mixson and Bert Roest (eds), *A Companion to Observant Reform in the Late Middle Ages and Beyond* (Leiden, 2015); Kaspar Elm, 'Verfall und Erneuerung des Ordenswesens im Spätmittelalter: Forschungen und Forschungsaufgaben,' in J. Fleckenstein (ed.), *Untersuchungen zu Kloster und Stift* (Göttingen, 1980), pp. 167–97; and James D. Mixson, 'Religious Life and Observant Reform in the Fifteenth Century', *History Compass*, 11:3 (2013), 201–14.

5 Nancy Bradley Warren, *Women of God and Arms: Female Spirituality and Political Conflict, 1380–1600* (Philadelphia, 2005), 11–35; Joan Mueller and Nancy Bradley Warren, *A Companion to Colette of Corbie* (Leiden, 2016); Anna Campbell, 'The Career, Cult and Canonization of St Colette of Corbie (1381–1447)' (unpublished Ph.D. dissertation, University of Reading, 2011), p. 65.

This chapter examines the impact of fifteenth-century monastic reform on spatial and architectural changes, focusing on the abbey of Sainte-Croix in Poitiers, a significant house in Western France. Sainte-Croix was influenced deeply by contemporary ideas about monastic reform, especially ideas about community and property growing out of the Observant movement, the Colettine reforms, and reform at Fontevraud, a significant monastery and head of its own order that underwent reform in the second half of the fifteenth century.

In order to facilitate reform goals of building community, architectural changes, such as larger dormitories and refectories that accommodated shared sleeping and dining, became necessary. Historians of female monasticism have produced a number of important studies of institutions and orders for this period, making it possible to examine the broader material impact of reform policies and situate Sainte-Croix in this larger movement.[6] In doing so, this chapter makes clear that material spaces had significant implications about the identity, spirituality, autonomy and control of female monastic women.

I have discussed the effect of fifteenth-century monastic reform on the Abbey of Sainte-Croix in Poitiers, France, in my book *Superior Women: Medieval Female Authority in Poitiers' Abbey of Sainte-Croix*, discussion that I hope to contextualise here in the larger late monastic reforming movement. Sainte-Croix was an ancient monastery founded by St Radegund in the sixth century inside Poitiers' Roman walls. By the fifteenth century, Sainte-Croix was a wealthy abbey with extensive holdings in and around Poitiers, and the abbess was an influential person in the local community. While Sainte-Croix was not formally part of Fontevraud's network of abbeys and priories, the two communities were closely interwoven. As they were in the same diocese, the bishop of Poitiers oversaw them both. They also shared abbesses in the late fifteenth century and the abbess of Fontevraud reformed Sainte-Croix after 1519; Fontevraud remained tightly in control of the abbey for the next century or more.

Sainte-Croix provides a useful case study for late medieval monastic reform, as a traditional Benedictine house independent of the Franciscans and of Fontevraud's

---

[6] See n. 1. Jones, *Ruling the Spirit*; Roest, *Order and Disorder*; Sara Ritchey, *Holy Matter: Changing Perceptions of the Material World in Late Medieval Christianity* (Ithaca, 2014); Constance Hoffman Berman, *The White Nuns: Cistercian Abbeys for Women in Medieval France* (Philadelphia, 2018); Anne E. Lester, *Creating Cistercian Nuns: The Women's Religious Movement and Its Reform in Thirteenth-Century Champagne* (Ithaca, 2011); Sharon T. Strocchia, *Nuns and Nunneries in Renaissance Florence* (Baltimore, 2009); June L. Mecham, 'Sacred Vision, Sacred Voice: Performative Devotion and Female Piety at the Convent of Wienhausen, circa 1350–1500' (unpublished Ph.D. dissertation, University of Kansas, 2004); Jennifer C. Edwards, *Superior Women: Medieval Female Authority in Poitiers' Abbey of Sainte-Croix* (Oxford, 2019).

network, yet greatly influenced by reforming trends from each. Much of the historiographical interest in monastic reform, particularly for female communities, has not attended to Poitou despite the enormous reach of Fontevraud or the forcefulness of Fontevraud abbess Renée de Bourbon's (1491–1534) and King Francis I's (r. 1515–47) reform there. Sainte-Croix was an ancient, wealthy, well-connected and well-known house in fifteenth-century France, and its reform was a significant process, one imposed externally with some internal support, through political control rather than theological encouragement. Reform at Sainte-Croix was bound up in local, ecclesiastical and royal politics as the bishop, the king, the abbess of Fontevraud and local Poitevin landholders attempted to gain influence and power over the nuns of Sainte-Croix. Reform involved reconstruction of existing or addition of new material spaces to build community literally, yet, as we will see, examining the practical aspects of the reform shaping the nuns' material world is also significant since that is the area that aroused complaint from the nuns themselves as these changes threatened their autonomy, self-determination and individualism.

Reform Ideals

'Reform' is a concept with a long history, calling out from the early Middle Ages for a renewal of monasticism's founding ideals after some period of 'decline' or 'corruption'. These are rhetorical manoeuvres intended to refocus an order or an institution on the monastic goals of poverty, obedience and chastity.[7] Calls for reform might come from spiritual concerns or practical necessities, but they are also opportunities to introduce something new under the guise of turning back towards founding traditions. Indeed, assertions of 'decline' or 'corruption' that justified reformers' interventions in specific houses may have had no basis, but were narratives of victorious reformers who controlled the sources left to historians.[8] None the less, calls for reform motivated lay people, clerics, and nuns themselves, who found opportunities for their own agenda, whether rooted in spirituality, charity or empowerment.

The Councils of Constance (1414–18) and Basel (1431) encouraged general reform in the early part of the fifteenth century by calling for investigation of

---

[7] James Mixson, 'Observant Reform's Conceptual Frameworks between Principle and Practice,' in James D. Mixson and Bert Roest (eds), *A Companion to Observant Reform in the Late Middle Ages and Beyond* (Leiden, 2015), pp. 60–84.
[8] Anne Huijbers, '"Observance" as Paradigm in Mendicant and Monastic Order Chronicles', in James D. Mixson and Bert Roest (eds), *A Companion to Observant Reform in the Late Middle Ages and Beyond* (Leiden, 2015), p. 119.

supposed corruptions in the church.[9] Reformers broadly encouraged obedience, community, poverty and enclosure, and like in many previous reform efforts emphasised a recommitment to monastic traditions and the eradication of supposed corruption and 'deformation', but that does not mean that corruption was really there to be found.[10] As Carlos Eire observed, common reforming 'buzzwords such as *reformatio*, *renovatio*, *restauratio*, *reparatio* and *instauratio* were frequently used by ever-growing numbers of the elite, and all of the terms had a similar meaning, "improvement".[11] New orders and movements, such as the Modern Devotion and the Observants, emphasised charity, poverty and community over a single leader. The popularity of these movements pressed traditional monasteries to grapple with reforming ideas, and houses such as Fontevraud, Windesheim and Bursfelde embraced reform and provided models for the reform of other houses with the support of the clergy and local nobility.[12]

Reformers emphasised community, enclosure, obedience and fiscal responsibility. Of course, not all monastics agreed that their practices were corrupt, in decline or in need of reform, and so reformers often faced resistance. For many monastic women, resistance to reform was an effort to preserve autonomy and self-governance, which is one reason Colette of Corbie claimed the power to select friars to perform the *cura monialium* and resisted Observant oversight of her houses.[13] Yet reform was popular among bishops, certain monastics, and even among the laity, including kings and royal and noblewomen, who were eager to organise,

---

[9] For the Conciliarist movement, see Francis Oakley, *The Conciliarist Tradition: Constitutionalism in the Catholic Church, 1300–1870* (Oxford, 2008); Brian Tierney, *Foundations of the Conciliar Theory* (Cambridge, 1995); Philipp H. Stump, *The Reforms of the Council of Constance (1414–1418)* (Leiden, 1994); Michiel Decaluwe, Thomas M. Izbicki and Gerald Christianson (eds), *A Companion to the Council of Basel* (Leiden, 2017).

[10] Tyler Lange, *The First French Reformation: Church Reform and the Origins of the Old Regime* (New York, 2014), p. 22; Heike Uffmann, 'Inside and Outside the Convent Walls: The Norm and Practice of Enclosure in the Reformed Nunneries of Late Medieval Germany', *The Medieval History Journal*, 4:1 (2001), 89.

[11] Eire, *Reformations*, p. 43.

[12] Van Engen, *Sisters and Brothers of the Common Life*, p. 157. The Observants were introduced in Poitiers in the abbey of the Cordeliers in 1492–3: Robert Favreau, *Le Diocèse de Poitiers* (Paris, 1988), p. 95; Grégory Goudot, 'From Lateran V to Trent: Reformations of the Religious Orders, Power and Society in a French Diocese: Clermont (1512–1560)', *Franciscan Studies*, 71 (2013), 135–46. The Franciscan order in France in particular expanded in this revival and, after an intense internal debate, embraced the Observant movement by 1517. Mecham, *Sacred Communities, Shared Devotions*, pp. 17–18.

[13] Lehfeldt, *Religious Women in Golden Age Spain*, p. 139; Warren, 'Monastic Politics', pp. 23–4; Campbell, 'The Career, Cult and Canonisation'.

systematise and standardise monastic practice within their jurisdictions as well as to place their own candidates in positions of control over monastic houses and territories. Their efforts were without question rooted in spiritual concerns, but also had practical implications for their own power and position.[14]

While there were certainly differences between this broad range of institutions, monastic reform consistently emphasised female claustration and communal living.[15] In order to achieve the goals of enclosure, poverty and community, reformers encouraged women religious to dine together, to sleep in shared dormitories, to serve together in the choir, and to hold their goods in common. Further, reformers reemphasised monastic cloister, stressing that the monastic community should remain separate from the world beyond the abbey walls.[16] These emphases were rooted in spiritual concerns. Reform-motivated construction provided communal spaces such as dormitories, refectories, infirmaries, chapter houses and the choir. As Manon Louviot observed, these spaces were 'central to the monastic community, especially because everyone could see and be seen by everyone else.' Providing space for the community to pray, dine and sleep in shared spaces focused their minds on devotion. Reserving the monastic space for the nuns emphasised the abbey as a sacred space where the nuns performed holy work. Walls defined holy space apart from the secular world and removed distractions that might profane the sacrality of the abbey. Communal dining with a reading to focus the mind allowed that sacrality to continue to meals, turning them into liturgical moments. Group sleeping arrangements further encouraged appropriate devotions and activities. Dormitories and refectories are 'particularly relevant for the purpose of studying spatial and social relations.'[17] As I will argue later, during the late fifteenth and early sixteenth centuries reformers oversaw construction campaigns that either retrofitted abbeys with the facilities they required as reformed communities, or added new buildings and elements that made reformed life possible within the cloister. Redesigned monastic buildings facilitated communal living and restructured hierarchies within the monastery,

---

[14] Annalena Müller, *From the Cloister to the State: Fontevraud and the Making of Bourbon France, 1642-1100* [sic] (Abingdon, 2021).

[15] Constance Proksch, *Klosterreform und Geschichtsschreibung im Spätmittelalter* (Cologne, 1994), pp. 280-9.

[16] Van Engen, *Sisters and Brothers of the Common Life*, p. 157; June L. Mecham, 'A Northern Jerusalem: Transferring the Spatial Geography of the Convent of Wienhausen', in Andrew Spicer and Sarah Hamilton (eds), *Defining the Holy: Sacred Space in Medieval and Early Modern Europe* (Aldershot, 2005), p. 142.

[17] Manon Louviot, 'Controlling Space, Disciplining Voice: The Congregation of Windesheim and Fifteenth-Century Monastic Reform in Northern Germany and the Low Countries' (unpublished Ph.D. dissertation, University of Utrecht, 2019), p. 124.

flattening social hierarchy by removing independent status and special perquisites such as small dining and living apartments.

Fontevraud and the Web of Reform in Western France

Reform was widespread across Europe in the fifteenth century, with particular support in Germany, Spain, Italy and France. As Carlos Eire noted, 'in the fifteenth century, Western Europe seemed full of reformers and would-be reformers [...] Talk of reform was in the air.'[18] However, Western France's active monastic reform needs better integration into this larger story.

In France, reform movements were underway by the mid-fifteenth century. Colette of Corbie reformed and founded both male and female houses according to the *Rule* of St Clare, emphasising strict poverty and total enclosure, while establishing designated friars to serve the spiritual needs of female houses.[19] She received papal approval for her reforms, separately from the Observant Franciscan friars, in 1406, and they continued after her death in 1447. Her success bolstered women pursuing monastic reform in Western France. Fontevraud initiated reform in the 1450s and reformed a number of Fontevrist houses by the 1470s. Benedictine monasteries in France embraced reform by the 1480s, with female houses mostly following the example of Fontevraud and male communities, such as Saint-Germain, starting a few decades later.[20] Fontevraud and Chelles were able to stimulate reform in a number of priories and abbeys through their vast monastic networks where reformers had pre-existing contacts and relationships. This is the same period in which Sainte-Croix came under Fontevraud's influence, when Anne d'Orléans became abbess of Sainte-Croix in 1484 while remaining abbess of Fontevraud. Reform also attracted the attention and support of King Francis I, who was personally involved alongside Renée de Bourbon, abbess of Fontevraud, in reforming French convents, including Sainte-Croix. Bishop of Poitiers Pierre d'Amboise advocated for reform of Sainte-Croix and another Poitevin abbey, La Trinité, bringing them both to Francis and Renée's attention.[21] Bishop of Paris Étienne Poncher also used his power of visitation as bishop of Paris to press reform on monasteries within his jurisdiction.

Fontevraud was a large double community in the Loire valley, established in the twelfth century about 80 km from Sainte-Croix, that became the head of

---

[18] Eire, *Reformations*, p. 43.
[19] Campbell, 'The Career, Cult and Canonisation', pp. 23, 75–81.
[20] Le Gall, *Les moines au temps des réformes*, pp. 20, 29, 35–6, 39; Goudot, 'From Lateran V to Trent', 135–46, at p. 136.
[21] Poitiers, Archives Départementales de la Vienne (henceforth ADV), 2H1/2 1503, 1519.

a network of dependent priories, using a modified version of the Benedictine *Rule*.[22] Fontevraud abbess Marie de Bretagne (1424–77) played a key role in the fifteenth-century reform movement. She hoped to address some of the impact of the Hundred Years War on her abbey, since the fighting had depleted the Fontevrist Order's resources. A full accounting in 1461 of the devastation by Guillaume de Bailleul showed that the population of the priories had declined steeply, with many priories completely empty.[23] Marie therefore requested a reformed rule as early as 1458, but found the version provided by papal agents unsatisfying, particularly its insistence on a three-year term limit for the order offices, and so designed her own rule, which received approval from Pope Sixtus IV in 1478.[24] Marie's monastic model emphasised community, strict enclosure – even adding to the rule a chapter on not leaving the monastery – and poverty, which was a change from Fontevraud's twelfth-century founder Robert d'Arbrissel's vision.[25] Annalena Müller argues that Robert d'Arbrissel's original design rejected claustration for Fontevraud's women since he preferred a more engaged, less secluded form of monasticism, so it is interesting to see Marie insist on it so forcefully. She

---

[22] Suzanne Tunc, 'De l'élection des abbesses de Fontevraud à leur nomination par le Roi', *Annales de Bretagne et des pays de l'Ouest (Anjou, Maine, Touraine)*, 99:3 (1992), 78–83. Chapter 56 of the Benedictine *Rule* suggests that superiors should dine at their own table with guests or members of the community whom the superior has selected for the honour: *The Rule of Saint Benedict*, ed. and trans. Bruce L. Venarde (Cambridge, MA, 2011); Marie's reforms significantly changed this freedom. See Annalena Müller, 'From Charismatic Congregation to Institutional Monasticism: The Case of Fontevraud', *The American Benedictine Review*, 64:4 (2013), 428–44. For more on the *Rule*, see Honorat Nicquet, *Notes sur la regle de Marie de Bretagne, et causes pour lesquelles l'Ordre de Font-Evraud est en un si grand desordre* (n.p., 1636).

[23] Château-Gontier, Bibliothèque municipale, ms. 12, J. Lardier, *La Sainte-Famille de Fontevrault* (1650), pp. 560–1.

[24] Jo Ann McNamara, *Sisters in Arms: Catholic Nuns through Two Millennia* (Cambridge, MA, 1996), p. 414; Yvonne Labande-Mailfert and Robert Favreau (eds), *Histoire de l'abbaye Sainte-Croix de Poitiers: Quatorze siècles de vie monastique* (Poitiers,1986), pp. 167–8; François Uzureau, 'La réforme de l'ordre de Fontevrault (1459–1641)', *Revue Mabillon*, 13 (1923), 141–6; Jean de Viguerie, 'La réforme de Fontevraud, de la fin du XVe siècle à la fin des guerres de religion', *Revue d'histoire de l'église de France*, 65 (1979), 107–17. See also Louise Coudanne, 'De la règle réformée de Fontevrault (1479) aux statuts d'Étienne Poncher: 1505', *Revue Mabillon*, 59 (1979), 393–408; Armand Parrott (ed.), 'Mémorial des abbesses de Fontevrault, issues de la maison royale de France', *Mémoires de la société académique de la Maine et Loire*, 36 (1881), 1–189.

[25] See Chapter VI, *De non exeundo a clausura*, and Chapter VII, *De non intrando clauseram: Regula ordinis Fontis-Ebraldi. La regle de l'Ordre de Font-Evrauld, imprimée par l'ordonnance de tres-illustre & religieuses princesse Madame Jeanne-Baptiste de Bourbon, fille L. de France, Abbesse Chef, & Generale dudit Ordre* (Paris, 1642).

expected reformed communities, including the abbess, to embrace both active and passive enclosure, as well as communal dormitories and refectories.[26]

Since Fontevraud's main house resisted her reform efforts, Marie left Fontevraud and settled at the priory of La Madeleine d'Orléans – a priory where she may have had some family protection – with a select group of women more receptive to reform.[27] Here her model was a great success, and became the blueprint for the reform of over fifty other houses.[28] Fontevrists helped to reform houses such as Les Filles-Dieu, Fontaine, La Madeleine d'Orléans, Chelles, Montmartre and Jouarre, among many others, as well as Fontevraud itself. Charmarie Blaisdell suggested that the Fontevrist houses embraced reform more peacefully than those of other orders because the abbess of Fontevraud had a tradition of tighter control over her order, so, even beyond the influence of Marie, Fontevraud's structure may have facilitated reform in that network.[29]

Fontevraud's model of reform within a network of monasteries is also demonstrated by Chelles, which embraced reform in 1504 and later sent more than forty nuns to other communities for the purpose of reform, including Gif, Malnoue, Faremoutiers, Jouarre and Montmartre.[30] As at Fontevraud, sisters from reformed monasteries in other networks spread out to reform other houses. When Étienne Poncher reformed the Benedictine abbey of Yerres in 1513 he sent fourteen nuns from the already reformed abbeys of Chelles and Malnoue to live among the women and implement reform.[31] This method of chain-reform was especially powerful, as women from reformed abbeys served as monastic ambassadors, set on convincing new sisters to embrace reform initiatives, such as introducing new liturgical forms.[32] Those nuns would, in turn, be able to travel to yet more abbeys.

---

[26] Müller, 'From Charismatic Congregation to Institutional Monasticism', 439. See also Uzureau, 'La réforme de l'ordre de Fontevrault', 141–6; Alfred Jubien, *Marie de Bretagne et la réformation de l'Ordre de Fontevrault* (Angers, 1872), pp. 1–27; P. Honorat Nicquet, *Histoire de l'ordre de Fontevrault* (Paris, 1642); Lardier, *La Sainte-Famille de Fontevrault*.

[27] Uzureau, 'La réforme de l'ordre de Fontevrault', 141–2; Müller, 'From Charismatic Congregation to Institutional Monasticism', 438. Reformers had challenges at Isenhagen in the 1440s and 1480s, as well: Heinz J. Schulze, 'Isenhagen', in Ulrich Faust (ed.), *Die Männer-und Frauenklöster der Zisterzienser in Niedersachsen, Schleswig-Holstein und Hamburg* (St. Ottilien, 1994), pp. 228–67.

[28] Le Gall, *Les moines au temps des réformes*, p. 38. For more on Marie de Bretagne's reform, see Alfred Jubien, *Marie de Bretagne et la réformation de l'Ordre de Fontevrault*; and Müller, 'From Charismatic Congregation to Institutional Monasticism'.

[29] Charmarie Blaisdell, 'Religion, Gender, and Class: Nuns and Authority in Early Modern France', in Michael Wolfe (ed.), *Changing Identities in Early Modern France* (Durham, NC, 1997), pp. 147–68, at p. 158.

[30] Le Gall, *Les moines au temps des réformes*, p. 63; McNamara, *Sisters in Arms*, p. 416.

[31] Blaisdell, 'Religion, Gender, and Class', p. 152.

[32] Gisela Muschiol, 'Migrating Nuns – Migrating Liturgy? The Context of Reform in

The woman who became abbess of Fontevraud after Marie de Bretagne, Anne d'Orléans, reformed six other priories and was elected abbess of Sainte-Croix in 1484 (see Table 9.1).[33] As we will see at Sainte-Croix in Poitiers, reformed abbeys also served as hosts for recalcitrant nuns expelled from their abbeys for resisting reform. In the reformed community these women were forced to embrace the shape of reformed monastic living. In Yerres, for example, when the women resisted reform, Poncher transferred six of the nuns to other communities.[34]

The Fontevrist reform spread across western and central France, eventually reaching Sante-Croix. The first hints of reform at Sainte-Croix arrived with Anne d'Orléans, Marie de Bretagne's successor as abbess at Fontevraud who gained the abbacy at Sainte-Croix in 1484 (see Table 9.1). Anne had shown an interest in reforming Fontevrist priories with Marie de Bretagne's statutes, although she did not pursue this with the same enthusiasm as her successor at Fontevraud, Renée de Bourbon.[35] It was unusual for Sainte-Croix's nuns to elect an outsider as abbess, and for an abbess to continue holding a position elsewhere, as Anne did, so it is possible that her election reflects interest in the Fontevrist reform at Sainte-Croix or, perhaps, meddling from an external authority, such as the king.[36] As abbess of Sainte-Croix, Anne contributed to reform there through some new construction projects, especially by working on the dormitory roof and repairing the nuns' refectory, but her modifications at Sainte-Croix were not extensive enough to accommodate the whole community.[37] At Anne's death in 1491, Sainte-Croix's prioress Jeanne de Couhé was elected abbess, but amidst great resistance from within and without the abbey.[38] During the contentious election in 1491, rival troops entered the monastery to influence the election, and André, the brother of Jeanne's opponent, Fontevrist nun Marguerite de Vivonne, occupied the abbey

---

Female Convents of the Late Middle Ages', in Teresa Berger (ed.), *Liturgy in Migration – From the Upper Room to Cyberspace* (Collegeville, 2012), p. 83.

[33] Bernard Palustre, 'L'abbesse Anne d'Orléans et la réforme de Fontevrault', *Revue des questions historiques*, 66 (1899), 210–17, at p. 216; Annalena Müller, 'Forming and Re-Forming Fontevraud: Monasticism, Geopolitics, and the *Querelle des Frères*' (unpublished Ph.D. dissertation, Yale University, 2014); de Viguerie, 'La réforme de Fontevraud', 108, 113.

[34] Blaisdell, 'Religion, Gender, and Class', p. 152. In Spain, some small monasteries were suppressed, and members sent to larger urban monasteries, but Lehfeldt found that some women ran back to their original houses: Lehfeldt, *Religious Women in Golden Age Spain*, p. 143.

[35] de Viguerie, 'La réforme de Fontevraud', 108, 111.

[36] We have no evidence that Anne was pressed onto the abbey, but we also have no evidence of her election. See Edwards, *Superior Women*, chap. 7.

[37] ADV 2H1/25.

[38] Edwards, *Superior Women*, chap. 7.

Table 9.1. Abbesses of Fontevraud and Sainte-Croix.

Abbesses of Fontevraud	Abbesses of Sainte-Croix
Marie de Bretagne (1457–77)	Isabeau de Couhé (1456–84)
Anne d'Orléans (1477–91)	Anne d'Orléans (1484–91)
Renée de Bourbon (1491–1534)	Jeanne de Couhé (1491–1511)
	Marie Berland (1512–20, d. 1533)
	Isabeau de Beauvau, admin. prioress (1522–34)
Louise de Bourbon (1535–75)	Louise de Bourbon (1533–35)
	Madeleine de Bourbon (1535–69)

with his men for months.[39] Tensions remained high after the abbacy was settled on Jeanne in 1492, and members of the community complained about her in 1509, charging Jeanne with neglect and prioritising her own family. The complaints – discussed in more detail below – focused on private facilities for nuns related to Jeanne and suggest that at least part of the community sought reform.[40]

A new reform impetus in Sainte-Croix accompanied the arrival of King Francis I and Renée de Bourbon (abbess of Fontevraud) in Poitiers in 1519. They were escorted by a group of soldiers, for a *Grand Jours*, an assize sent by the king and the Parlement of Paris to areas without their own local parlement, with the power to adjudicate civil and criminal matters, including oversight of local religious houses. When Francis and Renée arrived, Sainte-Croix was governed by Jeanne de Couhé's niece and successor, Marie Berland, who had weathered her own contested election controversy in 1511–12 (see Table 9.1).[41] Reform continued to interest part of Sainte-Croix's community, while others resisted, and this latter group appears to have had the upper hand by a slim margin. As a first step in the reform, Renée de Bourbon expelled women who rejected reform, sending them to live among communities where reform was more established.[42] Of the thirty nuns at Sainte-Croix in 1519, eleven, including the abbess Marie Berland, were sent away, and twenty-four nuns were brought in from Fontevraud, which gives a sense of how divided Sainte-Croix was over reform – these were the highest

[39] For a fuller discussion, see Jennifer C. Edwards, 'My Sister for Abbess: Fifteenth-Century Disputes over the Abbey of Sainte-Croix, Poitiers', *Journal of Medieval History*, 40:1 (2014), 85–107, and *Superior Women*, chap. 7; Labande-Mailfert and Favreau (eds), *Histoire de l'abbaye Sainte-Croix de Poitiers*.

[40] ADV 2H1/2 1509.

[41] Edwards, *Superior Women*, chap. 7.

[42] Blaisdell, 'Religion, Gender, and Class', p. 152, n. 26 and n. 27. Janet Burton, 'Medieval Nunneries and Male Authority: Female Monasteries in England and Wales', in Janet Burton and Karen Stöber (eds), *Women in the Medieval Monastic World* (Turnhout, 2015), p. 135.

numbers of nuns shifted during Renée's reforms. Marie Berland spent the rest of her life at Fontevraud, petitioning to return to Sainte-Croix without success.[43]

Material Reform

The reformers' goals required material changes to abbeys and priories in order to facilitate the communal living they envisioned, but material realities were also useful metaphors for the reform. The Dominican reformer Johannes Meyer (1422–85) ensured that nuns' spiritual lives were developed together by allowing communal spaces for devotion – readings in the refectory, celebrations of the liturgy, and even personal devotion conducted alongside their sisters.[44] This connection between communal material spaces and nuns' spiritual lives was crucial for Meyer, who suggested that spiritual decline led to a material one, pointing to the dilapidation of the abbey of Schönensteinbach as an example.[45] Similarly, the Benedictine reform chronicler Nikolaus of Siegen (1450–95) connected spiritual and material walls – the collapse of the former led to the collapse of the latter.[46] The material needs of the reform reflected inner spirituality, beyond facilitating community, by reorganising the abbey's space. Eradicating private spaces and creating shared facilities for dining and sleeping encouraged communal harmony in a number of ways. It ensured a more equal distribution of abbey spaces and resources to end hierarchical divisions and forestalled factionalism. It discouraged sinful behaviour or even the rumour of sinful behaviour, either of which disrupted the community. And it responded to concerns about personal property by taking away individual spaces that might be decorated or used to store personal items, redirecting property to the community and ensuring personal poverty. Physically orienting the nuns into the same places and removing the material, financial and cultural walls that divided them helped the sisters to build community.

Walls between the nuns and the laity, however, were essential. At a time when commitment to a life of Christian service did not require a veil or enclosure, monastic walls indicated a separate, sacred space, apart from the secular world.

---

[43] Edwards, *Superior Women*, chap. 7.
[44] Jones, *Ruling the Spirit*, p. 153. The walls of refectories also became important places for art that the nuns could enjoy in common, and that would also inspire the community in their shared spaces. See Kate Lowe, 'Elections of Abbesses and Notions of Identity in Fifteenth- and Sixteenth-Century Italy, with Special Reference to Venice', *Renaissance Quarterly*, 54:2 (2001), 389–429; Dominique Rigaux, 'The Franciscan Tertiaries at the Convent of Sant'Anna at Foligno', *Gesta*, 31:2 (1992), 92–8.
[45] See Johannes Meyer, *Women's History in the Age of Reformation: Johannes Meyer's Chronicle of Dominican Observance*, trans. Claire Taylor Jones (Toronto, 2019).
[46] Huijbers, '"Observance" as Paradigm in Mendicant and Monastic Order Chronicles', pp. 119–20 and n. 39.

The claustration of the women can be seen as segregating them from the world or protecting them from its dangers, and both meanings operated concurrently.[47] In France, the overlapping wars of the fifteenth century meant that walled protection was necessary, and Colette of Corbie insisted on walled abbeys in fortified towns for nuns' safety.[48] The abbey's walls defined the special status of its residents as religious and emphasised their shared mission in these sacred spaces. That became even more crucial to reformers as the choices for a religious life multiplied. Structures within the abbey created further levels of meaning. As access was more and more restricted, the significance and sacrality of space increased. When reform imposed increased barriers to the laity's access through the abbey church, they sought to limit temptations and dangers, as well as to reserve space for holy purposes. Just as monastic women were encouraged to focus on their interior spiritual life, they were physically moved to the interior of the abbey grounds. The architectural changes corresponded literally to spiritual expectations.[49] As Roberta Gilchrist has suggested, the architectural structure of the abbey connected strongly to the identity of those who lived in these spaces, both in the conceptual framework of those beyond the walls and in the interior spirituality of the nuns themselves.[50]

Spatial definition was necessary because, as Gilchrist observed in England's monasteries, they had previously become partitioned into more private spaces and cubicles:

> Bishops' visitations reported a gradual neglect of the monastic observance of common frater (eating communally in the refectory) in favor of several private messes, much like the private chambers which were replacing great halls in higher status secular settlements. These *familiae* developed into distinct households within the nunnery [...] appearing in injunctions from the late thirteenth century and prevalent by the fifteenth.[51]

---

[47] Anne Müller, 'Symbolic Meanings of Space in Female Monastic Tradition', in Janet Burton and Karen Stöber (eds), *Women in the Medieval Monastic World* (Turnhout, 2015), p. 304; Roberta Gilchrist, *Gender and Material Culture: The Archaeology of Religious Women* (London, 1994), [e-book] location 2872.

[48] Campbell, 'The Career, Cult and Canonisation', p. 96.

[49] Müller, 'Symbolic Meanings of Space in Female Monastic Tradition', p. 308.

[50] Gilchrist, *Gender and Material Culture*, [e-book] location 442–509.

[51] *Ibid.*, location 2074–5. Carola Jäggi made a similar point for European monasteries, with Uwe Lobbedey: Carola Jäggi and Uwe Lobbedey, 'Church and Cloister: The Architecture of Female Monasticism in the Middle Ages', in Jeffrey F. Hamburger and Susan Marti (eds), *Crown and Veil: Female Monasticism from the Fifth to the Fifteenth Centuries* (New York, 2008), p. 128.

Monastic women who preferred these private spaces may have been clinging to familiar spaces observed in secular homes, where wealthy and elite women possessed spaces of their own. Gilchrist observed that monasteries with small household arrangements large enough to provide dining and sleeping accommodations for only a few nuns, such as Elstow and Godstow, contained nuns who were very high-status women.[52] This pattern is borne out in Poitiers, an abbey that primarily contained social elites, and whose small, separated households provoked strife.

Reformers stressed communal living and promised to end the hierarchical divisions that had grown in abbeys, particularly as families privileged relatives over the rest of the community. Reformers also struggled with the strong push from some Franciscan circles to impose strict poverty on reformed communities. Going further than the standard prohibition against personal property, reformers such as Colette of Corbie barred the accumulation of even communal property, forcing monastics to rely entirely on alms. Land donations, entrance fees, prebends, and other sources of revenue common to monastic life came under attack from those who preferred a stronger commitment to monastic poverty, pressing these ideas at the Council of Constance.[53] These reforms targeted the separations that had grown within abbeys as nuns split apart to live in small houses that could only accommodate a handful of women, rather than in large dormitories and refectories. Some of these factional disputes stemmed from differences in social status, as noble and wealthy women preferred living arrangements that matched their pre-monastic experiences, and were more able to access funds to support such comforts. Such arrangements might include individual chambers, decorations, superior-quality bedding, separate dining facilities, and even better food. Such disparities easily caused dispute and factionalism. Concern that abbeys lacked adequate communal facilities was genuine. At Saint-Pierre-de-Lyon in 1503, one dormitory could only accommodate four of the abbey's thirty-three nuns.[54] The same situation was discovered at Saint-Pierre-aux-Nonnains in Reims and at Faremoutiers.[55]

At Sainte-Croix, separation in dining and sleeping arrangements led to factionalism and hostility, particularly because the private spaces were only available

---

[52] Gilchrist, *Gender and Material Culture*, p. 168.

[53] James D. Mixson, *Poverty's Proprietors: Ownership and Mortal Sin at the Origins of the Observant Movement* (Leiden, 2009), p. 8. Colette of Corbie did permit nuns to give over gifts to the convent so that they could be used by the whole community. Her notion of poverty was strict but still stressed monastic community: Campbell, 'The Career, Cult and Canonisation', p. 60.

[54] Le Gall, *Les moines au temps des réformes*, p. 226; Alfred Corvine, 'Une Visite de Saint-Pierre de Lyon en 1503', *Revue d'histoire de Lyon*, 11 (1912), 241–72, at p. 247.

[55] Le Gall, *Les moines au temps des réformes*, p. 226, n. 2.

to members of the abbess's own family. Sainte-Croix's nuns drew from the same group of local noble families, so here the issue was not social hierarchy but familial domination, as members from the de Couhé family controlled most of the abbey offices. The ability of the complaining nuns to resist also comes from their social background. Both factions of Sainte-Croix's nuns could draw on arguments about tradition, both those complaining that the smaller households interrupted community, and those pointing to the abbey's longstanding use of prebends and segregated living through priories.[56] Like other abbeys across Europe, Sainte-Croix had come to be dominated by wealthy and noble women whose demands on space and resources matched a secular rather than a monastic ideal.[57] The fifteenth-century reform that sought a course correction shifted instead to a more abstemious and communal form of life, one welcomed by members who did not have these status benefits or whose spiritual goals aligned with those of the reformers, and resisted by those who benefited from the existing system. As June Mecham showed, some of the nuns who held on to personal funds did so in order to benefit the community. Among the Heath convents she studied, Mecham found that aristocratic women used personal funds established by their relatives to provide resources for the abbey nuns and serve as patrons for abbey decorative programmes. This use of personal funding increased after reform eradicated other lines of revenue and created greater need in the community.[58] This is an important glimpse into the post-reform resistance that also served the nuns' best interests.

Individual sleeping arrangements, where nuns might have their own cell, also violated these reformers' spirit of community; dining in small groups without the liturgical readings, independent prayer, personal possessions and secretive activities; all turned the women away from communal living, thus making them targets of reform. By encouraging nuns to sleep and dine in shared spaces, reformers hoped to equalise the community as well as to encourage familiarity and sisterly relations. The ideal result, as suggested by Windesheim Congregation reformer Johannes Busch at Derneburg, was a community that quietly enjoyed meals at a 'common table' accompanied by the reading of scripture, with a shared dormitory.[59]

---

[56] The nuns described Sainte-Croix as a 'belle et notable abbaye' in which there were a 'grand nombre de religieuses nobles et de noble lignée de bonnes et grandes maisons': ADV 2H1/2 1509, Memoire, fol. 1; Robert Favreau, 'Une élection à l'abbaye Sainte-Croix de Poitiers en 1491', *Revue d'histoire de l'Église de France*, 65 (174) (1979), 75–87.

[57] Mixson, *Poverty's Proprietors*, pp. 14–15.

[58] Mecham, *Sacred Communities, Shared Devotions*, pp. 111–26.

[59] See Charitas Pirkheimer, 'Pictures of the Reformation Period', *The Dublin Review*, 66 (1898), 345–71; Johannes Busch, 'Liber de reformatione monasteriorum', ed. Karl Grube, *Des Augustinerpropstes Iohannes Busch Chronicon Windeshemense und Liber de refor-*

Sleeping arrangements held important ramifications for the community. Dormitories provided equal space and erased status markers between nuns such as wealth and nobility, but not when some nuns enjoyed private or small-group accommodations. Such arrangements invited comparison and dispute. Reformers were concerned that private cells encouraged individualism over community, allowing nuns to cling to extramural social and economic status. There were also concerns that private cells led to inappropriate activities such as the accumulation of personal possessions or night-time sinfulness. The dormitories were private to the nuns themselves, as Gilchrist observed: in nunneries the 'dormitory was located in the deepest space, whereas male communities were equally, and sometimes more likely to reserve the deepest space for the chapter house.'[60] But, by the late fourteenth century, as Gilchrist noted above, the trend was moving away from large communal dormitories, hence making this an area of concern for reformers.[61]

Refectories were important spaces where the entire community gathered together to dine. Nuns typically ate in silence while listening to a reading that focused minds on devotion. A communal text provided a lesson to the entire monastery, fostering a shared experience similar to their time in chapter. As a liturgical practice, reformers expected attentive reception of the reading. Communal dining in the refectory while listening to a reading was another opportunity for the sisters to focus on their spiritual lives *together*, and their silence allowed them to focus on the reading rather than on small talk or disputes, both as a spiritual exercise and as an effort to encourage harmony. When communities opted instead for private or small-group dining, these opportunities for community building were lost. Even more worrisome was when nuns were forced into smaller spaces because there were no spaces large enough to accommodate them.[62]

Concerns that this sort of divided dining and sleeping could lead to factionalism were fair: one group of nuns at Sainte-Croix complained in 1509 that Abbess Jeanne de Couhé unfairly privileged her own family when she had built a new dormitory only large enough for six women, and filled it with her own relatives

---

matione monasteriorum (Farnborough, 1968, orig. 1886); Cynthia J. Cyrus, *The Scribes for Women's Convents in Late Medieval Germany* (Toronto, 2009), p. 75.

[60] Gilchrist, *Gender and Material Culture*, location 2850. For more on medieval monastic architecture, see the work of Carola Jäggi, especially *Frauenklöster im Spätmittelalter: Die Kirchen der Klarissen und Dominikanerinnen im 13. und 14. Jahrhundert* (Petersberg, 2006).

[61] Erika Lauren Lindgren, *Sensual Encounters: Monastic Women and Spirituality in Medieval Germany* (New York, 2009), chap. 1.

[62] Lowe, *Nuns' Chronicles and Convent Culture*, p. 136.

while neglecting the larger dormitory.[63] The complaint alleged that the abbey buildings were in disrepair, especially the dormitory, and that the refectory had no windows or chimney.[64] A 1510 visitation from bishop of Poitiers Claude de Husson confirmed that the nuns ate in small groups in separate dormitories and that communal meals were impossible within the abbey's existing buildings.[65]

New, more communal spaces were not just for the regular community, but also included the abbess, whom reformers wanted to join nuns in refectories and communal dormitories.[66] Building community meant increasing fellowship for all nuns, reducing the abbess's independence, and addressing accusations of negligence and corruption. Emphasising strict passive enclosure also reduced the need for separate dining facilities for the abbess as she would no longer be entertaining visiting dignitaries once enclosure was enforced. Moreover, reformers encouraged abbesses to recommit to their oaths of poverty, which meant reducing their office's prestige and wealth.[67] When reforming an abbey, Renée de Bourbon immediately took control of the abbey's finances. She ended prebends and benefices that created independent lines of revenue, and put those back towards the community's finances.[68] The abbess was also responsible for redirecting external gifts to the abbey and away from individual women.[69] Bringing the abbess into the communal facilities encouraged humility and harmony for the whole community.

Some women at Sainte-Croix expected their abbess to take these steps, and were disappointed that Jeanne de Couhé did not. As part of their 1509 complaint, a faction of Sainte-Croix's nuns asserted that Jeanne failed to live in community with them, and accused her of neglect.[70] The latter charge was more significant, but the Parlement of Paris ordered Jeanne to address both concerns by paying for the community's food and eating with her nuns in the communal refectory. Jeanne invited local officials to observe her progress and the refectory's condition

[63] ADV 2H1/2, 1509; Edwards, *Superior Women*, p. 251.
[64] ADV 2H1/2 1509.
[65] ADV 2H1/2, 1510; Labande-Mailfert and Favreau, *Histoire de l'abbaye Sainte-Croix de Poitiers*, p. 201; Leslie Tuttle, 'From Cloister to Court: Nuns and the Gendered Culture of Disputing in Early Modern France', *Journal of Women's History*, 22:2 (2010), 11–33, at pp. 19–20.
[66] Winston-Allen, *Convent Chronicles*, pp. 83–6; Le Gall, *Les moines au temps des réformes*, p. 427; and Guy Marie Oury, 'Les Bénédictines réformés de Chezal-Benoît', *Revue d'histoire de l'Église de France*, 65:174 (1979), 89–106.
[67] Edwards, *Superior Women*, p. 249; Winston-Allen, *Convent Chronicles*, pp. 83–6; Le Gall, *Les moines au temps des réformes*, p. 427.
[68] de Viguerie, 'La réforme de Fontevraud,' 113; Le Gall, *Les moines au temps des réformes*, p. 286.
[69] Edwards, *Superior Women*, pp. 249–50.
[70] ADV 2H1/2 1509.

in a 1511 visitation that observed only sixteen of the abbey's twenty-seven nuns dining together.[71] Most of the remaining nuns were ill or tending them, but two healthy women just refused to participate.[72] This was part of the justification for King Francis I to reform the monastery with Fontevraud abbess Renée of Bourbon in 1519.

With this emphasis on communal spaces, reformed monasteries often had to build expensive new dormitories and refectories, as existing spaces could not accommodate the whole community, but the funds for such construction were not easy to gather. Francis I was generous in funding reform construction at monasteries between 1515 and 1522.[73] He sent Chezal-Benoit 1000 livres tournois (lt) in November 1520 so they could build a refectory, and 300 lt that same year to help construction at Sainte-Croix de Poitiers.[74] Nuns might be reluctant to commit such funds on their own to construction designed to facilitate reform, however, since reform meant giving up prebends and seeing priories collapsed back into the main house.[75] Several reformers, including Renée de Bourbon and bishop of Paris Étienne Poncher, suggested that both personal funds and family gifts needed to be redirected away from the decision-making of the nuns themselves.[76] At Chelles and Montmartre, Étienne Poncher set up a central depository and established an agent to direct funds to officers as necessary, so even the abbess did not have power to make decisions about the abbey's wealth.[77] Sainte-Croix's nuns, who complained that Jeanne de Couhé redirected the abbey's rent money to her lay relatives and that they no longer received their daily living allowance of 1 denier while their diet had been restricted, possibly welcomed this sort of revision of the abbess's financial responsibilities.[78]

[71] ADV 2H1/2; Labande-Mailfert and Favreau, *Histoire de l'abbaye Sainte-Croix de Poitiers*, p. 201.
[72] ADV 2H1/2 1511.
[73] Le Gall, *Les moines au temps des réformes*, p. 605. Chelles built a new dormitory, as well as new choir stalls to accommodate the whole community at prayer. New or expanded dormitories were also built at Yerres, Faremoutiers, Fontevraud, La Madeleine d'Orléans and Jumièges.
[74] Le Gall, *Les moines au temps des réformes*, p. 117; Ursmer Berlière, 'La Congrégation bénédictine de Chezal-Benoit', *Revue bénédictine*, 17 (1900), 29–50, 113–27, 252–74 and 337–61.
[75] de Viguerie, 'La réforme de Fontevraud', 113; Le Gall, *Les moines au temps des réformes*, p. 286.
[76] Müller, *From the Cloister to the State*, pp. 158–9.
[77] Le Gall, *Les moines au temps des réformes*, p. 429.
[78] A long complaint lists various sources of revenue available to the abbey, such as local houses or woods owned by Sainte-Croix, and claims Jeanne mismanaged them; the complaint also specifies unrepaired damages to Sainte-Croix's buildings, such as dilapidated chimneys: ADV 2H1/2, 1509. The prioress's documentation of the nuns' com-

Beyond the need to create spaces large enough to accommodate the entire community, reformed abbeys increasingly required funds for construction due to the success of their reforms. Several reformed abbeys grew in size with new members, perhaps as a result of increased attention on the monastery through its reform. These greater numbers of sisters in the community required expanded or newly created dining and sleeping accommodations simply as a practical matter. At Chelles, for example, the community went from fourteen nuns to eighty after the reform, while La Madeleine d'Orléans went from six to sixty. At Sainte-Croix in Poitiers, numbers increased from about thirty before the 1519 reform to over fifty in 1528 and then to eighty by 1540. Most of the reformed monasteries acquired new dormitories, as at Chelles, Sainte-Croix and Saint-Martin, while at Faremoutiers, Fontevraud and Saint-Pierre-de-Lyon existing dormitories were restored and/or expanded.[79]

Dormitories and refectories were not the only spaces of concern to reformers. Communities with increased populations put pressure on other areas of the abbey, especially the choir, the chapter room and the church. Chelles gained a new choir, Chelles and Fontevraud repaired choir stalls and/or increased their number, while Yerres enlarged the entire church. Yerres received a new chapter room, while La Madeleine d'Orléans was completely rebuilt.[80] Construction that improved an abbey's enclosure was also common, especially abbey walls, choir screens and devices that provided further separation between the nuns and the laity.

Enclosure

Enclosure was a defining feature of the conventual life and a key distinction from some of the central and late medieval religious movements.[81] Enclosure was an ancient ideal of female monasticism, strictly required in the sixth-century *Rule of Caesarius* that Sainte-Croix adopted at its foundation.[82] From its earliest iterations, enclosure was intended to protect religious women from the secular world, both its violence and its temptations, and these twin concerns remained in the late

---

plaints is unfortunately badly damaged: ADV 2H1/2, 1509. A contemporary customary lists the nuns' daily allowance as a jug of wine, a loaf of bread, and a cash payment: Pierre de Monsabert, 'Anciens usages de l'abbaye Sainte-Croix de Poitiers avant la réforme de 1519', *Revue Mabillon*, 12 (1922), 263–76.

[79] Le Gall, *Les moines au temps des réformes*, p. 605.
[80] Ibid., p. 605.
[81] Uffmann, 'Inside and Outside the Convent Walls', 91.
[82] Edwards, *Superior Women*, pp. 40–3; Albrecht Diem, 'Inventing the Holy Rule: Some Observations on the History of Monastic Normative Observance in the Early Medieval West', in *Western Monasticism* ante litteram: *The Spaces of Monastic Observance in Late Antiquity and the Early Middle Ages* (Turnhout, 2011), pp. 53–84.

medieval notion of claustration.⁸³ Enclosure further defined the holy space of the abbey; closing off windows and doors became a way of blocking out sin that might profane the abbey's sacred space.

While Benedict VIII's 1298 edict *Periculoso* seemed to enforce enclosure on all female monasteries, monastic women continued to go about their business without censure from their supervisors or neighbours. Erin Jordan has argued persuasively that, in practice, nuns going in and out of their monasteries to conduct abbey business, visit relatives, host dignitaries and employ workmen were not seen as 'breaking' enclosure.⁸⁴ Enclosure seems to have been a rhetorical position that distinguished monastic women, but one that did not necessarily limit an abbess's activity beyond her abbey walls: managing property, wielding high justice privileges in local courts, or exercising her rights to market days. These are, however, the very aspects of late medieval abbatial authority that reformers challenged. It is ironic to see Renée de Bourbon travelling to Poitiers to insist on the claustration of other nuns, or Colette of Corbie insisting on enclosure stricter than St Clare's while travelling constantly to impose reform, but the material realities of higher cloister walls, new grilles and other construction that segregated and contained monastic women were a key part of this late medieval reform.⁸⁵ Fifteenth-century reformers valued strict claustration for nuns and shifted responsibility for permitting entrance or exit from the abbess to the bishop.⁸⁶ Anxiety about new religious groups that emphasised community and service, but did not require vows or enclosure, encouraged traditional houses to stress their rule and claustration as part of a branding effort.⁸⁷ Such desires on the part of reformers did not always translate into the realities practised by nuns, however, who retained extensive connections and responsibilities in the community.

Bishops also had mixed feelings about reform. As Elizabeth Lehfeldt observed for Spain, *Periculoso* was a problem for more than the nuns: 'Almost immediately after its circulation, bishops and others betrayed an unwillingness to abandon the customary activity of nuns in medieval society and began making exceptions to the requirements of enclosure.'⁸⁸ Many men also entered the monastery on

---

⁸³ Müller, 'Symbolic Meanings of Space in Female Monastic Tradition', p. 304.
⁸⁴ Erin L. Jordan, 'Roving Nuns and Cistercian Realities: The Cloistering of Religious Women in the Thirteenth Century', *Journal of Medieval and Early Modern Studies*, 42:3 (2012), 597–614.
⁸⁵ Félix Pasquier (ed.), *Grands Jours de Poitiers de 1454 à 1634* (Paris, 1874); Campbell, 'The Career, Cult and Canonisation', p. 62.
⁸⁶ Edwards, *Superior Women*, p. 246–7; Winston-Allen, *Convent Chronicles*, p. 63.
⁸⁷ An effort to distinguish themselves as conventuals in an age of non-cloistered alternatives, see Van Engen, *Sisters and Brothers of the Common Life*, especially chap. 4.
⁸⁸ Lehfeldt, *Religious Women in Golden Age Spain*, p. 107.

a regular basis: canons to say a weekly mass, construction workers for building projects, and visiting family members or royal officials. Sainte-Croix's nuns continued to leave their abbey or to welcome guests inside, and faced very little criticism for their activities until the early sixteenth century. The abbess kept a boat, horses and a carriage; she left the abbey to administer her properties, to exercise her privileges of high justice, or to process with her community to the church of Sainte-Radegonde.[89] In fact, the nuns' departures were normal and necessary for the survival of their abbey and they mostly went unchallenged.[90]

Nevertheless, reformers persisted in advocating for enclosure and made structural changes to monasteries to facilitate the practice of claustration. New walls appeared at Sainte-Croix in Poitiers, increasing the size of the enclosure but blocking the nuns off from the city beyond. Renée de Bourbon funded a new wall at Fontevraud by selling her silver set.[91] During Saint-Pierre-de-Lyon's 1503 reform the windows of the abbey buildings that overlooked the street were sealed shut.[92] While some of the reformed nuns at Kirchheim complained about their enclosure, with one even scaling the abbey wall, the nun who described that incident in the abbey chronicle was anxious that enclosure might be lost, losing the community their Dominican identity.[93]

For bishop of Paris Étienne Poncher, the abbey's enclosure should include the dormitory, refectory, chapter room, the cloister, gardens and the church choir, spaces kept separate from areas visitors might access.[94] Much attention went to building elements that would facilitate enclosure and privacy. This included grilles or choir screens, such as at Fontevraud and Faremoutiers. Since Saint-Pierre-de-Lyon's abbey church was also a parish church, in 1503 reformers installed a grille between the choir and the nave to separate the nuns from the community.[95] At Yzeure, where the abbey church also served the parish, the queen of France Anne de Beaujeu (1461–1522) funded a new church to separate the two communities.[96] To ensure reform, Poncher added choir screens or grilles in abbeys he

[89] Edwards, *Superior Women*, chaps 6 and 7.
[90] Jordan, 'Roving Nuns and Cistercian Realities'. Jordan has also encouraged scholars to reconsider the idea that enclosure related to fears of pollution: Erin L. Jordan, 'Pro remedio anime sue: Cistercian Nuns and Space in the Low Countries', in Janet E. Burton and Karen Stöber (eds), *Women in the Medieval Monastic World* (Turnhout, 2015), pp. 279–98, at p. 287. Of course, some women found enclosure useful and comforting, and a way to maintain authority: Winston-Allen, *Convent Chronicles*, p. 10.
[91] Blaisdell, 'Religion, Gender, and Class', p. 150.
[92] Le Gall, *Les moines au temps des réformes*, p. 490.
[93] Uffmann, 'Inside and Outside the Convent Walls', p. 105.
[94] Le Gall, *Les moines au temps des réformes*, p. 316.
[95] Ibid., p. 317.
[96] Ibid., p. 317.

reformed. The choir screens were also intended to block the officiant, isolating the nuns.[97] At Ebstorf, for example, the nuns found the separation from the rest of the congregation caused by the new screen painful.[98] The abbey church at Sainte-Croix was not a parish church, a role played by the neighbouring church of Sainte-Radegonde in Poitiers, which was a dependent community the nuns used as a public face for Radegund's cult. Yet Sainte-Croix's church, too, received a new grille in the sixteenth century, which suggests how much more porous the abbey might have been despite claims about claustration.[99] The canonesses of the chapter of Windesheim, a network of houses created in the Modern Devotion movement in the Low Countries, following the guidance of Windesheim, typically used a gallery built into the west side of their churches as well as a screen to keep the canonesses regular from mixing with churchgoers down below or even being seen by them. The gallery did typically include pews.[100]

Such screens and new walls were not always popular. At Yerres the nuns tore down Étienne Poncher's choir grille immediately after it was constructed, and in 1506 the women of Saint-Pierre-de-Lyon destroyed the wall built by the reformers three years earlier. The nuns of Saint-Pierre complained to Parlement that the strict interpretation of enclosure that Philippe Bourgoing imposed on them violated their traditional privileges to go on procession.[101] At Sainte-Croix the women complained in 1503, when bishop of Poitiers Pierre d'Amboise imposed strict enclosure on nuns in Poitiers. Pierre threatened excommunication for any violations, prompting Jeanne de Couhé to complain to the papal legate and archbishop of Bordeaux, Cardinal André d'Espinay.[102] The cardinal was not very sympathetic to Jeanne's position, although he did clarify that priests could enter the abbey to conduct religious services.[103]

New material realities in reformed convents were not only about new structures. In 1488 Wienhausen's new abbess 'had the wall paintings in the nuns' choir repainted or restored by three members of her convent.'[104] The paintings depicted Christian heresy from Creation up to the Fall, as well as the story of

---

[97] *Ibid.*, p. 317.
[98] Uffmann, 'Inside and Outside the Convent Walls', p. 105.
[99] Labande-Mailfert and Favreau, *Histoire de l'abbaye Sainte-Croix de Poitiers*, p. 234.
[100] Wybren Scheepsma, *Medieval Religious Women in the Low Countries: The 'Modern Devotion', the Canonesses of Windesheim, and their Writings*, trans. David Johnson (Woodbridge, 2004), pp. 52–3.
[101] Le Gall, *Les moines au temps des réformes*, p. 490. Also: Blaisdell, 'Religion, Gender, and Class', p. 152, n. 31.
[102] Appeal from Jeanne de Couhé: ADV, 2H1/2, 7 September 1503.
[103] ADV 2H1/2, 1503; Labande-Mailfert and Favreau, *Histoire de l'abbaye Sainte-Croix de Poitiers*, p. 201.
[104] Muschiol, 'Migrating Nuns – Migrating Liturgy', pp. 83–100, at p. 98.

Christ, including Old Testament prophecies of his life and death, ending with an image of Christ Enthroned.[105] The images connect to the liturgy and, as Gisela Muschiol observes: 'The program of decoration in the nuns' choir [...] creates a quasi-presence of the pivotal biblical events, which time and again immerses the sisters celebrating the liturgy in the visualisation both of monastic history and of the history of salvation.'[106] The nuns of Wienhausen used these images to conceive of their abbey as a new Jerusalem and to travel through their abbey on a virtual pilgrimage.[107] The images focused the nuns' minds, inspired their devotion, and defined the abbey as sacred space suitable for a spiritual journey. When nuns from Wienhausen went to reform Medingen, they inspired similar artistic expression there.[108] The paintings refocused the nuns' minds by altering their material spaces. Unfortunately, since Sainte-Croix was torn down during the French Revolution and the years following, we do not have much information about the decorations Sainte-Croix might have held.

Conclusion

Many women participated in monastic reform, whether reforming other abbeys, inviting reformers to their abbeys, or working to effect reform in their own community. Reform was not simply imposed on female monasteries by outsiders. This becomes obvious when we look at the fierce resistance some communities put up against reformers. Disputes within a monastery show us that some nuns welcomed the changes reform could bring to their communities, particularly in shifting power relationships inside the community and yielding a more communal lifestyle. Equalising the status of the women in the monastery by cancelling prebends, reducing personal luxuries and emphasising community appealed to women committed to the monastic life but who were uncomfortable with wealth-based hierarchies within a community supposedly devoted to poverty. Reform promised equality, community and harmony, which noble status and personal wealth compromised. Some women also believed that reform, even claustration, gave them power to control their own lives by limiting secular interference in the abbey, and they pursued those changes eagerly.[109]

But other women resisted reform and clung to their traditions, perceiving reform as a limitation on their autonomy and authority.[110] These responses meant

---

[105] Mecham, 'A Northern Jerusalem', pp. 139–60.
[106] Muschiol, 'Migrating Nuns – Migrating Liturgy', p. 98.
[107] Mecham, 'Sacred Vision, Sacred Voice', pp. 305–47.
[108] Muschiol, 'Migrating Nuns – Migrating Liturgy', p. 98.
[109] Winston-Allen, *Convent Chronicles*, p. 10.
[110] Silvia Evangelisti, *Nuns: A History of Convent Life, 1450–1700* (Oxford, 2007), pp. 41–65.

reform was contentious and divisive for many monastic communities, and that the material needs of the reform were often contested. Reformers themselves might be unwelcome. Johannes Busch reported that a canoness at Derneburg locked him in a cellar during his visitation there, while Cistercian nuns at Mariensee, including the abbess, threw rocks at reformers from the church roof.[111] Francis and Renée may have arrived at Poitiers expecting such trouble: they arrived with a large number of armed troops – not what one might normally expect for the reform of a group of about thirty nuns.[112]

Concepts of space and gender in the monastic context have been in flux as scholars dig into documents of practice and recover the voices of monastic women considered silenced only an academic generation ago. Given the findings described here about the engagement of monastic women in reform within and beyond their own houses, we can broaden the view of reform's agents, leaving behind a vision of reform as a male imposition or a male reordering of female space. As Marie, Renée, Colette and other monastic female activists facilitating reform in the fifteenth century can demonstrate, this was an ideal that women shared, from its ideology to its execution. Erika Lindgren discusses the way women subverted the official designations of monastic spaces' function, and we might add the ways women invested in creating and enforcing these designations themselves.[113] This was not a dispute between men and women, or a simple top-down imposition, but one between advocates of different notions of monasticism with women on both sides of the debate, and calls coming from within each of the houses.

Reform in the fifteenth century reoriented the abbey's community. Women were thrust together in shared dining and sleeping facilities, at the same time that they were physically separated from the community beyond the gates. They lost their traditional avenues for revenue and financial autonomy at a time when they most needed resources to fund new construction. Yet, the reform was not exclusively imposed by others – factions of nuns welcomed reform and pursued its experts. These efforts reformed female spaces even as they were renegotiated.

Since the fifteenth-century reform movement affected the physical spaces of female communities, it is worth considering the impact of these physical changes on ideas of monastic space.[114] Heiki Uffmann argued persuasively that reform that enclosed monastic women shaped their concepts of space to focus almost entirely on 'the inner world of the religious community', while 'the architecture of nunneries, planned according to gender-specific norms, shapes the perspectives of the

[111] Busch, 'Liber de reformatione monasteriorum', ed. Karl Grube, pp. 562–4, 593.
[112] Edwards, *Superior Women*, chap. 7.
[113] Lindgren, *Sensual Encounters*, chap. 1.
[114] Müller, 'Symbolic Meanings of Space in Female Monastic Tradition', p. 302.

female writers. Their accounts often end at the convent walls. Their view is limited to the small area accessible to the religious women.' This was rather the point; even beyond physical separation from temptations or a dangerous world that the reformers had in mind, enclosure refocused the nuns' gaze on the interior of the monastery, on their spiritual lives and on their community. Building communal spaces that allowed the entire community to dine and sleep and meet and worship as a whole, and then removing them from external concerns, pushed monastic women together. This rearrangement of space shifted notions of authority within the community, stripping away traditional lines of income, flattening hierarchies that had developed, forcing even the abbess to eschew independent facilities that were an important and visible demonstration of her superiority in the community.[115] Reformed, communal spaces brought greater shared spiritual intimacy to the community while limiting their physical intimacy with the dangers and temptations of the broader world. At Sainte-Croix, as at many other abbeys, financial and authority privileges had been co-opted and abused by some members of the community and reform offered an opportunity to redress the factionalism that threatened the abbey; construction allowed the community to re-equalise the sisters while at the same time offering a recommitment to a spiritual life.

---

[115] Müller observed that 'space was also used in monasticism to strengthen the power and authority that operated within these communities. Given, for example, the higher status of the abbess or prioress, issues of interest are ceremonies of entry into the church, the refectory, or the chapter house; seating patterns; or art and architecture as markers of power': 'Symbolic Meanings of Space in Female Monastic Tradition', p. 314; Edwards, *Superior Women*.

CHAPTER 10

Who Made Reform Visible? Male and Female Agency in Changing Visual Culture

KATHARINA ULRIKE MERSCH

In recent years, many scholars have examined the impact of monastic reform on the visual culture of women's religious communities, in particular for fifteenth- and early sixteenth-century Germany.[1] It is common sense that nuns' production of tapestries, illuminated manuscripts and other works of art that formed part of a convent's visual culture served reform ideals, as the monastic rules prescribe manual labour. The topics depicted on such objects served to internalise spiritual ideas that were characteristic of certain branches of reform such as the Dominican Observance or the Augustinian Congregation of Windesheim. Therefore, adjusting or reviving visual culture was one of the distinctive features of reform in late medieval women's convents, alongside the production of new books and a renewal of liturgy. Scholars have argued that male reformers and provosts had a strong influence on the production of images within the female communities under their supervision. Other historians and art historians have observed that nuns and canonesses also had opportunities to shape the material and visual culture of reform.[2] Nevertheless, the question to what extent male clerics or the

---

[1] See, for example, June L. Mecham, *Sacred Communities, Shared Devotions: Gender, Material Culture, and Monasticism in Late Medieval Germany* (Turnhout, 2014); and Anne Winston-Allen, 'Networking in Medieval Strasbourg: Cross-Order Collaboration in Book Illustration among Women's Reformed Convents', in Stephen Mossman (ed.), *Schreiben und Lesen in der Stadt: Literaturbetrieb im spätmittelalterlichen Straßburg* (Berlin, 2012), pp. 197–212. These and other works from this field of study will be discussed in more detail below.

[2] For an orientation to the debates about the role of male offficials and the art objects produced by and for nuns in the context of reform, see Jeffrey F. Hamburger, 'Art,

women they took care of influenced artistic production in the service of reform remains contested.³ In this chapter I would like to examine this question in a systematic manner, drawing upon written sources and the visual evidence from fifteenth-century Germany. On what basis is it possible to distinguish between female and male agency when it comes to changing a female convent's visual culture during reform?

Some preliminary remarks concerning the general logic of reform and the ways researchers have dealt with it are necessary to understand how best to approach the problem addressed here. First, we have to distinguish two different methods of reform that scholars have deduced from written sources: reform could be implemented at the behest of the order, for example the Dominican order, or of a bishop, that is via an act of domination; or it could be implemented at the behest of the inhabitants of a women's community, indicating a more voluntary and active act.⁴ In the case that reform was imposed upon a convent, any change in a convent's visual culture was also likely to be imposed; when reform came from within the community, changes in visual culture were more likely to be voluntary. On the other hand, we have to take into account that both

---

Enclosure and the *cura monialium*: Prolegomena in the guise of a Postscript', *Gesta*, 31:2 (1992), 108–34; Mecham, *Sacred Communities*, especially chap. 6, 'The Art of Reform', pp. 159–204; Andrea Pearson, *Envisioning Gender in Burgundian Devotional Art (1350-1530): Experience, Authority, Resistance* (Aldershot, 2005), especially chap. 4: 'Nuns and Clerics: Ambiguous Authority in a Devotional Portrait Diptych', pp. 136–61; and Anne Winston-Allen, 'Women as Scribes and Illustrators in the Age of Reform: The Basel Connection', in Johanna Thali and Nigel F. Palmer (eds), *Raum und Medium. Literatur und Kultur in Basel in Spätmittelalter und Früher Neuzeit* (Berlin, 2020), pp. 177–200 and 534–9.

³ Considering the fact that women's agency in reforming their convents is itself contested (see, for the twelfth and thirteenth centuries, Fiona J. Griffiths, 'Women and Reform in the Central Middle Ages', in Judith M. Bennett and Ruth M. Karras (eds), *The Oxford Handbook of Women and Gender in Medieval Europe* (Oxford, 2013), pp. 447–63), it is not surprising that their agency in artistic production connected to reform is also contested. Sabine Wehking has addressed this problem in the case of some now lost panel paintings from the reformed convent of Medingen dating from 1499. The panels depicted the history of the convent, culminating in the re-establishment of the communal meal as a symbol for the *vita communis* and the election of the new abbess Margaretha Puffen during reform. Although the paintings were made to adorn the abbess's house, and even though written sources imply that both the provost Ulrich of Bülow and Abbess Margaretha Puffen arranged the panels to be painted, one often reads that only Ulrich of Bülow was responsible for the iconographic programme. Sabine Wehking (ed.), *Die Inschriften der Lüneburger Klöster: Ebstorf, Isenhagen, Lüne, Medingen, Walsrode, Wienhausen* (Wiesbaden, 2009), no. 58†.

⁴ Stefanie Monika Neidhardt, *Autonomie im Gehorsam: die dominikanische Observanz in Selbstzeugnissen geistlicher Frauen des Spätmittelalters*, Vita Regularis, 70 (Berlin, 2017), p. 85.

methods of implementation could be applied within one and the same community to a varying degree. A bishop or the superiors of the order might command the reform of a community; in the years that followed the process of reform could be voluntarily continued by the members of the community.[5] As a result, it is sometimes hard to connect art objects to reform, because in most cases we cannot tell whether a reform was completed by a certain date or not. It becomes difficult, therefore, to tell whether an image produced thirty or forty years after the initial occurrence of the term 'reform' in the written sources remained associated with those events. Sometimes the objects themselves provide information: for example, in the case of the Augustinian canonesses at Heiningen, the provost of the Augustinian canons in Sülte in Hildesheim ordered the convent's reform in 1450, and in 1451 bishop Magnus of Hildesheim did the same. The women finally accepted a reform in the tradition of the Congregation of Windesheim and were in contact with the reformer Johannes Busch for some time after 1459. We can verify that the convent carried on the reform voluntarily in the decades afterwards, because an embroidery depicting philosophy and the seven liberal arts from 1516 (Fig. 10.1) is linked to this prolonged process of renewal.[6] An inscription provides the crucial hint: it says that the women re-established the convent with their own hands and sweat, a rhetorical expression meaning that they reformed it.[7] I will come back to this later.

[5] *Ibid.*, pp. 88, 124. See also Heike Uffmann, *Wie in einem Rosengarten: Monastische Reformen des späten Mittelalters in den Vorstellungen von Klosterfrauen* (Bielefeld, 2008), pp. 170–1.
[6] See Katharina Ulrike Mersch, *Soziale Dimensionen visueller Kommunikation in hoch- und spätmittelalterlichen Frauenkommunitäten: Stifte, Chorfrauenstifte und Klöster im Vergleich* (Göttingen, 2012), pp. 290, 292–305.
[7] '[a]nno · d(omi)ni · m⁰ d⁰ xvi · uenerabilis d(omi)na · elisabet · tekiv[...] priorissa me · fieri [fec]it · per · has · deo · co(n)secratas · ac · professas · uirgines · mar/greta(m) · ho(r)nborch · svppriorissa(m) · a(n)na(m) lvnema(n)s · procvratrice(m) · ioha(n)na(m) · godel · alhedis <s[...] > · ivdit <s[...]ilber> · sacrista(m) · ioha(nnam) <[...]> · alhede(n) <[...]> · gesa(m) <[...]> · agneta(m) <[...]des> · anna(m) <gerden> · a(n)na(m) <[...]> · mar/gareta(m) <brockes> · katerina(m) <stelter> · elisabet <bergen> · a(n)na(m) <borstede> · gertrud(em) <voget> · lefeke(n) <groten> · c[.]negvnde(m) <a[...]enat> · elisabet <verbeck> · a(n)na(m) · lvbere(n) · a(n)na(m) <dreger> · a(n)na(m) <scutwehter> · margareta(m) <ravwel> · gesa(m) <hornborch> · a(n)na(m) <[...]ren> · mar/gareta(m) <v[.]chgelt> · margareta(m) <witcop> · beata(m) <brokes> · elisabet <rvsen> · lvcia(m) <g[...]> · katerina(m) <svstermans> · margareta(m) <binder> · a(n)na(m) <pa[...]> · gesa(m) <westval> · margareta(m) <bo[...]es> no(m)i(n)a · co(n)v(er)sar(vum) · margareta(m) <sc[...]> · alheid <ache[.]> · mechelt <lenten> · a(n)na <hamel> · sofia engel <lob[...]> · / harv(m) · religiosarv(m) · ac · devotarv(m) · uirginv(m) · svdore · ac · manvv(m) · labore · gloriosv(m) · istvd · m[o]nasteriv(m) · heni(n)gen · ex antiqva · ve/tvstate · dirvtv(m) · a · fv(n)dame(n)tis · noviter · erectv(m) · e(st) [...] pie · recordacionis · alheid <zilton> · margreta <gv(n)ter> · gesa <alen> · margreta <nolke> · m(ar)g(are)ta

230 KATHARINA ULRIKE MERSCH

Fig. 10.1. Heiningen, Embroidery with Philosophy and the Seven Liberal Arts, 1516, London, Victoria and Albert Museum, Inv. No. 289-1876. © Victoria and Albert Museum, London.

Of course, we have to take into account all existing sources, the written sources as well as the material evidence itself. And of course, every sort of source in its individuality can only offer limited information. Besides, the researchers who have dealt with these sources up until now may have varying concepts of gender

----

· agnes · dobke · lvcke · elisabet · gert(r)vd · / no(m)i(n)a · noviciar(vm) / belke · mechtildis · alhed · elisabeth [...]': Falk Eisermann, 'Die Inschriften auf den Textilien des Augustiner-Chorfrauenstifts Heiningen', *Nachrichten der Akademie der Wissenschaften in Göttingen 1, Philologisch-Historische Klasse*, 6 (1996), 227–59, at pp. 243–5.

and of female agency – or none at all. Therefore, it is necessary, too, to evaluate studies written by scholars of history, epigraphy and art history.

The Written Sources

With regard to written sources and especially ego documents, researchers such as Eva Schlotheuber, Heike Uffmann, Anne Winston-Allen and Sigrid Hirbodian have discussed how women experienced reform and have assessed the presumed scope for female action.[8] But only a few scholars have explored systematically the influence of the female convent members on visual culture; one of the first among them was Carola Jäggi, though she has not specifically addressed the topic of reform.[9] Therefore, I would like to add that when we take a look at the written sources that inform us about changing visual culture, we have to deal with the same problems that occur when reconstructing the process of reform itself. Sometimes it is hard to distinguish whether a reform was implemented from above or if it was established bottom up. That means it is difficult to determine whether the supervisors, the convent, or both, took the initiative to change the community's visual culture.

Chroniclers of reform such as the Dominican Observant friar Johannes Meyer often remained silent about women's initiatives to change visual culture (even if he did not conceal their ability to illuminate manuscripts), and only gave an account of the order's – and that means the men's – activities to promote reform.[10] According to Meyer, who only briefly mentions visual media in his account of the Dominican reform in his *Buch der reformacio Predigerorden* [*The Book of the Reformation of the Order of Preachers*],[11] the Dominican Master

---

[8] See, for example, Eva Schlotheuber, *Klostereintritt und Bildung: Die Lebenswelt der Nonnen im späten Mittelalter; mit einer Edition des 'Konventstagebuchs' einer Zisterzienserin von Heilig-Kreuz bei Braunschweig (1484-1507)* (Tübingen, 2004); Anne Winston-Allen, *Convent Chronicles: Women Writing about Women and Reform in the Late Middle Ages* (University Park, 2004); Uffmann, *Rosengarten*; Sigrid Hirbodian, 'Reformschwestern und Reformverliererinnen. Strategien und Handlungsmöglichkeiten geistlicher Frauen in den Reformen des 15. Jahrhunderts', in Andreas Bihrer and Dietmar Schiersner (eds), *Reformverlierer 1000-1800: zum Umgang mit Niederlagen in der europäischen Vormoderne* (Berlin, 2016), pp. 449-74.

[9] Carola Jäggi, 'Wie kam Kunst ins Kloster?: Überlegungen zu Produktion und Import von Werken der Bildenden Kunst in den Klarissen- und Dominikanerinnenklöstern der Teutonia', *Rottenburger Jahrbuch für Kirchengeschichte*, 27 (2008), 91-109.

[10] See Neidhardt, *Autonomie*, p. 129.

[11] Thomas Lentes, 'Bild, Reform und Cura Monialium. Bildverständnis und Bildgebrauch im *Buch der reformacio Predigerordens* des Johannes Meyer (†1485)', in Jean-Luc Eichenlaub (ed.), *Dominicains et Dominicaines en Alsace, XIIIe-XXe siècle. Actes du colloque de Guebwiller (April 1994)* (Strasbourg, 1996), pp. 177-95, at p. 185.

General, Conrad of Prussia, gave an image of the Crucifixion to each nun of the convent of Schönensteinbach in Alsace, when in 1397 they were enclosed solemnly to express the beginning of reform.[12] Meditating on these images was meant to guarantee that each individual could establish her own inner, psychological enclosure through which she interiorised the principles of seclusion at the heart of reform.[13] Meyer here does not mention the women's attitudes to nor their production of visual culture, even though it is now well known that the nuns of Schönensteinbach were quite productive illuminators.[14]

Concerning the Cistercian convent of Wienhausen, the written sources shed light on both the reformers' and the convent's opinions. Even though Abbess Katharina of Hoya had already of her own accord taken reform measures, such as building projects and the reinforcement of spiritual ideas within the convent's communication structure, the bishop of Hildesheim and duke Otto V of Braunschweig-Lüneburg in 1469 commanded the reform of the convent under the supervision of the Windesheim canon Johannes Busch, assisted by members of the Benedictine reform congregation of Bursfelde. The anonymous author of a chronicle written in Wienhausen in the seventeenth century complained that the people involved confiscated money, plate and other objects of value and acted so ruthlessly that even some images of saints were taken away and were never returned.[15] Apparently, the existing visual culture of Wienhausen was dear to the people living there (even in later times) although the reformers held it in low esteem. Indeed, in the reformers' view it was inappropriate: after members of the Congregation of Bursfelde had visited Wienhausen in 1483, they admonished the nuns that they should follow their order's customs concerning the images from now on and remove unnecessary objects. The nuns were to stop showing the decoration of their choir to visitors and producing new images.[16] But material evidence proves that the nuns did not desist from producing new images. As the subjects of these tapestries, mural paintings, illuminated manuscripts and devotional objects

---

[12] Johannes Meyer, *Buch der reformacio Predigerordens*, ed. Benedictus Maria Reichert (2 vols, Leipzig, 1908-9), book II, c. 9, p. 35. For an English translation see *Women's History in the Age of Reformation. Johannes Meyer's Chronicle of the Dominican Observance*, trans. by Claire Taylor Jones (Toronto, 2019).

[13] Jäggi, 'Kunst', p. 99; Lentes, 'Bild', p. 180; and Mecham, *Sacred Communities*, pp. 168-70.

[14] See Anne Winston-Allen, 'Making Manuscripts as Political Engagement by Women in the Fifteenth-Century Observant Reform Movement', *Journal of Medieval Religious Cultures*, 42 (2016), 224-47.

[15] Horst Appuhn (ed.), *Chronik des Klosters Wienhausen, erweitert um das Totenbuch und ein Register der Personennamen* (Celle, 1968), pp. 23-4. See Mersch, *Soziale Dimensionen*, p. 332.

[16] Hannover, Hauptstaatsarchiv, Cop. IX 02, no. 554. See Mersch, *Soziale Dimensionen*, p. 336.

such as the Veronica or scenes from the life of Christ suited the spiritual ideals of reform,[17] we may conclude that, in the end, the nuns of Wienhausen together with their abbesses Susanna Potstock (1470–1501) and Katharina Remstede (1501–49) were themselves responsible for changing the visual culture within their convent.

Sources from other convents are often less informative. The convent chronicles and annals tend only to mention the work itself without mentioning the potential influence of male reformers on the visual programme. For example, the annals from the reformed convent of Heiningen written from the beginning of the sixteenth century onward note that the embroidery depicting Philosophy shown here in Fig. 10.1 was created in 1516,[18] and that another embroidery depicting the sibyls was produced in 1517.[19] This entry in the annals did not say a word about who initiated the design of the ambitious iconographic programmes and the production of these large-scale textiles; the problem that I address in this chapter evidently did not concern the entry's author.

Occasionally only the nuns are mentioned in connection with textile production, as is the case for the Benedictine convent at Lüne, which was reformed according to the model of the Bursfelde Congregation. In 1481, the responsible bishop of Verden, Barthold of Landsberg, most likely delegated a commission of four clerics to visit the monastery and to announce that seven sisters from the already reformed convent of Ebstorf would introduce a similar change into the convent at Lüne. Among the sisters from Ebstorf was Sophia of Bodenteich, who replaced the former prioress of Lüne. Within the next 50 years, monastic life flourished; the provosts Nikolaus Graurock (†1493), Nikolaus Schomaker (1493–1506) and Johannes Lorbeer (1506–29) supported nuns to introduce and maintain an Observant lifestyle. Reform emphasised communal life and liturgy and extended to the restoration of the buildings and to manual work, such as textile production. Lüne is especially known for its embroideries that are also mentioned in the historiographical notes of the convent.[20] For example, a large embroidery showing

---

[17] *Ibid.*, pp. 333–8.
[18] Hildesheim, Dombibliothek, Codex Beverina 546d, fol. 9v.
[19] *Ibid.*, fol. 10r.
[20] Eckhard Michael (ed.), *Die Inschriften des Lüneburger St.-Michaelisklosters und des Klosters Lüne* (Wiesbaden, 1984), no. 45 (henceforth: *Inschriften*); Eckhard Michael, 'Bildstickereien aus Kloster Lüne als Ausdruck der Reform des 15. Jahrhunderts', *Die Diözese Hildesheim in Vergangenheit und Gegenwart*, 53 (1985), 63–78, especially at p. 67. See Tanja Kohwagner-Nikolai, *'Per manus sororum ...': niedersächsische Bildstickereien im Klosterstich (1300–1583)* (München, 2006), nos 36–44, pp. 325–75. For a contemporary account on the history of reform in Lüne see Ernst Nolte, *Quellen und Studien zur Geschichte des Nonnenklosters Lüne bei Lüneburg, Teil 1: Die Quellen: die Geschichte Lünes von den Anfängen bis zur Klostererneuerung im Jahre 1481* (Göttingen, 1932), pp. 127–8.

Fig. 10.2. Lüne, Embroidery with the Resurrection of Christ, 1504–7. © Museum für Kunst und Gewerbe, Hamburg.

the resurrection of Christ (Fig. 10.2), a work commenced in 1504 (according to the inscription) and completed in 1507 (as a chronicle from the monastery from about 1530[21] tells us)[22] is only attributed to certain nuns in the book of the sacristan: 'Item sexta feria Cantate [26 May] presentaverunt istee sorores KR, SV, ESR, CS, GR, AR et GH magnum tapete de Resurgente' ['On the sixth day after Cantate

---

[21] See Philipp Stenzig, *Die Chronik des Klosters Lüne über die Jahre 1481–1530: Hs. Lüne 13* (Tübingen, 2019), pp. 1, 8–9, 22–3.
[22] Ed. in Stenzig, *Chronik*, p. 119.

those sisters KR, SV, ESR, CS, GR, AR, GH presented the large embroidery of the Resurrection'].²³ The author obviously did not think it would be important to clarify in which way the sisters were responsible: did they only stitch the embroidery or did they develop the iconographic programme, too?²⁴

Carola Jäggi has pointed out that there are different ways of interpreting similar written sources. For example, she draws on Jeryldene Wood's argument that, when the male superior's initiative is mentioned, it could well be that the nuns were active before the male superiors found out that they were producing artwork, and that male supervisors only authorised their works *ex post* when writing about it.²⁵ Julian Gardner, on the other hand, has raised an important question:

> If the legislation for the enclosure of religious women has been correctly characterised as conceived and enacted by men for women, is it also right to conclude that altarpieces and other paintings were also expressive of male taste, or, at best, what men considered to be appropriate for nuns? Can one realistically expect that strictly enclosed religious communities, whose works of art were commissioned through male intermediaries, could reflect developments in female spirituality?²⁶

At first glance it seems plausible that enclosed nuns had few possibilities to get to know the visual world outside the convent walls well enough to choose actively from the range of products on the market or to be familiar with the latest fashion. But then again, reform sisters – as the above-mentioned case of Lüne proves – were well connected. Similar evidence is preserved from some Observant communities of the mendicant orders that were centres of artistic production (book illumination and tapestries). Given the fact that sisters from a reformed convent were sent to reform other convents, it is likely that – as Jane L. Carroll has emphasised – they 'introduced these and other artistic skills into the daily

---

[23] Michael (ed.), *Inschriften*, no. 60 with reference to Nolte, *Quellen*, p. 116.
[24] Instead of providing an answer to this question, which would necessarily be speculative, I would like to point out the significance of a proposal put forward in Therese Martin, 'The Margin to Act: A Framework of Investigation for Women's (and Men's) Medieval Art-Making', *Journal of Medieval History*, 42:1 (2016), 1–25, at p. 24: 'if the makers of the Middle Ages must remain unnamed' – or rather, in this case, their scope of action must remain uncertain – we 'must aim to start from a position of dispassionate neutrality. […] Let us show our readers the whole, complicated, messy picture.'
[25] Jäggi, 'Kunst', pp. 91–2 with reference to Jeryldene M. Wood, *Women, Art and Spirituality: The Poor Clares of Early Modern Italy* (Cambridge, 1996).
[26] Julian Gardner, 'Nuns and Altarpieces: Agendas for Research', *Römisches Jahrbuch der Bibliotheca Hertziana*, 30 (1995), 27–59, at p. 55.

regime of their new homes.'[27] It needs to be considered, too, that the nuns could exchange images with other nuns or their relatives outside the monasteries. The edition of the collection of letters from Lüne that Eva Schlotheuber and others are working on at the time of writing includes proof of this exchange, such as for example the letter of a nun who thanks a female relative in another convent for sending her devotional images.[28] And the nun mentions that she is sending her an image of St George in return. Some of these letters can be dated within the period of reform.[29] The nuns even sent images to male clerics to encourage them to meditate.[30] Accordingly, enclosure did not necessarily result in a total separation from the artistic developments in the world outside the convent.

But living in a reformed monastery might involve other problems: if we consider that reforming a convent regularly resulted in the abolition of private property and the reintroduction of common property, one could assume that only the convent as a whole could buy works of art. But then again, we have to consider the fact that throughout the centuries exceptions were common and even women living in strict communities could sometimes buy art objects.[31] Donation charters and testaments provide evidence for this practice.[32]

Hence, statements and assessments in written sources are diverse when it comes to male and female agency in changing visual culture. The historiographical accounts 'from above' tend to focus on male initiatives, the historiographical accounts from the convents do not seem to be too interested in questions about

---

[27] Jane L. Carroll, 'Woven Devotions: Reform and Piety in Tapestries by Dominican Nuns', in Jane L. Carroll and Alison G. Stewart (eds), *Saints, Sinners, and Sisters: Gender and Northern Art in Medieval and Early Modern Europe* (Aldershot, 2003), pp. 182–201, at p. 185.

[28] See, for example, Eva Schlotheuber, 'Daily Life, Amor Dei, and Politics in the Letters of the Benedictine Nuns of Lüne in the Fifteenth and Sixteenth Centuries', in Virginia Blanton, Veronica M. O'Mara and Patricia Stoop (eds), *Nuns' Literacies in Medieval Europe. The Kansas City Dialogue: Papers revised from a Conference held at the University of Missouri-Kansas City, June 5–8, 2012* (Turnhout, 2015), pp. 249–68.

[29] See the digital publication still labelled as work in progress: Eva Schlotheuber, Henrike Lähnemann, Simone Schultz-Balluff, Edmund Wareham and Philipp Trettin (eds), *Netzwerke der Nonnen. Edition und Erschließung der Briefsammlung aus Kloster Lüne (ca. 1460–1555)* (Wolfenbüttel, 2016) http://diglib.hab.de/edoc/ed000248/start.htm [accessed 27 December 2022], letter 224. See also letters: 265, 268, 270–1, 290, 316. For similar evidence in the chronicles of Observant women's communities in Italy see Wood, *Women*, pp. 102–6, 112.

[30] Schlotheuber et al. (eds), *Netzwerke*, letter 272.

[31] See Jäggi, 'Kunst', pp. 97–8.

[32] Ibid., pp. 192–3. See Corine Schleif and Volker Schier, *Katerina's Windows: Donation and Devotion, Art and Music, as Heard and Seen Through the Writings of a Birgittine Nun* (University Park, 2009), pp. 488–90.

who influenced what aspect of a work's design or production, and other written sources provide wide scope for interpretation or simply prove that women were interested in exchanging devotional images. This ambiguity may explain why research results differ so markedly.

The Material Evidence

With regard to the material evidence, certain types of media provide more information about women's agency in reforming visual culture within their convents than others. If we turn to book illustration, for example, we are able to trace the circulation of works produced in certain scriptoria and thereby reconstruct networks of reform, as for instance Anne Winston-Allen has demonstrated with regard to women's reformed convents in south-western Germany, to name but one researcher in this field of study.[33] It may be even more difficult to examine objects that weren't produced by the sisters themselves to glean details about their contexts of production. But the problem is even more complex. Carola Jäggi has drawn attention to the fact that many scholars acknowledge that nuns produced illuminated manuscripts and textiles, but casually presume that panel paintings and sculptures within the convent walls were all produced by monks or lay male artists. Yet this is by no means certain.[34] As the topic of this chapter is complex enough, I have to leave Jäggi's idea aside, because as far as I can see this remains a desideratum in basic research.

OBJECTS CREATED IN THE MONASTERIES

It may initially seem easier to assess male and female agency in changing visual culture for objects that were undoubtedly created in the communities, rather than for those received as gifts and donations. But here again the evidence is tricky to interpret. On one hand, this is due to the fact that, to commence such an investigation, one has to gather many different sources to prove that objects were created in the communities. For example, in the case of Elsbeth Töpplin, a sister from the Dominican convent of Schönensteinbach who was in charge of reforming the convent of St Maria Magdalena zu den Reuerinnen in Freiburg, researchers evaluated the manuscripts together with every conceivable sort of written source. Elsbeth copied and illustrated four or five manuscripts and she can

---

[33] Winston-Allen, 'Networking'. See also Jeffrey Hamburger's studies, for example, Jeffrey F. Hamburger, 'Magdalena Kremerin, Scribe and Painter of the Choir and Chapter Books of the Dominican Convent of St Johannes-Baptista in Kirchheim unter Teck', in James H. Marrow, Richard A. Linenthal and William Noel (eds), *The Medieval Book: Glosses from Friends & Colleagues of Christopher De Hamel* (Houten, 2010), pp. 124-49.

[34] Jäggi, 'Kunst', pp. 91-2.

be identified because Johannes Meyer mentioned her name in his *Buch der reformacio*. An entry in the anniversary book of the cloister of St Maria Magdalena zu den Reuerinnen also mentions her activity in copying books for the year 1509.[35] In fact, a traditional method of art history, formalism, helps to identify the illuminated manuscripts and objects in question. Nevertheless, Jäggi has identified a black spot in this method of research, as many scholars tend to ascribe a painting or illumination to a women's convent only if it is executed in a flat and 'naïve' style (in German, the term *Nonnenmalerei* – 'nuns' painting' – for a certain, simple style in book illumination is a perfect example for that common assumption). On the other hand, if an artwork stands out for its formal and stylistic qualities, many researchers tend to rule out without valid reason the possibility that it could have been produced within the walls of a female monastery.[36] It is evident that researchers sometimes apply the same logic to objects of art in men's convents when it comes to evaluating style – for good reason.[37] But nevertheless, one should be aware of this issue.

If women are depicted working on particular objects, this may count as a strong indicator for their agency in changing visual culture, but visual evidence for this is quite rare. And even in this case, it is difficult to determine whether women chose to represent themselves in this way on objects they themselves designed and produced. Jane L. Carroll and Stefanie Monika Neidhardt refer to two tapestries which were probably produced around 1500 in the Observant Dominican convents Heilig Grab in Bamberg and/or St Katharina in Nuremberg, depicting nuns working at a loom in the margins of the main programme (the Life of Christ). Art historians and historians argue that these depictions are not self-portraits but were conceived to demonstrate that manual labour was important within observant communities and to present an example of an ideal sister

---

[35] See Winston-Allen, 'Making Manuscripts', pp. 227–8, n. 12; Johannes Meyer, *Buch der reformacio Predigerordens*, vol. 2, ed. Reichert, p. 120.

[36] Jäggi, 'Kunst', pp. 108–9. See also Anne Winston-Allen, '"Nonnenmalerei": Iconography in Convent Women's Art of the Upper Rhine Region', in Barbara Fleith and René Wetzel (eds), *Kulturtopographie des deutschsprachigen Südwestens im späteren Mittelalter. Studien und Texte* (Tübingen, 2009), pp. 141–56. Winston-Allen has drawn attention to the fact that men sometimes painted in a similar style, *ibid.*, p. 148.

[37] Some stained glass windows in the church of the reformed Benedictine convent of Clus dating from 1486 include an inscription that ascribes the production to the convent members. Christine Wulf argues that this seems plausible as the execution is simple. But Wulf has a good reason to argue along these lines as there is little evidence for the production of stained glass windows in monasteries at all. Christine Wulf (ed.), *Die Inschriften des Kanonissenstifts Gandersheim und seiner Eigenklöster Brunshausen und Clus* (Göttingen, 2011), http://www.inschriften.net/gandersheim.html [accessed 27 December 2022], no. 20.

who embodied the essential features of the *vita contemplativa* and the *vita activa*.[38] But unfortunately we cannot discern who conceived this idea; we need further information that simply seems not to exist in this case.

Similar problems arise when we take a look at the mass production of moulded wax relief images that became common usage in the same period as late medieval reform movements. For example, the Cistercian women's convent in Rostock, reformed on behalf of Konrad Loste, bishop of Schwerin (1482–1503), produced several such moulded images from parchment and wax to form little triptychs. It is obvious that the sisters did not invent the programme, as for example a relief of Veronica with the apostles Peter and Paul mimics an engraving from Martin Schongauer, one of the most popular printmakers in late fifteenth-century Germany. The model used for these wax reliefs is attributed to a professional punch cutter, who made the form of the image into a stamp or die.[39] But did the nuns choose the images they reproduced of their own accord, or did the punch cutter or a male deputy select a model that they expected the nuns to like?

Thus, the argument has come to a point where it is necessary to distinguish between the production of images and the development of the underlying iconographic programme.[40] And at this point, it is necessary to take into account the iconographic programme itself, together with the sources that inform us about the separate process of production.

I will now focus on coats of arms and inscriptions that inform us who made an object and hint at who may have been present when an artwork was made. Both features provide crucial information. For example, the aforementioned inscription on the Heiningen embroidery with philosophy (Fig. 10.1) states that, in 1516, prioress Elisabeth Terwins commissioned her nuns to make the embroidery. The names of thirty-five sisters and five *conversae* are stitched in the inscription. The inscription records that these women reformed the convent.[41] But it also records that this was done under the guidance of some 'honourable men', Arnold Steinwick, Antonius Colhof and provost Heinrich Horensen from the nearby convent of Riechenberg. At the end of the text, several novices and convent members who were deceased are commemorated.[42] What do we make of this?

---

[38] Carroll, 'Woven Devotions'; Neidhardt, *Autonomie*, p. 211–12.

[39] See Kristina Hegner, 'Reliquiare und Klosterarbeiten des Mittelalters im Rostocker Zisterzienserinnenkloster zum Heiligen Kreuz'; Dirk Schumann (ed.), *Sachkultur und religiöse Praxis* (Berlin, 2007), pp. 223–40, at p. 236.

[40] This problem is also briefly addressed in Kohwagner-Nikolai, 'Per manus sororum ...', pp. 36–8.

[41] See above, n. 7.

[42] 'svb · regimine · honorabiliv(m) · uirorv(m) · religiosorv(m) · p(ro)fessor(vm) · i(n) ·

Did Arnold Steinwick, Anton Colhof and Heinrich Horensen instruct the nuns when they worked on the embroidery or did they merely supervise the implementation of reform? Leonie von Wilckens and Falk Eisermann assume that one of the canons from Riechenberg invented the iconographic programme.[43] This is not altogether unlikely, as we learn from other sources that Arnold Steinwick worked together with the prioress in reconstructing the monastery.[44] But then again, the sisters from Heiningen had been producing textiles for centuries, and they had a library at hand that provided them with texts that could inspire the iconographic programme of this embroidery. Comparable evidence from the convent of Riechenberg is lost.[45] Therefore, I would like to suggest a different reading of the inscription: maybe the prioress and her nuns not only produced the embroidery but elaborated its concept, too, while the men were in charge of reform in general.

The inscriptions and the layout of other tapestries from the same time and region, too, also obscure the men's activities while at the same time they highlight the women's agency. I am here referring to the rich tradition passed down from the reformed convent of Lüne. I have already mentioned the embroidery with the resurrection of Christ (Fig. 10.2). The relevant part of its Latin inscription does not refer to men at all. It simply states (in translation) that:

> In the year of the birth through the virgin 1504 the venerable *domina*, the prioress Sophia of Bodenteich, had this embroidery made by the hands of the sisters living here in Lüne in this period, to honour God and his beloved mother Mary and St Bartholomew, the royal apostle, our glorious patron, in the twenty-third year of reform. And in this same year the venerable *domina* blissfully ended her last day, may her soul rest in peace. Amen.[46]

---

rike(n)berch · s(an)c(to)r(vm) · d(omi)ni · arnoldi · ste(n)wick · qvi · ultra · xxx · a(n)n/os · et · p(ro)vidi · a(n)tonii · colhof · q(vi) · vltra · xx · a(n)nos · nobiscv(m) i(n) p(ro)speris · et · adversis · p(er)severantes · ordinati · ex · favore ·pii · pr(ior)is · hi(n)rici · hore(n)se(n) · co(m)missarii · n(ostri) / prioris · in · rike(n)berch': Eisermann, 'Inschriften', pp. 243-5.

[43] Michael Brandt (ed.), *Schatzkammer auf Zeit. Die Sammlungen des Bischofs Eduard Jakob Wedekin 1796-1870. Katalog der Ausstellung des Diözesanmuseums Hildesheim* (Hildesheim, 1991), no. 71 (Leonie von Wilckens); Eisermann, 'Inschriften', p. 255.

[44] Hildesheim, Dombibliothek, Codex Beverina 546d, fol. 11r. Gerhard Taddey, *Das Kloster Heiningen von der Gründung bis zur Aufhebung* (Göttingen, 1966), pp. 112-13.

[45] See Mersch, *Soziale Dimensionen*, pp. 301-2. Henrike Lähnemann has discovered similar thematic overlapping with the convent's library for the so called Wichmansburger antependium from Medingen, probably originating from the period of reform, see Henrike Lähnemann, '"An dessen bom wil ik stighen". Die Ikonographie des Wichmannsburger Antependiums im Kontext der Medinger Handschriften', *Oxford German Studies*, 34 (2005), 19-46.

[46] Michael (ed.), *Inschriften*, no. 60: 'Anno · partus · virginei · M° · quingentesimo · quarto ·

Moreover, several initials appear on the embroidery, which Eckhard Michael has ascribed to several nuns from Lüne. Nevertheless, Michael has stated that a learned theologian must have contributed the draft for the visual programme, even though he refers to other contemporary embroideries from Lüne that prove that the nuns were familiar with iconographic programmes influenced by theological ideas.[47] Michael's claim, however, leads to an assumption that seems counterintuitive, namely that the nuns in the course of reform were encouraged to do manual labour such as making embroideries, to read theological and devotional literature and to renew their liturgy, but were not able to combine these things to develop iconographic programmes.[48] But who else would have been able to do this, if not the nuns? The coats of arms on the embroidery represent the family of the abbess (Bodenteich), of her successor (Wilde), and of the families Lorbeer and Schomaker. This may indicate that the provosts Nikolaus Schomaker and Johannes Lorbeer could have been involved in developing the design of the textile (note that the abbess and her successor are represented in the same way). But were the provosts learned in a way that qualified them to develop a theologically ambitious programme? While little is known about Johannes Lorbeer, Schomaker at least was a *magister* and a licentiate of canon law.[49] While training in canon law most likely does not encourage artistic creativity, in any event he might have come into contact with theological speculation during his years of study. However, if the provosts developed the concept, might we expect their names to be mentioned in the inscription, too?

As several embroideries dating from the reform period are preserved from Lüne, it is possible to reflect on how the coats of arms depicted on these textiles

---

fecit · venerabilis · do(m)pna · priorissa · Sophia · de ·/ Bode(n)dike · istud · tapete · co(n) suere · per · man(us) · sororu(m) · monialiu(m) · hic · in · lune · tu(n)c · degenciu(m) · ad · honore(m) · dei · et · sue · dilecte · matris · Marie / ac · s(an)c(t)i · Bartholomei · regalis · apostoli · gloriosi · patroni · nostri · reformacio(n)is · hui(us) · Monasterij · anno / vicesimo · tercio · et · ip(s)o · a(n)no · eadem · venerabilis · do(m)pna · feliciter · suu(m) · diem · clausit · extremu(m) · cui(us) · a(n)i(m)a · requiescat · i(n) · pace · amen .'

[47] Ibid.
[48] This is what, for example, Brinkmann claims. See Jens-Uwe Brinkmann, *Kloster Lüne: Geschichte und Architektur* (Thunum/Ostfriesland, 2013), pp. 25–6: 'Die Vorlagen, nach denen gestickt wurde, schufen begabte Nonnen – wobei eine gewisse Naivität in den Zeichnungen nicht zu verkennen ist. Die geistlichen Programme der Arbeiten [...] dürften auf Anregung der Pröpste oder anderer Geistlicher zurückgehen.' This seems quite odd considering the fact that Eva Schlotheuber characterises the nuns in Lüne as well educated and speaks of a 'theological discourse they nurtured among themselves': Eva Schlotheuber, 'Intellectual Horizons: Letters from a Northern German Convent', in Ead., *'Gelehrte Bräute Christi': Geistliche Frauen in der mittelalterlichen Gesellschaft* (Tübingen, 2018), pp. 133–57, at p. 149.
[49] See Ida-Christine Riggert, *Die Lüneburger Frauenklöster* (Hannover, 1996), pp. 408–9.

Fig. 10.3. Lüne, detail of the bench cover depicting the legend of St Bartholomew (LUEKO Ha 001), 1493, photo: Kloster Lüne.

may contribute to our understanding of who was involved in the production of the embroideries. The first textile from Lüne that can be linked to reform – a bench cover dating to 1493 (Fig. 10.3) – lacks a similar inscription, but does include coats of arms, and its iconographic programme stresses female involvement in venerating the monastery's patron saint. Eight medallions on the bench cover are dedicated to the life of St Bartholomew; in the ninth medallion the saint – holding a knife and his skin as symbols of his martyrdom – is standing among a group of six veiled female figures that likely represent nuns. With speech scrolls in their hands, they venerate the 'glorious patron, St Bartholomew' and ask for his assistance. Just as on later embroideries, we see coats of arms representing the families of the abbess and the provost (Bodenteich and Graurock),[50] and in

[50] Michael (ed.), *Inschriften*, no. 45. For Nikolaus Graurock see Riggert, *Frauenklöster*, pp. 406–7.

addition the emblems of about twenty-six families in total can be identified on the bench cover.[51] A further bench cover dating to 1500 and dedicated to the legend of St Catherine has a similar design; it also depicts several coats of arms (Schomaker, Bodenteich and Landsberg). In this example, an inscription refers to the nuns of Lüne: 'In the year of the Lord 1500 this bench cover was completed by the hands of our sisters, who were then living in Lüne, at the time under the direction of the *domina* Sophia of Bodenteich.'[52] Michael assumes that in this case the coats of arms represent the families of the nuns involved in the production of the textile, although the inscription once again refers to the prioress and the manual labour of the nuns, who are also mentioned in the written sources. This pattern was evidently abandoned later, as an embroidery from 1503 with the Tree of Jesse implies.[53] The meaning of the coats of arms, therefore, is ambiguous.

It is no surprise, then, that other researchers have drawn different conclusions. Perhaps Sophia of Bodenteich was the moving spirit behind the rich artistic production at Lüne that commenced with the reform in 1481 because of the experience she brought with her from the convent of Ebstorf, where the production of bench covers had a long tradition.[54] This assumption can be supported with regard to Angela Karstensen's observation that the Lüne embroidery dedicated to the life of the infant Christ, with images of prophets and the sibyls, dating from 1500, depicts a fable that is represented similarly in older Ebstorf architectural sculptures.[55] From the perspective of focusing on the women's experience[56] and knowledge, the coats of arms incorporated into the textile designs merely indicate that figures such as bishop Barthold of Landsberg from Verden and the provosts Nikolaus Graurock and Nikolaus Schomaker were important to the convent in

---

[51] See Michael (ed.), *Inschriften*, no. 56.

[52] See *Ibid.*, no. 55.

[53] Inscription in translation: 'In the year of grace 1503 the *domina* Sophia of Bodenteich commissioned this embroidery to be stitched by the sisters who were then living at Lüne, to honour God and his beloved mother Mary and Saint Bartholomew, our patron. In the 23rd year of reform.' Coats of arms: Schomaker, Bodenteich and Landsberg. See Michael (ed.), *Inschriften*, no. 58. In the book of the sacristan it says: 'quarta feria Circumdederunt in die Vincentii martiris presentaverunt sorores GS, EH, KR, SV, ESR et CS tapete cum Yesse': Nolte, *Quellen*, p. 115. See also the *Chronicle of Lüne*, ed. in Stenzig, *Chronik*, p. 94: 'Item ipso anno consuerunt sorores tapete, in quo continetur Yesse cum arbore'. For the written sources see *Ibid.*, n. 114, pp. 94–5.

[54] Kunst- und Ausstellungshalle der Bundesrepublik Deutschland, Bonn and Ruhrlandmuseum Essen (eds), *Krone und Schleier: Kunst aus mittelalterlichen Frauenklöstern* (Munich, 2005), no. 482 a–d, pp. 528–9.

[55] Angela Karstensen, *Der Auferstehungsteppich zu Kloster Lüne: Bildtradition und Singularität* (Berlin, 2009), pp. 73–5.

[56] See Mecham, *Sacred Communities*, p. 181.

ways that are no longer identifiable.[57] (It is possible that Nikolaus Graurock is not the only one represented by this coat of arms, as several women with the name Graurock were also nuns in Lüne.[58])

The embroidery with images of prophets and sibyls does mention Schomaker's name, and it also depicts the coats of arms of the Schomaker and the Bodenteich families. The inscription reads in translation:

> In the year 1500 of the birth of our Lord the *domina* prioress Sophia of Bodenteich, in the twentieth year of her term of office, took care of and arranged for this embroidery to be put together by the hands of the sisters living at this moment in the monastery of Lüne to praise and to honour the highest God and his beloved mother Mary, the royal and glorious apostle Bartholomew, our patron; in the eighth year of the venerable provost and our father *dominus* Nikolaus Schomaker.[59]

Nikolaus's name is mentioned, but with no reference to how he might have contributed to the iconographic programme or the production of the textile. Michael has argued that he was perhaps the one who introduced Phillip Barbieri's treatise on the sibyls to Lüne, because Schomaker was active in a region where the treatise, which provides the basis for the depictions of the sibyls, on the embroidery was known before he arrived at Lüne. Yet Michael has also acknowledged that this is by no means certain.[60] I would like to point out that we come across Nikolaus Schomaker's name here in a dating clause that also refers to the dates of office of Sophia of Bodenteich. Other dating clauses in the inscriptions on the textiles from Lüne refer only to the period of Sophia's office (the bench cover dedicated to the legend of St Catherine),[61] or they refer to Sophia's term of office and the years that have passed since reform was introduced (the embroidery dedicated to the resurrection of Christ).[62] The date clause on an embroidery from 1503 that shows sixteen scenes from the life of Christ mentions only the years of reform: 'In the year 1503 the *domina* Sophia of Bodenteich, prioress, had this embroidery stitched together by the hands of the sisters in Lüne to honour God and his mother Mary and our patron St Bartholomew in the thirteenth year of reform'.[63]

---

[57] *Krone und Schleier*, no. 482 a–d, pp. 528–9.
[58] See the Chronicle of Lüne, ed. in Stenzig, *Chronik*, pp. 70–1.
[59] See Michael (ed.), *Inschriften*, no. 57.
[60] See *Ibid.*, no. 57. The Lüne chronicle only mentions the manual labour of the *sorores*, Nolte, *Quellen*, p. 115, the Chronicle of Lüne, ed. in Stenzig, *Chronik*, p. 88.
[61] See Michael (ed.), *Inschriften*, no. 55.
[62] See *Ibid.*, no. 60.
[63] *Ibid.*, no. 59.

Here again, the coats of arms refer to the family of the prioress (Bodenteich), to the family of her successor (Wilde) and to those of the provosts' families, Lorbeer and Schomaker.[64] Once again, the inscription refers only to the prioress and her nuns. Comparable date clauses can also be found in the Lüne chronicle.[65] In my opinion, this comparison of date clauses indicates that Nikolaus Schomaker was important to the monastery (as was Sophia of Bodenteich). But the fact that his name occurs in a date clause does not necessarily imply that he was involved in producing the embroidery or in developing its iconographic programme. Indeed, we find the initials of the *filatrices*' names on the embroidery as well ('HE / AL / KE / MRO / AG / ESM filatrix'[66]). Given this rather detailed explanation of the women's activities in making the object, if Nikolaus Schomaker had been involved in the production of the textile it would seem inappropriate if his contribution to the design of the embroidery was not also mentioned in the inscription. Likewise, the written sources only mention the sisters' involvement.[67]

On the Lüne textiles, therefore, most inscriptions mention the women's work and Sophia of Bodenteich's initiative, but no inscription mentions the provosts' initiative, even if Nikolaus Schomaker's name is once used in a date clause. The coats of arms regularly represent the families of Sophia and the convent's provosts, and a few textiles are adorned with a greater number of emblems that may represent the families of the nuns who embroidered them. In comparison, those parts of the inscription that definitely refer to the process of stitching seem to offer the most reliable information concerning men's and women's agency. The coats of arms may provide a hint as to where to look for further information, i.e. the background of the people involved. Sophia definitely was familiar with the production of textiles with religious iconographic programmes. The provosts' potential competence with regard to the development of iconographic programmes remains obscure.

---

[64] *Ibid.*, no. 59.
[65] For example, for the year 1497: 'Item in ipso anno dominus prepositus et pius [pater] noster, magister Nicolaus Schomaker, fecit prolongare chorum nostrum, anno reformationis XVII°, et anno prepositure sue VI°, anno prioratus domine Sophie de Bodendike, pie matris nostre, XVII': The Chronicle of Lüne, ed. in Stenzig, *Chronik*, p. 83. Please note that the author here does mention what Nikolaus Schomaker had done for the monastery, a detail lacking in the embroidery's inscription.
[66] Michael (ed.), *Inschriften*, no. 59.
[67] The community's chronicle states for 1507: 'Item ipso anno presentauerunt sorores tapete cum septem apparitionibus'. An entry in the sacristan's book states that four sisters, again designated with initials, presented the embroidery with the apparitions of Christ in February 1507: Michael (ed.), *Inschriften*, no. 59 with reference to Nolte, *Quellen*, p. 115, see also the Chronicle of Lüne, ed. in Stenzig, *Chronik*, p. 120.

To sum up: nuns' agency in producing the visual programme of their textiles is evident as the cases presented here are examples of their manual labour within the convent. When it comes to identifying the creators of iconographic programmes it seems to me that many researchers tend to focus on men who are being represented via coats of arms or whose names are mentioned in inscriptions, even if the texts do not imply any active male involvement. But if we include recent methodological approaches based on a combination of the analysis of art objects with an analysis of the written sources,[68] it may be easier to understand the possibilities that women, even those in enclosed communities, had to change their visual culture. When asking who would have been competent to develop an iconographic programme, it is also useful to investigate the background of the nuns (which does not mean that one should ignore the men's potential competence). And we should take into account that enclosed women circulated and received images, as the letter collection of Lüne proves.

DONATIONS AND GIFTS

The situation is even more complex when we turn to donations and gifts, because it is even more difficult to identify the person who developed an iconographic programme. In addition, it is sometimes nearly impossible to assess a donated object's relation to reform, as the following illustrative examples demonstrate.

Donations may be attributed to a certain person because of heraldic designs. Moreover, when the visual programme in question can be related to spiritual ideas important to reform, researchers tend to attribute the donated object to one of the nuns. For example, a sheet from Wienhausen depicting the hunt of the unicorn in the *hortus conclusus* with the Virgin Mary and archangel Gabriel is likely to have been made in a workshop from Touraine (Fig. 10.4). As the coat of arms of the Remstede family is attached to the sheet, Horst Appuhn has assumed that the abbess Katharina Remstede gave it to the convent, because the subject is considered a symbol for the practice of strict enclosure that was introduced in Wienhausen on the occasion of reform.[69]

---

[68] See, for example, Mecham, *Sacred Communities*. Mecham does not address the question pursued in this chapter. For a broad methodological approach for transdisciplinary work see Mersch, *Soziale Dimensionen*, pp. 21–32.

[69] Horst Appuhn, 'Der Wappenteppich der Äbtissin Katharina Remstede im Kloster Wienhausen, eine Lüneburger Wirkerei von 1501', *Lüneburger Blätter*, 11/12 (1961), 9–11. In fact, hangings with the *hortus conclusus* could – even in men's convents – simply serve as decoration for altars dedicated to St Mary, see Otfried Krafft, 'Aus verlorenen Sinnenwelten. Stifterinnen und Heilige, Sachkultur und Kunst in einem Inventar der Augustinereremiten von Schmalkalden (1518) (mit Edition)', *Jahrbuch für mitteldeutsche Kirchen- und Ordensgeschichte*, 15 (2019), 331–82, at p. 364.

Fig. 10.4. Wienhausen, woven wall hanging depicting the hunt of the unicorn and the *hortus conclusus* (WIEN Ha 14), *c.* 1500. © Kloster Wienhausen.

We also need to keep in mind that some of the objects one intuitively associates with reform simply because their imagery fits into the spiritual contexts of observance may have been gifts from people outside the monastery. One example is the leather binding of an incunabulum with a plate depicting the hunt of a unicorn within the *hortus conclusus*. This book containing works of Bernard of Clairvaux was given to Magdalena Holzschuherin, a nun in the Observant monastery of St Klara in Nuremberg, by her uncle Sebald Reich, because the provost of St Laurence told him that this would be a good idea.[70] Did these men have in

---

[70] See the note at the beginning of the book: '1498 jar Am Montag nach Concepcionis gloriose virginis schenckt der Ersam Sebolt Reich seiner Mumen Magdalena Holzschuherin daß puch in ir studium/ vnd sind angeben worden von dem wirdigen hochgelerten heren doctor zu der zeit pffarrer zu sant lorenczen herr Sixt Tucher/ got mach sie teilhaftig alles des gutten das dar von allen den geschicht die dar an leßen oder horen

mind that the gift (including the binding) might encourage the ideals of reform or are we just trained to perceive the motif of the *hortus conclusus* as a label of reform for women?

Conclusion

While the narratives of male chroniclers of reform tend to shed little light on female agency in the context of changing visual culture, other written sources do. We can at least find evidence that the nuns and canonesses were accustomed to produce and exchange images. If we keep these general findings in mind when analysing the material evidence, we can perhaps find new ways – compared to older basic research studies – of identifying the creators of iconographic programmes. At the same time, it would be helpful to closely examine which works of art were definitely connected to reform processes and which were not.

Nevertheless, there is one last issue that needs to be addressed. I have dealt with the problem of identifying women's agency in changing visual culture, but, with regard to methodology, we face serious problems in identifying men's agency, too. I would like to mention this only briefly: it would be so much easier if we could compare the art objects that were produced in women's convents with those produced in the convents of the men who supervised them. But until now I have not identified a way to adequately consider this issue, perhaps because visual culture in men's convents in late medieval reform movements is still a research desideratum. Another possible explanation may be that much more material evidence from men's communities in the area examined in this chapter is lost. Or could it be that nuns enclosed behind convent walls had more time at hand to produce images than the monks and regular canons who were responsible for the spiritual, liturgical and economic reform of women's convents and who wrote books about their efforts?

---

leßen': http://www.inka.uni-tuebingen.de/?inka=27000355 [accessed 27 December 2022], *Krone und Schleier*, no. 338, p. 430.

CHAPTER 11

Nuns, Cistercian Chant and Observant Reform in the Southern Low Countries

JOHN GLASENAPP OSB

OVER the course of the long fifteenth century, myriad efforts rallied to return religious life to its perceived early customs and authoritative sources. Kaspar Elm once described these initiatives, known collectively as the Observant movement, as an 'almost incomprehensible variety of local reform'.[1] Controversial practices such as simony and private property bitterly divided communities and prompted calls for change. Intensifying matters further, the common observance and vitality of female abbeys in this period was disproportionately compromised as a result of economic insecurity. Secular and religious leaders alike took notice, and women's religious discipline became the object of heightened scrutiny and

---

[1] Kaspar Elm, 'Verfall und Erneuerung des Ordenswesens im Spätmittelalter: Forschungen und Forschungsaufgaben', in J. Fleckenstein (ed.), *Untersuchungen zu Kloster und Stift* (Göttingen, 1980), pp. 188-238, translated by James D. Mixson as 'Decline and Renewal of the Religious Orders in the Late Middle Ages: Current Research and Research Agendas', in Kaspar Elm and James D. Mixson (eds), *Religious Life between Jerusalem, the Desert, and the World: Selected Essays by Kaspar Elm* (Boston, 2016), pp. 138-88, at p. 138. See also Kaspar Elm (ed.), *Reformbemühungen und Observanzbestrebungen im spätmittelalterlichen Ordenswesen* (Berlin, 1989); Kaspar Elm, Peter Joerißen and Hermann J. Roth (eds), *Die Zisterzienser: Ordensleben zwischen Ideal und Wirklichkeit: Eine Ausstellung des Landschaftsverbandes Rheinland, Rheinisches Museummamt, Brauweiler, Aachen, Krönungssaal des Rathauses 3. Juli–28. September 1980* (Bonn, 1980); Kaspar Elm, 'Mythos oder Realität? Fragestellungen und Ergebnisse der Zisterzienserforschung', in Nicole Bouter (ed.), *Unanimité et diversité cisterciennes: Filiations, réseaux, relectures du xiie au xviie siècles; Actes du Quatrième Colloque* (Saint-Étienne, 2000), pp. 17-48; James D. Mixson and Bert Roest (eds), *A Companion to Observant Reform in the Late Middle Ages and Beyond* (Leiden, 2015); Kathryne Beebe, 'Observant Reform in the Late Middle Ages', in Bernice M. Kaczynski (ed.), *The Oxford Handbook of Christian Monasticism* (Oxford, 2020), pp. 300-13.

external intervention, with or without the approval of the sisters. These leaders imagined temporal scarcity and structural decrepitude to be a product of spiritual laxity, not vice versa. Consequently, histories of late medieval religion have long painted a picture of almost universal religious corruption and decadence in this period, for which the Observance offered a corrective.[2] But in the last several decades scholarship has uncovered a much more complex picture, one that has begun to rehabilitate the intellectual engagement of women.[3]

Reform of women's communities in the fifteenth century was typically initiated and supervised by men but carried out through lengthy visitations and exchanges among nuns themselves. While examples abound of nuns' resistance to external coercion, contributing to their image as recalcitrant and disorderly, Anne Winston-Allen has argued that nuns generally welcomed opportunities for education and stricter discipline, provided they were grounded in their own rule.[4] These opportunities for teaching and learning were most often administered by women for women through a process that was overwhelmingly oral. Therefore, what this education entailed in individual communities, the extent to which male supervisors were involved, and how men responded to those interactions are questions that histories predominantly reliant on documentary accounts have been ill suited to address. Historians investigating such questions can benefit from other sources attesting to these engagements.

This chapter examines how musical revisions made to the chant books by the nuns of the Cistercian abbey of Beaupré in Grimminge, East Flanders (Baltimore, Walters Art Museum, W. 759–62) reflect a changed understanding of both local tradition and twelfth-century authority, namely that of St Bernard of Clairvaux and the standardised version of Cistercian chant created under his supervision. Few details are known about the Observant movement that transformed the abbey of Beaupré besides its origin at the female Cistercian abbey of Marche-les-Dames in Namur in 1406. Nuns of Beaupré were the first within this otherwise female Cistercian movement to introduce their reform to Benedictine women, beginning at the abbey of Ghislenghien in 1480. The Cistercian monks of Jardinet, who

---

[2] Bert Roest, 'A Crisis of Late Medieval Monasticism?', in Alison I. Beach and Isabelle Cochelin (eds), *The Cambridge History of Western Monasticism in the Latin West* (2 vols, New York, 2020), vol. 2, pp. 1171–90.

[3] For an orientation, see: Eva Schlotheuber, 'Intellectual Horizons: Letters from a Northern German Convent', in Elizabeth Andersen, Henrike Lähnemann and Anne Simon (eds), *A Companion to Mysticism and Devotion in Northern Germany in the Late Middle Ages* (Leiden, 2013), pp. 343–72; and Claire Taylor Jones, *Ruling the Spirit: Women, Liturgy, and Dominican Reform in Late Medieval Germany* (Philadelphia, 2018).

[4] Anne Winston-Allen, *Convent Chronicles: Women Writing about Women and Reform in the Late Middle Ages* (University Park, 2004), p. 130.

were granted temporary *cura monialium* over the sisters of Beaupré and many surrounding women's communities, followed suit and began leading the reform of male Benedictine abbeys, beginning with Lobbes in 1497. Archival evidence, combined with those new chant books that survive from this cluster of reformed Benedictine abbeys, demonstrates that most of the Benedictine monasteries in question adopted Cistercian chant in the course of their reforms. Whether it was the nuns of Beaupré or the monks of Jardinet who first championed standardised Cistercian chant at the expense of local and Benedictine traditions, the chronology of events makes clear that the initial effort to introduce Cistercian chant in Benedictine monasteries was spearheaded by women and followed by men. In this respect, the nuns belonged to a liturgical current flowing out of the Council of Basel in which many independent groups sought to revive authentic versions of Gregorian chant.[5] This set of liturgical manuscripts fills out the fragmentary archival record and brings to light substantive conversations about authority and tradition held between nuns and monks, mutual influence between men and women, intensive musical teaching and learning between monasteries, exchanges of resources, some heated exchanges, and occasional infighting over chant and liturgical practices.

The Authority of Cistercian Chant

The corpus of chant that was standardised in its final form in the 1140s and carried the imprimatur of St Bernard of Clairvaux marked the second attempt by the Cistercians to produce an authoritative repertoire. The first effort, led by Stephen Harding, third abbot of Cîteaux, was roundly panned as a failure. Sometime between 1108 and 1112, Abbot Stephen sent delegations of monks to Milan, the city of St Ambrose, in search of authentic versions of Ambrosian hymns, as well as to Metz, the fountainhead of Gregorian chant in the Carolingian period.[6] Over time, it became increasingly clear that the copies that both groups retrieved were

[5] Mary Kay Duggan, 'Bringing Reformed Liturgy to Print at the New Monastery at Marienthal', *Church History and Religious Culture*, 88:3 (2008), 415–36.

[6] The *terminus ante quem* for the first revision comes from the 'Monitum' to the Cistercian hymnal in which Stephen refers only to the New Monastery and not to any daughter-houses. The first daughter-house, La Ferté, was founded in 1113. The text survives in a single source, Nantes, Bibliothèque municipale, MS 9, fol. 144r. Latin editions of the text may be found in John Michael Beers, *A Commentary on the Cistercian Hymnal = Explantio super hymnos quibus utitur Ordo Cisterciensis: A Critical Edition of Troyes Bib. Mun. MS. 658* (London, 1982), p. xxvi; Chrysogonus Waddell, 'The Origin and Early Evolution of the Cistercian Antiphonary: Reflections on Two Cistercian Chant Reforms', in M. Basil Pennington (ed.), *The Cistercian Spirit: A Symposium in Memory of Thomas Merton* (Shannon, 1970), pp. 190–223, at p. 206. An English translation

not faithful witnesses of the earliest tradition and were riddled with problems and incongruities, including apocryphal texts and non-Biblical events.

By the 1140s, the consensus among the growing body of Cistercian abbots had turned against Stephen Harding's liturgy.[7] If authenticity could not be recovered from a single urtext, the later generations of Cistercians determined that the authoritative form of the chant could nevertheless be reconstructed using reason alone. A second chant committee, overseen by St Bernard of Clairvaux, was appointed for the task. They first formulated a theologically grounded music theory, to which they determined the original Gregorian melodies must have adhered. The group produced four texts to accompany and explain their new antiphoner, gradual and hymnal.[8] The issue of modal unity was central to their editorial decision-making. For example, consistent use of a B-flat (a commonly accepted modification, though not diatonic in any mode) necessarily, if unintentionally, transposes the mode of the chant. Therefore, restrictions on its use were required lest the melody morph into a corrupted version of the original in a foreign modality. In St Bernard's Prologue to the Cistercian antiphoner, he pronounced the text and music of the chants authoritative and forbade any variation:

> I, indeed – summoning some of these very brethren who have been found to have superior knowledge of the theory of the chant and skill in its practice – together we have collected [...] a new Antiphoner, the following volume. This, we believe, is beyond reproach as to its music and text [...] We therefore desire that in our monasteries it be everywhere followed, both in word and note, exactly as it has been painstakingly revised, and set out in this volume. And by the authority of the entire Chapter, at which all the abbots accepted and confirmed it, we therefore forbid the slightest change to anything by anyone.[9]

---

appears in E. Rozanne Elder (ed.), *The New Monastery: Texts and Studies on the Earliest Cistercians* (Kalamazoo, 1998), p. 78.

[7] Alicia Scarcez argues that the objection to the corpus as a whole was ultimately cultural. Stephen Harding had imposed a Germanic (Eastern) chant dialect onto a community accustomed to the Latin (Western) tradition of Cluny and Marmoutier, and it was never fully accepted. Alicia Scarcez, *L'antiphonaire cistercien primitif d'après les sources musicales de 1136/1140: Le premier chant de Cîteaux retrouvé* (Münster, 2020).

[8] These are the *Tonary of St Bernard*, the *Regule*, the *Tractatus*, and the Prologue to the gradual, edited in Christian Meyer, 'Le tonaire cistercien et sa tradition', *Revue de musicologie*, 89:1 (2003), 57–92; Claire Maître, *La réforme cistercienne du plain-chant: Étude d'un traité théorique* (Brecht, 1995); David Wulstan (ed.), *The Letter of St Bernard and the Tract on the Cistercian Revision of the Antiphoner: The Text Newly Edited, Principally from the Mount Melleray Manuscript* (Lions Bay, 2015); 'Tractatus Cantandi Graduale', in *PL*, vol. 182, col. 1151–4.

[9] 'Ego vero accitis de ipsis fratribus nostris qui in arte et usu canendi instructiores atque

As Solutor Marosszéki has argued, the most significant and unprecedented aspect of the so-called 'Bernardine' recension was not the correction of problematic chants per se, but rather the construction of a totalising intellectual system.[10] Whether or not the Cistercian reformers in the late fifteenth century were versed in the analytical justifications of the Bernardine corpus, Cistercian chant carried a theoretical weightiness and a quasi-patristic authority that local independent traditions, such as those of Benedictine houses, never did.

Moreover, St Bernard enjoyed heightened stature in the fifteenth century. Scholars such as Berndt Hamm, Giles Constable and Jean Leclercq have highlighted the prominence of twelfth-century authors, particularly Bernard of Clairvaux, in the circles of the *Devotio moderna* and the Observant reformers. Erasmus, for example, looked to Bernard as the last of the Fathers.[11]

The Reform of the Abbey of Beaupré

The Abbey of Beaupré was founded by a group of nuns from the Cistercian abbey of La Cambre in 1228 under the patronage of Alix de Boelare, just outside the city of Geraardsbergen (French: Grammont). Little survives from the abbey of Beaupré before the fifteenth century besides three (later rebound as four) of the

---

periciores inventi sunt [...] novum tandem Antiphonarium in subiectum volumen collegimus et cantu, sicut credimus, et littera irreprehensibile [...] Ita ergo ut demum mutatum est et in hoc volumine continetur, volumus in nostris de cetero monasteriis tam verbo quam nota ubique teneri, et mutari omnino in aliquo ab aliquo auctoritate tocius capituli, ubi ab universis abbatibus concorditer susceptum et confirmatum est, prohibemus.': Bernardus of Claivaux, *Letter of St Bernard*, ed. Wulstan, pp. 8-9.

[10] Solutor Rodolphe Marosszéki, *Les origines du chant cistercien: Recherches sur les réformes du plain-chant cistercien au xiie siècle* (Rome, 1952).

[11] Berndt Hamm, 'Von der Spätmittelalterlichen Reformatio zur Reformation: Der Prozeß normativer Zentrierung von Religion und Gesellschaft in Deutschland', *Archiv für Reformationgeschichte*, 84 (1993), 7–82. An English translation is found in John M. Frymire, 'Normative Centering in the Fifteenth and Sixteenth Centuries: Observations on Religiosity, Theology and Iconology', *Journal of Early Modern History*, 3 (1999), 307–45; Jean Leclercq, 'Monastic and Scholastic Theology in the Reformers of the Fourteenth to Sixteenth Centuries', in Ellen Rozanne Elder (ed.), *From Cloister to Classroom: Monastic and Scholastic Approaches to Truth; The Spirituality of Western Christendom, III* (Kalamazoo, 1986), pp. 178–201, at p. 193; Giles Constable, 'The Popularity of Twelfth-Century Spiritual Writers in the Late Middle Ages', in Anthony Molho and John A. Tedeschi (eds), *Renaissance Studies in Honor of Hans Baron* (Dekalb, 1971), pp. 5–28; Giles Constable, 'Twelfth-Century Spirituality and the Late Middle Ages', in Osborne B. Hardison, Jr. (ed.), *Medieval and Renaissance Studies: Proceedings of the Southeastern Institute of Medieval and Renaissance Studies; Summer, 1969* (Chapel Hill, 1971), pp. 27–60.

original six volumes of its deluxe antiphoner copied in 1290.[12] Like many monasteries, the community experienced considerable financial hardship throughout the fourteenth and fifteenth centuries. This circumstance left the community exposed to external intervention. In 1462, the General Chapter temporarily placed the nuns under the care of Jean Eustache, the founding abbot of Jardinet.[13] Under his leadership, the abbey of Jardinet became a major catalyst of female reform by supplying books, confessors and visitators to abbeys of nuns in the region.[14]

Jean Eustache was not warmly received by all at Beaupré, however, and this may be an explanation for his absence in Beaupré's obituary (Brussels, KBR, MS No. 18200–01). Several of the sisters appealed to their influential parents to block his involvement. The Lord of Ravenstein approached Philip the Good on their behalf to halt the reform. Unfortunately for the dissenting nuns, the sympathies of the duke, and in particular his wife, Isabella of Bourbon, were not with the status quo. They ruled that the reform under Jean Eustache would proceed.[15]

The abbey of Beaupré became enveloped in a female Cistercian Observant movement that radiated from the abbey of Marche-les-Dames to encompass most Cistercian nunneries in a region of the southern Low Countries between Arras and Liège. Little is known of what was taught, learned or implemented in any of

---

[12] The antiphoner was long believed to have been produced at the nearby Cistercian abbey of Cambron, although Alison Stones has cast doubt on any connection between the antiphoner and Cambron. See:*Gothic Manuscripts 1260–1320*, pt. 1, vol. 1, *Text and Illustrations* (London, 2013), p. 63. See also Henry Yates Thompson, *Illustrations of One Hundred Manuscripts in the Library of Henry Yates Thompson* (7 vols, London, 1916), vol. 6, pp. 4–9; Sydney C. Cockerell, 'LXXXIII. Antiphoner of the Cistercian Abbey of Beaupré, near Grammont', in *A Descriptive Catalogue of Twenty Illuminated Manuscripts Nos. LXXV to XCIV...in the Collection of Henry Yates Thompson* (Cambridge, 1907), pp. 55–74; Lilian M. C. Randall, *Medieval and Renaissance Manuscripts in the Walters Art Gallery*, vol. 3, pt. 1, *Belgium, 1250–1530* (Baltimore, 1997), pp. 26–56.

[13] According to a statute of 1462, the reform of Beaupré was initiated 'ad instantiam et petitionem illustrissimi domini ducis Burgundiae et dominae ducissae seu consortis' ['at the insistence and request of the most illustrious lord, the Duke of Burgundy, and of the lady, his wife, the Duchess']: Joseph Marie Carnivez (ed.), *Statuta Capitulorum generalium Ordinis Cisterciensis ab anno 1116 ad annum 1786: Ab anno 1457 ad annum 1490* (8 vols, Louvain-la-Neuve, 1933–41), vol. 5, 1462, §56, p. 111.

[14] Xavier Hermand, 'Les relations de l'abbaye cistercienne du Jardinet avec des clercs réformateurs des diocèses de Cambrai et de Tournai (seconde moitié du XVᵉ siècle)', *Revue Mabillon*, 13 (2002), 237–63; Xavier Hermand, 'Réforme, circulation de scribes et transferts de manuscrits dans les abbayes cisterciennes du diocèse de Liège au XVᵉ siècle: À propos de sept volumes provenant de l'abbaye du Jardinet (Namur, Musée provincial des arts anciens du Namurois, Fonds de la ville, 48, 49, 50, 51, 67, 70, 71)', *Scriptorium*, 64:1 (2010), 3–80.

[15] Ursmer Berlière, 'Abbaye de Beaupré à Grimminge', in *Monasticon Belge*, vol. 7, bk 3, *Province de flandre orientale: Liège* (Liège, 1980), pp. 307–28, at p. 317.

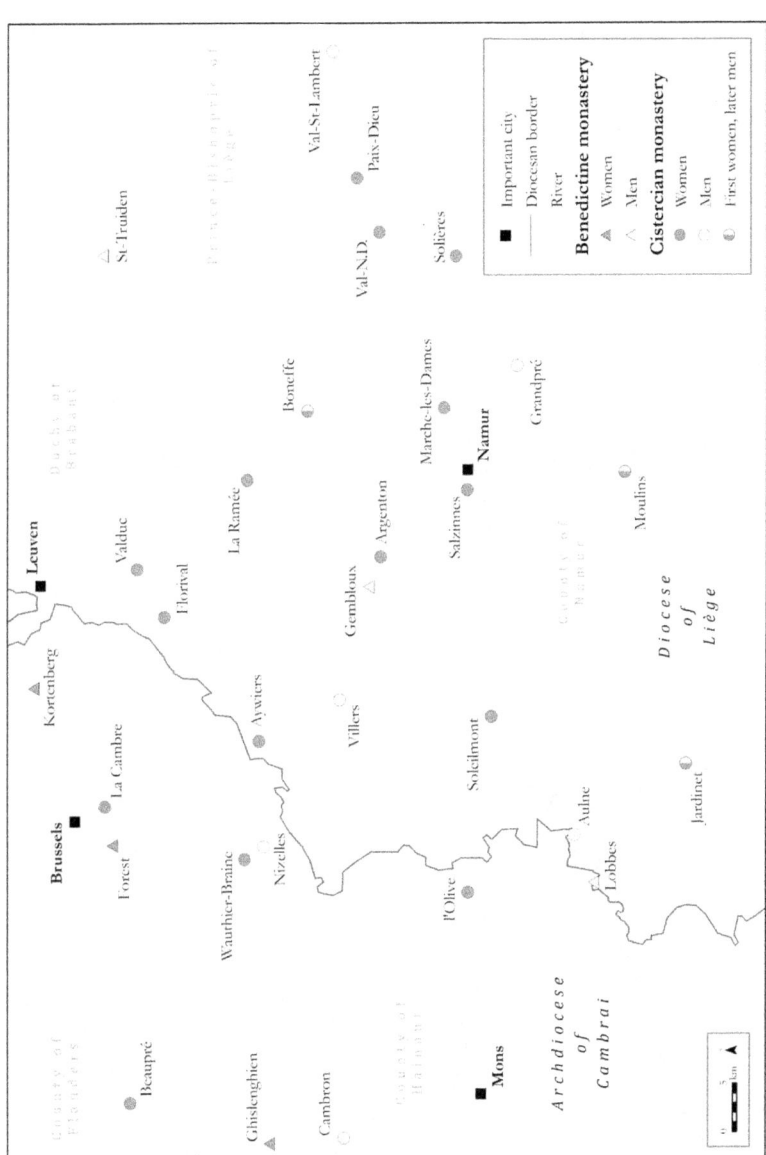

Map 11.1. Reformed Benedictine and Cistercian monasteries in central Belgium. © Hans Blomme.

Table 11.1. Transmission of reform, from Marche-les-Dames to Forest Abbey.

Marche-les-Dames	Soleilmont	Argenton	Valduc	Beaupré	Ghislenghien	Forest Kortenberg
1406 →	1415 →	1439 →	1460–3 →	1463 →	1480–1 →	1500 c. 1500

the affected houses. A chronicle from the abbey of Valduc (Dutch: Hertogendal) written in 1488 by Joes van Dormael, a monk of Villers and confessor to the nuns of Valduc, is the sole account of Beaupré's reform. It claims that a nun from Beaupré was sent to Valduc in 1463 for instruction in the reform along with nuns from several other abbeys.[16]

Two sources from related Cistercian nunneries offer clues about what the reform of Beaupré may have entailed. A visitation report for the nuns of Valduc written in 1473 by their father abbot at Villers, Francken Calabers, suggests what practices the nun from Beaupré may have observed and instituted. Although the document is not directly related to the reform of Valduc, as Roger De Ganck cautions, it does describe the standards of discipline upheld in the following decade. The text begins by demanding regular and punctual attendance at services and urging the proper style of singing. Abbot Calabers reminded the women that only the sick and infirm were relieved from their obligation to attend the office. They must take care in choir not to mutter, to sing off-pitch, or to allow their voices to wobble or crack ['niet grommende oft die stemme valsende oft brekende'] (fol. 1). Instead, they should chant with joyfulness, diligence and zeal.[17] He then proceeded to outline rules for enclosure and the reception of guests, times of abstinence from meat, simplicity of clothing, and allowances for reading in the vernacular both privately and in the refectory. Finally, he admonished the nuns to seek permission from their confessor (rather than the abbess) to leave the enclosure.[18]

---

[16] Cyriel Vleeschouwers (ed.), 'Joes van Dormael's Kroniek der Hervorming binnen de Brabantse Cisterciënserinnenabdij Hertogendaal (1488)', *Ons Geestelijk Erf*, 47 (1973), 173–220.

[17] Calabers' language echoes that of statute 'LXXV. De falsis vocibus' in the *Instituta generalis capituli* in Chrysogonus Waddell (ed.), *Narrative and Legislative Texts from Early Cîteaux: Latin Text in Dual Edition with English Translation and Notes* (Nuits-Saint-Georges, Abbaye de Cîteaux, 1999), pp. 360, 489–90. On twelfth-century Cistercian references to singing style, see especially Chrysogonus Waddell, 'A Plea for the *Institutio Sancti Bernard quomodo cantare et psallere debeamus*', in M. Basil Pennington OCSO (ed.), *Saint Bernard of Clairvaux: Studies Commemorating the Eighth Centenary of His Canonization* (Kalamazoo, 1977), pp. 180–207.

[18] Roger De Ganck, 'De "Reformatie-beweging" bij de Zuid-Nederlandse cisterciënzerinnen in de 15de eeuw', *Cîteaux: Commentarii cistercienses*, 32 (1981), 75–86. De Ganck

The disciplinary norms outlined by Calabers are largely echoed in the sole official document describing the reform programme. The Cistercian abbey of Flines was another women's community that became involved in the same reform movement and whose confessor was also a monk of Jardinet. Dated precisely one hundred years after Marie le Bervy implemented her new observance on 15 December 1406, the Flines nuns were presented with a list of articles of reform drafted on 15 December 1506 by Abbot Nicole Spaens of Nizelle, who had been appointed the nuns' visitator by their father immediate, Abbot Jean Foucault of Clairvaux. Like Abbot Calabers' visitation report, the document opens by encouraging regular participation and punctuality at the liturgy. The sisters are urged to celebrate the liturgy 'thoughtfully and slowly' ['meurement et à traict'].[19] Subsequent reform articles address the specific building requirements necessary for stricter claustration, namely, the installation of more windows. In addition to the ubiquitous prohibitions on simony and private property, there are regulations concerning pittances, communal goods, the eating of meat, simplicity of clothing and the reception of guests.[20]

While both texts foreground the quality of singing in the liturgy, neither is concerned with the melodies themselves. The new observance that the nuns of Beaupré learned at Valduc almost certainly did not include overhaul of the liturgy. The idea must have been conceived later at Beaupré or perhaps at Jardinet. Yet, many other groups outside the Cistercian Order around the same time were revisiting their liturgies in search of authentic models, particularly among Benedictines. Reform at the Benedictine abbey of Melk (*c.* 1417) was modelled on the abbey of Subiaco, where a group of Viennese monks travelled to learn the ideal observance and correct liturgy from the cradle of Benedictine monasticism.[21] The early architects

---

noted that this text is written in the same hand as Joes van Dormael's chronicle (Brussels, KBR, MS IV 811; previously Brussels, National Archives, Brabant Ecclesiastical Archive, supplement 20562).

[19] Andrea G. Pearson has translated this phrase as 'promptly and on time' and argued that it correlated with the image of a clock representing punctual attendance at the liturgy in a diptych depicting the reform. Jean Bellegambe, *Virgin and Child with Rosary, St Bernard with Cistercian Monk, Guillaume Bollart with the Abbess of Flines, Jeanne de Boubais on the reverse*, after 1507, oil on panel, 15⅞ x 20 in (40.3 x 50.8 cm), The Frick Art Museum, Pittsburgh, https://collection.thefrickpittsburgh.org/objects/34 [accessed 27 December 2022] in 'Nuns, Images, and the Ideals of Women's Monasticism: Two Paintings from the Cistercian Convent of Flines', *Renaissance Quarterly*, 54:4, pt. 2 (2001), 1356–1402, at p. 1386.

[20] Edouard Hautcœur (ed.), 'Documents sur la réforme introduite à l'abbaye de Flines, en 1506', *Analectes pour servir à l'histoire ecclésiastique de Belgique*, 9 (1872), 213–26.

[21] Ursmer Berlière, 'La réforme de Melk au XVᵉ siècle', *Revue Bénédictine*, 12 (1895), 204–24, 289–309; Barbara Frank, 'Subiaco, ein Reformkonvent des späten Mittelalters. Zur Erfassung und Zusammensetzung der Sublacenser Mönchsgemeinschaft in der Zeit von 1362 bis 1514', *Quellen und Forschungen aus Italienischen Archiven und Bibliotheken*,

of the Bursfeld reform, Johann Dederoth and his successor Johannes Hagen, won final approval in 1452 for their new ordinal based on 'countless hours of textual research in the oldest available regional manuscripts to "remove superfluous material and purge apocryphal and inauthentic reading."'[22] Though work on the ordinal was completed in 1448, the edition became embroiled in a rival project at the Benedictine abbey of St Jacob of Mainz, and its formal approval set the archbishop of Mainz at odds with the papal legate.[23] In 1511, Philippe Bourgoing, former prior of Cluny, assembled a group of theological scholars to review and modify the Cluniac liturgy to align it better with the *Rule* of St Benedict.[24] Most fruits of these labours have not survived, and little musicological analysis of the remaining efforts has yet been undertaken.

Revision of the Beaupré Antiphoner

While discussion about the liturgy at Beaupré may have been percolating through the community for some time, editing the antiphoner did not commence for many years after the reform in 1463. The changes must have occurred after 1476, since they included the addition of the feast of the Visitation, which was universally adopted by the General Chapter in that year.[25] Though there are several possible explanations for the gap between the monastery's reform and the revisions to the antiphoner, including time to raise the necessary funds, to cultivate the right

---

15 (1972), 526–656. The reformed liturgy adopted by Melk has been studied by Robert Klugseder, 'The Medieval Office Tradition of the Benedictine Monastery of Saints Ulrich and Afra, Augsburg' (unpublished Ph.D. dissertation, University of Regensburg, 2007).

[22] Paulus Volk (ed.), *Urkunden zur Geschichte der Bursfelder Kongregation* (Bonn, 1951), pp. 54–5. Quotation and translation from Duggan, 'Bringing Reformed Liturgy to Print', p. 417.

[23] Mary Kay Duggan, 'Politics and Text: Bringing the Liturgy to Print', *Gutenberg-Jahrbuch*, 76 (2001), 104–17; Mary Kay Duggan, 'Fifteenth-Century Music Printing: Reform, Uniformität, and Local Tradition', in *Niveau, Nische, Nimbus: Die Anfänge des Musikdrucks nördlich der Alpen* (Tutzing, 2010), pp. 17–32; Paulus Volk, 'Die erste Fassung des Bursfelder *Liber ordinarius*', in *Fünfhundert Jahre Bursfelder Kongregation: eine Jubiläumsgabe* (Münster, 1950), pp. 126–92; Dieter Mertens, 'Der Streit um den Bursfelder *Liber ordinarius*', *Studien und Mitteilungen des Benediktiner-Ordens und seiner Zweige*, 86 (1975), 728–59; Gerhard Müller, 'Reform und Reformation: Zur Geschichte von Spätmittelalter und früher Neuzeit', *Jahrbuch der Gesellschaft für Niedersächsische Kirchengeschichte*, 83 (1985), 13–29, at p. 21; Philipp Stenzig, 'Der liturgische Kontext', in *Die Chronik des Klosters Lüne über die Jahre 1481–1530: Hs. Lüne 13* (Tübingen, 2019), pp. 27–61.

[24] Jean-Marie Le Gall, *Les moines au temps des réformes, France (1480–1560)* (Seyssel, 2001), p. 354.

[25] Bernard Backaert, 'L'évolution du calendrier cistercien', *Collectanea ordinis cisterciensium reformatorum*, 12 (1950), 81–94, 302–16; 13 (1951), 108–27.

expertise, or to procure the correct exemplar, there are no grounds to assume that reform of the liturgy was an ordinary component of the initial reform imposed on the nuns. Therefore, it remains highly plausible that the modifications to the nuns' chant were choices they made in the wake of reform. In fact, the chant revisions almost certainly occurred under the abbacy of the second abbot of Jardinet, Martin de Lannoy, elected in 1477. Prior to his election (held at the abbey of Beaupré because of fighting associated with the Burgundian wars in the vicinity of Jardinet), Abbot Martin had been the longtime confessor to the nuns of Beaupré. Archival documents from Beaupré indicate that he had 'assisted' the women in their reform, and yet there is no indication of liturgical change at the abbey in his decades of service as confessor.[26] Given his long familiarity and good rapport with the sisters, it is reasonable to assume that he may have been as influenced by them and their work on chant as they were by him.

Sixty-five new leaves were added to the extant volumes of the Beaupré Antiphoner in the years after 1476, including offices for the feasts of the Visitation, Corpus Christi and St Mary Magdalene. Approximately a hundred leaves are missing from the extant volumes, the vast majority of which were removed by the nuns themselves at this time.[27] Proper offices were the primary target. Local non-standard chants for the feasts of SS John the Baptist, Benedict, Catherine and the 11,000 Virgin Martyrs of Cologne were expunged. Some of these were replaced with new inserts containing the standard Cistercian versions, and some were simply discarded. Nevertheless, vestiges of what had been replaced do remain on several of the pages left in the antiphoner. These remnants consistently differ from the standard Cistercian assignments, and a large number of the rejected chants appear to be *unica*.

The excision of these leaves also meant the loss of several illustrations. Two initials did survive the purge of their offices, however, and bear witness to the importance of these feasts to the local community and what the nuns stood to lose in the revision process. One of these, in the second volume of the antiphoner (W. 760, fol. 122v), features St John the Baptist flanked by two kneeling nuns in brown habits and black veils who represent the Beaupré community. All

---

[26] Martin de Lannoy is the first name in a list of confessors, chaplains and *familiares* (servants, paid workers and other employees) of the abbey recorded in a miscellany from Beaupré (Brussels, KBR, Fonds Goethals no. 74, fol. 60r) copied in the late eighteenth century with a heading that it had been pulled from an old register ('tirez d'un vieu registre'). He is described as 'pater de nôtre monastere l'espace de 30 ans' where he 'acista à la reformation' of Beaupré. Additionally, he was identified as the long-time confessor of Beaupré in the martyrology of the abbey of L'Olive and received one of the longest and most detailed entries in the obituary of Beaupré (Brussels, KBR, MS No. 18200–1), where he is called 'pater et confessor' of this monastery before the reform with a later hand adding '30 annos' interlinearly.

[27] Randall, *Medieval and Renaissance Manuscripts*.

Fig. 11.1. Beaupré Antiphoner, initial 'B' with St John the Baptist for the non-standard first Vespers responsory 'Baptista Christi et praecursor', W. 760, fol. 122v. © The Walters Art Museum, Baltimore.

three feasts of St John the Baptist had been local to Beaupré (Nativity, Octave of the Nativity and Decollation), and his cult suffered the most losses in the revisions. Another image is now housed at the Ashmolean Museum in Oxford as part of John Ruskin's teaching collection (Oxford, Ashmolean Museum, Ruskin Collection, Standard Series 7). It is the most ornate page of the entire antiphoner set. This leaf begins the feast of St Catherine and was originally found in W. 760 following fol. 182, where residue on the facing page is still visible. The only office provided in the manuscript for this saint, Vespers, originally occupied two full folios, with the second half of the final Magnificat antiphon concluding on the following leaf. Based on the surviving portion in the bound manuscript, this chant for St Catherine appears to be an *unicum* and explains the removal of these pages.

During the revision process, Roman numeral foliation was added and the antiphoner was rebound. This numeration now runs continuously, including over the place where the missing leaves for St Catherine were originally located. Nevertheless, a second set of pagination with Arabic numbers was added during a subsequent rebinding (*c.* 1700, according to Michelle Brown), and the Ashmolean

Fig. 11.2. Excised leaf from the Beaupré Antiphoner for the Feast of St Catherine. © Ashmolean Museum, University of Oxford.

leaf does contain this page number.[28] Evidently, the folio was removed by 1500, preserved separately, added back c. 1700, and finally removed again in the 1850s by John Ruskin.[29]

The fact that the Ashmolean leaf was preserved separately by the community at Beaupré for two centuries after its initial removal from the antiphoner suggests the ambivalence the nuns could have felt about the changes to the antiphoner. Motivated by zeal for Cistercian chant, the nuns were asked to discard some of their most precious artistic heritage. For someone in the community, it may have seemed too extreme to part with such a visually magnificent leaf altogether. Lying disbound in its excised state, it would have served as a reminder of the price of reform at Beaupré.

The Adoption of Cistercian Chant in Benedictine Abbeys

The re-invigorated appreciation for the twelfth-century Cistercian repertoire, evidenced in the Beaupré Antiphoner, had implications beyond the community of Beaupré alone. After the reform of their monastery in 1463, nuns of Beaupré were tasked with the reform of the abbey of Ghislenghien in 1480. These sisters were the first Benedictines to become affiliated with an otherwise Cistercian women's movement.[30] Subsequently, a delegation of reformed nuns from Ghislenghien

---

[28] Lilian M. C. Randall, 'The Fragmentation of a Double Antiphonal from Beaupré', in Linda L. Brownrigg and Margaret M. Smith (eds), *Interpreting and Collecting Fragments of Medieval Books* (Los Altos Hills, 2000), pp. 210–29, at p. 216, n. 17.

[29] John Ruskin described the difficulty dismembering a 'large missal' in diary entries on 30 December 1853 and 1 and 3 January 1854, and produced an engraving of Christ's baptism in the Jordan from W.761 shortly thereafter. Sydney C. Cockerell thought the rebound missal was the Beaupré Antiphoner, in 'Antiphoner of the Cistercian Abbey of Beaupré', p. 62.

[30] The earliest account of Ghislenghien's reform comes from Joes van Dormael's chronicle, in which he claimed that two nuns from Ghislenghien were recommended to the abbey of Valduc by Bishop Henri de Bergues to learn the reform. This version is attested nowhere else, however. Confusion over names likely resulted because the abbey of Ghislenghien was more properly known as known as Val-des-Vierges (Dutch: Maagdendaal or Maagdendaele), and Ursmer Berlière has claimed that the community to which Joes van Dormael meant to refer is the much more proximate Cistercian abbey of Maagdendaal (French: Val-Virginal) in Oplinter, Flemish Brabant. 'Abbaye de Valduc, à Hamme-Mille', in *Monasticon Belge*, vol. 4, bk 2, *Province de Brabant* (Liège, 1968), pp. 531–48, at p. 539, n. 4. All other sources, including those from Ghislenghien and Beaupré, agree that it was Beaupré that reformed Ghislenghien. The *Gallia christiana* relates that the reform of Ghislenghien was conducted by two nuns from Beaupré who came to Ghislenghien. Denis de Sainte-Marthe, 'Gislenghemium', in *Gallia christiana, in provincias ecclesiasticas distributa; qua series et historia archiepiscoporum, epis-*

then permanently transferred to the Benedictine abbey of Forest (Dutch: Vorst) to lead the reform in that house. The reigning abbess of Forest was deposed by the bishop of Cambrai in 1500 after a decade-long series of financial troubles following losses to the abbey that were suffered during fighting between the Hapsburg Maximilian I and King Charles VIII of France. The new abbess of Forest, Marguerite I de Liedekerke, was elected from the recently-arrived group from Ghislenghien.[31]

Despite the convent's economic woes, one of Abbess Marguerite's first acts was to commission a sumptuous, large-format, five-volume antiphoner, now in private ownership. The set was executed by Julien de Gavre in the 'Ghent-Bruges' style and completed in 1502.[32] It contains the distinct Cistercian versions of the chant melodies. Additionally, an un-notated sixteenth-century breviary (Brussels, KBR, MS 3822-3823) was rubricated explicitly as Cistercian use both at the beginning of the psalter (fol. 19r) and at the beginning of the breviary section (fol. 106r). The designation illustrates that these black nuns were not unwitting about the origins and associations of their new liturgy.

Though the new Cistercian antiphoner for the nuns of Ghislenghien was not produced until 1507 (only the winter cycle of the Ghislenghien Antiphoner survives as Lund, Lund University Library, MS 56), Marguerite I de Liedekerke's commission of the Forest Antiphoner suggests that the Cistercian liturgy was already well established at Ghislenghien by 1500 when the outgoing group transferred to Forest. Abbess Marguerite and her fellow sisters from Ghislenghien would have introduced, taught and championed Cistercian chant at Forest on the model of Ghislenghien just as the nuns of Beaupré surely had during Ghislenghien's reform.

---

coporum, et abbatum Franciæ vicinarumque ditionum ab origine ecclesiarum ad nostra tempora deducitur, et probatur ex authenticis instrumentis ad calcem appositis (16 vols, Paris, 1725), vol. 3, p. 150.

[31] Ursmer Berlière, 'Abbaye de Forest', in *Monasticon Belge*, vol. 4, bk 1, *Province de Brabant* (Liège, 1964), pp. 189-217, at p. 206.

[32] Because Marguerite I de Liedekerke belonged to the de Gavre family, both Hubert Nelis and Anne-Marie Legaré have surmised that Julien de Gavre may have been a relation of the abbess. Nelis has also suggested he may have been a chaplain or spiritual director to the nuns of Forest. Unfortunately, his identity is unknown. Hubert Nelis, 'Antiphonaires enluminés de l'abbaye de Forest (1500-1502)', *Revue belge d'archéologie et d'histoire de l'art*, 1:1 (1931), 213-21; Anne-Marie Legaré, 'Du nouveau sur l'enluminure en Hainaut à la fin du Moyen Âge: L'antiphonaire de l'abbaye de Forest (Westmalle, Abbaye des Trappistes, Ms. 9)', in Brigitte Dekeyzer and Jan Van der Stock (eds), *Manuscripts in Transition: Recycling manuscripts, texts, and images; Proceedings of the International Congress held in Brussels (5-9 November 2002)* (Leuven, 2005), pp. 407-17; Guido Hendrix, *Handschriftenbezit en boekengebruik Trappisten van Westmalle 1794-1994* (Leuven, 1994), pp. 132-44.

The liturgical changes at Beaupré, Ghislenghien and Forest followed different, even contradictory, paths. While at Beaupré chants for the office that did not conform to Cistercian use were systematically removed and occasionally replaced, some allowances were made for local feasts in the Benedictine houses. For example, twelve leaves were excised from the Beaupré Antiphoner for the feast of the 11,000 Virgins (based on a gap in the Roman numeral foliation between clix and clxx in W. 760 following fol. 148). Remnants of the original chants for this office survive in the manuscript on either side of the removed section and indicate that the liturgy for the 11,000 Virgins at the abbey of Beaupré differed from standard Cistercian use. Yet the Forest Antiphoner contains those same non-standard assignments as well as the rest of the full office (a mix of standard and non-standard chants). Likewise, the local office for the feast of St Alena, whose relics were housed at Forest Abbey, was retained in the new antiphoner for Forest (vol. 3, pp. 377–404 (misnumbered on the page as 357–84)) and breviary (KBR, MS 3822-3, fols 377–8). Since the Cistercian liturgy at Forest was introduced by fellow Benedictines, the reformers from Ghislenghien may have been more lenient about exceptions than the Cistercians had been. Nevertheless, retention of these offices was undoubtedly the outcome of some discussion, possible resistance, and eventual compromise among the women, likely with the approval of the confessor and abbot of Jardinet.

Both the liturgical revisions at Beaupré and the adoption of Cistercian chant at Ghislenghien took place during Martin de Lannoy's abbacy. Meanwhile, the confessor to Ghislenghien during their reform, Jean de Binche, was described in the chronicle of Jardinet as subprior of that community.[33] Both women's abbeys were thus related through their connections to Jardinet. Although we cannot be sure why the abbey of Beaupré was chosen to direct the reform of Ghislenghien, it may be that Martin de Lannoy, who had overseen the reform of Beaupré, considered it a fitting exemplar. If the review of the Beaupré Antiphoner was completed or underway by 1480, then the abbey of Beaupré would have been all the more qualified to introduce Cistercian chant at Ghislenghien.

The position of Jardinet as the nexus of both Benedictine reform and the promotion of Cistercian chant under Martin de Lannoy was reaffirmed by his successor, Jardinet's third abbot, Arnoul de Solbrecq (1484–1502).[34] While this

---

[33] Georges Dereine, 'Une chronique de l'abbaye du Jardinet (Walcourt)', *Cîteaux: Commentarii cistercienses*, 33 (1982), 153–94, at p. 154.

[34] No mention survives of the confessor at Forest Abbey, but Xavier Hermand has commented that monks of Jardinet were involved in their reform 'sans doute'. Because a contingent of nuns from Ghislenghien permanently transferred to Forest for the reform, one of whom became abbess for the next forty-one years, influence from Jardinet was at the very least indirect. Xavier Hermand, 'La réforme de l'abbaye de Saint-Trond et

Observant movement was first introduced to Benedictine nuns under Martin de Lannoy, Arnoul de Solbrecq continued in this direction with the first reform of Benedictine monks at Lobbes in 1497. A booklist written around 1500 at Jardinet contains twenty categories of books, the majority of them liturgical, to be sent to support the ongoing reform of Lobbes. The list, which mentions several antiphoners, a missal, three processionals, a psalter with hymnal, in addition to an 'usus ordinis Cisterciensis', and 'plura breviaria quibus utuntur fratres' ['many breviaries that the brothers used'], raises the possibility that a major liturgical undertaking, specifically of a Cistercian type, was underway.[35] Alas, no liturgical books survive from Lobbes itself.

Shortly after the reform of Lobbes, followed by that of the Benedictine women's communities at Forest and (the attempted reform) at Kortenberg in 1500, Arnoul de Solbrecq formally left the Cistercian Order in 1503, along with twelve other monks from Jardinet, to transfer permanently to the Benedictine abbey of Gembloux.[36] The abbey of Gembloux then affiliated with the Benedictine Congregation of Bursfeld in 1505. Numerous liturgical books from Gembloux postdating their reform survive. A new antiphoner (Brussels, KBR, MS 5645) likewise contains the Cistercian office, even though adoption of the Bursfeld liturgy was ordinarily a precondition for admittance to the congregation. The Gembloux manuscripts are the strongest indication that Martin de Lannoy and Arnoul de Solbrecq were not only promoters of Cistercian chant (and may have had to negotiate a compromise with the abbey of Bursfeld to preserve it), but also regarded it as superior on musical grounds independent from considerations of institutional identity and uniform discipline.[37]

---

les réseaux monastiques au début du XVIe siècle: Autour d'un recueil de textes réformateurs; Bruxelles, Bibliothèques royale, 20929–20930', *Revue bénédictine*, 112 (2002), 356–78, at p. 371; Xavier Hermand, 'Les relations de l'abbaye cistercienne', 255, n. 95.

[35] Derolez, Albert and Benjamin Victor (eds), *Corpus Catalogorum Belgii: The Medieval Booklists of the Southern Low Countries, vol. 2, Provinces of Liège, Luxemburg and Namur* (Brussels, 1994), pp. 193–5.

[36] A portrait in the *Gesta abbatus gemblocensium* depicts Arnoul de Solbrecq as monastic reformer of both Benedictines and Cistercians. In his right hand, he holds the two crosses of Jardinet and Gembloux and, in his left, the key of St Peter and a bundle of rods symbolising his status as reformer. A. Papin, *Gesta abbatum gemblocensium* (Brussels, KBR, MS 10293–10294), available digitally at https://uurl.kbr.be/1734473 [accessed 27 December 2022]. See Jean-Baptiste Lefèvre, Histoire et institutions des abbayes cisterciennes (XIIe–XVIe siècle)', in *Monastères bénédictins et cisterciens dans les Albums de Croÿ (1596–1611)* (Brussels, 1991), pp. 109–86, at p. 171; Jean-Baptiste Lefèvre, 'Réformes cisterciennes en Namurois et leur rayonnement (XIIe–XVIe siècle)', in Jacques Toussaint (ed.), *Les cisterciens en Namurois, XIIe–XVIe siècle* (Namur, 1998), pp. 47–54, at p. 52.

[37] See notes 16–19.

Following the likelihood that monks of Jardinet imposed Cistercian chant on the Benedictine monks of Lobbes, as we know they did on the Benedictines of Gembloux, Arnoul de Solbrecq's successor as abbot of Gembloux, Mathieu Petri, sent a delegation of six monks in 1514 to the abbey of Sint-Andries in Bruges (Saint-André-les-Bruges) when that house sought admission to the Bursfeld Congregation. Though none of Sint-Andries's liturgical books from these years survive, a chronicle from the monastery records that the group from Gembloux created an uproar when they arrived there. The chronicler reports that 'in these men [from Gembloux], [the monks of Sint-Andries] were indeed deceived, for they unleashed total confusion through their reform and brought great damage and harm to our monastery'.[38] Ursmer Berlière attributed the altercation to the attempt by the Benedictines from Gembloux to foist their liturgy on the monks of Sint-Andries.[39] Given the context outlined in this chapter, it is near certain that the contingent from Gembloux once again attempted to impose Cistercian chant on their fellow Benedictines.

Three years later, in 1520, Abbot Mathieu Petri's successor at Gembloux, Antoine Papin, extended similar assistance to the Benedictine monks of Sint-Truiden (French: Saint-Trond), while they also pursued incorporation into the Bursfeld Congregation. The abbot of Sint-Truiden at the time was Guillaume de Bruxelles. He had formerly been active in the same Cistercian women's Observant movement while confessor of the Cistercian nuns of Flines during their reform.[40] He then left the Cistercian Order and affiliated with the Benedictines once he was appointed abbot of Saint-Amand shortly before his move to Sint-Truiden. Abbot Guillaume similarly acquired a number of new manuscripts for Sint-Truiden. Those books, including an antiphoner copied in 1539 (Liège, ULiège Library, MS 24) and a gradual produced between 1540 and 1542 now housed at the Bibliotheek Hasselt Limburg, do not contain the Cistercian liturgy.[41] They suggest that the

---

[38] 'Hic abbas [sancti Andreae] [...] petiit ab abbate Gemblcensi aliquos ex suis religiosis, quatenus per ipsos reformatio Bursfeldensis introduceretur in sua abbatia, sed in istis hominibus vere deceptus fuit, nam pro reformatione omnem confusionem introduxerunt, et multa damna ac detrimenta praestiterunt nostro monasterio.': Arnold Goethals, *Chronica monasterii Sancti Andreae juxta Brugas ordinis sancti Benedicti*, ed. W. H. Jacob Weale (Bruges: Gailliard, 1868), 172, n. 2.

[39] 'Le 29 avril 1517 [moines de Gembloux] introduisaient dans ce monastère des usages nouveaux et les livres liturgiques de leur abbaye d'origine, ce qui n'alla pas sans protestations et disputes.': Ursmer Berlière, 'Abbaye de Saint-André-lez-Bruges', in *Monasticon Belge*, vol. 3, bk. 1, *Province de Flandre occidentale* (Liège, 1960), pp. 86–129, at p. 112.

[40] Camille de Borman (ed.), *Chronique de l'abbaye de Saint-Trond* (Liège, 1877), pp. 358–9.

[41] Diederik van Breedzip, 'Graduale van de abdij van Sint-Truiden', *Bibliotheek Hasselt* (https://hasselt.bibliotheek.be/catalogus/diederik-van-breedzip/graduale-van-de-abdij-van-sint-truiden/library-v-limburg-extern_4315574) [accessed 30 April 2022]. The

dissemination of Cistercian chant into reformed Benedictine houses in the region had halted by this time, possibly after the fiasco at Sint-Andries.

Confraternities and Reform

The adoption of Cistercian chant by a Benedictine community was not a practical or expedient decision. Association with Cistercians offered none of the benefits that, for example, formal admittance to the Bursfeld Congregation did, such as provincial chapters, regular visitation, privileges and exemptions, networks of support, freedom from commendatory abbots and abbesses, freedom from episcopal jurisdiction, protection from unwelcome reformers of other Orders like Johannes Busch, and even autonomy from the local bailiff.[42] Nevertheless, communities could replicate some aspects of such networks for themselves through grassroots confraternities. The bond forged among the nuns of Ghislenghien, Forest and Beaupré, as well as Beaupré's Cistercian motherhouse of La Cambre through shared liturgy and kinship was strengthened by a confraternity agreement attested in a ceremonial and book of prayers (Brussels, KBR, MS II. 3319) copied in the early eighteenth century:[43]

> Nous avons association, a[vec] les Dames de Forêt, de même avec les Dames de Ghislenghien, et [nous] chantons une Messe, au trépas de chaque Dame et pour les Soeurs, un 7 [P]seaumes. Au trepas d'une Dame de la Cambre, nous disons un 7 [P]seaumes et pour les Soeurs, de même. Beaupré s'a tellement maintenu en disciple de l'ordre et les Dames ont reformé La Cambre, et Ghislenghien, quoique [el]les sont de l'ordre de S. Benoît.

---

    library of Sint-Truiden suffered a catastrophic fire in 1538, and this volume would have replaced the one lost.

[42] Eva Schlotheuber, 'Die Zisterzienserinnengemeinschaften im Spätmittelalter', in Franz J. Felten and Werner Rösener (eds), *Norm und Realität: Kontinuität und Wandel der Zisterzienser im Mittelalter* (Berlin, 2009), pp. 265–84, at p. 270.

[43] A mortuary roll from Forest Abbey (Manchester, John Rylands Library, Latin MS 114) contains a list of ten monasteries with which Forest was in confraternity at the time of Abbess Elisabeth 'sConincs's death on 19 July 1458, and Beaupré, Ghislenghien and La Cambre are not on the list. Considering these communities had no prior connection, the confraternity can confidently be associated with the reform of these houses. See Montague Rhodes James, *A Descriptive Catalogue of the Latin Manuscripts in the John Rylands Library at Manchester* (Manchester, 1921), vol. 1, pp. 201–10 (cat. 114); Frank Taylor, 'Additional Notes to James's Catalogue', in *Descriptive Catalogue of the Latin Manuscripts* (Munich, 1980), p. 39; Stacy Boldrick, 'An Encounter between Death and an Abbess: The Mortuary Roll of Elisabeth 'sConincs, Abbess of Forest (Manchester, John Rylands Library, Latin MS 114)', *Bulletin of the John Rylands Library*, 82:1 (2000), 29–48.

[We have association with the nuns of Forest; the same with the nuns of Ghislenghien, and we sing a Mass upon the death of each nun and a set of seven Psalms for lay sisters. At the death of a nun of La Cambre, we recite a set of seven Psalms; the same for the lay sisters. Beaupré has maintained itself well in the discipline of the order, and the nuns reformed La Cambre and Ghislenghien, even though they are of the order of St Benedict.][44]

Confraternities frequently entailed other privileges in addition to prayers for the deceased, such as the right to join each other's choirs and to take refuge in another's house or property during times of war or calamity.[45] Communities could associate for any number of reasons, but in several cases a confraternity accompanied the adoption of other shared customs. For example, to circumvent the General Chapter's resistance to congregations, several Dutch Cistercian monasteries instead joined together as a fraternal union, the *Colligatio Galiaeensis*. Their association involved a 'common observance, the mutual exchange of priors, the sending of confessors, and last but not least the remembrance of the dead'.[46] As informal alliances that fell outside institutional oversight, confraternities could form unimpeded between male and female communities as well as between houses of different orders, establishing relationships on their own terms.

Confraternities appear elsewhere among houses in the same reform movement. The female abbeys of Argenton and Valduc entered into an association in 1467 shortly after Valduc reformed under the supervision of nuns from Argenton. The Cistercian women's abbey of Maagdendaele in Oudenaarde joined the society in 1469 after a group from Valduc transferred to Maagdendaele to lead the reform

---

[44] All translations mine unless indicated otherwise. The claim that Beaupré reformed La Cambre is unattested elsewhere.

[45] Ursmer Berlière, 'Les confraternités monastiques au Moyen-Âge', *Revue liturgique et monastique*, 11 (1925–6), 134–42; W. G. Clark-Maxwell, 'Some Letters of Confraternity', *Archaeologia or Miscellaneous Tracts Relating to Antiquity*, 75 (1926), 19–60; Id., 'Some Further Letters of Fraternity', *Archaeologia or Miscellaneous Tracts Relating to Antiquity*, 79 (1929), 179–216; Jean-Pierre Gerzaguet, 'Les confraternités de l'abbaye de Marchiennes au Moyen-Âge (XIIᵉ–XVᵉ s.)', *Revue bénédictine*, 110 (2000), 301–54; Giles Constable, 'Commemoration and Confraternity at Cluny during the Abbacy of Peter the Venerable', in Giles Constable (ed.), *The Abbey of Cluny: A Collection of Essays to Mark the Eleven-Hundredth Anniversary of Its Foundation* (Berlin, 2010), pp. 313–38.

[46] 'Dennoch sicherten die gemeinsame Observanz, der gegenseitige Austausch von Prioren, die Entsendung von Beichtvätern und nicht zuletzt das […] Totengedächtnis.': Kaspar Elm and Peter Feige, 'Reformen und Kongregationsbildungen der Zisterzienser in Spätmittelalter und früher Neuzeit', in Kaspar Elm, Peter Joerißen and Hermann Josef Roth (eds), *Die Zisterzienser: Ordensleben zwischen Ideal und Wirklichkeit. Eine Ausstellung des Landschaftsverbandes Rheinland. Rheinisches Museumamt, Brauweiler. Aachen, Krönungssaal des Rathauses 3. Juli–28. September 1980* (Bonn, 1980), p. 247.

there.[47] In the case of Ghislenghien, the chronicler of Valduc, Joes van Dormael, claimed that the confraternity was initiated by the bishop of Cambrai following their reform, presumably to ensure continuing exchange, support and informal supervision as stakeholders in one another's communities:

> And he [Bishop Henri de Bergues] sought and also humbly requested a confraternity among them, which was granted to him, as he wished, with an open letter, sealed by the abbess and the convent.[48]

That the confraternity agreement among Beaupré and its three related houses was freshly copied into the aforementioned ceremonial and book of prayers (MS II. 3319) approximately two hundred years later powerfully demonstrates the strength of the spiritual networks forged through reform and the serious responsibility that communities assumed for those they influenced. The association endured even after the liturgical resemblance among the Benedictine and Cistercian houses dissolved in the seventeenth century. The liturgical evidence from these houses in the last quarter of the fifteenth century reveals the nuns' conscious and careful deliberation of liturgical change. It also intimates some degree of ambivalence towards reform consistent with the attitudes expressed in the sisters' chronicles studied by Winston-Allen and others. The revisions to the chant books of these abbeys in the final decades of the fifteenth century demonstrate an intensified commitment to twelfth-century Cistercian forms, especially those associated with St Bernard. The incorporation of special feasts in the Forest Antiphoner of precisely the same type as those removed from the Beaupré Antiphoner suggests some degree of malleability, negotiation and prioritisation in the reform of each house. Stripped of all local particularities, the liturgy at Beaupré became fully and authoritatively Cistercian for the first time in its history in the late fifteenth century. The black nuns of Ghislenghien and Forest, however, embraced a more complex and dynamic monastic identity that was shaped by personal exchanges, grassroots networks of their own design, and new ideas. In each community, the women's changing understanding of what it meant to be a nun of that monastery found its principal expression in and through the liturgy, just as it had for centuries before the Observant reform.

---

[47] Vleeschouwers, 'Joes van Dormael's Kroniek', 207.
[48] 'Ende des versocht hij oec ende badt oetmoedichleec om tconfraterniteit van hier binnen, dwelc hem, alsoet wel betaemde, willichleec gheconsenteert was met eenen openen brieve, bezeghelt vander abdissen ende convent.': Vleeschouwers, 'Joes van Dormael's Kroniek', 210.

Index

abbess   58, 69, 70, 73, 84, 138, 140, 146, 150, 151, 170, 175, 204, 210–11, 216, 218–19, 221–3, 225–6, 228, 240–2, 245, 256, 263, 267, 269
   See also Agnes, abbess of Clonard; Anne d'Orléans, abbess of Sainte-Croix; Castellana, abbess of San Giovanni della Pipia; Imelda de Giroldis, abbess of San Giovanni della Pipia; Jeanne de Couhé, abbess of Sainte-Croix; Katharina of Hoya, abbess of Wienhausen; Katharina Remstede, abbess of Wienhausen; Lucia de Bezanis, abbess of San Giovanni della Pipia; Margherita Casanova, abbess of San Giovanni delle Pipia; Marguerite I de Liedekerke, abbess of Forest; Marie Berland, abbess of Sainte-Croix; Marie de Bretagne, abbess of Fontevraud; Ottabona, *ministra*, *rectrix* and abbess of San Cristoforo; Renée de Bourbon, abbess of Fontevraud; Ricburg, abbess of Lamspringe; Susanna Postock, abbess of Wienhausen
Aethelwold, bishop of Winchester   57, 59, 62, 66, 71–2, 74, 79
   Life of   58–9
Agnes, abbess of Clonard   93
   See also Clonard, co-located houses
Agnes, roman martyr   18, 38–43, 45–7, 116
   See also hagio-liturgical motifs - *sponsa Christi*
   Officium of   37, 42, 45, 46
   Passio of   35–42, 46, 53

Annaghdown   89, 91, 93, 96
   See also co-located houses
Anne d'Orléans, abbess of Sainte-Croix and Fontevraud   208, 211–12
   See also Fontevraud, Sainte-Croix
Ardcarn   91, 93
   See also co-located houses
Arnold Steinwick, provost of Heiningen   239–40
Arnoul de Solbrecq, abbot of Jardinet   264–6
Arrouaise   22
   Arrosian Observance   84–5, 87–8, 92–4, 97
   See also Annaghdown, Ardcarn, Clonard, Clonfert, Clonmacnoise, co-located houses, Derrane, Duleek, Durrow, Kells, Roscommon, Termonfeckin,
Augustinians   22, 82, 84–5, 87–9, 94–6, 108, 113–14, 117–18, 124, 129, 182, 185, 187, 188–91, 193–7, 200, 201, 227
   See also Arrouaise, congregation, Hamersleben, Heiningen, San Giovanni in Monte, San Vittore, Sant'Orsolina/San Lorenzo, Santa Maria Annunziata, Windesheim
Crutched Friars   95

Beaupré   250–1, 253–4, 256–62, 264, 267–9
Beaupré antiphoner, Baltimore, The Walters Art Museum, W.760   253–4, 258–62, 264, 269 and Oxford, Ashmolean Museum, Ruskin Collection, Standard Series, 7   260–2
   See also Cistercian chant

272 INDEX

Benedictines   13, 22, 75, 79, 96, 106, 109,
    111, 113–14, 118, 126, 129, 136, 138, 142,
    144, 157, 161–3, 169, 182, 186–8, 191–
    2,197, 200–1, 204, 210, 233, 236, 238,
    250, 251, 253, 257, 258, 262–7, 269
  See also congregation - Bursfelde,
    Drübeck, Forest, Hadmersleben,
    Lamspringe, Leominster, Lüne,
    Nunnaminster
Benedictine reform   61, 74, 77, 79,
    150, 182, 185, 194, 204, 208, 210,
    213, 232, 251, 257, 264–7
Berthold of Landsberg, bishop of
    Verden   233, 243
bishops, promoting reform   26, 51, 58–9,
    114–5, 137, 139, 142–6, 182–92
  See also Aethelwold, bishop of
    Winchester; Berthold of
    Landsberg, bishop of Verden;
    Dietrich, archbishop of Trier;
    Dunstan, archbishop of
    Canterbury; Étienne Poncher,
    bishop of Paris; Folco Scotti,
    bishop of Pavia; Gille, bishop
    of Limerick; Hernando de
    Talavera bishop of Ávila and
    Granada; Hildeward bishop of
    Halberstadt; institutionalisation;
    Malachy, archbishop of
    Armagh; Niccolò Albergati,
    bishop of Bologna; Omobono,
    bishop of Cremona; Oswald,
    bishop of Worcester and
    archbishop of York
Branca de Portugal, infanta, *senhora* of
    Lorvão and Las Huelgas   161–2
  See also Las Huelgas, Lorvão

Castellana, abbess of San Giovanni della
    Pipia   139, 141, 143–4
  See also San Giovanni della Pipia
Catherine of Lancaster, Queen   170–1
Chelles   208, 210, 219–20
Cistercians   20, 81–2, 84, 92, 96–7, 126,
    132–58, 175, 180, 183–7, 191, 193, 198,
    200–1, 225, 232, 239, 250–69
  See also Beaupré, Della Barona, Flines,
    Ghislenghien, *Iesu Christi*,
    Jardinet, La Ferté, Las Huelgas,
    Lorvão, Marche-les-dames,
    San Cristoforo, San Giovanni
    della Pipia, Sancta Maria della
    Colomba, Valduc, Wienhausen.
chant   250, 254, 256–69
Cistercians and nuns   133–5, 143, 146,
    148–50, 184, 253–6
  General Chapter   133–4, 148, 159, 174,
        194, 254, 258
  reform   132–53, 159–68
Clonard   91, 93–4, 97
  See also co-located houses
Clonfert   89, 91, 95
  See also co-located houses
Clonmacnoise   89, 91, 93
  See also co-located houses
co-located houses   20, 85–7
  See also Annaghdown, Ardcarn,
    Clonard, Clonfert,
    Clonmacnoise, Derrane,
    Dual-sex monastery, Duleek,
    Durrow, Kells, Roscommon,
    Termonfeckin
  aftermath and end   87, 93, 96–7
  archaeology   92, 97
  architecture and spatial lay-out   16,
        88–9, 91–2
  definition   87–9
  outside Ireland   96
  reform   87, 92
Colette of Corbie   203, 206, 208, 214–15,
    221, 225
Colettine reform   203–4
confessor (of nuns)   254, 256–7, 259, 264,
    266, 268
  See also Martin de Lannoy
congregation   11, 85, 182–92, 197–201, 223
  Bursfelde   206, 232–3, 258, 265–67
  Camaldolese   185–6, 188–9, 200–1
  Castilian Congregation of
        Todesillas   170
  Celestines   186
  Congregation of Observance   176, 178
  Lateran canons (also known as Santa
        Maria in Fregionaia)   183,
        189–190, 192–4, 197
  of women   186–7, 197–8
  Olivetans   186
  Santa Maria Annunziata (also known
        as Annunziate)   183, 190–2,
        195–6
  Santuccia Carabotti of Gubbio   186–7
  Vallombrosan   185, 188
  Windesheim   216, 227, 229
Constanza de Castilla, prioress of Santo
    Domingo de Madrid   158, 174–7
  Book of Devotions and Offices (*Libro
    de Devociones y Oficios*)   158,
    175
council
  Fourth Lateran Council (1215)   136–9,
        146, 153, 184, 198
  of Basel (1431)   205, 215
  of Constance (1414–18)   170, 176, 205, 215
  of Winchester (*c.* 973)   57–59, 78

cura monialium 21–3, 91, 99, 117–18, 126–8, 133–5, 137, 143, 146, 150, 152–3, 191, 206, 251, 254
See also confessor, provost

Della Barona 147–8
Derrane 89, 91
See also co-located houses
Dietrich, archbishop of Trier 28–9, 35, 48, 50, 52, 54–5
See also Liutrud
Dominicans 155, 170–1, 173–6, 178, 180, 183, 187, 189, 190, 192, 197, 200–1, 213, 222, 227–8, 231, 237–8
See also Johannes Meyer, Maria Magdalena zu den Reuerinnen, Sancti Spiritus de Toro, Santo Domingo el Real de Madrid, Schönensteinbach
Prior Provinical and reform of nuns 138–9, 141, 176
Drübeck 111, 113–14, 117–18, 129–30
dual-sex monastery (double monastery) 21, 87, 111, 128
See also Arrouaise, co-located houses, Hamersleben, Huysburg
Duleek 89, 91, 94
See also co-located houses
Dunstan, archbishop of Canterbury 57, 71–2, 74, 79
Durrow 89, 91, 94, 96
See also co-located houses

Edgar, king of England 57, 70, 78
Elisabeth Terwins, prioress of Heiningen 239
See also Heiningen, Textiles - Philosophy Embroidery
Elisabetta, prioress of Sancta Maria Annunziata 196
See also congregation - Santa Maria Annunziata
enclosure
architecture of 16–7, 93, 165, 176, 220, 222
practice of 8, 22–3, 149, 169, 206–10, 213–4, 218, 220–4, 226, 232, 235–6, 245–8, 256
Étienne Poncher, bishop of Paris 208, 210–11, 219, 222–3

Flines 257, 266
Folco Scotti, bishop of Pavia 145, 147–9, 151
Fontevraud 87, 97, 204–6, 208–13, 220, 222
See also La Madeleine d'Orléans, Renée de Bourbon

Forest 256, 263–5, 267–9
antiphoner (in private ownership) 263–4, 269
Francis I, king of France 205, 209, 212, 219, 225
Franciscans 96, 180, 183, 187, 189, 192, 196, 203–4, 208, 215
See also Colette of Corbie, Poor Clares

Gerhard, provost of Lamspringe 127
See also Lamspringe, provost
Ghislenghien 250, 256, 262–74, 267–9
Gille, bishop of Limerick 82–5
De statu ecclesia 83
Glodesind of Metz 27–28, 43–7, 54
See also John of Saint-Arnoul, Sainte-Glossinde
Consecratio of 43, 45–6
Life of 18, 27, 35, 43–6, 52, 53
Gregory IX, Pope 139, 141, 143, 147–9, 153, 176
Gregory XII, Pope 192–5, 197

Hadmersleben 113–14, 117–18, 128–9
Heinricus, pater monasterii 111, 113, 128
Hadrian IV, Pope 130
hagio-liturgical motifs
sponsa Christi 38–9, 42–6, 52–3, 56
virginity 30, 36, 40–1, 50, 115
Halberstadt 101, 118
See also bishops
Hamersleben 108, 110–14, 117–19, 130
Heiningen 108, 229, 233, 239–40
See also textiles - Philosophy embroidery
Hernando de Talavera, bishop of Ávila and Granada 168, 174
treatise of 168, 174
Hildeward, bishop of Halberstadt 28, 29
Hohenbourg 1–2
Honorius III, Pope 147
Huysburg 109, 113–14, 118, 130

identity
ambiguous identity and reform 17–21, 88, 96–7, 142, 153, 195–6
and religious order 18–20, 61–2, 134–5, 137, 149, 149–50, 153, 264–9
collective 22–3, 119–28, 229
institutional 1–2, 18–9, 78–80, 100, 135–7, 150–3, 159, 180–2
Iesu Christi 144, 147–49, 153
See also San Cristoforo
Imelda de Giroldis, abbess of San Giovanni della Pipia 138–40, 144
See also San Giovanni della Pipia

274 INDEX

institutionalisation
  See also identity
  of men's religious communities 182–3, 188–90
  of women's religious communities 15, 20, 87, 96, 132–53, 190–1, 195-6

Jardinet 250–1, 254, 257, 269, 264–6
Jean Eustache, abbot of Jardinet 254
Jeanne de Couhé, abbess of Sainte-Croix 211–12, 216–19, 223
  See also Sainte-Croix
Johannes Busch 216, 225, 229, 232, 267
Johannes Meyer 213, 231–2, 238
  Buch der reformacio predigerorden/
  Book of the reformation of the order of Preachers 231, 238
John of Saint-Arnoul 27, 35, 43–4, 46–7, 52–3
  See also Glodesind

Katharina of Hoya, abbess of Wienhausen 232
  See also Wienhausen
Katharina Remstede, abbess of Wienhausen 233, 246
  See also textiles - Unicorn hanging
Kells 89, 91, 94, 95
  See also co-located houses

La Ferté 148–50, 251
La Madeleine d'Orléans, priory of Fontevraud 210, 219–20
  See also Fontevraud
Lamspringe 118–19, 127
  See also manuscripts, Ricburg
Las Huelgas 159–63, 165, 167, 175
  See also Branca de Portugal, liturgy
Las Huelgas Beatus; New York, Pierpont Morgan Library, Ms. 429 159, 163, 165, 167
Lasia Roncastaldi, prioress of Sant'Orsolina/San Lorenzo 190
  See also Sant'Orsolina/San Lorenzo
Leominster 69–71, 74, 75, 78–80
  Leominster Prayerbooks; London, British Library, Cotton MSS Galba A.xiv 18, 63–70, 73–79, Nero A.ii 68–9, 72–8 and Titus D. xxvi 68, 75
Leonor Sánchez de Castilla, prioress of Sancti Spiritus de Toro 171, 174
liturgy 15–16, 121–5, 158–9, 166–8, 175, 249–69
  See also Cistercian chant, manuscripts and hagiography 30–1, 55–6

and prayer 45, 49, 51, 53, 71–9, 116, 129
consecration of abbesses 32
consecration of deaconess 32
consecration of domestic virgins 52–3
consecration of virgins 30–1, 33–8, 41–56, 115–6
consecration of widows 32–4, 52
women's liturgical agency 15–6, 52–5, 79–80, 174–5, 263-4
Liutrud, deo sacrata and hermit in the Perthois (Champagne) 27–30, 47, 49–51, 54
  See also Dietrich of Trier
  Life of 18, 28, 35, 47, 52, 54
Lorvão 161–2, 167
  See also Branca de Portugal
Lorvão Beatus (Lisbon, Arquivo Nacional de Torre do Tombo, Cod. 160) 159, 163, 167
Lucia de Bezanis, abbess of San Giovanni della Pipia 138–9, 143
  See also San Giovanni della Pipia
Lüne 233–4, 236, 240–6
  See also textiles

Mafalda, infanta 161
Malachy, archbishop of Armagh 82, 84–5, 89, 92
male-female relations (in religious life) 21–3, 84–5, 99–100, 110, 117–9, 121, 124–31, 142, 227–48, 259, 263–5, 267–9
  See also co-located houses, confessor, cura monialium, dual-sex monastery, provost
manuscripts
  See also Beaupré - Beaupré antiphoner, Forest - Forest antiphoner, Las Huelgas - Las Huelgas Beatus, Leominster - Leominster prayerbooks, Lorvão - Lorvão Beatus
  Cambridge, Corpus Christi College, MS 201 (Regularis Concordia) 60–1
  female patronage of 27, 158–80, 263
  Hildesheim, Cathedral Treasury, MS. 37 (Ratmann Sacramentary) 106–7
  Los Angeles, The John Paul Getty Museum, MS 64 (Stammheim Missal) 106
  Wolfenbüttel, Cod. Guelph. 475 Helmst. (Lamspringe) 101, 116–8, 127

women and manuscript
    exchange   19, 159–79, 237–8
women and manuscript
    production   64–8, 71–80, 109,
    110, 118–19
Marche-les-Dames   250, 254, 256
Margherita Casanova, abbess of San
    Giovanni del Pippia   140
    See also San Giovanni del Pippia
Margherita Lambertenghi   195–6
    See also Santa Maria Annunziata
Marguerite I de Liedekerke, abbess of
    Forest   263
    See also Forest
Maria Magdalena zu den
    Reuerinnen   237–8
Marie Berland, abbess of Sainte-
    Croix   212–13
    See also Saint-Croix
Marie de Bretagne, abbess of
    Fontevraud   209, 211–12
    See also Fontevraud
Martin V, Pope   176, 191, 194
Martin de Lannoy, abbot of Jardinet   259,
    264–5
    See also provost
Mary Magdalene   122–5
Matthew, apostle   36, 41, 55
    Passio of   35–39, 41–2, 50, 51, 55
Modern Devotion/*devotio moderna*   202,
    206, 223, 253

Niccolò Albergati, bishop of
    Bologna   189, 190–2, 194, 197
Nikolaus Graurock, provost at
    Lüne   242–4
    See also Lüne
Nikolaus Schomaker, provost at
    Lüne   233, 243–45
    See also Lüne
Nunnaminster   58–60, 62, 66, 68, 75

Observant reform   4, 11, 22, 155–8, 167–8,
    192, 203–6, 208, 231, 233, 235, 238,
    247, 249–50, 253–4, 265–6, 269
Omobono, bishop of Cremona   139, 142
Oswald, bishop of Worcester and
    archbishop of York   57, 71, 74, 79
Ottabona, *ministra, rectrix* and abbess of
    San Cristoforo   145–7, 149–50
    See also San Cristoforo

Pontificale Romano-Germanicum
    (PRG)   26–7, 30–1, 49
    female ordines in   31–5, 45–7, 50, 52–5
    hagiographical connections of   35–43,
    51–2, 55

Poor Clares   170, 176
    See also Collette of Corbie,
    Franciscans
poverty, monastic ideal   205–9, 213, 215,
    218, 224
prioress   118–19, 170–1, 174, 190–1, 196,
    211–12, 220, 226, 233, 240, 243–4
    See also Constanza de Castilla,
    prioress of Santo Domingo de
    Madrid; Elisabeth Terwins,
    prioress of Heiningen;
    Elisabetta, prioress of
    Annunziata; Lasia Roncastaldi,
    prioress of Sant'Orsolina/
    San Lorenzo; Leonor Sánchez
    de Castilla, prioress of Sancti
    Spiritus de Toro; Sophia of
    Bodenteich, prioress of Lüne
provost   28, 100, 106, 111–15, 117–19, 127–
    8, 227–9, 233, 239, 241–5, 247
    See also Arnold Steinwick, provost of
    Heiningen; Arnoul de Solbrecq,
    Abbot of Jardinet; Gerhard,
    provost of Lamspringe;
    Heinricus, pater monasterii;
    Jean Eustache, abbot of Jardinet;
    Martin de Lannoy, abbot of
    Jardinet; Nikolaus Graurock,
    provost at Lüne, Nikolaus
    Schomaker, provost of Lüne
    and visual culture   227, 235, 239–40,
    247
Pusinna, hermit and sister of Liutrud   28,
    29, 47, 61

reform
    See also Augustinians, Benedictines,
    Cistercians, congregation,
    Dominicans, Franciscans,
    institutionalisation, Observant
    Reform
    and nuns' agency   1–3, 7–12, 144,
    150–3, 227–31, 235–6
    and nuns' visual culture   100,
    227–48
    and status of women in the
    Church   7–11, 34, 52–5, 83–6,
    57–9, 114–7, 130–1
    as negotiated reality   1–5, 11–2
    ecclesiastical   4, 26, 58–9, 81–2, 96,
    114–15, 135–6, 145–8, 182–3, 192
    gender and reform   8–12, 129–31,
    156–7, 182–3, 198–9, 206–7, 225,
    227–39
    historiography   3–12, 154–6
    interpretive questions   26, 55, 136,
    228–9

reform (cont'd)
  women's adaptive strategies 60-1,
    79-80, 262
  women initiating reform 57-9, 156-
    7, 161, 169-79, 195-6, 209-11,
    224-5, 243, 251, 263
Regularis concordia 57-60, 71-80
  adapted 19, 60-1, 74
Renée de Bourbon, abbess of
    Fontevraud 205, 208, 211-13,
    218-219, 221-2, 225
Ricburg, abbess of Lamspringe 226
Roscommon 89, 91, 94
  See also co-located houses
Rule
  debates about 1-2, 21, 57-62, 79-80,
    96, 137, 142, 146, 149-50, 152-3,
    174-5, 187, 196, 209-10, 221, 264,
    266
  of Augustine 88, 92, 96, 168, 181, 185,
    196, 189
  of Benedict of Nursia, Benedictine
    Rule 2, 57-9, 62, 66, 78-80,
    113, 122, 146, 181, 184-5, 189, 209,
    258
    adapted for female use 59, 209
  of Caesarius 220
  of St Clare 208

Sainte-Croix, Poitiers 20, 204, 211,
    219-20, 222, 225
  See also Jeanne de Couhé
Sainte-Glossinde 35, 27, 44-5
  See also Glodesind of Metz
San Cristoforo 137, 144-53
  See also Iesu Christi, Ottabona
San Giovanni della Pipia 137, 138-44,
    151-3
San Giovanni in Monte 182, 188-91, 194,
    197-8
San Vittore 185, 188-90, 194, 201
Sancta Maria del Boschetto 139, 141-2, 151
Sancta Maria della Colomba 143
Sancti Spiritus de Toro 171, 174
Sant'Orsolina/San Lorenzo 182, 188,
    190-1, 197-8, 200
Santa Maria Annunziata see congregation
  - Santa Maria Annunziata

Santa Maria in Fregionaia see
  congregation - Lateran canons
Santo Domingo el Real de Madrid 174
  See also Constanza de Castilla,
    prioress of Santo Domingo de
    Madrid
Santo Domingo in Toledo 170, 174
Schönensteinbach 232, 237
Sophia of Bodenteich, prioress of
    Lune 233, 242-5
  See also Lüne, textiles
sponsa Christi (as normative ideal) 38-
    47, 52-4, 56, 115-6
St Odile 1-2
Susanna Postock, abbess of
    Wienhausen 233

Teresa, infanta 161-2
Termonfeckin 89, 91-3, 96-7
  See also co-located houses
Textiles 17, 23, 99-131, 229, 239-46
  See also visual culture
  Berlin fragment, 'Scenes of the Life of
    Christ' 99-131
  corporate identity 117-18, 129-31
  Lüne benchcovers 242-4
  Philosophy embroidery 229-30, 233,
    239-40
  Prophets and Sybils
    embroidery 243-5
  Resurrection of Christ 234-5, 240-1
  Unicorn hanging 246
  women as makers of 99, 109-10,
    239-46

Valduc (Hertogendal) 25-7, 262, 268-69
visitation 97, 135, 143, 146, 149-50, 169,
    208, 218-19, 225-7, 267
visual culture 16-7, 98-131, 224, 227-48

Wienhausen 223-24, 232-3, 246
  See also Katharine of Hoya, Katharina
    Remstede, Susanna Postock
Winchester 60, 65-6, 68, 71, 80
  council of 57-9, 78
  See also Aethelwold, bishop of
    Winchester

Other volumes in
Studies in the History of Medieval Religion

Details of volumes I–XXXV can be found on the Boydell & Brewer website.

XXXVI: Jocelin of Wells: Bishop, Builder, Courtier
Edited by Robert Dunning

XXXVII: War and the Making of Medieval Monastic Culture
Katherine Allen Smith

XXXVIII: Cathedrals, Communities and Conflict in the Anglo-Norman World
Edited by Paul Dalton, Charles Insley and Louise J. Wilkinson

XXXIX: English Nuns and the Law in the Middle Ages:
Cloistered Nuns and Their Lawyers, 1293–1540
Elizabeth Makowski

XL: The Nobility and Ecclesiastical Patronage in Thirteenth-Century England
Elizabeth Gemmill

XLI: Pope Gregory X and the Crusades
Philip B. Baldwin

XLII: A History of the Abbey of Bury St Edmunds, 1257–1301:
Simon of Luton and John of Northwold
Antonia Gransden

XLIII: King John and Religion
Paul Webster

XLIV: The Church and Vale of Evesham, 700–1215:
Lordship, Landscape and Prayer
David Cox

XLV: Medieval Anchorites in their Communities
Edited by Cate Gunn and Liz Herbert McAvoy

XLVI: The Friaries of Medieval London: From Foundation to Dissolution
Nick Holder

XLVII: 'The Right Ordering of Souls': The Parish of All Saints' Bristol
on the Eve of the Reformation
Clive Burgess

XLVIII: The Lateran Church in Rome and the Ark of the Covenant:
Housing the Holy Relics of Jerusalem, with an edition and translation of the
Descriptio Lateranensis Ecclesiae (BAV Reg. Lat. 712)
Eivor Andersen Oftestad

XLIX: Apostate Nuns in the Later Middle Ages
Elizabeth Makowski

L: St Stephen's College, Westminster: A Royal Chapel and English Kingship,
1348–1548
Elizabeth Biggs

LI: The Social World of the Abbey of Cava, *c.* 1020–1300
G. A. Loud

LII: Medieval Women Religious, *c.* 800–*c.* 1500: New Perspectives
Edited by Kimm Curran and Janet Burton

LIII: The Papacy and Ecclesiology of Honorius II (1124-1130):
Church Governance after the Concordat of Worms
Enrico Veneziani

LIV: Women and Monastic Reform in the Medieval West, *c.* 1000–1500:
Debating Identities, Creating Communities
Edited by Julie Hotchin and Jirki Thibaut

LV: Thomas of Eccleston's *De adventu Fratrum Minorum in Angliam* "The
Arrival of the Franciscans in England", 1224–c.1257/8: Commentary and Analysis
Michael J. P. Robson

LVI: Religious Conflict at Canterbury Cathedral in the Late Twelfth Century:
The Dispute between the Monks and the Archbishops, 1184–1200
James Barnaby

LVII: The Reception of Papal Legates in England, 1170–1250:
Narrating the *Adventus* Ceremony
Emil Lauge Christensen

LVIII: The Passion and Miracles of St. Thomas Becket
by Benedict of Peterborough
Translated by Rachel Koopmans

www.ingramcontent.com/pod-product-compliance
Lightning Source LLC
Chambersburg PA
CBHW070308230426
43664CB00015B/2674